Employing Bureaucracy

EMPLOYING BUREAUCRACY

Managers, Unions, and the
Transformation of Work
in American Industry, 1900–1945

SANFORD M. JACOBY

New York   Columbia University Press   *1985*

Library of Congress Cataloging in Publication Data

Jacoby, Sanford M.
  Employing bureaucracy.

  Includes index.
    1. Personnel management—United States—History—
20th century.   2. Labor and laboring classes—United
States—History—20th century.   3. Bureaucracy—
United States—History—20th century.   4. Trade-unions—
United States—History—20th century.   I. Title.
  HF5549.2.U5J32   1985   658.3′00973   85-3841
  ISBN 0-231-05756-3

Columbia University Press
New York   Guildford, Surrey
Copyright © 1985 Columbia University Press
All rights reserved

PRINTED IN THE UNITED STATES OF AMERICA

Clothbound editions of Columbia University Press books are
Smyth-sewn and printed on permanent and durable acid-free paper.

To the memory of my mother and father

Contents

Acknowledgments

I am deeply grateful to many friends and colleagues for their ideas and support. David Brody, Clair Brown, Ellis Hawley, Diane Lindstrom, Michael Reich, George Strauss, and Lloyd Ulman read at least one version of the entire manuscript. Walter Fogel, Joan Hannon, Daniel Mitchell, Joseph Pratt, and Peter Seixas gave useful advice on various parts of the manuscript. Abraham Ackerman, David Arsen, Sean Flaherty, Candace Howes, Charles Jeszeck, Rebecca Morales, Stacey Oliker, and Greg Topakian provided help of various kinds at critical junctures.

The UCLA Faculty Research Committee and the Eleanor Roosevelt Institute provided financial assistance. UCLA's Institute of Industrial Relations contributed funds for research assistance.

Passages in this book have been taken from two previously published papers: "Industrial Labor Mobility in Historical Perspective," *Industrial Relations* (Spring 1983), pp. 261–282; and from "The Origins of Internal Labor Markets in American Manufacturing Firms" in Paul Osterman, editor, *Internal Labor Markets,* MIT Press, 1984.

Special thanks go to Laura Kent, for editorial assistance; and to Vickie Bean, Wilma Daniels, Lori Ramirez, and Pat McNally for expertly typing the manuscript.

Above all, I want to thank my family and my wife, Susan Bartholomew, for their encouragement and love.

S.M.J.

Employing Bureaucracy

INTRODUCTION

In 1972, a dramatic strike took place at a General Motors assembly plant in Lordstown, Ohio. The strikers, many of whom were young and well-educated, walked out in protest over working conditions at the plant. They said they were seeking something more from their labor than high wages, pensions, and job security. One young worker wanted "a chance to use my brain," a job "where my high school education counts for something."[1]

The strike received national attention and unleashed a torrent of books and articles about job satisfaction, the work ethic, and the quality of working life. Their authors sounded a common theme: that workers were dissatisfied because their jobs were uninteresting, meaningless, and lacking in opportunities for personal growth. This view was shared by a diverse group, ranging from liberal corporate managers to Marxist students of the labor process. But there was little agreement over what should be done to improve the situation. Work reform experts prescribed remedies such as job enrichment and more participative forms of management;[2] radical scholars argued that these were Band-Aids at best, that employers had intentionally drained most jobs of their conceptual content and would never willingly restore it.[3]

But hindsight and national survey data suggest that the Lordstown experience was not typical and that researchers in the 1970s gave insufficient attention to the so-called "extrinsic" features of the work environment—pay and other economic benefits, job security, and opportunities for promotion. Attitude surveys show that these are still very important to blue-collar workers. For example, workers who regard their income as adequate and their job security as good are five times more likely to be very satisfied with their jobs than are those who think that their income is inadequate and their job insecure.[4] Dissatisfied workers complain more about extrinsic factors like hours, earnings, job insecurity, and company policy than they do about intrinsic factors such as "the work itself."[5]

The point is not that intrinsic rewards are unimportant or job enrichment unwelcome. Rather, these findings demonstrate that the blue-collar worker's definition of a "good job" turns on matters that are relatively mundane: A good job is one that pays well, offers stability and promotion opportunities, and protects against arbitrary discipline and dismissal.

We tend to take these things for granted, in part because a sizable proportion of today's jobs fit this definition. Yet industrial employment conditions were much different as recently as fifty years ago: Workers had little protection from the vagaries of the labor market. Wages and employment levels were unstable and tenure insecure. Foremen meted out rough and arbitrary discipline. Most employers looked upon their workers as indolent children or beasts of burden and treated them accordingly.[6] Good jobs, as they are defined today, were scarce and hard to come by.

The present work is an attempt to understand how industrial labor was transformed and to identify the historical process by which good jobs were created. It is, therefore, an account of the bureaucratization of employment, since many of the features that define good jobs—stability, internal promotion, and impersonal, rule-bound procedures—are characteristic of bureaucratic organization.

Bureaucracy is a loaded word; it carries a host of connotations. To modern organization theorists, the bureaucratic features of employment are an inevitable and automatic result of the technical imperatives imposed by large and complex organizations. As Talcott Parsons put it, "Smaller and simpler organizations are typically managed with a high degree of particularism . . . But when the "distance" between points of decision and operation increases, uniformity and coordination can be obtained only by a high degree of formalization."[7] Recent radical accounts of the evolution of the labor process take issue with this view, seeing bureaucratic devices such as calculable rules and career ladders as mechanisms of employer control over the work force. From this perspective, bureaucracy is not neutral; it is rationality shaped to serve the employer's interests.[8]

When I began this study, I had to consider both of these points of view. Eventually I discovered that neither of them provides a satisfactory guide to historical developments in the United States. Thus, I found that size mattered but that, contrary to modern organization theory, there was no lockstep relation between how big a company was and how its employment system was organized. Giant manufacturing establishments were a common feature of the industrial environment by 1890, yet in many of them, blue-collar employment did not acquire bureaucratic characteristics until four or five decades later. Moreover, medium-sized firms (those with fewer than a thousand workers) were often among the first to get rid of the traditional system of factory labor administration. Management in these firms employed bureaucracy to solve a variety of problems, many of them unrelated to size.

But management was not the only group to use bureaucracy and to derive benefit from it. Through their unions, workers sought to bureaucratize employment in order to enhance their bargaining power, shield themselves from turbulent competition, and ensure managerial consistency and fairness. In fact, managers in some companies resisted or delayed bureaucratization even as their employees promoted it. These managers were concerned that structure and rules would hinder their discretion, although they were sometimes willing to impose these things on themselves in order to forestall what they regarded as a greater evil—unionization. This situation differs considerably from the view of radical theorists that bureaucracy was "systematically and consciously" designed by employers to increase their control.[9]

Thus, a problem shared by both schools is their tendency to view bureaucracy as an expressive totality,[10] all of whose features are prevaded by a dominant principle: for organization theorists, the imperatives of size and efficiency; for radicals, the logic of control. A related problem is that both theories portray management as the agent of all organizational change, rationally adjusting employment structures either to shifts in technology and market forces or to new forms of worker resistance.

This study takes a different approach. It treats bureaucratic employment practices as the outcome of a prolonged struggle to overcome the insecurity and inequities produced by a market-oriented employment system. The struggle was played out both within management and between management and other groups; its result was by no means inevitable. At a broader level, this struggle was part of what Karl Polanyi called "the double movement" of two great organizing principles in society. One was the principle of economic liberalism, which used laissez-faire and contract as its methods; the other was the principle of social protection, which relied on protective legislation, restrictive associations, and other methods of market intervention.[11]

Each of the world's major industrial nations experienced this struggle as part of its transition to modernity, a passage marked by several dramatic shifts: from the entrepreneurial firm to the large corporation; from the old to the new middle class; and from local protests to national unions and labor parties. These transitions all occurred within the century after 1850, although nations modernized at different times and at different speeds during this period. They differed as well in the timing and sequence of the various shifts that constituted the transition. England, for example, had powerful trade unions very early in its passage to modernity, something that was not true of Japan. As a result of these dissimilarities, each nation varied considerably with respect to the constellation of forces—economic, social, and political—that played out Polanyi's double movement.[12]

In most nations, regulation and stabilization of the labor market were achieved through bargaining by workers organized into trade unions, and through legislation supported by middle-class reformers and labor parties. To some extent this was also true of the United States, except that the absence of an effective labor party made middle-class reform activity especially important. In addition, American management manifested a comparatively strong strain toward self-regulation, given the relative weakness prior to the 1930s both of government regulation and of trade unionism. The relationships are, however, complex: Unionism's limited scope gave American managers room to act preemptively whenever they felt threatened by an increase in labor's bargaining power, as during World War I. The result, as John R. Commons observed at the time, was that in the United States, "the restraints which laborers place on free competition in the interests of fair competition [are being] taken over by employers and administered by their own labor managers."[13]

The differences between the United States and other nations are to some extent attributable to the large proportion of immigrants in America's industrial labor force. Language barriers, tensions inherent in ethnic heterogeneity, and the high mobility of immigrant workers militated against the formation of workplace and other organizations. The newcomers' lack of roots, their frequent moves from one place to another, made for instability in America's cities and workplaces and at the same time permitted the persistence of a market-oriented employment system that was equally unstable.

For economic liberals, the creation of a free labor market was one of the great achievements of the nineteenth century. The employment contract allowed workers and employers to enter, design, and terminate their relationship at will, without interference from the state or traditional moral authority. Hence it facilitated the movement away from the eighteenth century's highly personal employment relationship, constrained by mutual obligations, to an impersonal and freer relationship of contractual equality. But the liberal formula had numerous defects; and Commons, like other critics of his day, pointed out several of them. First, a large corporation and a single employee could hardly be regarded as equal in bargaining power when it came to forming the contract, especially when the latter could find no alternative employment. Second, in accepting the contract, the employee agreed to submit to the authority of the employer (or his agent, the foreman), causing the relationship to revert to one of domination and subordination. Third, the employer's power to terminate the contract at will, and to control the supply of jobs, had far graver consequences for the worker than the worker's mutual right to quit had for the employer.[14]

Commons thought that, in the United States, protective legislation and trade unionism were bringing some measure of equality and fairness to the labor exchange. But he thought that this also was occurring through the restraints or "working rules" that American employers were taking over from regulative bodies and placing upon themselves. These rules filled in the contract's empty spaces with procedures and regulations specifying how employers, foremen, and workers should conduct themselves; hence they made the contract more an agreement than a command. From this, said Commons, came a movement away from "coercion" and toward the establishment of legality, of "rights, duties, and liberties." Moreover, these working rules signified that the employee was part of a "going concern," a relatively permanent relationship. Rules governing layoff and dismissal, for example, reduced some of the transience associated with the labor contract; they established "a new equity" that protected the worker's job. In the familiar legal formula, employment was shifting back from contract to status, as the industrial worker's job became a "position" with circumscribed rights and duties, including safeguards against its loss.[15]

Between 1900 and 1945, two forces—one supporting the status quo and the other pressing for change—contended within the American manufacturing firm. On the one side were foremen, production managers, and plant superintendents—persons committed to the existing employment system for both economic and philosophical reasons. These men had a manufacturing orientation: Their overriding concern was to get the product out as quickly and cheaply as possible. In administering employment, they looked for quick results and maximum flexibility; the work force was to be adjusted to changes in technology and to fluctuations in output, never the other way around. Hence they favored strict discipline for the worker and freedom from the restraint of rules and commitments for themselves. They also shared an ideology, a set of beliefs, about the industrial worker—that he was lazy, grasping, and untrustworthy—and about their responsibility to him—which was that they had none, beyond paying the going wage rate. Liberality and security would, they thought, corrode the work ethic. This ideology meshed with their production orientation and with the policies that flowed from it, forming a structure of mutually reinforcing ideas, a world view.

On the other side was a disparate group of trade unionists, social reformers, and personnel managers. Each was trying to make the employment relationship more orderly and stable, but for different reasons. Unions sought to give industrial labor some of the security, dignity, and status rights associated with white-collar occupations; that is, they wanted to create new social norms for manual employment. Social reformers were sympathetic to these goals (if not always to organized labor) both because of humanitarian impulses and fears of more radical change from below. They criticized industry's employment practices as backward, crude, and wasteful. They were not, however, antagonistic to industrial capitalism; rather, they wanted to make it more rational and viable. Yet these middle-class professionals also had interests of their own; they were more than mere servants of power. They encouraged the proliferation of bureaucracy and top-down reform because these were likely to give them a greater directive role in public and private affairs.

Within management, the conflict between the traditional and the bureaucratic approach to employment was epitomized by clashes between the production division and the new personnel departments that began to appear after 1910. The personnel manager's point of view differed from that of most line managers, in part because of the personnel department's function in the managerial hierarchy. The creation of a personnel department signalled that employment policy would now be treated as an end in itself rather than as a means to the production division's ends. One of the personnel manager's chief responsibilities was to stabilize labor relations, a task that required trading off short-term efficiency in the interests of achieving high employee morale over the long run. In practice, this meant preempting many of the union's employment policies and placing stringent checks on line managers, especially foremen. Production officials were not happy about this turn of events. They were especially skeptical of the personnel manager's claim that good employee relations contributed to high productivity, since most of them believed just the opposite.

But personnel management was more than a new slot in the corporate hierarchy. Unlike marketing or finance, it was deeply affected by developments external to the firm, such as changes in social attitudes and norms regarding industrial employment. Because it had its roots in various Progessive reform movements, personnel management attracted to its ranks educators, social workers, and even former socialists. It was influenced by new middle-class beliefs in the necessity of market intervention, the beneficial effects of rational administration, and the power of the educated expert to mediate and mitigate social conflict. Many early personnel managers thought of themselves as neutral professionals, whose job was to reconcile opposing industrial interests and make employment practices more scientific and humane.

Personnel management and the new bureaucratic approach to employment did not gradually take hold in an ever-growing number of firms. Instead they were adopted during two periods of crisis for the traditional system of employment—World War I and the Great Depression. These were periods when the unions gained strength, when social experimentation was popular, and when the government intervened in the labor market. As this uneven growth suggests, many companies did not immediately see much value in a bureaucratic employment system. Normally, top management in these firms either paid little attention to employment (which they regarded as relatively unimportant) or were ideologically committed to the production manager's world view. Shedding traditional employment practices required a change in managerial values as well as external pressure from government and unions.

This view is somewhat different from that favored by modern business historians. For example, Alfred D. Chandler, Jr., argues that the rise of managerial capitalism was almost entirely an economic phenomenon, and that "neither the labor unions nor the government has taken part in carrying out the basic functions of modern business enterprise."[16] Chandler's claim is correct with respect to those functions that top management considered essential to the enterprise, such as marketing or production. But it does not hold true for the employment sphere: here, although market forces mattered, they were not all that mattered. Chandler misses this point because he accepts the American manager's bias that employment is a distinctly secondary corporate function. Hence, despite the comprehensiveness of his work, he omits any discussion of personnel and labor relations. This omission gives a misleading picture of the modern business enterprise as something that was not, and very likely cannot be, greatly affected by social norms and restraints.

Caveats

Before presenting an overview of this book, I would like to mention several features of its organization and focus. First, the book frequently refers to "the internal labor market," a construct used by economists to analyze bureaucratic employment practices. In an internal labor market, firms use administrative mechanisms to set wages and to allocate labor, rather than relying upon the external labor market. Institutional labor economists conducted the first studies of the internal labor market in the 1940s and 1950s as part of a project to bring economic theory into line with the demise of the classical labor market and traditional employment practices.[17] They described the internal labor market as an enterprise-based employment system, marked by hiring from within, employment security, and a web of decision rules. Then in the 1960s and 1970s, a new body of economic research attempted to provide an economic rationale for the institutionalists' descriptive findings: Internal labor markets were said to be a way for firms to reduce the costs (e.g., screening, turnover, and skills transmission) associated with training workers in firm-specific or idiosyncratic skills.[18]

These newer theories give us an elegant, if singular, explanation for the existence of internal labor markets. But the theories tend to be ex-post-facto rationalizations of postwar American practices. They do not tell us why internal labor markets have not always existed, if they are so efficient, or why their features are so different in other industrial nations.[19] Moreover, the theories ignore the possibility that employers at any time can select from an array of efficient organizational forms but that their actual choices are constrained by social, cultural, and even political considerations. Several of these theoretical problems are attributable to the lack of a historical perspective in recent research on internal labor markets. This book attempts to provide that missing perspective and, in so doing, tries to rebuild the bridge between labor economics and economic history.

A second feature of this book is its focus on the employment practices of manufacturing firms. Many economists treat manufacturing as more important than other sectors of economic activity: to Marxists, it is the site of productive labor; to post-Keynesian theorists, it is the wellspring of technological change.[20] But I did not choose to analyze manufacturing firms for these reasons. Instead, my choice was dictated by the richness of the historical data available on industrial employment methods; in comparison, data on other sectors are sparse. One consequence of this choice is that the book has relatively little to say about women, who accounted for only a small fraction of the manufacturing labor force.

Finally, this study is based on the experiences of a variety of industries and uses survey data to report on the practices of many hundreds of firms. This approach allows me to draw broad generalizations about what were central tendencies at various points in time. But it has its drawbacks: It cannot provide the wealth of information about microlevel variables that can emerge from a detailed case study. I did use material on several companies that others had already studied. But I was unable to gain entry to any new corporate archives except those which contained little or no information on the company's employment practices.

Overview

The opening chapters describe the traditional employment system found throughout industry between 1875 and 1915. The foreman, the labor market, and worker responses to them are the focus of chapter 1. Although the traditional system was profitable, it was not without costs, for both the employer and society. By the 1890s, a search for ways to reduce these costs had begun, a wide-ranging effort to create order in the firm, the labor market, and the society in which they were embedded.[21] Leading this search were various groups of college-educated professionals: industrial engineers and welfare workers hired by employers (chapter 2), as well as activists in the vocational guidance movement who became interested in employment reform (chapter 3). These groups coalesced around a series of problems—worker alienation, unemployment, labor turnover, and labor unrest—and it was as would-be solvers of these problems that they made connections with each other and formed a new profession, personnel management, in the decade before World War I (chapter 4).

At first reluctant to accept personnel management, employers became markedly more receptive to change between 1916 and 1920. The war period saw meteoric growth in the personnel management profession and an expansion of its influence within the firm. Chapter 5 examines the factors responsible for this growth and looks at its effects on the traditional employment system. After 1920, the waning of a wartime sense of urgency slowed the pace of employment reform. Personnel management continued to spread during the 1920s, as did bureaucratic employment practices, but the institutional dynamism of the war period was gone (chapter 6).

The early years of the Great Depression saw an unraveling of many of the policies that had been established during the preceding fifteen years. But this regression ceased in 1933, as companies began to adjust to an upsurge in unionism and to increased public scrutiny of private employment practices. Between 1933 and 1935, the rapid growth in the number of personnel departments and the improvement of their status in the corporate hierarchy were little short of phenomenal (chapter 7). Nevertheless, this second wave of institutional reform was too little and too late to halt the spread of unionism; after 1935, initiative shifted from management to the unions. This development is discussed in chapter 8, which closes with a discussion of World War II, when government invervened in the labor market to an unprecedented extent and when industry's new bureaucratic employment system became firmly established.

CHAPTER 1

THE WAY IT WAS: FACTORY LABOR BEFORE 1915

At the beginning of the nineteenth century, most commodities in the United States were produced either in the workshops of artisans or at home. Skilled tradesmen—carpenters, cobblers, potters—crafted their wares in small shops, owned by merchants or master craftsmen, that had not yet been significantly affected by machine methods. Goods made at home were usually consumed there, although in urban areas the putting-out system was common: Merchants distributed raw materials and tools to household workers, who then wove the cloth or made the shoes and returned the finished product to the merchants for distribution and sale. By the end of the century, however, everything had changed: Most commodities were now manufactured in factories, which were enormous agglomerations of machinery and men.

America's first factories were New England's textile mills, which supplanted home methods of production between 1790 and 1840. These early mills shared a number of features that distinguished the factory system from other modes of production: a reliance on power-driven machinery; the integration of different production processes at a single site; an elaborate division of labor; and finally, new methods of administration based on the overseer or foreman.

The overseer was the key figure in the early New England mills. Large mills employed a number of them, each in charge of a room full of machinery and workers. Although there was an agent who dealt with the mill's owners, the overseer did most of the work of maintaining mechanical and human order. In addition to tending machines, he selected the workers, assigned them to their tasks, and made sure that they labored diligently. Indeed, one advantage of the textile factories was that they permitted more effective labor supervision than was previously possible. Under the putting-out system, merchants could manipulate only the piece prices they paid; effort was controlled by the worker, who could take anywhere from two days to two weeks to turn in his goods. But in the factory, workers had less discretion over their work pace and methods. As one Rhode Island merchant wrote in 1809, "We have several hundred pieces now out weaving, but a hundred looms in families will not weave so much cloth as ten at least constantly employed under the immediate inspection of a workman."[1]

Until the 1840s, the factory system was limited chiefly to the textile industry. By 1880, it had become the dominant production mode in most manufacturing industries. As Carroll D. Wright observed in his introduction to the census of manufactures for 1880:

> Of the nearly three millions of people employed in mechanical industries of this country at least four-fifths are working under the factory system. Some of the other [than textiles] remarkable instances of the application of this system are to be found in the manufacture of boots and shoes, of watches, musical instruments, clothing, agricultural implements, metallic goods generally, firearms, carriages and wagons, wooden goods, rubber goods, and even the slaughtering of hogs. Most of these industries have been brought under the factory system during the past thirty years.

Despite this dramatic growth, the factory did not immediately displace older organizational forms. In the iron and steel industry, rural forges and small foundries coexisted during the 1860s and 1870s with giant rail mills employing more than a thousand workers. Similarly, although steam-powered machinery provided the impetus to establish shoe factories in the 1850s, certain types of women's shoes and slippers were manufactured on a putting-out basis until the end of the century.[2]

Older methods persisted in yet another way. Many of the industries that shifted to the factory system after 1850 continued to depend on techniques from the earlier period. In these industries, the factory was often no more than a congeries of artisanal workshops which had been mechanized and enlarged. A steady infusion of craft skills was still required, particularly when the factory turned out small batches of an unstandardized product. As a result, proprietors in these industries were content to let their foremen and skilled workers make most of the decisions about the timing and manner of production.[3]

At one extreme, this practice took the form of internal contracting, which was less a system of production management than a ceding of managerial control to the contractor. The contractor, who was a highly skilled foreman, arranged with the proprietor to deliver the product within a specified time at a specified cost. The proprietor provided the contractor with tools, materials, and money, and then left him in charge of production. The contractor hired and supervised a group of skilled workers, who in turn might employ their own unskilled helpers. This system was most common in metalworking industries—sewing machinery, locomotives, guns—where a high degree of skill was needed to process component parts to exacting tolerances.[4]

At the other extreme were industries that left production decisions entirely to the skilled workers, with no foreman or contractor involved. For instance, at the Columbus Iron Works during the early 1870s, workers negotiated with the firm's owners on a tonnage rate for each rolling job undertaken by the firm. The gang members decided collectively how to pay themselves, how to allocate assignments, whom to hire, and how to train helpers. Unlike internal contracting, this was a highly egalitarian method for production management; no one interposed between the skilled workers and the owners.[5]

Neither the syndicalism of the rolling mill workers nor internal contracting was, however, very common. Rather, in most nineteenth-century factories, salaried foremen and skilled workers shared responsibility for administering production. Although the salaried foreman occupied a position inferior to the internal contractor's, he nevertheless had authority to make most of the decisions about how a production task was to be accomplished, including work methods, technical processes, and work organization.

The foreman exercised his authority within limits set by the skilled workers, who guarded their autonomy in production through a multitude of working rules that governed methods of shop organization and through what one historian has called the craftsman's "moral code." The code included output quotas set by the workers to protect themselves from overexertion, as well as an

ethos of manly defiance to any foreman who tried to subvert traditional shop rules.[6]

Foremen had their own moral code, one which owed a great deal
to the skilled worker's shop culture. They were arrogant, proud,
conservative men, mindful of the position to which their skill and
knowledge had elevated them. Often they wore white shirts to
work and seated themselves at raised desks in the middle of the
shop floor. But despite their former status as skilled workers, most
foremen were strenuously antiunion. They were well aware that
their authority depended on severing ties to their pasts. As one
observer noted, "They spurn the rungs by which they did ascend."[7]

By the 1880s, winds of change were beginning to erode the power
of foremen and skilled workers over production management. The
new industries, such as electrical machinery and chemicals, were
based on a technology that had little continuity with artisanal
techniques. The older industries, like iron and steel, had mechanized to the point where craft skills were no longer essential to
production. After the introduction of continuous flow methods in
steel manufacturing, the foreman was left with little authority.
Most production decisions were now made by engineers and me-
tallurgists. Among skilled steelworkers, who had once been
"strong, even arrogant in their indispensability," the "strong sense
of independence disappeared." In machine-paced industries like
textiles, the overseer was forced to share authority with an increasing number of specialists equal or superior in rank: the chief engineer, the chief electrician, and the supervisors of piping and the
waste house. Other than making occasional repairs or inspecting
goods to insure their quality, the overseer had fewer and fewer
responsibilities in production. In textiles, as in steel and other
industries, most of the foreman's tasks were related to employing
and supervising labor. Here, however, the methods of the 1850s
persisted, with little modification.[8]

I. Foremen in Control, 1880–1915

Whereas the foreman's degree of control over production varied
by industry, his authority in employment matters was uniform
across industries. Whether in a machine shop or on the assembly

line, the foreman was given free rein in hiring, paying, and supervising workers. To the worker, the foreman was a despot—rarely benevolent—who made and interpreted employment policy as he saw fit. Any checks on the foreman's power emanated from the workers he supervised, not from the proprietor.

Recruiting and Hiring

The foreman's control over employment began literally at the factory gates. On mornings when the firm was hiring—a fact advertised by signs hung outside the plant, by newspaper ads, or by word of mouth—a crowd gathered in front of the factory, and the foreman picked out those workers who appeared suitable or had managed to get near the front. At one Philadephia factory, the foreman tossed apples into the throng; if a man caught an apple, he got the job. Foremen could be less arbitrary. For instance, they frequently hired their friends, the relatives of those already employed, and even their own relatives: "Oftentimes he [the foreman] is connected by blood ties with those who come under his control and he will inevitably be swayed by considerations of previous friendship no matter how hard he may strive not to be." New foremen might dismiss current employees to make room for their friends and relatives, as occurred in a Lawrence textile mill during the 1880s. The overseers "made changes very freely in the departments commited to them, and the result was that for several months a feeling of great insecurity prevailed among the hands."[9]

In addition to blood ties, foremen relied on ethnic sterotypes to determine who would get a job and which job they would get. The Irish and Germans were considered good skilled workers, while Poles and "Hunkies" were thought to be suited for heavy labor. Jews were said to be dexterous, Rumanians dishonest, Slovaks stupid, and Italians "so susceptible to the opposite sex that they could not be satisfactorily employed." When an investigator in the steel mills asked for a job on a blast furnace, he was told "only Hunkies work on those jobs, they're too damn dirty and too damn hot for a white man."[10]

To get a job, workers often resorted to bribing the foreman with whiskey, cigars, or cash, a practice that one study found to be "exceedingly common" in Ohio's factories. The study included an affidavit from an immigrant worker who, to get a factory job, had paid the foreman a five-dollar bribe. Several days later the foreman told the man that he would be fired unless he paid another five dollars right away, because someone else had just paid ten dollars for a similar job.[11]

Assignment to a job was determined in large part by favoritism or ethnic prejudice. The foreman had little interest in or knowledge of an employee's previous work experience. If a newly hired employee proved unsatisfactory, he was easily replaced by someone else. Although intradepartmental promotions occurred, transfers and promotions between departments were rare, as were definite lines of promotion (except on skilled work). The foreman had a parochial view of the factory and was reluctant to give up his best workers to another foreman.

Few companies kept detailed employment records before 1900. Only the foreman knew with any accuracy how many workers were employed in his shop and how much they were paid. In a large firm, a worker could quit his job in the morning and get taken on by the foreman of another department in the afternoon. In 1915, the top managers of a large hosiery factory reported that they had little idea of how many people their firm hired and dismissed each week.[12]

The one exception to this lack of information was the bureau that specialized in screening skilled labor for open-shop employers. Henry Leland, founder of the Cadillac Motor Company, started the Employers' Association of Detroit in 1897 to ensure that Detroit remained an open-shop city. The organization kept records on every individual who had worked for a member firm and blacklisted those who were "agitators" and union supporters. To get a job at a member firm, a worker had to apply through the Employers' Association. By 1911, the association's employment bureau had in its files names of more than 160,000 workers, a figure equalling nearly 90 percent of the Detroit labor force. Other employer organizations (including the National Metal Trades Association and the National Founders Association) set up similar local agencies to blacklist radicals and trade unionists and to supply member firms with the names of "good men" who needed work.[13]

Although direct recruitment was common during the nineteenth century, it was not usually done by the foreman. Instead, employers either sent their own special recruiters to the New York docks to secure immigrant workers or else relied on private agencies like the American Emigrant Company, which kept scouts in several foreign ports to recruit emigrating workers. After the 1890s, however, immigration flows had become large enough and cyclically sensitive enough to meet industrial demand. Consequently, direct recruitment was rare, except in sectors like construction and the railroads, where work was seasonal and labor requirements for certain projects could run into the thousands.[14]

During the heyday of mass immigration, employers recruited through the immigrants' own informal network: Newcomers to America headed for areas where their countrymen, often men from the same European villages, had found jobs. As more men of a given nationality arrived, benefit societies were organized, priests appeared, and wives and children were sent for. Gradually a new ethnic community developed in the area. The news that a company was seeking help was transmitted to friends and relatives in the old country; sometimes, tickets were purchased for them. Letters might also warn of a shortage of jobs.[15]

Wages and Effort

The foreman also had considerable power in determining the wages of the workers he hired, whether for piecework or daywork. As a result, different individuals doing the same job were often paid very different rates. Because top management monitored labor costs but not the wage determination process, the foreman had an incentive to hire individuals at the lowest rate possible. It was common practice for a foreman "to beat the applicant down from the wage he states he wishes to the lowest which the interviewer believes he can be induced to accept." Moreover, by being secretive about wage rates and production records, foremen could play favorites, varying the day rate or assigning workers to jobs where piece rates were loose. Since each foreman ran his shop autonomously, rate variations across departments were also common. In their report on the stove industry, Frey and Commons found that "molding [piece] prices were far from equal on similar work in the same shop or district."[16]

Despite—or perhaps because of—the latitude they gave him in determining rates, the firm's owners expected the foreman to hold down labor costs. This meant paying a wage no greater than the "going rate" for a particular job. But it also meant keeping effort levels up in order to reduce unit costs. When the going rate rose, effort became the key variable to be manipulated by the foreman.

The methods used by foremen to maintain or increase effort levels were known collectively as the "drive system": close supervision, abuse, profanity, and threats. Informal rules regulating such work behavior as rest periods were arbitrarily and harshly enforced. Workers were constantly urged to move faster and work harder. Sumner Slichter defined the drive system as "the policy of obtaining efficiency not by rewarding merit, not by seeking to interest men in their work . . . but by putting pressure on them to turn out a large output. The dominating note of the drive policy is to inspire the worker with awe and fear of the management, and having developed fear among them, to take advantage of it."[17]

Driving was more prevalent with daywork, where the effort wage was indeterminate. But it occurred with straight piecework too, when foremen sought to prevent workers from restricting output. An official of the machinists complained that "in many cases the rapidity with which the workingmen have been driven under the piecework and similar systems have been the means of driving the mechanics to the insane asylum." Under the bonus wage systems that began to appear after 1890, wages did not rise in proportion to output. Thus, unit labor costs fell with additional production, creating an incentive for the foreman to drive his men even harder and arousing the unions' anger over these new "scientific" payment plans.[18]

The drive system depended, ultimately, on fear of unemployment to ensure obedience to the foreman. Workers were more submissive when jobs were scarce, as was often the case before World War I. A discharge was usually devastating, since few workers had savings to cushion the hardships of unemployment and only meager relief was available. On the other hand, a tight labor market tended to undermine the foreman's authority, forcing him to rely more heavily on discharges to maintain discipline. Data from a metalworking plant illustrate this point. In 1914, a depressed year, the plant had 225 dismissals, many of them for "unadaptability" or "slow work"; this suggests that workers who could not keep up to standard were fired during hard times. By 1916, when the economy had improved and workers could afford to be feisty, the number of dismissals rose to 467, and a relatively large number of workers were fired for "insurbordination," "troublemaking," and "positive misconduct." But whether times were tough or easy, the foreman was free to fire anyone as he saw fit, and discharges were meted out liberally. One critic of this system told the story of an assistant superintendent making his rounds through the shop: "Bill," he said to the foreman, "has anyone been fired from this shop today?" "No," the foreman meekly replied. "Well, then, fire a couple of 'em!" barked the assistant superintendent, in a voice that carried. "It'll put the fear of God in their hearts."[19]

Employment Security

Employment instability involved more than high dismissal rates. In its cyclical and seasonal forms, unemployment regularly touched a large portion of the working class. Between 1854 and 1914, recessions or depressions occurred every three or four years, with about twenty-five of these sixty years spent in contraction. In Massachusetts, unemployment was high even during relatively prosperous periods such as 1900–1906, when about one in every five of the state's manufacturing workers was unemployed for at least part of each year. Even Massachusetts' trade union members, a relatively skilled group, were not immune to job loss. An average of 29 percent of these workers had a spell of joblessness each year between 1890 and 1916. The amount of time spent in unemployment was considerable: In 1890 and again in 1900, over 40 percent of the nation's unemployed were jobless for more than four months.[20]

Because of dismissals and seasonal instability, unemployment was widespread throughout the labor force even during good years. Paul H. Douglas, the noted labor economist, estimated that approximately two-thirds of the unemployment that occurred in the three decades after 1896 was due to seasonal and chronic, as opposed to cyclical, causes. During the 1900s, workers in highly seasonal industries—men's clothing, glass containers, textiles— were on average employed only about three-fourths of a full working year. Employment tended to be more stable in consumer goods industries which produced items unaffected by style changes. But in 1909 even the most stable industry—bread and bakery goods— had monthly employment levels that varied 7 percent from peak to trough. That same year, the industrial average fluctuated 14 percent over the year, rising to 45 percent in the automobile industry. The seasonal instability of employment perpetuated the drive system. Activity became frenzied during the busy season as firms rushed to fill orders. Capacity utilization rates and employment levels rose by magnitudes rarely encountered today. A Fall River textile worker said that during the industry's busy season, "The Board of Trade drives the agent, the agent drives the superintendent, he drives the overseer, and the overseer drives the operative. They drive us, and we drive each other."[21]

However, the existence of widespread unemployment is not by itself an indication of the impermanence of the employment relationship. Had there been some understanding that laid-off workers would be recalled when needed, periodic unemployment need not have severed the relationship. But few firms made systematic attempts to rehire their workers after layoffs. For example, statistics from a large Chicago metalworking plant, whose records distinguished between new hires and rehires, reveal that only 8 percent of all new hires during the 1908–1910 period were rehires of workers who had been laid off during the depression that began late in 1907. Average industrial rehire rates were probably much lower. Of course, rehiring was more common in seasonal industries, since layoffs and their durations were more predictable. Even here, however, reemployment was by no means guaranteed. A government study of seven dressmaking establishments found that from 32 percent to 75 percent of those employed during the spring busy season were rehired after the summer lull.[22]

In addition to rehiring, mechanisms to maintain the employment relationship during downturns included guaranteed employment plans and work-sharing arrangements. By 1920, only 15 companies had employment guarantee plans. Work-sharing plans, though more prevalent, were usually initiated by trade unions in cooperation with unionized employers. Employers in nonunion firms maintained that work-sharing was cumbersome and inefficient.[23]

Few workers had anything resembling equity in their jobs. When layoffs came, it was the rare employer who ordered his foremen to reduce the work force systematically. Employment security was determined by the same arbitrary criteria as hiring. Bribes were a common means of ensuring job security. Shortly after the turn of the century, a group of Lithuanian workers in a rubber factory were forced to hand over a regular portion of their wages to the foreman as a sort of unemployment insurance. In other shops, according to an article in *Engineering Magazine,* everyone had to "pay some sort of tribute to his foreman. The tribute is usually in the form of money or service, but there are cases where the tribute is of a nature which cannot be mentioned in an open paper."[24]

In short, prior to World War I employment for most manufacturing workers was unstable, unpredictable, and frequently unjust. The worker's economic success and job satisfaction depended on a highly personal relationship with his foreman, with management and "the company" playing only a minor role. A foreman interviewed in 1920 noted that "before the war, most workmen worked where they did not so much because of the company they worked for but because of the foreman. To them the foreman represented the company, and workers in the barroom and other hangouts didn't talk so much about this company or that company as they did about this foreman or that foreman they had worked for." There *was* an implicit system of employment here, but it was not bureaucratic. Foremen had many favors to offer those whom they had befriended or those who had bought their friendship. Personal ties and loyalty counted for much, although later reformers were horrified by the particularism and brutality that infused the drive system. Those changes that made employment practices more rational, stable, and equitable were not a managerial innovation; rather, they were imposed from below.[25]

II. The Union Response

Trade unionism helped to curb the foreman's arbitrary exercise of power and gave the skilled worker some control over the terms of his employment. The trade union ensured that strict rules and equitable procedures would govern allocative decisions. While only a minority of all workers belonged to unions, those unions were a persistent reminder that the employer's authority, and that of his agents, could be circumscribed through collective action.[26]

Prior to the 1880s, local trade unions unilaterally adopted working rules or "legislation" that governed wages and working conditions for union members. Enforcement depended upon members' refusing—under threat of punishment by the union—to obey any order that contravened the union's rules. But after 1880, as the unions and their national organizations grew more powerful, the status of these rules changed from unilateral group codes to contractual and bargained restrictions on the employer and his foremen. These contracts were extensive documents that strictly regulated work methods and effort norms as well as such issues as apprenticeship standards and wage scales. An 1889 Memorandum of Agreement for members of the Amalgamated Association of Iron, Steel and Tin Workers at the Homestead Works contained fifty-eight pages of "footnotes" defining work rules for union members.[27]

Hiring

Controlling access to a trade was a fundamental element of the unions' power, and regulating apprenticeship standards was an important method for effecting this control. By limiting the number of apprentices or by lengthening the time required to become a journeyman, the union ensured that there would not be an oversupply of men in the trade and thus that the living standards to which union members were accustomed would not deteriorate. Moreover, by overseeing the training process, the union made certain that persons entering the trade were exposed to the virtues of unionism and had absorbed its moral code.

By the turn of the century, however, the apprenticeship system was fading out in many occupations where an ever finer division of labor reduced the demand for versatile craftsmen who knew all the "secrets" of a trade. The ratio of apprentices to the total number employed in manufacturing steadily declined, from 1:33 in 1860 to 1:88 in 1900. In testimony to Congress in 1901, Samuel Gompers noted that "the apprenticeship system is not so generally in vogue now as formerly. The introduction of new machinery . . . and the division and subdivision of labor have rendered a high class of skill, in which workmen have whole work, scarcely necessary (except the demand for the highest skill in a particular branch)."[28]

Nevertheless, the unions had other ways to bolster their control. One important mechanism was the closed or preferential shop, which restricted the foreman's discretion to hire whomever he chose and enhanced the demand for union labor. This protected union members against discrimination in hiring and guaranteed that vacancies would be filled by them. In some trades, the closed shop led to more restrictive union admissions policies so that a fixed number of potential vacancies could be divided among a smaller body of members. Some unions required that the foreman apply to a union hiring hall when in need of labor; this practice allowed the union to dispense jobs to the workers of its choice. Such arrangements also allowed unions to provide employment for older members and to prohibit the use of tests and other screening devices deemed objectionable. But basically they were a powerful demonstration to the worker that his well-being was best served by allegiance to the union rather than to his foreman.[29]

Wages and Effort

In their approach to wage determination, trade unions sought to protect not only absolute wage levels but also relative and effort wages. The central feature of this approach was the so-called standard rate, which all union members were supposed to receive. Reflecting the principle of equal pay for equal work, the standard rate ruled out all incentive wage systems under which earnings did not rise in proportion to output and effort, as well as all payment systems which "graded" workers: that is, classified them by some criterion such as merit or competence or sometimes even seniority. (One union said that seniority allowed the employer to get "first class service from a man getting less than a first class wage.") The unions' strong emphasis on the standard rate was based on the premise that foremen would always prefer to deal with individuals and that grading was the surest way to divide and conquer.

The unions were opposed to grading on other grounds as well. First, they argued that grading was unnecessary since apprenticeship standards insured that all journeymen were equally competent. Second, they feared that grouping workers by competence would undercut the standard rate and lead inevitably to the substitution of relatively cheap labor for higher priced men. Third, they believed that grading encouraged specialization within the trade, thereby lessening the demand for all-around craftsmen and eroding wage levels. Finally, they viewed grading and other meritocratic wage determination methods as an affront to their egalitarianism and their insistence on occupational autonomy. When the United Typothetae, an employers' association, proposed a graded wage system in 1887, the Typographical Union replied that "it would be impossible to satisfactorily grade all workmen except by an elaborate system of examination which would be appalling to undertake."[30]

In practice, however, the unions permitted the payment of different rates for the various steps within a trade and for especially skilled or dangerous work. Among machinists and molders, for example, journeymen who had recently advanced from apprenticeship could be paid wages below the standard rate. Other unions allowed grading by skill, but only if the different grades were nonsubstitutable. The photoengravers permitted half-tone etchers to be paid more than line-etchers, but the latter—however capable—were never permitted to do half-tone work.[31]

The standard rate represented a level of well-being for which union members had fought and to which they felt entitled. Consequently, organized workers viewed wage cuts as a threat to their living standards and stood ready to strike in defense of the standard rate. As early as 1870, textile manufacturers in Fall River, and then coal operators in Ohio's Hocking Valley, deliberately provoked strikes by cutting the wages of their unionized workers, hoping to break the unions in the ensuing disputes.[32]

Unions were equally concerned about how hard members had to work to receive their pay. To check the foreman's driving and to protect the effort wage, skilled workers made effective use of "the stint," the deliberate restriction of output. In many instances, the union specified output limits in the trade agreement and imposed fines on pieceworkers whose earnings were excessive. Typically, however, union members policed themselves. Skilled workers who restricted their output did not think of themselves as Luddites but instead as "sober and trustworthy masters of the trade" whose stinting demonstrated "unselfish brotherhood."[33]

While the stint was also used to deter foremen from playing favorites in assigning piecework jobs, the unions had other ways to limit favoritism. For example, in 1896 the molders demanded that piece rates be listed in a price-book, so as to prevent foremen from paying different rates for similar work. In one stovemaking shop, both the foreman and a union representative were given keys to the locker in which the price-book was kept. In the Chicago meatpacking industry, the cattle butchers devised a detailed system of promotion lines governed by seniority that was intended to curtail favoritism in job allocation and to create a sense of equity among the union's members. Foremen and other managers were strongly opposed to the practice. As John R. Commons observed, "These rules of promotion do not find favor with the superintendents, who contend that forced promotion takes a man away from work he does well."[34]

Elsewhere, promotion lines were devised primarily to enhance the prospects of a shop's incumbent workers. During the 1870s, unskilled helpers in the steel industry demanded that they be given preference over outsiders whenever a skilled position became vacant. By the late 1880s, the steelworkers' union had adopted rules calling for promotion lines governed by seniority. "We endeavor," said the union, "to prevent men from learning the skilled positions before they have served in the minor ones. If they are permitted to learn the skilled jobs, it would necessarily mean that those holding the minor positions would have no opportunity for improvement."[35]

Security

In an effort to reduce unemployment, trade unions adopted rules regulating manning levels and working hours, as well as output quotas. Workers in seasonal industries like construction were encouraged to slow down as the slack season approached. While such strictures may have had some stabilizing effect on the demand for union labor, they could not prevent periodic outbreaks of unemployment. When layoffs threatened, the unions attempted to mitigate the impact of unemployment through work-sharing and through seniority rules.

Work-sharing was practiced by a variety of unions—the needle trades, the boot and shoe workers, the machinists, the coal miners—and took a variety of forms. Groups of workers might alternate shifts of a week or less. Alternatively, some union shops closed early or shut down for a day or two each week. In industries such as brewing, the employers and the union made joint arrangements to share the work; in other trades, the unions unilaterally withdrew their members on certain days of the week.[36]

A few unions responded to downturns with rules requiring that layoffs be made in accordance with reverse seniority. This was less common than work-sharing, in part because employment was so volatile in many industries that seniority rules would have divided the union into two groups, those who had steady jobs and those who did not. Further, seniority layoffs were unsuited to those trades with a tradition of mobility, where few workers remained with an employer for any length of time. Hence, some of the first unions to rely on seniority layoffs were found on the railroads and in newspaper printing, industries in which employment was relatively stable and workers were attached to their employer rather than to their trade. The first written agreement recognizing seniority as a factor in layoffs was signed by railroad workers in 1875; fifteen years later the typographers adopted their famous "priority law," which required that layoffs be made in strict accordance with seniority.[37]

Another cushion against the shock of unemployment was the requirement that advance notice be given of impending layoffs. Innocuous as this rule may seem, employers were under no obligation to give notice, and unprepared workers often suffered. A shopman on the Baltimore & Ohio railroad recalled, "Our boss was always afraid to tell you there was going to a be a layoff. I have seen McSweeney write on the door with a piece of chalk, 'No work tomorrow.' He waited so long that he could not get around to tell the men in time."[38]

Whether the unions chose seniority or work-sharing, their regulations undermined one of the foreman's chief prerogatives under the drive system—determining the incidence of layoffs. Neither scheme allowed foremen to discriminate against union members or to pit workers against each other in a struggle to retain their jobs. Indeed, the printing and railroad unions became interested in seniority-based layoffs at a time when both industries were experiencing an increase in favoritism, nepotism, and, especially, discrimination against union members.[39]

The strongest protection the unions devised against unfair treatment were the restrictions they imposed on the foreman's power to discipline and discharge. These restrictions were of two types. In some industries, the union followed a craft tradition of unilaterally promulgating rules with respect to discipline and dismissal. That is, the *union* determined standards of behavior; fined or expelled members who fell below these standards; and provided its own internal grievance procedure. The closed shop was critical to the operation of these systems: Only if union membership was a prerequisite of employment could the union secure compliance with its rules. For example, the milkwagon drivers' union agreed in its contracts to fine or suspend any member proved guilty of "drunkenness, or dishonesty, incompetency, smoking or drinking while on duty." Moreover—and this is key—the company agreed to dismiss anyone whom the union expelled. Hence, a union member's job security depended less on his relation to any single employer or foreman than on his standing in the union, which controlled access to future employment via the closed shop.[40]

A second type of restraint was found in those union contracts that gave the *employer* the right to set standards and to administer discipline. The contracts required, however, that discipline be meted out only when the employer had "just and sufficient cause." Occasionally these causes were spelled out, but usually the meaning of such phrases as "justice" and "reasonable rights" was determined by an appeals body: a third-party arbitrator, a joint committee made up of equal numbers of union and management representatives, or simply some high-level manager who was sufficiently removed from the shop floor to render a dispassionate decision. If a worker was found "not guilty" at his "trial" or "hearing," he could be awarded pay for time lost and given his old job back.[41]

Many unions mandated a hierarchical structure for dispute resolution. For example, a worker in the anthracite coal industry during the 1900s would first take up a complaint with his foreman. If not adjusted, it would be submitted to the pit committee and mine superintendent. Then the grievance would go to a regional board of conciliation and, if conciliation failed, to an umpire. Prior to World War I, well-developed grievance procedures terminating in arbitration were found in only a few industries, including coal, the railroads, and the needle trades. Elsewhere the procedure had fewer steps and usually culminated in a meeting of the union officers and the employer.[42]

These disciplinary provisions, together with the closed shop and seniority rules, undermined the fundamental assumption of the drive system: that employment was a relationship of indefinite duration terminable at the employer's will. The unions held the alternative concept that employment was a permanent relationship between the union (a set of workers) and the employer (a set of jobs). In the building trades, this set of jobs spanned establishment boundaries; on the railroads, and in the printing, metalworking, and needle trades, these jobs were found within a single firm. In either case, the union behaved as if it owned this set of jobs: With the closed shop, only union men could fill the jobs; under work-sharing, the jobs could not be dissolved. The union's various security mechanisms kept the employer from turning to the open market to fill vacancies. Moreover, through its allocative, wage, and dismissal practices, the union embedded the employment relationship in a web of impersonal, equitable rules. Indeed, by 1915 the unions had come very close to creating a bureaucratic employment system for their mostly skilled members.

III. The Less Skilled

The unskilled worker dissatisfied with his job had few options. He could complain to higher officials, but they invariably supported the foreman in any dispute. Daniel McCallum, president of the Erie Railroad, justified this practice by asserting that "obedience cannot be enforced where the foreman is interfered with by a superior officer giving orders directly to his subordinates." More was involved here than the application of a military model to industry. As one economist perceptively observed, managers feared that any show of liberality would "give the workmen exaggerated notions of their rights and management desires to keep the workers' minds off their rights." In the early 1900s a group of nineteen unskilled rubber workers presented their employer with signed affidavits that described how they had been forced to bribe a foreman to retain their jobs. All nineteen were fired within two weeks.[43]

Occasionally the unskilled were able to establish their own workplace organizations, which regulated employment in much the same way as the craft unions did. During the 1880s, the Knights of Labor included local assemblies made up of less skilled workers who banded together to press for higher wages and to protect themselves from arbitrary foremen. Some of the locals even achieved the closed shop and a seniority-based layoff system. But unskilled workers had relatively little bargaining power and were rarely able to sustain sizable, stable organizations.

The absence of organization did not, however, deter them from engaging in militant activity. In steel, for instance, pitched battles were fought at Cleveland (1899), East Chicago (1905), McKees Rocks (1909), and Bethlehem (1910), with the unskilled, immigrant work force on one side and the militia and police on the other. The particularly violent strike at McKees Rocks was touched off when the company fired a group of workers who had protested pay practices and fee-charging by the company's foremen. But these strikes, while spectacular, were sporadic and seldom successful.[44]

Limitation of output was a somewhat more effective means of checking the foreman. The Commissioner of Labor's 1904 report on *Regulation and Restriction of Output* found that stints and slowdowns were "enforced in nonunion establishments" and were widely accepted "among all wage earners." But lacking the discipline provided by a union, and sundered by ethnic conflicts and language barriers that stymied cooperation, unskilled workers— even those belonging to assemblies of the Knights of Labor—had less success with this method than did their skilled counterparts.[45]

Because his actions were so ineffectual, the unskilled worker seeking higher wages or better working conditions usually had no alternative but to quit. Data from the 1900s and 1910s show labor turnover levels that were extraordinarily high by modern standards, especially among less skilled workers. Many companies experienced monthly separation rates in excess of 10 percent. In one Milwaukee engine factory, whose experience was typical of other factories, the separation rates for unskilled and semiskilled workers in 1912 were three times as high as the rates for skilled workers in the tool and pattern department. A government official termed labor turnover "the individualistic strike": Just as the number of strikes by skilled trade unionists tended to increase during a recovery period, so did the number of quits by the less skilled.[46]

High turnover rates also reflected the immigrant backgrounds of the unskilled. Almost two-thirds of the immigrants arriving in the United States between 1870 and 1910 were unskilled, and they became the backbone of the manufacturing labor force. Around the turn of the century, when the foreign-born constituted nearly one-quarter of the labor force, they represented about half of all unskilled laborers in manufacturing. Foreign-born workers accounted for 58 percent of all workers in iron and steel manufacturing, 61 percent in meatpacking, 62 percent in bituminous coal mining, and 69 percent in the cotton mills.[47]

While it is well-known that immigration flows were large and cyclically sensitive, it is less well-known that emigration flows followed the same pattern. Between 1870 and 1914, one person left the United States for every three that arrived. While emigration decreased and immigration increased during good years, the annual proportion of emigrants to immigrants never fell below 20 percent. Emigration rose during depressed years, as recent immigrants—the first to lose their jobs—decided to return home. Ninety percent of the Bulgarians who made up most of the unskilled labor force in an Illinois steel mill had left town by the end of the 1908 depression. That year, immigration fell, and the national proportion of emigrants to immigrants rose to 75 percent. Although more immigrants stayed than left, the large backflow contributed to the instability of the unskilled labor force and to high rates of turnover.[48]

Immigrants often came to the United States with no intention of permanently settling here. Many were single men or married men with families back home. This was true of about half of the unskilled Italian laborers living in Buffalo in 1905, and of four in five of the nation's immigrant steelworkers. These men came to make their "stake," planning to return to Europe to buy land, open shops, or pay off debts. The transience of the immigrant labor force was part of an older European pattern of peasant mobility. In Italy, landless day laborers roamed from place to place looking for work, often spending weeks or months away from home. Slovaks worked seasonally on their plots and then supplemented their incomes as roving peddlers; Polish peasants went to Germany. The fact that many immigrant workers viewed their stay in the United States as temporary made it difficult to organize them into unions. A strike just lengthened the time a man was away from home and family, while the prospect of returning home made one's privations more bearable.[49]

Finally, quitting was a form of resistance to the rigors of factory life. Here there was a continuity of experience among the early New England textile workers, their French-Canadian and Irish replacements, and the southeastern Europeans who filled the factories after 1880. Each group brought to the factories a preindustrial work ethic that was attuned to the seasons, migratory, and uncomfortable with industrial discipline. Ellen Collins quit the mill at Lowell in the 1840s complaining about her "obedience to the ding-dong of the bell—just as though we were so many living machines." During the 1870s, managers of New England textile mills complained that absenteeism and quits made it difficult to run their machines on the hottest summer days. One manufacturer said in 1878 that "our mill operatives are much like other people and take their frequent holidays for pleasure and visiting." Forty years later, the quit rate at a Connecticut silk mill quadrupled during the hot summer months of 1915. Thus, each group successively went through the process of internalizing factory discipline; this was one of the props to high turnover before 1920.[50]

Although they were relatively less mobile, skilled workers also had a tradition of itinerancy that formed at the intersection of artisanal work habits and the requisites of learning a trade. It was supported by craft institutions, especially the trade union, and by repeated waves of immigrant artisans carrying similar traditions to the United States.

A familiar figure in industrializing societies, the footloose craftsman moved from shop to shop, acquiring the secrets of his trade. Employers often approved of this type of mobility. The labor supervisor at National Cash Register wrote in 1907 that for a skilled worker, "it is of value, not a detriment, if he has had several employers—he is learning the trade." Reinforcing this mobility was a work ethic that emphasized manliness and independence. Acceptance of demeaning working conditions, or even long tenure, would compromise that ethic. One trade union representative noted that, for many skilled workers, "a job may be satisfactory in every respect, quite as good as they are likely to find anywhere, yet they will leave because they do not want to remain in one shop too long. . . . It rests upon a fear of losing their independence, of getting into a frame of mind wherein they will come to attach disproportionate importance to the retention of a certain job."[51]

The craft union facilitated the skilled worker's propensity to move. The constitutions of the early national unions required local secretaries to furnish reports on the conditions of the trade in their area and to help traveling members find jobs. Some unions loaned their members money to finance a search for work if none was to be found near home. But this loan system was on the decline by the beginning of this century, partly "because, as in the case of the iron molders, it was made use of to secure a free holiday."[52]

IV. A Market of Movement

Because the employment relationship was one of weak attachment on both sides, the industrial labor market prior to 1915 was a market of movement, characterized by high rates of mobility. Indeed, the few available company records indicate a pattern of continuously high turnover rates before World War I. The earliest turnover data come from the New England textile industry of the 1830s and 1840s, and they show that the young Yankee women who worked in the mills were an unstable labor force. Most were unmarried and could return to their parents' farms if they were dissatisfied or if work was scarce. But the immigrants who began to replace native workers in the 1850s had high turnover rates too. A study of 151 Scottish weavers recruited by Lyman Mills in 1853 found that nearly 80 percent of the women had left the firm within three years.[53]

A similar picture emerges in other companies, especially those employing relatively more men. A Massachusetts firm that manufactured textile machinery recruited large numbers of French-Canadians between 1860 and 1890. But "so rapid was the turnover" that, of every three workers hired, only one stayed with the firm. Rates of persistence were also very low at the Boston Manufacturing Company. For quinquennial periods between 1850 and 1865, only 10-12 percent of the male workers employed at the beginning of a period were still working for the firm five years later.[54]

Nineteenth-century employers sometimes complained about what one of them called "the nomadic system of employing men." Employers often responded to high quit rates by withholding the wages of those who left without prior notice, a practice that also deterred strikes. When a Massachusetts mill owner was asked in the 1870s to explain these wage forfeitures, he replied, "If a mill did not keep back workers' wages, it would simply awake to find all its hands gone by the morning."[55]

The better records available for the first two decades of the twentieth century show continuing high levels of turnover throughout the manufacturing sector. But because the overall data are so fragmentary, especially for the nineteenth century, some other source of information is needed to gauge labor turnover levels.

Geographic Mobility

One indirect way of measuring turnover is to examine geographic mobility rates, the amount of movement into and out of a place over time. This measure is imperfect, since some separations involve changes between jobs in the same area, and some moves are made by persons outside the labor force. Accurate estimates would demand knowledge of the proportion of job separations that involve a move (currently about 40 percent) and the proportion of moves that entail a job separation (currently over 60 percent). Unfortunately, we have no way of knowing whether, or how much, these proportions have changed since the nineteenth century because we do not know the net effect of opposing forces. For instance, the spread of home ownership and the equalization of economic opportunity between regions have acted to depress the proportion of separations that entail a move. On the other hand, cheaper transportation and better information on distant labor markets have had the opposite effect. Nevertheless, the relationship between geographic and job mobility suggests that it is valid to use the former to track major shifts in the latter.[56]

For many years, the standard measure of geographic mobility was the level of net migration in a city, state, or region. Net migration represents the intersection of two population flows but gives no indication of their absolute size. Recently urban historians have begun to estimate gross migration flows for various cities by using city directories, voter registration rolls, and property tax files. The results have been startling.

For example, net migration into and out of Boston during the ten years after 1880 totaled 65,179 individuals, whereas the gross flows involved nearly one and one-half million people. Moreover, rather than being a decade of particularly high rates of movement, the 1880s saw Boston's lowest decennial mobility rates between 1830 and 1920. Sixty-four percent of the adult men living in Boston in 1880 were still living there ten years later. In contrast, the average decennial persistence rate for other decades was only about 40 percent.[57]

The Boston experience was not unique. Persistence rates in most other urban areas were just as low as Boston's during the 1830-1920 period. Evidence indicates that males were less mobile during the late eighteenth and early nineteenth centuries. But after 1830, geographic mobility increased throughout the United States and remained at high levels at least until 1920. This ceaseless movement into and out of American cities supports the supposition that industrial turnover rates were continuously high before World War I.[58]

This supposition is further buttressed by the finding that, between 1830 and 1920, geographic mobility varied inversely with occupational status: Skilled and less skilled manual workers had lower persistence rates than white-collar workers. In other words, whatever stability existed in American cities during this period is in large part attributable to the relative immobility of such persons as professionals, merchants, teachers, and clerks. This may explain why the middle class regarded stability as a virtue.[59]

Extensive mobility during these years was an indicator of the tenuousness of the employment relationship and the fluidity of the labor market. But did this ceaseless movement across space and between employers improve the worker's economic status? Sumner Slichter thought so, describing the prewar labor market as one in which "the behavior of men was dominated by the idea of opportunity—a market in which there was a considerable number of men ready to give up one job in the hope of getting a better one." Slichter's remark, made in the 1940s, reflected his perception that the workers of his day had become too concerned with security, to the detriment of individual initiative and labor market efficiency. Coming at this issue from a different body of research, Stephan Thernstrom was more skeptical about the economic benefits conferred by mobility. He asked whether "the exceptional volatility of the American working class, especially its least skilled workers, does not point to the existence [prior to 1920] of a permanent floating proletariat made up of men ever on the move but rarely winning economic gains as a result of spatial mobility."[60]

Whichever interpretation is correct, there is no doubt that employment under the drive system was a tenuous relationship. Both parties in the relationship took full advantage of their legal rights, acquired early in the nineteenth century, to quit or to dismiss at will. In fact, this was the only worker right consistently recognized by the courts of the day, and most managers did little to discourage its exercise. During the McKees Rocks dispute of 1909, the president of the struck company was succinct in his opinion of the strikers: "If a man is dissatisfied, it is his privilege to quit."[61]

CHAPTER 2

SYSTEMATIC MANAGEMENT AND WELFARE WORK

Employers were satisfied with the profitability of the decentralized drive system. Since immigrant labor was abundant, they were indifferent to improving employment methods. And, since they tended to view the worker as dumb, docile, or unreliable, they believed that any attempt to win his cooperation by improving employment conditions would be futile: "Labor will simply take advantage of liberal treatment."[1]

But the drive system was not without costs. First, it entailed administrative costs that could be reduced by more bureaucratic methods of coordination and control. Beginning around 1880, employers started to revamp the organization of their increasingly large enterprises, turning to professional engineers for assistance. These industrial engineers applied their expertise to production problems, setting up rationalized manufacturing systems and focusing their managerial skills on the foreman's autonomous realm.

A second set of costs involved the worker's response to the drive system, including recurrent labor unrest, erratic working habits, and radical political sentiments. During the nineteenth century, employers had used strikebreaking and dismissals to cope with these problems. Now, however, a growing number believed that they would have to take more positive steps if they were to win the worker's cooperation and loyalty. Whatever the motivation—a Christian sense of stewardship, a desire to forestall the labor movement by preemption, concern about public opinion, or fear of impending social unrest—the period after 1900 saw a greater willingness on the part of employers to experiment with a variety of paternalistic techniques designed to make workers more sedulous, sober, and loyal.

Both industrial engineering and welfare work had a major impact on the way that American industry administered its employment policies and thought about its labor problems. Although their approaches to these matters differed drastically, these two groups prepared the ground for the proliferation of personnel departments during World War I. In this chapter (and the two that follow), the ideas and events that led to a partial eclipse of the foreman's drive system are examined.

I. Systematic Management

America's manufacturing industries expanded dramatically during the late nineteenth and early twentieth centuries. Manufacturing employment nearly doubled between 1880 and 1900, and nearly doubled again between 1900 and 1920. Accompanying this growth was a trend toward larger establishments: from 65 workers per iron and steel establishment in 1860, to 103 in 1870, to 333 by 1900. New industries such as electrical machinery and motor vehicle manufacturing soon rivaled steel and textiles in establishment size.[2]

Not only the scale but also the speed of manufacturing operations increased, as human labor was replaced by power machinery and handling equipment. This reduction in the amount of time required to process each unit of output, together with the growth in the volume of production, meant that unit costs were steadily reduced. Consequently, the manufacturing firm was able to channel internally generated cash flows into the acquisition of other firms that produced inputs or substitutes for its products.[3]

The unprecedented size and complexity of the manufacturing firm created many administrative difficulties. As we have seen, most proprietors had been content to let their foremen and highly skilled workers manage production. But rapid growth put pressure on this decentralized system. The flow of production was hindered by the lack of coordination between the various departments of a firm. Data on costs were not kept or were gathered only irregularly, making it difficult to compare the performance of various units. If production speed was to be increased, greater coordination and systemization were required.

Employers increasingly turned to professional engineers for assistance in solving these problems. The years between 1880 and 1920, when the number of engineers grew from 7,000 to 135,000, have been called the "golden age" of America's engineering profession. Part of this growth was attributable to the rise of industries based on science, such as chemicals and electrical manufacturing, for which engineers designed new products and processes. But in addition to their technical achievements, engineers were responsible for developing new methods of organization and management. During this period, discussions of plant administration and cost accounting were found chiefly in engineering publications. Much of the pioneering work on these topics was done not by engineers in the new science-based industries but by mechanical engineers in the older metalworking industries, where the highly developed division of labor necessitated greater coordination of operations. Moreover, these older industries already had an entrenched system of production management. If growth was to continue, control of production would have to be wrested away from foremen and skilled workers.[4]

After 1880, articles on production management began to appear more frequently in the *Transactions* of the American Society of Mechanical Engineers and in commercial publications like *Engineering Magazine*. The gist of these articles was that the rapid growth of machine shops and other metalworking establishments had led to internal disorder and that greater coordination and systemization were required if production speed was to be increased. As John Tregoing, a mechanical engineer, observed in his *Treatise on Factory Management* (1891):

> The first and foremost want of many of our large factories is not work, but a thorough revision of the machinery that manages and directs the whole concern. It is not a want of brains; it is not the difficulty of working out a vast and complicated scheme; it is not a matter of involving the company in a large outlay of money—it is simply a question of *method*, the application of a few simple rules, and a respect for the time-honored principle that Order is the first Law of the Universe, and the nearer our approach to it, the more harmonious will our arrangement work.

The lack of method perceived by engineers like Tregoing resulted from a breakdown of coordination between the various departments of the manufacturing firm, a breakdown that impeded the horizontal flow of production through the works. In addition, the proliferation of lower-level management positions made it more difficult for top management to get the information necessary for effective decision-making and to maintain control over foremen and other managers. Joseph A. Litterer, a business historian, has dubbed these breakdowns "organizational uncoupling"; the engineer's attempts to rectify this uncoupling led to what Litterer refers to as the "systemetic management movement."[5]

At first, systematic management was no more than a hodgepodge of remedies for the waste and confusion found in the machine shops. Engineers stressed the need to develop greater coordination between production units and stronger links between the various levels of management. Analogies were drawn to the military's hierarchical system or to the human body, with the firm's top managers (along with the engineers) representing the brain. Some pictured the factory as an enormous machine, whose parts all had to fit together for high-speed, frictionless performance.

To facilitate the coordination of production, the engineers recommended forms, records, standard procedures, and instructions. Henry Towne, an engineer and president of Yale and Towne Lock Manufacturing Company, wrote several influential articles outlining the system of shop management in use at his firm: After an order was received, it was numbered and tagged by the head office, sent to the production superintendent for assignment, and then given to the appropriate foreman, who sent back to the superintendent on another special form an estimated completion date for the order. Henry Metcalfe, who had served as superintendent of several large arsenals run by the Army's Ordnance Department, introduced the use of routing slips, which were prepared by the head office and which indicated the sequence of departments an order would pass through and the operations to be performed in each department.[6]

Many engineers became infatuated with these techniques; and for the next twenty years the engineering publications—especially those with a mania for this sort of thing, such as *System*—were filled with articles describing new types of forms. Sometimes a firm's top managers were overwhelmed by the mounting paper-work. In 1907, Henry Ford and his righthand man, Charles Sorenson, "spent a Sunday morning emptying drawers of cards and tickets—the plant's cost system—on the floor of the factory record office." Nevertheless, the use of standard forms and instructions spread throughout industry and eventually came to be considered essential features of good management, providing a check on the foreman's failure to keep records or to cooperate with other foremen and insuring that production would be carried out exactly as specified. Of the production record system in use at Carnegie's steel plants, Charles Schwab said in 1896 that "greater economies are effected by strict supervision over all departments than in any other direction."[7]

Another major innovation was the development of detailed cost-accounting systems. Prior to the 1880s, data on costs were not kept or were gathered only irregularly. As late as 1885, a trade association in the iron and steel industry—unable to find the information needed for a federal tariff study—complained that many firms "do not keep their records with sufficient minuteness." The engineers were largely responsible for an increase in the detail and frequency with which cost data were collected. The development of accurate information on costs, including overhead and labor costs, enabled management to compare the performance of different units and to pinpoint problem areas in the firm. By 1901, the U.S. Steel Corporation had implemented a uniform accounting system at all of its plants, each of which sent monthly reports to the New York office detailing the costs of their various operations. The blast furnace forms alone contained over eight thousand items.[8]

The systematic management literature also recommended that some of the foreman's duties be routinized and parceled out among staff employees. Thus, new clerical and white-collar positions, such as time keeper and cost clerk, were created to keep track of production. Other traditional duties of the foreman, such as assembling raw materials for production and keeping stock of tools and inventory, were made the responsibility of special clerks.

Under these new production control systems, foremen retained some essential functions. They assisted in gathering cost data, submitted records, and wrote out orders for parts and materials. Nevertheless, the innovations introduced by the engineers significantly reduced the foreman's autonomy. He was told which units to produce, what method to use, and in what order to perform the operations. In short, his directive and conceptual duties in production were taken over by persons far removed from the shop floor. Foremen did not take kindly to their loss of power and prerogatives. According to one efficiency engineer, they "resented taking instructions from abrasive, soft-handed college men who had never themselves poured a mold or run a machine." But even though the systematic management movement reduced the foreman's role in production, it left relatively untouched the other major area under his control—employment.[9]

Incentive Wages

That employment received far less attention than production in the systematic management literature must not be construed as indicating a lack of concern or interest. Instead it represented the engineer's somewhat simplistic belief that most employment and labor relations problems could be solved through a properly devised incentive wage. The first incentive wage schemes used in American industry were piece-rate wages, which became increasingly popular after 1880. But engineers were skeptical that productivity gains could be achieved by piecework, pointing to the worker's refusal to exceed traditional output norms and to the growing disparity in labor costs between the United States and its competitors in England and Germany in the 1890s.[10]

American engineers began to experiment with more sophisticated incentive plans. For example, Frederick A. Halsey's "Premium Plan of Paying for Labor," presented to the American Society of Mechanical Engineers (ASME) in 1891, gave the worker a bonus for any output he produced beyond a minimum level (which was set by the engineer). But the most famous of these new wage-incentive plans was Frederick W. Taylor's differential piece rate, which he described in a paper to the ASME in 1895. Unlike Halsey's plan, which based its minimum rate on customary effort levels, Taylor's differential piece rate was set "scientifically" by breaking a task down into its component parts, timing these parts, eliminating "unnecessary motions," and then arriving at a minimum time for task completion. The plan's fame rested on two factors: first, on Taylor's claim to have found a scientific method for determining a fair day's work and the "one best way" of performing a task; and second, on his characterization of the plan as "a step toward a partial solution of the labor problem."[11]

Taylor argued that the plan could reduce labor unrest because it circumvented one of the problems associated with conventional piecework: the employer's tendency to cut piece rates when workers produced more and thereby garnered higher earnings. By guaranteeing the employer an increasing return on the worker's output, Taylor's plan lessened the likelihood of wage cuts. This supposedly inhibited strikes and encouraged workers to pursue the lure of higher incomes. With a properly designed wage-incentive plan, said Taylor, "both sides take their eyes off the division of the surplus until this surplus becomes so large that it is unnecessary to quarrel over how it shall be divided."

Taylor admired skilled workers, viewing them as rugged individualists driven mainly by a desire for economic gain. But he was hostile to their trade unions, which he described as a "hindrance to prosperity." Taylor thought that his wage-incentive plan would stimulate "each workman's ambition by paying him according to his individual worth" and would thus weaken the unions by weakening their hold on the "ambitious" skilled worker. Indeed, his plan was the essence of individualism: Instead of establishing wage rates for whole classes of jobs, it set a different incentive rate for each job, thereby striking at the heart of the unions' approach to wage determination, the standard rate.[12]

Although most unions had willingly accepted payment by the piece, they were violently opposed to wage-incentive plans like Taylor's, fearing that such plans would erode traditional effort norms and would cheapen trades by breaking them down into simpler jobs. But the deeper concern was that these plans would make collective wage bargaining difficult, if not impossible, ultimately turning the wage bargain into an individual matter between the worker and his employer. As John R. Commons observed, "The fear of the unionist is the fear that his organization cannot cope with the infinite number of little variations from schedule, or with variations that the schedule does not provide for." Consequently, the introduction of time study and production standards in unionized shops often led to strikes, some of them quite spectacular. Unions sought and obtained federal legislation banning the use of stopwatches in government arsenals and shipyards; and Taylor twice had to defend his incentive plan at congressional hearings instigated by the unions.[13]

Scientific Management

Taylor was best known for his "scientific management" system, which synthesized various systematic management methods then being proposed by other mechanical engineers. His reputation was based less on any particular innovation than on his uncompromising attitude toward traditional management methods and his skills as a publicist for his blend of commercial, scientific, and ethical principles. By the time of his death in 1915, Taylor had become a national figure, and scientific management had penetrated social and cultural realms far removed from the shop floor.

Like other systematic management reforms, Taylor's system completely changed the foreman's role in production. Taylor proposed that the foreman's production responsibilities be allocated to a "planning department" and a group of "functional foremen." The planning department was envisioned as the firm's production control center, housing a variety of staff positions related to cost analysis, time study, process innovation, and standardization. Taylor argued that, if all "brain work" done by foremen was transferred to the "brain workers" in the planning department, production costs would drop sharply. The idea of functional foremen, though more original, was rarely adopted: It entailed dividing the foreman's "all-around" duties into eight specialized jobs and assigning each job to one of the functional foremen, on the assumption that such division of labor was always more efficient.[14]

In several plants where scientific management was introduced, foremen were as angered as skilled workers by Taylor's innovations, objecting particularly to his minute systemization and to their loss of prerogatives. When he was employed at Midvale Steel in Philadelphia, Taylor devised a shop bulletin board that used special tags to indicate future work assignments for different machines in the shop. The board had to be covered with thick glass to prevent foremen from tearing the tags off. At the Simonds Roller Bearing Machine Company, which hired Taylor as a consultant in 1897, all of the foremen resigned when Taylor set up a planning office. And when the installation of Taylor's system at the Watertown Arsenal led to a massive walkout by skilled machinists in 1911, a number of the arsenal's foremen supported the striking workers.[15]

Personnel Management

Because the main thrust of systematic and scientific management was the reorganization of industry's production methods, neither Taylor nor other engineers had much to say about the foreman's employment duties, except those related to wage determination. Indeed, some scholars argue that the efficiency engineers contributed little to the development of modern methods of employment administration. But even though the engineers were silent about the *content* of personnel management—recruitment, promotion, dismissals—they did establish an organizational rationale for its *form*—the specialized staff department.[16]

Some elements of the engineers' approach to production management—orderly procedures, accurate records, and the departmentalization of routinized functions—came into play with the establishment of personnel departments by a few forward-looking companies in the decade after 1900. One such department, initiated by Goodyear Tire and Rubber in 1900, concerned itself with the orderly processing of new employees and the keeping of employment and pay records. Although these were essentially clerical functions, the idea of creating staff personnel departments was in the air, and the engineers were responsible for that.[17]

Occasionally engineers specifically called for the establishment of specialized employment departments. Taylor's *Shop Management* listed seventeen functions within the planning department, and three of these—an employment bureau, a pay unit, and a shop disciplinarian—were core activities around which personnel departments formed after 1910. Several of the nation's first personnel departments were sited in firms with strong ties to Taylor. For instance, Henry Kendall's Plimpton Press set up its personnel department in 1910, at which time several of Taylor's associates were under contract to the firm. The head of the department was given charge of all hiring and of maintaining employee records, for which he used special cards.[18]

At a more general level, the path that personnel management followed after 1910 paralleled the path taken by production. The foreman's employment duties were transferred to staff departments. Information formerly regarded as part of the foreman's "secret" store of knowledge, such as wage rates and job content, was appropriated by the personnel manager much as the secrets of production had been appropriated by the engineer (a process that the engineers called "the transference of skill and knowledge"). Personnel managers used much the same rhetoric that engineers had used to attack foremen: they were not specialists, they were overly busy, their methods were not scientific.[19]

Nevertheless, having noted that the engineers set an organizational precedent for the personnel department, one must add that their writings on employment matters lacked richness of detail. Taylor's descriptions of the shop disciplinarian and the employment bureau were skimpy and vague, and a special 1912 report on scientific management, written by Taylor's disciples, had nothing to say about labor beyond a discussion of incentive pay. Because of this single-minded focus on wage incentives, critics of scientific management faulted the engineers for their "naive ignorance of social science." Said Robert F. Hoxie of the University of Chicago: "They tend naively to assume that when the productivity of the concern is increased and the laborers are induced to do their full part toward this end, the labor problem . . . is satisfactorily solved." In a 1914 survey of thirty-five companies that had introduced some aspect of scientific management, Hoxie found "little uniformity" in employment methods and said that "at best a separate labor department is established."

Thus, personnel management had wider sources than industrial engineering. Even the personnel department at Plimpton Press, a company well within the Taylor fold, owed its character more to a welfare work philosophy than to scientific management. Its personnel manager was, in the words of Henry Kendall, someone a worker could "go to for advice in regard to his present employment, for suggestions in regard to outside education or instruction, one who is in sympathy with him, and with whom he can rest his grievances." This kind of personnel manager, ready to be the worker's counselor and confidante, was a far cry from Taylor's planning clerk or shop disciplinarian.[20]

II. Welfare Work

Between 1886 and 1889, a period of labor unrest, some forty companies launched profit-sharing plans for their employees and, at the same time, began to provide various amenities like lunchrooms and landscaped grounds. This marked the start of America's welfare work movement. So diverse were the activities covered by the term that a 1916 government study defined welfare work as "anything for the comfort and improvement, intellectual or social, of the employees, over and above wages paid, which is not a necessity of the industry nor required by law."[21]

Like scientific management, welfare work sought to prevent strikes and to improve production, though its methods were more indirect, focusing on the worker after he had put down his tools and left the shop. It was rooted in the belief that the worker himself—the intemperate, slothful worker or the ignorant immigrant, prey to radical nostrums—was directly responsible for labor unrest, social tension, and the decline of the work ethic. To countermand these tendencies, firms experimented with programs ranging from thrift clubs, complusory religious observances, and citizenship instruction, to company housing, outings, and contests. The idea was that the firm could be used to recast the worker in a middle-class mold: uplifting him, bettering him, and making his family life more wholesome.

Welfare work blossomed during the era of juvenile reform, domestic science, settlement work, and other well-intentioned but paternalistic attempts to remake the working-class family. It attracted its practitioners and publicists from the "helping professions"—social workers, settlement workers, educators—who sought to protect the working-class family from the exigencies of industrial life, even while calling into question the family's ability to function without expert assistance.[22]

Welfare workers gave a great deal of attention to the family, believing that many of the employee's defects could be traced to an improper home life. Companies sought to turn the workplace into a replica of the ideal middle-class home by placing potted plants around the factory's interior, landscaping its grounds, and even hanging curtains at its windows. One automobile factory had a recreation room decorated with oriental rugs, lace curtains, ferns, and a Victrola. Another factory organized a "Little Mothers" club where women learned hygiene and infant care. Many companies paid their male employees a premium called a "family wage," which was supposed to make it unnecessary for their wives to work. White Motor Company, a firm that adhered to this policy, also gave hiring preference to married men, proclaiming that "comfortably housed, sane-thinking families . . . are not fertile soil for revolutionary propaganda."[23]

At another level, welfare work attempted to evoke a sense of family life within the firm itself. Observing that firms had grown too large and impersonal, employers tried to reproduce the close personal ties of the nineteenth-century workplace. This nostalgia derived from a belief that labor relations had been less adversarial in the entrepreneurial firm, when owners knew all of their employees by name. The welfare work director at National Cash Register in 1901 attributed "most of the trouble of the present day" to "the loss of this personal relation and feeling of mutuality of interest." He further noted that "in this day of the large corporations, the employers are out of touch with their workmen. That this works untold harm cannot be doubted."[24]

Among the methods used by welfare workers to promote the image of the corporate family and to boost its "team spirit" were company picnics, company athletics, company songs, company contests, and company magazines filled with inconsequential gossip about these activities. The names of these magazines underscored the "one big happy family" theme: *The American Sugar Family, The Minute Family, Ourselves, Us,* and, at a soap company, *The Family Wash.*[25]

To create a sense of familial warmth and friendliness, welfare workers also tried to build close personal ties to employees. The welfare director at the Cleveland Hardware Company visited the home of every worker one week after hiring and at least once a year after that. Mary B. Gilson, welfare director at Joseph & Feiss Company, regularly went to workers' homes to check on living conditions, family relationships, and illnesses. She argued that the "intelligent" employer knew that, by checking into the causes of absences and headaches, "he is helping to make better workers and better citizens and a more stable and steadily prosperous body of employees." The welfare worker was the employee's confidante, extending a hand of friendship from an otherwise impersonal corporation.[26]

The role of welfare worker, like that of social worker, was congruent with the stereotype of the woman as sympathetic and nurturing. Not surprisingly, then, a relatively large proportion of welfare workers were women, many of them former social workers. In fact, home visiting as a technique was popularized by Mary Richmond, a prominent social worker. Richmond said that "friendly visiting" was a way for the social worker to "get back into genuine relations with people of smaller incomes." Social workers were encouraged to become friendly with their clients, braving what Vida Scudder called "smells hitherto unknown" to visit people in their homes and to provide advice on proper living.[27]

But the home visit often became the occasion for a patronizing lecture. Mary B. Gilson advised employees on marital choice, furniture arrangement, even personal appearance. She said, for instance, "It is no longer a debatable question that elaborate clothes and jewelry and powder and paint have a demoralizing effect on the character and ability of a working girl." In her autobiography, Gilson recalled that "there was no facet of life we did not touch." Because of their frequent contact with employees, welfare workers could also serve as a conduit of information on the worker's union proclivities and living habits. In 1915, more than half of a group of surveyed firms reported that they used their nurses and welfare secretaries to search out employee "malingering."[28]

The family theme extended to the employer, who supported welfare work out of a paternalistic sense of duty and a Christian belief that great wealth carried great responsibility. John D. Rockefeller, Jr., a devout Baptist, was chastened by the horror of the Ludlow Massacre and the public's condemnation of his seeming aloofness. He became an ardent advocate of welfare work, which he saw as a form of stewardship: the "duty of everyone entrusted with industrial leadership to do all in his power to improve the conditions under which men work and live."[29]

Because employers felt a special sense of obligation toward their female employees, welfare work was common in industries that employed large numbers of women: food processing, clothing, communications, and retailing. For instance, welfare work was introduced at International Harvester in 1901, when Gertrude Beeks, a prominent social reformer, was hired to develop "betterment" programs for the firm's mostly female twine-makers. Beeks became a sort of housemother to the women: listening to their problems, organizing a summer camp for them, and introducing improvements like mirrors in their dressing rooms. The H. J. Heinz Company of Pittsburgh, a leader in welfare work, employed Aggie Dunn as a social secretary to the 1,200 women employed in its packing plant. "Mother" Dunn kept watch on the women's attendance and acted as a counselor to troubled employees.

Welfare work also helped to undermine whatever union proclivities existed among women. In 1903, after International Harvester had merged the Deering and the McCormick companies, the women at Deering's twine mill went out on a sympathy strike with the firm's male machinists. The twine-makers at the McCormick mill did not join the walkout, however, perhaps because of Gertrude Beeks' efforts on their behalf. And when Beeks visited H. J. Heinz to study its welfare programs, she was told that the secret of the company's success lay in the fact that they "do not employ a single union man."[30]

Craftsmen and Woodsmen

Another aspect of welfare work was its effort to divert industry's skilled workers from the unions by means of quasi-pecuniary incentives, including profit-sharing, pension, and home ownership plans. These plans proliferated during times of labor militance. Often introduced when a strike seemed imminent, they usually included a clause restricting benefits to those who had remained loyal to the firm. For example, the stock bonus plan initiated by U.S. Steel in 1903, during a period of strikes and labor unrest, stipulated that the bonus was to be paid only to those employees who had "shown a proper interest in [the company's] welfare and progress." To steelworkers, the message was clear: Stay out of trouble or risk forfeiting a hefty bonus. Similarly, one of the company's subsidiaries announced a pension plan in 1902, but the pensions were to be granted at the employer's discretion and could be denied for misconduct, disloyalty, or indeed any other reason. The result of such pension plans, said a 1915 government study, "is to prevent [union] activity on the part of the employee."[31]

At a more subtle level, these pecuniary welfare programs undermined workers' collective efforts at self-improvement. Providing insurance in case of illness or death was an important function of the trade union and of the Friendly Societies which flourished during the nineteenth century. But corporate welfare programs encouraged individuals to protect their interests not by mutualism but by devoting themselves to the interests of their employers. Moreover, unlike trade union benefit funds, the potential beneficiaries of company programs almost never had a say in the administration of those programs.

Because these plans were intended to deter strikes and unions— phenomena that did not usually involve the unskilled—most of them excluded unskilled workers either directly or by limiting eligibility to long-service employees who had contributed money to the plan. But their focus on skilled workers reflected another motive: the desire to retain skilled labor. While unskilled workers were available in abundance during the period of unfettered immigration, skilled craftsmen were sometimes hard to find and to keep.[32]

Housing programs provide a good example of how employers dealt with both these problems simultaneously. The welfare director of one large firm advised other companies to "get [workers] to invest their savings in their homes and own them. Then they won't leave and they won't strike. It ties them down so they have a stake in our prosperity." The first housing project in the steel industry was launched after the Homestead Strike of 1892, when homes were made available to skilled workers at a substantial discount. The prospect of home ownership was attractive to most workers, who were unlikely to quit a company that had enabled them to buy a house at below-market prices. At the same time, a worker who lost his job might lose his home. This consideration was a powerful deterrent to union activity. Recognizing its leverage in this area, U.S. Steel would threaten to move its plants to other communities during periods of labor unrest.

The housing programs of other companies were similarly designed. An executive of the Aberthaw Construction Company, a firm that specialized in building company housing, said in 1917 that "nearly all" of the company housing then being constructed in the nation was intended for skilled workers. This exclusivity worried some observers. As a 1914 article in *Iron Age* noted: "The problem of maintaining a force of skilled workmen is realized by every employer [and] much attention has been given to the welfare of high-priced workmen while they are outside the shop. . . . But the unskilled employee of the shop or foundry gets little attention."[33]

Welfare work was also common in geographically isolated industries like mining, lumbering, and textiles. Here one found company towns, in which the employer provided for all of the worker's needs from housing to schools, churches, and recreation. The welfare programs in these communities were born out of the economic necessity of attracting labor to undeveloped areas. But the company town also served as a form of social control. Because the company owned the town and wrote its laws, large demonstrations were usually illegal, and union organizers could be forcibly removed from the area.[34]

Thus, industrial welfare programs affected most segments of the labor force. Although precise data are not available, the findings from the government's 1916 survey of welfare work give some sense of the distribution of these programs: Of the 431 companies included in the survey, 37 percent came from industries employing a predominantly female work force, 28 percent from industries employing a predominantly male work force, and 10 percent from industries usually found in isolated areas.[35] Other figures suggest that, in addition to breadth, welfare work had depth: In 1914, the National Civic Federation listed over 2,500 companies as being engaged in some form of betterment work. But even though it was practiced widely, welfare work nevertheless generated considerable controversy.[36]

Opposition

Some of welfare work's strongest opponents were industrial engineers like Frederick W. Taylor, who argued that profit-sharing and other welfare programs were "a joke" and of "distinctly secondary importance" relative to wage-incentive plans. Taylor criticized welfare work because of the "remoteness" of the reward; he believed that personal ambition was "a more powerful incentive to exertion than a desire for the general welfare." Underlying this logic was a view of the worker as a rational materialist, who would cease striking and stinting when given a direct economic incentive to work hard. Though crude, Taylor's psychological model was based on an appreciation of the skilled worker's manliness and hard-headed economism. Over the years, Taylor had absorbed some of the craftsman's culture. He enjoyed shocking Harvard audiences by using profane shop language, and he thought that polite society, like welfare work, was too effeminate. Others opposed welfare work on similar grounds—it was too maternalistic. Charles W. Post, a prominent cereal manufacturer, said:

> Patronizing and coddling grown men and women is not looked favorably upon by the Infinite Power which governs us all. . . . It is intended by the Creator that mankind obtain "welfare" as the result of service and often-times hard service. It is not to be fed to him in a silver spoon and his chin held up while he takes it.[37]

Indeed, the workers themselves often criticized welfare programs as poor substitutes for higher wages and a demeaning intrusion into their private lives. At a Maine textile mill, a group of angry young women told the firm's welfare secretary, whom they called "Sanitary Jane," that they were just as clean as she was and would not submit to further hygienic examinations. Union members were especially suspicious of welfare work, recognizing that it was often motivated by the employer's desire "to destroy all the sentimental appeal in the betterment activities of the union." Yet welfare workers were surprised and hurt when their programs evoked hostility and resentment. One welfare secretary told a conference of colleagues:

> I made up a beautiful collection of welfare work pamphlets, telling what the other companies were doing along welfare lines. Next day I went to a meeting addressed by a woman and heard her refer to welfare as "hell-fare." I took the collection with me, but did not have as much confidence in the pamphlets as when I collected them.[38]

Companies responded to these criticisms in several ways. First, many of them changed the names of their welfare departments to "Industrial Service" or "Employee Service" departments, because, as one welfare secretary explained, a person "who does not like to accept charity will nevertheless receive a service because a service is offered by a friend." Second, they adopted the engineer's own efficiency criterion as a way of rebutting the charge that welfare programs lacked economic rationality; as one steel manufacturer put it, "in dollars and cents it pays to treat employees as they think they deserve." The welfare secretary of a large publishing company claimed that his service department was "conducted along economic lines, as every other department is conducted; every dollar spent on it must yield 100 cents in return." Finally, companies increasingly turned to outside organizations to run welfare programs that workers might have resented had they been directly provided by the employer.[39]

The YMCA

The Young Men's Christian Association (YMCA) first became involved in welfare work during the 1870s, through its religious activities with railroad workers. With permission from employers, the YMCA set up special rooms to hold prayer meetings and Bible classes in nineteen major railroad stations across the country. An early supporter of these activities, railroad magnate Cornelius Vanderbilt erected a large building to house the programs which the YMCA had organized for his employees. By 1888, when the building was completed, these programs had become more secular, so it contained game rooms, libraries, lunch rooms, an infirmary, bowling alleys, and a gymnasium. The idea spread rapidly, and some ninety Railroad Association buildings had been constructed by 1901. Each association was directed by a "secretary" appointed by the YMCA's national Railroad Department. Between 1890 and 1911, the years of the railroad YMCAs' greatest growth, this department was headed by Clarence J. Hicks, who later administered welfare programs for various Rockefeller concerns, including Colorado Fuel & Iron Company and Standard Oil of New Jersey.[40]

Because the funding for its railroad work came wholly from private employers, the YMCA had to make a convincing case that sober, pious employees were more productive and loyal. One YMCA secretary claimed that a worker belonging to the YMCA would work harder than "the man who goes to his work from the saloon or some other low resort." The YMCA's work, he noted, "produces splendid results on the economic as well as on the moral side [and] all intelligent railroad officials are learning that this work is a great thing for the investor." The YMCA aimed its programs at the skilled worker, who was more likely than the unskilled worker to be Protestant, hence a suitable object of concern. But the skilled worker was also likely to be a union member, and the period was one of considerable labor unrest on the railroads. To deflect the charge that it was a tool of the employer, the YMCA adopted a "Zone of Agreement" policy pledging strict neutrality in any labor dispute. But this "neutrality" was questionable at best: Although it met regularly with employers, never once did the YMCA hold a meeting with union representatives. As a YMCA magazine warned in 1895: "It must never be forgotten by any railroad YMCA man that the company is the source from which it derives its main support."[41]

The YMCA eventually branched out of railroad work and began to organize welfare activities for industrial workers in cities and in isolated lumber camps, mining camps, and mill towns. To administer these programs, it established an Industrial Department in 1902. In a report written that same year, its first director, C. C. Michener, defined a distinctive role for the YMCA. Noting that employer-run welfare programs had "not produced the desired results" because "they were solely company matters and the company planned everything and paid the bills," Michener argued that the YMCA could get better results by taking welfare work out of the employer's hands.[42]

Various strategies were used to reach industrial workers in urban areas. For instance, at some companies, the YMCA ran programs—including sing-alongs, speeches, and skits—inside the factory, at the lunch hour or between shifts. Shop bands were organized and portable organs set up right on the shop floor. Another strategy was to use the pooled contributions of employers in neighboring factories for the construction of YMCA buildings. In South San Francisco, four local meatpacking companies donated funds for a YMCA building, which was then used exclusively by their employees. Finally, some companies shouldered the entire cost of erecting and maintaining a YMCA building for their workers. These could be found in major cities—there was a Sears, Roebuck YMCA in Chicago—as well as in company towns like Gary, Indiana, and Wilmerding, Pennsylvania. By 1920, there were 154 industrial YMCA buildings; in Chicago alone, the YMCA's industrial service work reached over 130 companies. The YMCA provided not only the programs but also the welfare secretaries to administer them. The industrial "Y" was "a social headquarters with recreation facilities, refreshment features, shops, socials, foremen's meetings, . . . special work for colored workers, motion pictures, moral and religious work, classes in English and citizenship for foreigners."[43]

In geographically isolated areas, the YMCA worked to shut down the saloons, offering in their place more wholesome diversions like lectures, music groups, sports, table games, and Bible classes. While these efforts may have aroused the enmity of thirsty workers, employers testified that the YMCA promoted labor peace as well as sobriety. A coal operator from West Virginia said, "The result of our small investment in the YMCA is almost beyond our belief. Men who formerly got drunk are sober. Whereas we had trouble getting men, there is a waiting list. No local strikes now, but the best of good will."[44]

Despite its pledge of neutrality, the YMCA's industrial programs were intended to benefit, and were controlled by, corporate sponsors. Employers sat on the YMCA's local boards, provided its financial support, and even audited its expenditures. While never openly attacking the unions, the YMCA issued frequent warnings about the dangers of labor radicalism. C. C. Michener thought that industrial YMCAs served as a "corrective [to] socialistic influences"; his successor, Charles Towson, said in 1914 that the YMCA would deter groups like the IWW by bringing "sentiment and sympathy" to the workplace.[45]

Employers allowed the YMCA to conduct their welfare programs for several reasons. First, the YMCA promoted the very values that employers considered desirable in their workers: temperance, honesty, industriousness, and thrift. Second, by letting an overtly religious and avowedly neutral organization conduct its welfare activities, business could avoid the charge that it was trying to mold worker values. When Clarence J. Hicks went to Colorado Fuel and Iron in 1915, he dismantled many of the company's older welfare programs and had the firm subsidize the construction of an industrial YMCA in Pueblo. Hicks said that he "talked to the corporation about getting away from paternalism and letting the YMCA do this work." Finally, the YMCA's welfare philosophy emphasized harmony in the workplace and patience in the face of adversity—virtues more consistent with maintenance of the status quo than with social reform or militant unionism.[46]

The Welfare Professional

Nonetheless, welfare work had a strong reform impulse behind it. Many welfare workers, including those employed by the YMCA, sincerely believed that their programs would improve workers' lives and soften some of industry's cruder aspects. According to Mary B. Gilson, most people went into the field "with faith in its power to meliorate industrial conditions." Welfare workers drew upon the diverse intellectual currents of Progressivism, mixing the Social Gospel with the latest ideas in education, social work, and public health.[47]

Those engaged in welfare work were well educated and dedicated to public service. They tended to have backgrounds in social and settlement work, municipal reform, and religious activities. International Harvester's welfare staff during the 1900s provides a good example. Before she was hired by the McCormicks in 1901, Gertrude Beeks worked for a local reform organization, the Civic Federation of Chicago. A close friend of Jane Addams, she was active in the city's settlement house movement. During Beeks' tenure as welfare secretary, the company hired Henry Bruere to administer an educational and cultural institute for its workers. Bruere had previously been a settlement house worker in Boston; in later years, he was a leader of New York's municipal reform movement. During this period the YMCA opened some facilities on the premises of Harvester's plants, and in 1911 Clarence J. Hicks left his post at the YMCA to head up Harvester's welfare department.

Out of these common roots there developed a professional subculture and a network of contacts. Welfare secretaries exchanged information on their activities and visited each other's factories. They also organized classes; for instance, Graham Taylor taught a course on welfare work at Chicago Commons, a settlement house. Students from local companies heard lectures on worker's compensation, plant safety, cooperatives, and trade unions. The new schools of social work and business also began to offer courses in welfare work.[48]

Several outside organizations pushed the welfare movement in the direction of greater professionalism. One such group was the American Institute for Social Service (AISS), which was organized during the 1890s by a minister and a social worker who wanted to promote industrial welfare work. In addition to publishing a magazine called *Social Service,* the AISS maintained a research library for use by its corporate clients. The National Civic Federation (NCF), a much larger and more prestigious group, opened a Welfare Department in 1904. The department provided technical advice on welfare work to its corporate members, issued numerous publications, and held regular conferences at which welfare secretaries discussed the latest techniques and developments in their field. Gertrude Beeks, who headed the department, even organized an employment service for welfare secretaries.[49]

This increasing professionalization was attributable to the growing complexity of welfare work. Before the turn of the century, anyone "broadly and deeply religious" who was capable of "infusing life and warmth into all" could become a YMCA railway secretary. But as welfare programs grew more sophisticated and came to provide a greater variety of services, the YMCA began to demand qualifications of a higher order. By World War I, over 700 secretaries were doing the YMCA's railroad and industrial welfare work. They were aided by a large technical staff at national headquarters, who prepared handbooks, published newsletters, and set up conferences for the secretaries and others interested in industrial service work. Conferences were held at regional campgrounds and at the YMCA's large facility at Silver Bay on Lake George, which was also used as a training center for welfare secretaries.[50]

Welfare work was gradually turning into an area that required expertise and special competence. Using social work as a model of how paternalism could be fused with professionalism, welfare workers developed systematic methods for identifying and remedying employee problems. Like social workers, they took university courses in domestic science, psychology, and sociology. Their claim to special competence in building employee morale and resolving grievances—in "human relations"—became a justification for their status in the managerial hierarchy. As one writer noted, the welfare worker had to be "a man or woman of bold judgment, of sympathetic understanding, of tact in dealing with people of various kinds and other qualities which tend to promote harmony all through the plant."[51]

Yet welfare workers regularly encountered resistance from production managers and foremen, who resented any intrusions into their domain and who, like many employers, doubted that uplift activities enhanced productivity or loyalty. Gertrude Beeks' hostile encounters with the plant superintendent at International Harvester eventually caused her to resign. To production men interested only in cost and speed, welfare work was little more than high-sounding gibberish.

Conflict with other managers could be reduced if welfare activities were centralized and if the welfare worker's powers were vested in a special department. Among the first companies to set up functional welfare departments were National Cash Register and Westinghouse Air Brake. By 1915 many of the larger firms engaged in welfare work had created such departments. U.S. Steel's Bureau of Safety, Sanitation, and Welfare, organized in 1911, had the authority to systematize and standardize welfare work throughout the corporation's subsidiaries; the Employee Service Department at Cincinnati Milling Machine Company was in charge of the company's lunchroom, recreation activities, medical department, and benefit programs. With a few notable exceptions, however, these welfare departments were not involved in most aspects of employment management.[52]

The NCR Experiment

One of these notable exceptions involved the National Cash Register Company (NCR), which launched its extensive welfare program during the 1890s, under the direction of Lena Harvey. NCR's activities ran the gamut from an employee clubhouse, medical services, and a relief association to a library, theater, and choral society. But Harvey had little say in employment matters and exercised no control over the company's foremen.[53]

In stark contrast to its progressive welfare programs, the brass foundry at NCR was run in dictatorial fashion by a tough, hard-driving foreman named McTaggart. He would "call them [the molders] together from time to time and deliver speeches to them, and his remarks would drive them for more work—more work seemed to be his way always." The molders organized a union but on three occasions—in 1897, 1899, and 1901—McTaggart fired both its leaders and its members. On the last occasion, however, the molders went on strike, joined by members of some of the twenty other unions that had contracts with NCR. In retaliation, John Patterson, NCR's flamboyant owner, locked out all of the firm's 2,300 workers. After a long and bitter dispute, some of the unions agreed to a settlement, but the foundry resumed operations as an open shop. The company gave McTaggart a long "vacation," dismissed Lena Harvey, and established a new Labor Department, headed by Charles U. Carpenter.[54]

The Labor Department continued to administer NCR's existing welfare programs. Like John Patterson, Carpenter valued the work begun by Miss Harvey and wrote that it "[does] not seem possible to cultivate any better feeling on the part of the employee toward his employer unless some attempt is made to restore the old-time 'personal touch.'" But Carpenter expanded the Labor Department's scope far beyond welfare work, creating two new units in the Labor Department: an employment department and a records department. By 1904 fewer than half of the Labor Department's staff were assigned to welfare work.

To insure that there would be no more McTaggarts, the new units now performed several of the activities that had once been carried out by the company's foremen. First, the employment department assumed the right to hire employees; it also began to keep track of tardiness and absenteeism by using time tickets and punch clocks. The department's head, H. A. Worman, focused his hiring efforts on skilled workers, whom he called "the backbone of the factory organization . . . the one[s] to be hired most carefully." In making hiring decisions, Worman used confidential information obtained from former employers (presumably about an applicant's union proclivities), saying that "employers are coming to understand that their interests in this respect are mutual." Second, the Labor Department tried to establish "a just and scientific wage system" by taking over the foreman's job of administering wages and adjusting rate inequities. (Seventy percent of the firm's employees were on piecework.) Third, Carpenter required that no employee be fired without his prior approval. Moreover, employees were permitted to appeal their dismissals to the Labor Department. Finally, Carpenter gave himself the authority to intervene in disputes between workers and foremen.

Realizing that the company's foremen would have to be trained "in the best methods of handling men," Carpenter held weekly meetings with them to discuss worker grievances and to outline NCR's policy on various employment issues. The very notion of corporate labor policy was itself a major innovation. Carpenter thought that "a foreman should not be permitted to adopt his own policy and enforce his own rules in regard to such matters but should be forced to follow the line laid down by the company and compelled to work in harmony with its general policy."[55]

In short, Carpenter transformed NCR's traditional employment practices by creating a centralized system of hiring and firing, by codifying rules and grievance procedures, and by consolidating all welfare work under a single administrative unit that was overseen by a "fair minded, practical, educated expert" (as he immodestly described himself). These reforms signalled a major change in the management of employment, incorporating many of the safeguards that the unions had devised to protect their members from foremen like McTaggart and thereby undercutting the unions.

Carpenter's philosophy of labor relations was: "The time to stop trouble is before it begins." By restricting the foreman's autonomy, he insured against future strikes like the one McTaggart had provoked. By reducing wage inequities, he removed another cause of strikes at NCR. But Carpenter was no friend of organized labor. When Gertrude Beeks visited NCR in 1902, Carpenter told her that he kept a list of workers "whose records are at all objectionable ... to weed them out, including socialists." He boasted that he could make NCR into an open shop "tomorrow," without precipitating a strike. Indeed, by 1913 not one of the twenty unions that had been at NCR in the 1890s was still around.[56]

NCR's methods were far more advanced than those of most

other companies in the period before the war. Elsewhere, the welfare department was almost never on an equal footing with the firm's other major divisions; rather, it was subordinate to the conservative, cost-conscious manufacturing department. Even at International Harvester, a bellwether company in many respects, the welfare department did not achieve functional autonomy until 1918. As a result, most prewar welfare departments had no control over such matters as hiring, wage determination, training, employment security, and union relations. In these companies, said one observer, the welfare secretary

> has not yet been assimilated into the operating organization, he has little authority to determine the labor policy of the company. He deals largely with matters outside the regular routine of industry operations, he has to do primarily with the men while *off* the job rather than *on* the job.

In short, because they lacked independent authority and a mandate to intervene in the employment sphere, welfare departments could do little to restrain the foreman's drive system, which continued to coexist with extra-work paternalism, as the two had coexisted at NCR during the 1890s.[57]

Nevertheless, welfare work represented a distinctive role within the company. Labor management was becoming the province of the specialist, and labor-related policy was becoming an object of rational administration. The creation of welfare departments marked the beginning of an effort to develop employment policies which were not subordinate to the firm's short-run emphasis on production and which recognized the value of maintaining employee morale. Like systematic management, welfare work created an organizational precedent for the personnel department. But the roots of personnel management lay not only in these movements, but in another that was taking shape outside of industry.

CHAPTER 3
VOCATIONAL GUIDANCE

In the four decades spanning the turn of the century, the industrial education movement focused public attention as never before on the school as an instrument of social policy. Proponents of industrial education argued that tighter links between the schools and the economy would enable the nation to cope more effectively with the stresses and strains of becoming an industrial urban society. They believed that many social problems—poverty, political unrest, alienation, and a perceived decline in the work ethic—could be traced to a clash between old values and habits and new technological demands. In their view, the immigrant working classes, hopelessly mired in harmful thought and behavior patterns brought from Europe, were unable to adjust to the rigors of industrialism. But their children held the key to a happier and more orderly future.

A key concept of industrial education was the vocation, which was akin to a career or a calling, except that industrial education almost always trained students for manual occupations. Educators hoped that, by imparting some of the stabilizing influences of a professional career, a well-chosen vocation would bolster the work ethic and deter unrest and crime. The theory of industrial education was straightforward. The school was supposed to guide students toward a vocation that suited their interests and abilities and then to train them for it. But behind this simple idea was a strong impulse toward using the school as a mechanism for social control. Through psychological testing and counseling, vocational guidance encouraged working-class children to choose manual rather than professional occupations. Vocational education then prepared them for their destined place in the labor market.

But vocational education and guidance had another, more benign side. They were a form of uplift, intended to reduce poverty and unemployment. Educators sought to ensure that children from urban ghettos would take stable, career-like jobs rather than working intermittently at unskilled jobs. Giving a child a vocation meant placing him in a good job: virtually always a manual job, to be sure, but nevertheless respectable. A few educators went even further, arguing that the schools should be used to regulate the youth labor market and that employers should adopt vocational techniques and should provide good jobs to young graduates. Thus, a number of vocational guidance enthusiasts shifted their efforts away from the schools, focusing instead on industrial employment reform. Vocationalists became some of the most active proponents of personnel management, and they infused the new profession with an abiding interest in employee selection and career development.

In short, vocational guidance took a very different route to personnel management than did welfare work and scientific management. The latter arose within the factory to cope with essentially private problems, such as the disorder and depersonalization accompanying the growth in firm size. In contrast, vocational guidance was part of a movement which arose in the public sphere, in response to broad social concerns, and which later brought many of those concerns to bear on private employment practices.

I. Manual Training and Vocational Education

As the United States entered the industrial age in the 1880s and 1890s, its public schools came under increasing fire from a diverse group of educators, businessmen, and social reformers. A common criticism was that the schools had not kept pace with rapid economic and social change; somehow they had to be modernized to ease the nation's transition to urban industrialism. One innovation that attracted wide interest was manual education, or "hand learning."

Manual training idealized the skilled craftsman of the preindustrial era, who was fast disappearing as the division of labor increased. The mythic Yankee artisan—hard-working, broadly educated—personified the values of an earlier period that the manual training movement hoped to preserve. Proponents felt that, if children were taught traditional trades, they would become industrious and thrifty and would learn to take pride in their work. The pedagogical theory underlying this belief was vague; it assumed an almost mystical link between working diligently with one's hands and developing one's mind and moral virtues. In essence, the movement represented a reaffirmation of the work ethic, which was regarded as the moral bedrock of society. According to one educator writing in 1893, manual training exercises inculcated "habits of neatness, accuracy, order and thoroughness; they exercise the judgment, will and conscience; they present an incentive to good work in all directions."[1]

Manual training had something for everyone. Pedagogues thought that it would make the schools more practical and eliminate outdated teaching methods such as rote learning. Employers liked its emphasis on the work ethic and looked to manual training to expand the supply of skilled labor. Social reformers saw it as a means to end the alienation of modern factory work, to uplift the poor, and to reduce vagrancy and idleness.

The work ethic and associated values were to be restored by having boys learn such skills as woodcarving, metalworking, potting, and gardening; girls were to be instructed in sewing, cooking, and laundering. Training in "all-around" rather than particular marketable skills was stressed. When manufacturers urged that more practical subjects such as mechanical drawing and industrial design be included these were incorporated into some programs. Generally speaking, however, the manual education curriculum aimed not so much at preparing students for particular slots in industry as at reviving or preserving the broad skills associated with traditional trades, skills in which conception and execution were unified.

The reform impulse in manual training was based on the belief that social problems could be solved by changing the individual. Some advocates, following the lead of John Ruskin and William Morris in England, emphasized the aesthetic and anti-industrial element in hand learning. Ruskin and Morris hoped to restore the creative impulse in work as well as the dignity of labor; they saw manual training as a prologue to a socialist commonwealth of artisan guilds. But for most American advocates of manual training, its liberative potential was less important than its transmission of work-related values, which could remedy such problems as poverty, intemperance, and idleness. Although lip service was paid to the notion that manual training was suitable for all children, in practice it was focused on urban, working-class students and on other groups thought to be in need of a good dose of the work ethic, such as southern blacks and Indians.[2]

But manual training had a number of shortcomings. Chief among these was its limited vocational applicability. Many of the "all-around" trades had become obsolescent as a result of technological change and the growing specialization of labor. This is not to say that industry had no need for skilled labor. Indeed, after 1890 there was a steady demand for machinists, repairmen, and maintenance workers, especially those with industry-specific skills. The problem was that these were not the kinds of skills being taught in manual training classes.

Corporation Schools

One response to this deficiency was the corporation school. Between 1900 and 1915, many large companies set up their own private training schools so they would not have to rely on the public schools or on union apprenticeship programs to meet their need for skilled labor. In 1913, a group of these companies created the National Association of Corporation Schools (NACS), which had over 140 corporate members by 1918. The largest group of NACS members were railroads, machinery, and metalworking companies. Corporation schools were also used to train clerical and technical workers, so a considerable number of NACS members were public utilities, department stores, and banks.[3]

Because the corporation school provided workers with general trade skills, rapid turnover and the raiding of newly trained employees by competitors soon became serious problems. At General Electric's Lynn plant, less than one-fourth of its trade apprenticeship graduates remained with the firm, and other NACS members encountered similar difficulty holding on to their graduates. As economist Paul Douglas commented, "The employer must face the question: considering the transient nature of the working force, does it pay *him* (not does it pay the industry) to train young workers?"[4]

Intended primarily to increase the supply of skilled labor, corporation schools also had a strong antiunion thrust. NACS members thought that they could weaken the unions by developing a corps of skilled workers who would give their allegiance to the institution that trained them. Magnus W. Alexander, training director for General Electric, remarked: "It stands to reason that young people trained by industry in industry will, if they are properly trained, develop a spirit of loyalty to their employer and toward industrial employers in general."[5] Trade unions had always made loyalty to the union and respect for union brothers an important part of their apprenticeship training. By taking the training function away from the unions, corporation schools sought to instill in the trainee "the ideals and standards of the organization, and to infuse him with the right attitude toward work." Graduates often went on to become foremen, employees whose loyalty to the firm was taken for granted.[6]

Smaller companies were equally concerned about the shortage of skilled labor and about union control of apprenticeship programs. But because they could not afford to establish their own private trade schools, they began to call for public funding of vocational education. The strongest private support for vocational education came from the National Association of Manufacturers (NAM), an open-shop employers' association founded in 1895 whose members were small and medium-sized firms that felt threatened by increased competition from European and larger American firms. Attributing Germany's growing domination of world markets to its system of public trade schools, the NAM demanded similar trade training in America's public schools. In short, it wanted to see manual training replaced by vocational education geared to the specific needs of local employers.[7]

Vocational Education

Many educators sympathized with the NAM's position and agreed that the schools should be more closely integrated with the production process. The influential 1906 report of the Massachusetts Commission on Industrial and Technical Education attacked manual training as "a sort of mustard relish or appetizer" that was "without reference to any industrial end." Another critic said that proponents of manual training should "face the facts of modern large-scale production with its specializtion of labor. . . . The sooner they cease to think in terms of the handicraft era, the greater will be the chance of creating an educational system that is worthwhile."[8]

While this new emphasis on marketable skills reflected a realistic recognition that the handicraft era was indeed gone, it also signaled a shift to a more practical and market-oriented vision of the purposes of education. Historians have noted that, after the turn of the century, educators became "less concerned with retaining traditional ways of life and more committed to channeling, rationalizing, and making more efficient the industrial process." Educators even adopted the parlance of the businessman and the industrial engineer, speaking of waste, cost-effective education, the importance of school administration, and above all, the economic benefits of education. "Industry," said the National Education Association in 1910, "has for education a fundamental and permanent significance."[9]

Yet vocational education was more than an infusion of business values and priorities into the schools. It was also a response to the rapid growth in high school enrollments. Until the 1890s, working-class students rarely went far beyond elementary school, where children of all classes and backgrounds received an identical education. In fact, the common school was touted as America's democratic alternative to the class-segregated schools of Europe. The high school at this time was a college-preparatory institution, geared to the small number of relatively wealthy students who attended it. By the early 1920s, however, rising enrollments had dramatically transformed it from an institution for the "classes" to an institution attended by the "masses."[10]

This influx posed a dilemma for educators. According to the ideology of the common school, the new high school students should be given the same academic education as other students. But many educators believed that these new students were incapable of studying history and literature. They were said to be "manually minded." Even John Dewey acknowledged that the "distinctively intellectual is not dominant" in such persons. Moreover, an academic education was deemed irrelevant for them since their "evident and probable destinies," as Harvard's Charles Eliot put it, barred them from nonmanual pursuits.[11]

Keenly aware that separate vocational schools contradicted the democratic principles of the common school, supporters of vocational education turned the ethos of equality upside-down. They made the curious argument that it was unjust to give all students the same education; a common curriculum was discriminatory because it was designed only for the college-bound and failed to meet the needs of other students, forcing the "manually minded," who found their studies irrelevant and incomprehensible, to leave school prematurely. Leonard P. Ayres, the author of *Laggards in Our Schools,* attributed high attrition rates to the fact that the schools "are adjusted to the power of the brighter pupils. They are beyond the powers of the average pupils, and far beyond those of the slower ones."

A few critics like John Dewey warned that any narrowly conceived scheme of vocational education could become "an instrument in accomplishing the feudal dogma of predestination." But most educators were untroubled by this possibility, believing vocational education to be democratic because it was true to the hard facts of nature. As the Social Darwinists were fond of pointing out, children were not equally endowed. Said Charles Eliot:

> Does democracy mean that all people are alike? Does it mean that all children are equal? We know they are not. Many of us have seen that in the same family, with the same inheritances and the same environments, the children often illustrate an astonishing variety of disposition and capacity. If democracy means to try to make all children equal, it means to fight nature, and in that fight democracy is sure to be defeated.[12]

While Eliot was concerned with preserving privilege, a sizable number of social reformers and child welfare activists embraced vocational education out of a belief that it would enhance social mobility. The rationale for this belief was presented in a study conducted by a young sociologist, Susan M. Kingsbury, for the 1906 Massachusetts report on industrial education. Kingsbury's study was concerned with the state's 25,000 children between the ages of fourteen and sixteen who were not enrolled in school. These were the "wasted years of the child's life," since children left school to take "blind alley" jobs—as errand boys, millhands, helpers, and lumpers—that "did not permit of development or advancement to a desirable occupation," that bred bad working habits "resulting in instability of character," and that sometimes exposed them to immoral influences. "When the child has reached sixteen or seventeen, he or she must begin again at the bottom." Out of the ranks of these school dropouts came the "floaters," those workers who drifted from job to job, thus contributing to unemployment, labor turnover, and poverty.

Kingsbury blamed the schools for the high dropout rates. She maintained that, if these children were to be induced to remain in school, they needed "less academic work" and more "practical training . . . and academic work as applied to industrial problems" so that they could acquire the "intelligence and responsibility" needed to land a good job, a vocation.[13] Kingsbury went beyond many of her contemporaries by linking poverty and instability to occupational, rather than personal, characteristics. But her solution was traditional: Change the individual by giving him or her vocational education. She did not advocate any direct reform of the labor market.

Thus, vocational education was a reform movement to the extent that it steered students away from the worst jobs and probably gave them a better sense of their place in the industrial structure than they could get from McGuffey's Reader or from pottery classes. But its advocates wanted to mesh the schools so closely with the labor market that most working-class children would stand little chance of entering a nonmanual occupation or attending college. Here, educators were driven by the prejudice that children from different social classes varied greatly in their innate capacities and abilities. But how could they make sure that students ended up in suitable courses and schools? To give children what they and their parents wanted was democratic; to tell them what they needed was not. Some mechanism was required that would allow children to choose but that would make their choices consonant with the educator's perception of need.

II. Origins of Vocational Guidance

A settlement house called Civic Service House opened in Boston's North End in 1901. Its first director was Meyer Bloomfield, a recent Harvard graduate who had been raised on New York's Lower East Side, where he attended classes at University Settlement. Bloomfield felt a responsibility toward those immigrants still living in the tenements and sought to bring them closer to the world he had entered since leaving New York. He proposed a settlement house that would concentrate on education and community organization, as opposed to purely social and recreational programs.[14]

Bloomfield's proposal was influenced by the English settlement model, which sought to bridge the division between the classes by having the intellectuals bring the fruits of the university to the working class. Samuel Barnett, organizer of Toynbee Hall in East London, tried to recreate a college setting in the slum's settlement house. Toynbee Hall had a quadrangle, diamond-paned windows, and a dining room whose halls were lined with college shields. Barnett thought that the settlement would become the locus of neighborhood political activities: Residents and settlement workers would cooperate in pressing for community improvements and local political representation. He called this idea "Practicable Socialism."

Established with funding from Mrs. Quincy Agassiz Shaw, a wealthy Boston philanthropist and daughter of the noted biologist, Civic Service House offered evening classes in the English language, American government, and history, taught by students from nearby colleges like Harvard and Boston University.[15] The settlement was also involved in local political activity. It belonged to the Good Government Association—a coalition of liberal businessmen, social reformers, and neighborhood associations (dubbed the "Goo Goos" by a local wag)—which worked to unseat Mayor John Fitzgerald and to implement election rule reforms that would "place power in the people." In addition to participating in municipal reform activities, Civic Service House was used as a meeting place for local unions. Bloomfield and his assistant, Phil Davis, were active in organizing several local trade unions in the garment and other industries, as well as the Women's Trade Union League. In

1903, when the AFL held its convention at Faneuil Hall, Phil Davis brought William English Walling and Mary O' Sullivan to Civic Service House to outline the League's proposed structure and to choose Mary Morton Kehew as its first president.[16]

Although the setlement house workers were well received by the labor movement, labor leaders occasionally charged them with being more interested in investigation than in action. Another frequent criticism was that they were too ready to give up a strike in favor of arbitration. Like other middle-class professionals, the settlement workers felt that they had a special responsibility to "stand between and try to make peace on the basis of justice," as Graham Taylor put it. Meyer Bloomfield, along with his close friends and Civic Service House supporters A. Lincoln Filene and Louis D. Brandeis, helped to devise the influential Protocol of Peace which settled the bitter 1910 strike of New York's waistmakers. The Protocol provided for a permanent Board of Arbitration to rule on worker grievances which the union and the employer's association could not resolve on their own.[17]

The third staff member at Civic Service House was Ralph Albertson, who was an assistant and close friend to reformer Frank Parsons. In 1904 Phil Davis decided to establish at Civic Service House a workers' college modeled after the Workingman's Institute at Toynbee Hall. Albertson got Parsons interested in the idea, and together they organized the Breadwinners' College, which opened at Civic Service House in 1905.

Frank Parsons

Frank Parsons was a most unusual individual. Born in 1854, he was trained as a civil engineer but supported himself as an author of legal textbooks. This work earned him a position at Boston University's Law School, where Meyer Bloomfield was one of his students. (Parsons had been denied a position in the university's economics department on the grounds that he was too radical.) In addition to his academic work, Parsons was a tireless champion of reform causes. In a number of muckraking books, he argued for public ownership of natural monopolies such as electricity, telegraphs, and the railroads; he testified on this subject before the

U.S. Industrial Commission in 1901. A recognized expert on municipal reform, he wrote two books calling for the initiative, the referendum, direct primaries, and women's suffrage. Parsons believed that progress "never came from the upper classes," and he ran on the Radical ticket in Boston's 1895 mayoral election.[18]

Parsons was concerned with the problems of the worker as well. After the 1893 depression, he called for aid to the unemployed through public works projects and later castigated the "monopolists" whose employees meant "no more to them than so many cogs in the machinery of their powerhouses." In 1905 he organized a national campaign in support of the eight-hour day, which he believed would lead to "more opportunity for self-development, a higher citizenship and nobler manhood." Parsons had a vision of utopia in which the government would own and manage natural monopolies, leaving the "common people" to run worker-owned cooperatives. Everyone would be paid a minimum wage, wealth would be distributed equally, and people would work for honor rather than personal gain. The final stage in Parson's utopia was "Familyism," when the golden rule and brotherly love would prevail.

Distinguishing himself from more radical socialists like Debs, Parsons argued for peaceful evolution rather than class struggle. He was particularly impressed by New Zealand's extensive social welfare programs and wrote an 800-page book describing that nation's social democracy. Thus Parsons' diverse interests touched on most of the main points of Progressive reform. His writings and political activities drew praise from men like John R. Commons and Mayor Samuel "Golden Rule" Jones, and won him the friendship of Louis D. Brandeis and Oliver Wendell Holmes, Jr.

But for all his prescient ideas, Parsons was no saint. He was something of a racist, and he susbscribed to the elitist notion of achieving reform through social engineering: "Life can be molded into any conceivable form," said Parsons. "Draw up your specifications for man . . . and if you will give me control of the environment and time enough, I will clothe your dreams in flesh and blood." He believed that change could be effected through social uplift and the intervention of right-thinking men in public affairs. Opposed to unrestricted immigration, he feared that reform would be halted if America lost its "heroic blood by the foul admixture of serfhood . . . pouring in from Europe." No doubt this attitude explains his infatuation with Anglo-Saxon New Zealand.[19]

Before becoming head of Breadwinners' College, Parsons served as dean of Ruskin College in Illinois and later helped to establish Ruskin College in Missouri. Both institutions were inspired by John Ruskin's idea of bringing higher education to the worker, the same idea that later led to the founding of Rand and Brookwood colleges. When Breadwinners' College opened, it offered evening classes in history, civics, English language, economics, and music. A diploma was granted at the end of two years. Lecturers, drawn from local universities, included philosophers Morris Cohen and Josiah Royce, and a young Harvard undergraduate named Walter Lippmann.

The students at Breadwinners' College were young immigrants from the surrounding community. Some followed in Bloomfield's footsteps, attending college and then going on to respectable professional careers; successful graduates included a local judge and a Labor Department official. But most remained stuck in dead-end jobs in the North End's candy factories and warehouses.[20]

Lecturing on the "The Ideal City" to the Economic Club of Boston in 1906, Parsons said that young people needed assistance in choosing a vocation and that such a choice should entail more than "just hunting for a job." Meyer Bloomfield was so impressed by Parsons' talk that he invited him to speak at a reception for the graduating class of a local evening high school. Sixty boys were invited to the roof garden of Civic Service House to listen to "the Professor" and to discuss their plans with him.[21]

Parsons' view of vocational choice reflected a kind of reform Darwinism. It combined the idea of innate individual differences and natural selection for the occupational structure with the need for active social intervention to ensure that individuals ended up in the niches—no higher or lower—for which their biology had destined them. In one of his earlier books, Parsons wrote:

> The training of a race horse, and the care of sheep and chickens have been carried to the highest degree of perfection that intelligent planning can attain. But the education of the child, and the choice of his employment are left very largely to the ancient, haphazard plan—the struggle for existence and the survival of the fittest. . . . Men work best when they are doing what nature has specially fitted

them for. And the same laborers will achieve immensely fuller and richer results if they are spurred on by interest, or love, or patriotism, than if these interests or emotions have no partnership in their service. . . . A sensible industrial system will therefore seek to make these feelings factors in every piece of work, to put men, as well as timber, stone and iron in the places for which their nature fits them,—and to polish and prepare them for efficient service with at least as much care as is bestowed upon clocks, electric dynamos or locomotives.

In this passage, Parsons shows that he regards expert, rational intervention—"intelligent planning"—as superior to the operation of the market. His vision of a "sensible" industrial order resembles Taylorist notions of social efficiency: Harmony is achieved when the human machine is put in its proper place. These concepts would constitute the intellectual basis for vocational guidance: the well-intentioned but coercive practice of guiding individuals to the "places for which their nature fits them."[22]

That some sort of agency was needed to guide young people in their choice of schools and occupations was an idea whose time had come. The Kingsbury report had been released in 1906, and the National Society for the Promotion of Industrial Education (NSPIE) was created that same year.[23] In the fall of 1907, Parsons submitted to Mrs. Shaw a plan for establishing the Vocation Bureau of Boston at Civic Service House. Mrs. Shaw approved the plan, and the bureau opened several months later, directed by Parsons. Ralph Albertson (then working as an employment supervisor at Filene's department store) and Phil Davis were made associate directors. The list of the bureau's trustees—a virtual Who's Who of progressive reform activity in Boston—included liberal businessmen (Henry S. Dennison, A. Lincoln Filene, J. H. McElwain), union leaders (Mary Kehew, John Tobin), and educators (Paul Hanus and George H. Martin).

An independent unit during its first year of operation, the bureau counseled everyone from Harvard seniors to an ex-bank president. The majority of its clients, however, were high school students or young people of high school age. Even at this early stage, Parsons was concerned with the professionalization of vocational guidance. For those wishing to become vocational counselors, he advocated a course of lectures, research, and trial counseling. At the end of this training period, said Parsons, the counselor would be "an expert, qualified to test the abilities and capacities of young men, apply good judgment, common sense and scientific method . . . and give appropriate counsel with the insight, sympathy, grasp, and suggestiveness the service calls for."[24]

Parsons' counseling techniques set a standard for the early vocational guidance movement. The heart of his method was the personal interview. The applicant was asked to write an essay about himself and to fill out an extensive "self-analysis" form that posed such questions as: "Am I the kind of man I wish my sister to associate with, become intimate with, and marry?" Then Parsons used this information to make an analysis by "seeking in every line for the significance of" five factors, which he listed in an order that suggests his biases: (1) heredity and circumstance, (2) temperament and natural equipment, (3) face and character, (4) education and experience, and (5) dominant interests.

Parsons thought that the final decision about occupational choice should be left to the individual, but that the counselor could "help him so approach the problem that he will come to wise conclusions himself." His report of a sample case provides a fascinating insight into his counseling technique. The client, a nineteen-year-old boy who wanted to be a doctor, is described as "sickly looking, small, thin, hollow-cheeked, with listless eye and expressionless face." Parsons first asked the boy if he thought a doctor should be well and strong and then told him, "And you are not strong." There followed a series of rhetorical questions which Parsons himself answered: "You haven't the pleasant manners a doctor ought to have," "your hand was moist and unpleasant when you shook hands," and so forth. Next, Parsons described two men: One is handsome, cordial, well-read, and acquainted with many people who can help him to attract patients; the other resembles the boy. At Parsons' prodding, the boy agreed that he did not bear much likeness to the first man. Then Parsons moved in with the clincher: "Do you really think, then, that you would have a good chance to make a success of the medical profession?" The boy replied, "I never thought of it this way before, I just knew it was a good business, highly respected, and that's what I wanted."[25]

Emphasizing the importance of "scientific method" in counseling, Parsons developed a plethora of devices to aid him in his work: statistical analyses of occupational earnings and employment changes, analysis forms, and pamphlets such as "Suggestions for a Plan of Life." He expressed the hope that vocational bureaus would be equipped with "every facility that science can devise for the testing of the senses and capacities." Parsons relied on simple psychological tests and even on phrenology and handshakes in judging his applicants.[26]

Yet for all his manipulativeness and his lapses into pseudo-science, Parsons still managed to infuse vocational guidance with a spirit of reformist zeal. He tried to broaden the horizons of urban youths, giving his young clients extensive reading lists that were heavy on authors like Charles Zuebelin, Jane Addams, and Frank Parsons, and encouraging them to read widely on their own in history, economics, and politics. Also indicative of his reformist attitudes was his belief that counseling, by steering young people away from the casual labor market, could reduce youth unemployment and could prevent young workers from "drifting" between jobs. "Boys generally drift into some line of work by chance, proximity, or uninformed selection," said Parsons. By determining a boy's "adaptability" for particular jobs and by giving him a "well considered plan to insure his success," vocational guidance offered a rational and generally humane alternative to this haphazard process.[27]

Guidance in the Schools

When Parsons died in 1908, Meyer Bloomfield took over the Vocation Bureau. Meanwhile, vocational education was spreading not only throughout Massachusetts but also to other states. Articles debating its pros and cons appeared regularly in the newspapers. In this atmosphere of heightened public attention and controversy, Boston's Superintendent of Schools, Stratton D. Brooks, sought some legitimate way to select students for the city's new industrial high schools. Brooks believed that the effect of vocational education had been "to move forward suddenly the time of choice, and it is this necessity to choose early a definite career that renders desirable a consideration of vocational direction." In May 1909, he wrote to Edward A. Filene, asking his help in securing the assistance of the Vocation Bureau. Responding to this request,

Bloomfield quickly drew up a plan for bringing vocational guidance into the city's schools.[28]

The bureau's early efforts were focused on training special teachers to be vocational counselors; by the end of the first year, each elementary and high school in the city had a counselor. Bloomfield and his associates met with students, teachers, parents, and employers to explain the aims and benefits of guidance counseling. Special attention was given to elementary school graduates, the group from which vocational high school students were recruited.

The bureau's work in the schools soon became known throughout the nation, partly as a result of Bloomfield's public relations efforts. In 1910, with assistance from the Boston Chamber of Commerce, Bloomfield organized the first National Conference on Vocational Guidance, which was held in Boston in conjunction with the NSPIE's annual convention. Bloomfield organized another national conference in New York in 1912 and a third conference in Grand Rapids in 1913. At the Grand Rapids meeting, the National Vocational Guidance Association (NVGA), a national organization to promote vocational guidance, was created. For many years the NVGA held its conventions jointly with the NSPIE, reflecting the close link between vocational guidance and vocational education.[29]

Bloomfield, like Parsons before him, was keenly interested in professionalizing vocational counseling. He gave a summer course at Harvard in 1911 "in view of the present demand for competent advice to young people," and taught similar courses at Berkeley, Boston University, Colorado, and Teachers College in New York. Bloomfield stressed the need for "expert guidance" yet warned that the counselor should not prescribe a vocation for the student. The counselor was there simply for "suggestion, inspiration, and cooperation."[30]

In cities across the country, vocational guidance and vocational education developed alongside each other. Guidance counseling became a way of nudging students into vocational courses and legitimating the choice to their parents. The Conference on Vocational Guidance defined the "large aim" of guidance as "developing the methods and materials by which the public schools may help fit their individual graduates for the work they are likely to do." One counselor remarked, "A guidance bureau should be like a type-distributing machine, which will take a hopperful of type, of all the letters of the alphabet, and place each in its particular niche in the one place of all places where it fits." Thus, one task of the counselor was to adjust the student's educational goals, if they seemed unrealistic. An educator from Oakland, California, observed: "The boys are to a large extent aiming at something they can never achieve. The function of the schools is first to rationalize these aspirations and then to carry forward the present plans for occupational training."[31]

Another task of the vocational counselor was to make sure that the child did not simply follow his own interests or the wishes of his parents, since "as a rule the parent does not know his own child." New York City's Board of Education urged counselors to let the child arrive at his own decision, but only after he had been guided by the counselor. Vocational guidance, said the Board, "means leading him and his parents to consider the matter themselves, to study the child's tastes and possibilities, to decide for what he is best fitted, and to take definite steps for securing for him the necessary preparation or training." Thus, the counselor had to know how to exert a high degree of subtle pressure.

Counselors turned to science to buttress the authority of their advice. The burgeoning discipline of psychology provided them with empirical evidence of the variability and heritability of capacity, as well as with a scientific method for classifying individuals. While experts argued over the relative roles of heredity and environment in determining interests and abilities, they tended to agree that vocational interests were stable. Edward L. Thorndike, a prominent psychometrician, thought that a child's vocational interests were "a much more permanent fact of his nature than his relative degrees of interest in different lines of thought and action." They were, he said, "symptomatic to a very great extent of present and future capacity or ability."

If interests and ability were permanent and measurable, then tests could be used to determine what a child was interested in and fitted for; the results of these tests would constitute incontrovertible evidence to place before him and his parents. Educators hardly needed to be told that testing was more persuasive than manipulation or cajolery. As Thorndike said of the vocational counselor:

He may use whatever shrewdness, diplomacy, and political skill he has, but no amount of these will do the peculiar work which the sincere, unvarnished assertion of a person known to be an expert to the effect that a certain thing is so, that this is the best way, and that such-and-such are the reasons, will do for him.[32]

Testing and classification became the predominant concerns of most vocational counselors, who developed complex techniques for rating students, elaborate record-keeping systems, and new testing methods. Vocational guidance now was the science, as well as the art, of allocating the "manually minded" to their appropriate niches and of scaling down their aspirations; occasionally, however, hidden talents were discovered.

III. Bloomfield and the Reform Wing

Some leaders of the vocational guidance movement were skeptical of testing. Meyer Bloomfield doubted whether psychological tests could be of much use to counselors. "Laboratory psychology," he said, "is nor far enough advanced to enable one to fathom bent and aptitude. The fact must not be lost sight of that the vocation bureau is neither a laboratory nor a clinic." He and others believed that guidance should be more than an effort to fit children to particular jobs or curricula. Under Bloomfield's leadership, these reformers tried to develop guidance as a tool for changing social and industrial conditions rather than adapting children to them.[33]

Bloomfield thought that the immigrant child faced special obstacles in his struggle to achieve respectability and security. His problems were not going to be solved by his parents because, said Bloomfield, they worked day and night, had little time for their children, and knew nothing of American institutions. Nor could those problems be solved by the traditional Smilesian virtues of self-help and hard work, which manual training had sought to inculcate. The ethic of "personal and individual effort, however valuable," said Bloomfield, "cannot deal adequately with modern conditions." The child needed special assistance, a boost from the guidance counselor.

Bloomfield, whose own ghetto-to-Harvard career was a perfect example of the promise of American mobility, noted that, in the ghetto, "the gifted as well as the ungifted live. . . equally doomed to undeveloping and cheaply paid labor." The guidance counselor, substituting for the supposedly overworked and ignorant parent, could give the immigrant child the advice he needed to get a respectable job and to compete with middle-class children. "To whom shall children turn," Bloomfield asked rhetorically, "for counsel and information about the vocation?"[34]

Bloomfield worried that the unguided child might end up in what he called a "vocational cul-de-sac," one of the many blind-alley jobs in which working-class youths were employed. John M. Brewer, who ran the Vocation Bureau after Bloomfield left, defined a blind-alley job as one "which offers little opportunity for growth in skill or knowledge, advancement, or extension of usefulness with consequent increase of earning power, and which does not usually lead to a better occupation." These were the jobs that the Kingsbury study had identified as "distinctly bad in influence," jobs that offered no "opportunity for advancement." Kingsbury had hoped that vocational education would steer children away from blind-alley jobs by giving them the practical skills demanded by employers. Bloomfield went several steps further, arguing that guidance should be used to help children make informed vocational decisions and, more important, to change the labor market.[35]

Unlike Kingsbury and Parsons, Bloomfield envisioned an activist role for the schools. If giving students skills and guidance was not enough to ensure that they would get good jobs, then the schools would have to improve the characters of the jobs available to them. The schools were already assisting industry by teaching children marketable skills, so industry had a reciprocal obligation to provide decent jobs. Moreover, the schools had the right to monitor employers. Said Bloomfield:

> It is proper that those who give employment to boys and girls shall ask for more efficiency. . . . But it is equally a right and duty of those entrusted with the nurture of the rising generation to make the vocations render account too. What happens to the boys and girls under the new influences in employment is not alone a question between them and their individual employer, nor between them and their parents, but it is essentially one for the community.[36]

Investigations and Follow-Ups

Reformers in the vocational guidance movement took the position that the primary duty of the schools was to protect the child for the benefit of society and that this duty gave them the right to investigate and change working conditions for young workers. This view was close to that held by child welfare advocates, a number of whom were active in the vocational guidance movement: Bloomfield had campaigned for a child labor law in Massachusetts in 1909; Owen Lovejoy and other members of the National Child-Labor Committee regularly addressed meetings of the Vocational Guidance Association.

In 1913, Lovejoy lashed out against the idea that guidance counseling should do no more than help graduates find jobs: "Business says—'Here are the jobs; what kind of children do you have to offer?' We must reverse the inquiry and say to business, 'here are our children; what kind of industry do you have to offer?'" He also criticized guidance counselors for failing to try to change the character of the jobs taken by graduates: "We reveal that we have not yet risen to the point of looking upon our industrial occupations as sacred callings ministering to the necessities of our race, but as the unfortunate fate of those who through poverty, inexperience or lack of personal initiative are unable to get on top and draw profits from the labor of others."[37]

The reformers suggested several steps that the vocational guidance movement might take to organize and reform the youth labor market. All agreed that vocational counselors should collect information on local employers in order to determine the quality of the jobs being offered. The Vocation Bureau of Boston listed open jobs in a card file, using yellow cards for "undesirable" jobs and red card for "objectionable or dangerous" jobs. By studying jobs, said one guidance reformer, "the school can learn . . . what it can do to fit the children for the industrial life into which they go, and at which point it must stand absolutely firm and say to industry it will do nothing to fit its children for conditions so far from human—work which a monkey could do, if it kept at it."

Another proposal was that counselors follow up young people placed in jobs by the school, to investigate their employment conditions and adjustment problems. Bloomfield thought that the schools should be empowered to take young graduates out of a workplace if it was found to be unsatisfactory. Another reformer argued that followups should even go so far as making sure that the foreman did not place a Polish boy next to a Bohemian boy, since they were sure to fight with each other.[38]

Standards

To conduct surveys and followups, counselors needed a standard by which to evaluate conditions in industry. The guidance reformers saw two basic problems in the jobs open to children. First, these jobs tended to be intermittent. The 1909 Report of the Royal Commission on the Poor Laws had found that blind-alley jobs (it used that term) contributed to unemployment. Some thought that this weakened the child's work ethic. Said Paul Douglas, unemployment "for adults is bad enough; for children it is positively vicious. It breaks down habits of industry which are slowly forming, and exposes them to all sorts of positive dangers." Others, like Meyer Bloomfield, were more concerned with the long-term effects of irregular employment on a young person's job prospects: "Such employment as that of errand boy are not necessarily demoralizing. But callings like this are apt to waste the years during which a boy should make a beginning at a skilled or developing occupation. The probabilities are that younger but trained competitors eventually oust the untrained." Bloomfield accepted vocational education as one solution to this problem but thought that vocational guidance also had a contribution to make, especially if counselors encouraged firms to stabilize employment and scrutinized the jobs offered to school-leavers.[39]

A second problem with the jobs open to young workers was that they offered few promotional opportunities. John M. Brewer defined a good job as one that relieves "the worker of the monotony of machine-like labor by change of work and rotation of tasks; it must have a comprehensive plan of promotions whereby vacancies in the higher positions can be filled by persons occupying those below." Similarly, Frank M. Leavitt, a Pittsburgh school official, said that a "good industry" was "one in which there are clearly defined lines of progress from the lowliest 'job' up to some of the prominent responsible positions in the organization, thus providing an incentive for both work and study." In the surveys he conducted of occupations open to children in the Boston labor market, Bloomfield put great value on promotional opportunities; and in one of his books, he drew diagrams of the course a youth might follow in various industries as he made his way up from an entry job to a managerial position.[40]

The emphasis on internal promotion as a desirable feature of employment grew out of the ubiquitous discussion of careers in the vocational literature. People whose occupations followed the traditional pattern of a professional career were idealized for their willingness to work hard and defer immediate gratification. The hope was that somehow these traits might be transferred to those working in nonprofessional occupations. In an influential article, Charles Eliot labeled the force that pushed professional workers to labor diligently at their vocations the "life-career motive":

> Professional students in the United States exhibit keen interest in their studies, work hard, advance rapidly and avail themselves of their opportunities to gain knowledge and skill to the utmost limit of their strength and capacity, no matter whether the profession for which they are preparing be divinity, law, medicine, architecture, engineering, forestry, teaching, business or corporation service.

Eliot thought that persons infused with the life-career motive had not only more satisfying and successful work lives but also more fulfilling personal lives because of the regular cycle of hard work and achievement:

> There is nothing low or mean about these motives and they lead on the people who are swayed by them to greater serviceableness and greater happiness—to greater serviceableness because the power and scope of individual productiveness are thereby increased; to greater happiness, because achievement will become more frequent and more considerable, and to old and young alike, happiness in work comes through achievement.[41]

The methods used by vocational counselors to imbue their students with the life-career motive included discussions about traditional careers as well as object lessons in career values. Jesse B. Davis, president of the National Vocational Guidance Association in 1915, urged vocational counselors to teach students lessons about "cooperation, obedience, right-thinking, initiative and leadership." John M. Brewer pointed out the relationship between these values and social stability. The child who leaves school without acquiring the life-career motive, said Brewer, "may develop distrust, pessimism, temptation, and finally, immorality and bad citizenship."[42]

But the vocational counselor's moral suasion would go for naught, according to the reformers in the vocational guidance movement, if the only jobs available to school graduates were unstable, monotonous, and lacking in opportunities for promotion. Eliot's Harvard students worked hard not only because they were imbued with the life-career motive but also because the jobs for which they were preparing would develop their intelligence and satisfy "the instinct for educational experiences in the work they are doing," in Bloomfield's words. Bloomfield argued that young workers became demoralized if they labored at jobs requiring "long hours of dull and sterile work." Vocational guidance might help steer some graduates away from dead-end jobs. But what of those who still ended up in them? First "they become job hoboes," said Bloomfield, and then they become "the unemployables." Paul Douglas pointed out that, for these young workers, "a change of jobs is rarely a change upward, merely a change to another unskilled and routine task. . . . These changes moreover, breed irresponsibility in the child himself."[43]

The school's task went beyond awakening the life-career motive to improving the jobs held by young workers, bringing to them some of the security and advancement opportunities associated with professional careers. By encouraging employers to establish lines of promotion and to stabilize employment, the schools could do more to strengthen the work ethic and to further social integration than they could ever achieve through lessons in "moral guidance." Hence the jobs held by wage earners had to become more like the jobs held by salaried professionals. As Owen Lovejoy told the 1913 Vocational Guidance Conference, this goal required that guidance counselors "break down the present class distinctions which already cleave society and wreck so many lives." For Bloomfield, such efforts represented an extension of his attempt to bridge the educational and cultural gap separating the classes. From his settlement work, he brought to vocational guidance a deep concern with upward mobility.[44]

But were the schools up to the task of restructuring private employment policies? Bloomfield had occasional doubts. For instance, he wrote in 1913: "On the whole, experience seems to support the proposition that the school system is not the most suitable agency to attempt the organization of the labor market for the young." Others also expressed their doubts. In 1915, the superintendent of Minneapolis' schools said that "the responsibility

of influencing the conditions of industry in favor of human welfare
... is unquestionably beyond the power of any vocational guidance
movement that is likely soon to develop." This pessimism reflected
the reformers' inability to generate widespread support, especially
as vocational guidance became integrated into the education bureaucracy and restricted its concerns to the testing, counseling, and
classifying of students. By 1918 a well-placed observer of the guidance movement, John M. Brewer, noted that it was "difficult to
find examples of employment supervision" by the schools; they
lacked "authority and equipment for adequate work."[45]

IV. Vocational Guidance and Personnel Management

Although the schools had little effect on private employment
practices, guidance reformers still believed that vocational guidance
could promote "a more intelligent and generous treatment of employees by business houses." And vocational guidance did have a
major impact on industry. That impact came not through the
schools, however, but through the new profession of personnel
management, which Bloomfield and others used as a vehicle for
introducing vocational principles to industry.

The Boston Association

In 1910, Frederick J. Allen joined the Vocation Bureau of Boston
as assistant director and "Investigator of Occupations." Allen
wrote several pamphlets issued by the bureau that described occupations for young workers in the Boston area, the first being
"The Machinist." Other occupations described in the pamphlets
included baker, banker, and confectioner. In gathering information
for these studies, Allen made the acquaintance of managers and
educators throughout the greater Boston area. From these contacts,
Allen and Bloomfield selected sixty persons as "the most public
spirited" and invited them to Civic Service House in 1911 to discuss
"the selection, training and management" of workers. In December
1912, having met regularly for several months, this group held a

conference at which a permanent organization was formed, the
Boston Employment Managers' Association (EMA).[46]

At the time, only a few firms in the Boston area had employment
or personnel managers. Years later, Bloomfield recalled that Allen's
studies of local firms had found "not one which gave more than
incidental and occasional consideration to the subject of personnel
organization." A contemporary noted that fewer than a half dozen
personnel managers were charter members of the Boston EMA;
the rest consisted largely of educators and reformers. Many of the
early supporters of Bloomfield's effort to promote professional
personnel management were proselytizers drawn from the ranks
of the vocational guidance, industrial education, and labor market
reform movements. Personnel management was not well known
outside of these movements, although Bloomfield and other vocationalists laid the foundation for its phenomenal growth after
1915.[47]

One motive underlying the creation of the Boston EMA was a
desire to publicize personnel management and to use it to
strengthen ties between the schools and industry. Speaking at a
1916 meeting of the association, A. Lincoln Filene said that "the
employment manager is the connecting link between the schools
and business, and we are beginning to recognize the importance of
the position he holds." Bloomfield thought of personnel management as an attempt to bring "close harmony" between training,
guidance, and industrial employment. If industrial education was
to train students in needed skills, if guidance was to place students
effectively, and if the schools were to have any influence over
private employment policies, then the personnel manager was the
logical person for educators to work with. Bloomfield could not
imagine guidance counselors having regular contact with
foremen.[48]

A second motive for establishing the Boston EMA was alluded
to by Bloomfield in testimony before the U.S. Commission on
Industrial Relations in 1913: "We thought the men who do the
hiring of men ought to get some idea of what fitness and future
means in the career of the worker." As we have seen, those active
in the vocational guidance movement felt that the school's careful
selection and training of students for appropriate vocations would
count for little if industry failed to take a similar interest in the

"life-career" motive of its workers. Introducing personnel managers to vocational methods was one way to insure that the graduate would continue to receive guidance after leaving school. As advocates of vocational guidance frequently pointed out, the same techniques used by the schools had wide applicability to industry.[49]

Vocational guidance had close organizational ties to the early personnel management movement. The first national conference of personnel managers in 1916 was held under the auspices of the NSPIE, the umbrella organization that pushed for federal support of industrial education; in 1917, when Bloomfield was president of the National Vocational Guidance Association, the NVGA sponsored the second national conference held at Philadelphia. Prominent vocational educators such as Paul H. Hanus and Charles A. Prosser, both personal friends of Bloomfield, appeared regularly at the conferences Bloomfield organized to promote personnel management.[50]

A third motive for the establishment of the Boston EMA was the conviction that personnel management could "help unravel the tangled problem of misemployment, under-employment and unemployment, and the waste of human capacity." Since the schools could do little to bring about reforms in this area, the personnel manager might be the appropriate person to introduce policies that would stabilize employment and eradicate blind-alley jobs. Other groups interested in labor market reform, such as the American Association for Labor Legislation, were also attracted to personnel management as a way of solving the unemployment problem.[51]

Vocationalism in Industry

Vocationalists had long criticized industry for its "wasteful" recruiting techniques. Consequently, their involvement in the personnel management movement led to a further rationalization and tightening of the linkages between the schools and industry. Charles A. Prosser, president of the NSPIE, thought that personnel management gave industry an opportunity to develop working relationships with the schools. At a conference in 1916, he urged that personnel managers inform guidance counselors of the labor needs of their firms and then, in return for the schools' cooperation, agree to hire graduates of local schools. The Cheney Silk Mills at Manchester, Connecticut (whose personnel manager, H. L. Gardner, was a member of the Boston EMA), made this kind of agreement with nearby schools. The schools developed trade courses to meet the firm's specifications, and the firm reciprocated by increasing its contributions to the school district. Strawbridge and Clothier, the Philadelphia department store, and the Dennison Manufacturing Company agreed to hire local high school students as junior employees during the summer months. (The personnel managers of both firms were charter members of the Boston EMA.) Thus, through the personnel manager, schools began to establish the contacts that had been touted as one of the benefits of vocational education.[52]

The early personnel management movement was deeply influence by the vocational guidance philosophy which held that it was possible to find the right person for the right job. Like Frank Parsons, the typical personnel manager attached great weight to individual differences in interest and ability; both believed that, if these differences could be accurately gauged and matched to job requirements, industrial harmony would be achieved. This belief found its practical expression in the tremendous interest that personnel managers displayed in testing and other rational selection techniques. Among the earliest industrial users of employment tests were companies with close ties to the Boston EMA. In 1917 Roy W. Kelly, author of the first American personnel management textbook and director of Harvard's Vocational Guidance Bureau, credited vocational guidance with having created "the spirit of industrial management that looks to a wiser selection of employees."[53]

Identifying jobs and collecting information on job characteristics was the other side of this concern with individual differences. Personnel managers adopted the guidance counselor's penchant for standardizing occupational terminology and writing detailed descriptions of job requirements (so-called job analysis). E. M. Hopkins, personnel manager at Strawbridge and Clothier, thought that "one of the most essential moves for the employment office" was "to survey requirements of the work and opportunities for the workers in respective departments." Meyer Bloomfield encouraged these activities, noting in 1915 that "so little analysis of the work

required has been undertaken that we have practically no specifications, no blueprints of job requirements, in order to enable an
applicant to measure himself against the actual demands."[54]

Like vocational counselors, personnel managers emphasized detailed record-keeping. Although this emphasis was partly attributable to the influence of the efficiency engineers, the information
collected by personnel managers, and the uses to which it was put,
bore a strong resemblance to what was being done in the schools.
Personnel managers began to keep productivity and performance
records similar to the report cards and records being introduced
into the schools. The purpose of these records, said one personnel
manager, was "to advise [the employee] when he may profitably
aspire to a more responsible position." While few people questioned the school's motives for introducing ability tests and records,
trade unions were deeply suspicious of the motives of the employer,
given the antiunion ends that such activity might serve. After 1910
the railroads began to keep extensive performance records and to
use vocational tests. During the giant Illinois Central-Harriman
strike of 1911-1915, the unions demanded that employment records, employment tests, and compulsory physical exams be
abolished.[55]

Most significant, personnel managers absorbed the vocationalists' concern with careers and promotions. In emphasizing the need
to extend professional career patterns to manual workers, personnel managers used language reminiscent of Eliot's definition of the
life-career motive. For instance, Boyd Fisher, head of the Detroit
Employment Managers' Association, said in 1916:

> I know of few plants where routine factory work is a sufficient
> career, but I see no reason why it should not be. Doctors look
> forward cheerfully to going on being doctors. Lawyers have no
> difficulty in deciding that their life work is the law. Other professions
> are satisfying to those who follow them, and yet such is the nature
> of factory work that at present it savors a bit of the desire to
> perpetuate class distinctions to suggest that factory workers content
> themselves with the prospects of continuing as factory workers.[56]

Organizations and individuals with close ties to the vocational
guidance movement were especially interested in developing internal promotion plans for workers. For instance, Dennison Manufacturing, Filene's, and Cheney Brothers—companies whose person-

nel managers belong to the Boston EMA—devised some of the earliest nonunion internal promotion plans. Bloomfield's successor at the Vocation Bureau, Roy W. Kelly, conducted the first national survey of promotion plans for industrial workers, and the Federal Board for Vocational Education, which was created by the Smith-Hughes Act, published a personnel textbook in 1919 which emphasized how promotion plans could be used to "transform the life of labor into something worthy of a career."[57]

Proponents of promotion plans pointed out that these plans would contribute to labor peace by building morale and loyalty. Philip J. Reilly, personnel manager at Dennison's, said that his company's promotion plan "engenders loyalty and *espirit de corps*." Sumner Slichter criticized industry for failing to adopt definite promotion systems and argued that productivity would improve if workers had something to look forward to. In the current jargon, promotion systems would make the worker future-oriented:

> The importance of a lack of a fairly definite prospect of advancing to a better paying or more attractive work has been inadequately appreciated. Most men feel the need of a goal to put the zest of the struggle and contest into their work; the hope of better things tomorrow to take their minds off the difficulties of today. Every factor which lessens the hope for better things tomorrow renders the hardships of today doubly onerous.[58]

Thanks in part to the efforts of vocationalists, then, promotion plans became a leading item on the agenda for industrial employment reform. Of course the idea that an internal promotion plan would improve morale, loyalty, and productivity was not exclusive to the vocational guidance movement. Nonetheless, the guidance reformers, with their emphasis on careers and on the need to eliminate blind-alley jobs, helped to assure that more attention was given to promotion policies.

V. Postcript: Job Ladders and Class Struggle

Recently there have been some attempts, notably by neo-Marxist writers, to explain the origins of industry's use of promotion ladders for manual workers. In an oft-cited article on the steel industry,

Katherine Stone argues that the policy of internal promotion along multiple job ladders was first initiated at a time when technological developments were reducing the distinctions between unskilled and skilled workers.[59] Stone says that employers introduced internal promotion plans to prevent this trend toward "homogenization" from culminating in greater solidarity between workers previously divided by skill. Promotion along job ladders not only served to pit workers against each other in the struggle to advance to better jobs but also differentiated the interests of workers moving along different ladders. Other radical scholars have advanced Stone's argument as a general principle of managerial practice during the period between 1890 and 1920.[60] Because of the importance of their work, it is well to examine Stone's analysis in detail.

The most persuasive part of Stone's argument is her contention that skills were being leveled during this period, as the number of skilled and unskilled jobs was reduced relative to the number of semiskilled jobs. One of the most careful studies of mechanization conducted at this time concluded that "the aggregate effect may be . . . a leveling process producing fewer skilled but also few really unskilled jobs." Numerous examples of the reduction in skill level may be cited: A machine superintendent noted that 75 percent of his shop's jobs could be learned in less than a week; a government survey found that over a quarter of all jobs in the automobile industry required no previous experience; and a worker could be trained for the assembly line in the electrical manufacturing and appliance industry in as little as ten days. Some observers took a more agnostic position on the issue, noting that mechanization increased the number of highly skilled maintenance and repair jobs at the same time as it undermined traditional crafts. Leo Wolman argued that the notion of a leveling trend, "depending as it does upon the refined definition of terms and exhaustive knowledge of industrial processes makes statistical verification of this view impossible."[61]

The truth about the extent of deskilling lies somewhere between the extremes. According to a study of jobs in the steel industry before and after the mechanization referred to by Stone, the proportion of skilled jobs dropped, and the proportion of semiskilled jobs increased, but there were still many unskilled jobs (see table 3.1). Of course, how jobs are classified is a factor here. Many jobs

Table 3.1. Occupational Distribution in Steel Manufacturing Plants, 1884–1907

	Percent Laborers	Percent Semiskilled	Percent Skilled
1884	49	14	37
1907	62	21	17

SOURCE: Isaac A. Hourwich, *Immigration and Labor: The Economic Aspects of European Immigration to the United States* (New York, 1912), pp. 396, 400.

that were easy to learn and paid low wages were classified as semiskilled largely because they entailed working with machines. As one student of the subject noted: "There appears to be a strong tendency to regard all machine operators as semiskilled, even though the work is very simple, and the rate of pay slightly, if any, above that for common labor."[62]

Stone's view of the consequences of deskilling is more questionable. She says that employers devised job ladders which "pitted each worker against all the others in rivalry for achievement and undercut any feeling of unity which might develop among them." More probably, internal promotion plans *reduced* rivalry by weakening the foreman's power to assign workers to jobs that were clean, safe, or well-paid. Under the drive system, competition for good jobs was intense, while criteria for promotion were vague and, in practice, inequitable. But with the introduction of a definite promotion plan, the number of competitors for a single job was reduced since the lines leading to it were clear. Moreover, promotion ladders made it less likely that a vacancy would be filled by an outsider. Finally, these plans gave workers more bargaining power when faced with technological change; job titles and promotion patterns were codified, making them more rigid than before. This explains both the early union interest in promotion plans and, as will be discussed, the sluggish pace at which management introduced such plans.

Stone says: "Around the turn of the century, employers began to recognize the dangers inherent in the homogenization of the workforce," and they formulated this problem as "worker discontent caused by dead-end jobs." Rather than changing the jobs themselves, employers simply changed the arrangement of jobs so as to give workers a sense of mobility and an incentive to work harder. Stone is correct here, but she misses the significance of these developments by failing to note that those most concerned with

the deadening effects of blind-alley jobs were middle-class reformers and a few progressive employers, not employers at large. The
reformers' critique of deskilling was in some cases as trenchant as
that of modern critics. They focused attention as never before on
the character of the jobs offered by industry, maintaining that
manual workers could be impelled by the same motives as those
that caused white-collar professionals to labor diligently at their
vocations: desire for advancement opportunities, for employment
security, and for equitable treatment. This was no small claim in
an era when most employers regarded workers as brutish or machine-like and paid no attention at all to motivation, preferring to
leave that to their foremen.

It is not clear what the alternative would have been. Stone and
writers like Braverman seem to favor a return to the craft system
of organization, when conception and execution were unified in
broadly skilled jobs. But besides being unrealistic, this suggestion
is insensitive to the plight of the less skilled worker. When the
internal contract system was still operating in the iron and steel
industries, a sheet shearer made twelve dollars a day and paid his
helper two dollars. Chances for promotion from helper to journeyman were uncertain, particularly for immigrant workers. The system hardly seems preferable to an internal promotion ladder.[63]

Finally, Stone's argument that promotion plans splintered
worker solidarity because "workers on different job ladder rungs
had different vested interests" ignores the fact that the internal
promotion plans introduced between 1910 and 1930 were usually
accompanied by an internal transfer system that allowed workers
to shift among departments within the plant. Vocationalists
thought of transfer systems as the internal analogue to a worker's
picking and choosing among jobs in the external labor market until
he had found one that was right for him. Transfer systems were
supposed to "enable the worker to find his niche" and "aid the
worker in getting varied experience." Dennison Manufacturing had
a policy of "transferring employees from one department to another to promote them as well as to give another chance to the
promising employees who failed to 'make good' on their first jobs."
Just as guidance counselors followed up recent school graduates,
the personnel manager at Dennison's kept track of new employees
and transferred them if they were dissatisfied or "incompetent."[64]

Workers' interests were differentiated not by internal promotion plans but by their ethnicity, by the still-strong cleavages between the skilled and the unskilled, and by the worker's complete dependence on the whims of his foreman. A system of transfers and tryouts would have been impossible under the balkanized drive system. Foremen were strongly opposed to company-wide promotion, transfer, and tryout systems, feeling that these developments undermined their authority. As one observer wrote in 1919: "Foremen are apt to assume the attitude that 'if you do not work in my department you cannot work elsewhere,' and will do everything in their power to prevent dissatisfied workmen from being replaced."[65]

CHAPTER 4

PROBLEMS, PROBLEM-SOLVERS, AND A NEW PROFESSION

Each of the groups that fed into personnel management focused on a different aspect of work relations: The engineers looked at job design and administrative practices; welfare workers were concerned with the factory environment and the worker's edification; and vocationalists emphasized employment policies and procedures. These separate strands began to come together in the years before America's entry into the war. Efficiency—the engineers' watchword, with its connotations of scientific method and bureaucratic order—infused the welfare work and vocational guidance movements at the same time that the engineers started to take employment reform and worker uplift seriously. It was as would-be solvers of a number of problems that troubled both employers and society—industrial alienation, unemployment, and turnover—that these groups made connections with each other and became integrated into a larger enterprise: the personnel management profession.

I. Motivating the Alienated

Of the various tendencies inherent in America's new industrialism that disturbed reformers and intellectuals in the early 1900s, none worried them more than the declining efficacy of the work ethic. This perceived decline was thought to be the source of problems ranging from individual alienation and boredom to social instability and unrest. Often the worker himself was blamed for this decline; he was an immigrant, or a drunkard, or a mental misfit. But it was also widely recognized that work itself was no longer satisfying; it had become too specialized and monotonous, offering at best merely pecuniary rewards.[1]

Henry C. Metcalf, head of the vocational guidance committee of the National Association of Corporation Schools (NACS), believed that the continuing division of labor was eroding the work ethic. Workers, he said, "are chafing under too narrow specialization, especially when that is accompanied by work conditions which tend to repress the development of individual and human personality." Welfare workers leveled similar charges. Lee Frankel and Alexander Fleisher, who were in charge of welfare activities at the Metropolitan Life Insurance Company, attributed labor instability to the deskilling of jobs. Labor turnover, they noted, "is not due to a shortage in labor but rather to the increasing subdivision of labor processes which has made work more monotonous and the transition from one occupation to another more easy."[2]

In fact, welfare work may be seen as an effort to deal with this problem, by providing extra-work activities to satisfy needs that factory jobs could not fulfill: for cultural and aesthetic stimulation, for educational development, and even for personal challenge (company athletics was one substitute). Vocational guidance represented another such effort: Work would be less stultifying if individuals held jobs that interested and suited them and if these jobs could provide some of the intrinsic rewards associated with a professional career. Both approaches were based on the belief that a satisfied worker was not only more stable and ambitious but also more productive, a modern notion that prefigured the "worklife quality" programs of our own age. One young economist criticized employers for having "disregarded the fact that efficiency is increased by contentment. It is the satisfied worker who puts his whole heart into his work."[3]

Neither the welfare workers nor the vocationalists, however, penetrated to the heart of the industrial worker's malaise; they proposed no fundamental change in the content of factory labor. Ultimately, their proposed solutions involved little more than adjusting the worker to the drudgery of his job. But their failure to come up with adequate solutions did not deter them from vehemently criticizing engineers in general, and Frederick W. Taylor in particular, for having made industrial labor dull, enervating, and meaningless.

The charge was somewhat unfair, since it overstated the influence of the engineer. As early as the 1880s, those associated with the manual training movement had expressed deep concern over the growing division of labor and its negative effects on craftsmanship, the work ethic, and creativity. But rarely did they point an accusing finger at the engineer, who was just beginning to apply his techniques to work design and incentive pay systems.

The attack on industrial engineering must be viewed in the context of growing national criticism of scientific management, sparked by a number of highly publicized strikes, a congressional investigation, and the Hoxie report of 1915. Vocationalists and welfare workers alike faulted the engineer not only for his bias in favor of deskilling but also for his crude, economistic view of labor productivity and labor peace. They argued that the engineer failed to pay sufficient attention to the "human factor," by which they meant the worker's attitudes, interests, and psychological needs. As Henry C. Metcalf put it: "Scientific management we now know has not fully caught the vision of the organic nature of human relations in industry. There is much justice in the criticism of the narrowing influences of the shop under scientific management."[4]

Eventually, these criticisms were heard by the engineering profession. In 1910 Joseph W. Roe, a professor of industrial engineering at Yale, started a program at the Sheffield School to train engineers in "industrial service work." The idea caught on at other engineering schools and was encouraged by the YMCA's Industrial Service Department, which developed a curriculum—covering such topics as how to handle employees, the human factor, elements of welfare work and vocational guidance, trade union history, and the worker's standard of living—for use in these programs. Most industrial service programs also included field work designed to give engineering students contact with and sympathy for the working classes. The students were employed as census enumerators in urban ghettos and as teachers of English to groups of immigrant workers. By 1916, over 150 engineering colleges sponsored industrial service programs intended to bring out "the human side of engineering."[5]

Similarly, engineers like Harrington Emerson began to devote more attention to vocational psychology after 1910, arguing that it offered a solid basis for the "scientific selection of employees." Meetings of Emerson's Efficiency Society now were devoted to topics such as employee selection, vocational guidance, and industrial education. Paul Hanus, a professor of vocational education, was on the society's board of directors, as was Lillian M. Gilbreth, a noted psychologist who had studied with Hugo Munsterberg at Harvard. Gilbreth combined scientific management with the new psychology of individual differences in her research as well as in her personal life.[6]

But the most dramatic shift in orientation occurred in the Society for the Promotion of Scientific Management (later the Taylor Society). After Taylor's death in 1915, the society came to be dominated by men and women committed to combining progressive social ideals with efficient management practices. Many became active in the personnel management movement; employers in the society—Henry S. Dennison, Richard Feiss, Henry P. Kendall—developed model personnel departments for their companies. Some of Taylor's followers actively promoted the idea of joint management in industry, including employee representation and even collective bargaining, views that put them at the liberal end of the management spectrum.

Ideas such as these, which were intended as an answer to critics of scientific management, represented a sharp departure from Frederick W. Taylor's own thinking, especially his singularly monetary approach to motivation. Robert Bruere and Ordway Tead, both society members, became leading advocates of the need to recognized the "creative spirit" and "esprit de corps" among industrial workers. Both men argued that the worker had an "instinct" for craftsmanship and creativity and that this instinct was being repressed by industry. Individuals would work effectively only when allowed to express their creative instincts and when given some control over, and knowledge of, the production process. Tead even went so far as to admit that Taylor's system "takes all planning away from workers, making each operation a meaningless, machine-like job at which no craftsmanship can be exercised and from which no joy can be derived." As a way of giving workers a heightened sense of participation in production, Tead and Bruere called for shop councils and worker involvement in time study and rate setting.[7]

In 1918, with the assistance of other Taylor Society members, Tead and Bruere founded the Bureau of Industrial Research, which conducted and published research on personnel management and labor relations. The bureau also provided technical assistance in these areas to groups like the Interchurch World Movement (for whom it conducted the famous study of the 1919 steel strike) and to private firms. Tead and Bruere were hired in 1919 by Morris Leeds, a fellow Taylorist, to help install a personnel department at Leeds' Philadelphia manufacturing firm.[8]

The ideas of Robert B. Wolf, another Taylor Society member, were less radical but no less unorthodox than Tead and Bruere's. In his papers to the society, Wolf argued that "non-financial incentives" were as effective in raising the effort levels of workers as wage bonus plans were. Wolf believed that these incentives—which included such motivational devices as group production contests, promotion and transfer plans, shop councils, and even welfare programs like thrift and pension plans—"brought out the creative faculty of the men to the fullest extent." Wolf also noted that "increasing financial returns have failed to stimulate productivity. . . . The constant demand for shorter hours and the increasing labor turnover are proof that work in most of our industries not only does not attract but actually repels the workmen." Unlike Tead and Bruere, Wolf was trained as an engineer and employed as a production manager, so his critique of deskilling and his espousal of nonfinancial incentives are all the more impressive. By admitting that these incentives could serve as a substitute for wage bonus plans, Wolf anticipated the Taylorists' subsequent acceptance of previously heretical motivational assumptions and techniques. Ordway Tead declared in 1920 that "the sole and primary incentive to effort and interest is not the pay envelope. . . . The most deep-rooted incentives are non-financial."[9]

One of the Taylor Society's earliest advocates of change was Robert G. Valentine, who had a varied career as an English professor, U.S. Commissioner of Indian Affairs, and chairman of the first Massachusetts minimum wage board. Valentine was also very friendly with organized labor and worked as a consultant to several unions. In 1914, shortly after he became active in the society, Valentine was asked by Henry P. Kendall of the Plimpton Press to mediate a labor dispute between the Press and the typographers. Frederick W. Taylor, having advised Kendall to resist the union's demands for the preferential shop and for a halt to the introduction of scientific management, was shocked when he discovered that Kendall had accepted Valentine's advice to bargain with the union. Kendall rebuked Taylor for his attitude, telling him that Valentine was headed in the right direction and that scientific management would eventually have to recognize and deal with organized labor.

As a self-styled "Industrial Counselor," Valentine developed the technique of the labor audit, whereby "a patient, accurate, dispassionate, sympathetic, tactful" outsider would survey a firm's labor relations and employment methods to suggest improvements. In a talk to the Society for the Promotion of Scientific Management, Valentine first described the purpose of the labor audit and then argued that "a perpetual human audit" could be carried out if a firm established a personnel department with powers equal to those of the manufacturing division. The talk broke fresh ground for the society by emphasizing the independence of labor and production problems and by advocating personnel management; it was twice printed in the Taylor Society's bulletin.[10]

By 1920 the Taylor Society had become the most ardent of the various engineering associations in its support of personnel management. This new orientation resulted in part from the society's willingness to admit non-engineers as members; more important, it indicated the Taylorists' ability to accept criticism and to absorb new ideas. Harlow S. Person, director of the society for many years, taught personnel management courses in New York after the war and periodically invited Meyer Bloomfield and other critics of scientific management to address the society. Even on the sensitive issue of the engineer's suitability to manage employment affairs, the Taylorists came to agree with the welfare workers and vocationalists. In a speech to a YMCA conference in 1920, Person noted that engineers were not qualified to be personnel managers because "the training of the engineer has been confined to the studying of the reactions of dead matter, purely technical education. . . . This does not equip a man to handle human relations or to assume human leadership."[11]

Thus, the efficiency engineers reached a rapprochement with their critics by accepting the need for a new approach to worker motivation and the work ethic, managerial problems that had wider social significance. Another area of common concern was unemployment, a societal problem that both groups proposed to solve by changing managerial techniques.

II. Managing Unemployment

At the turn of the century, unemployment was a devastating experience for most working-class families. As radical orators were fond of pointing out, it was the scourge of capitalism. The severity of the 1893 depression moved even Samuel Gompers to attack the system: "In a society where such abnormal conditions prevail there must of necessity be something wrong at the basic foundations. . . . The ownership and control of the means of production by private corporations which have no human sympathy . . . is the cause of the ills and wrongs borne by the human family." Believing that capitalism could be made less brutal without being eliminated entirely, a generation of reformers dedicated themselves to finding a solution to the unemployment problem.[12]

Unemployment, Not the Unemployed

The severe depression that began in 1893 marked a turning point in social attitudes toward the unemployed. For the first time it was widely acknowledged that the unemployed might not be entirely to blame for their situation. Charity organizations like the New York Association for Improving the Condition of the Poor now admitted that, in some cases, unemployment was "not due usually to moral or intellectual defects" on the part of individuals "but to economic causes over which they could have no control."[13]

Economists began to study unemployment as a serious problem separate and distinguishable from poverty. In a paper delivered to the American Economic Association in 1894, Davis R. Dewey, an economist at the Massachusetts Institute of Technology, asked: "Who are the unemployed and what does this term denote? . . . The term *unemployed* as used today is a new term in our economic vocabulary. Does it, however, correspond to new economic conditions or may it not be a new term applied to an element which has existed for centuries, that is, the poor?" Dewey answered himself by noting that if the unemployed were merely the "able-bodied poor, sturdy beggars, shiftless ne'er-do-wells, weaklings, and intemperates," the economist "need not trouble himself with any new analysis with respect to such phenomena." But, he argued, in addition to the poor, there now existed a new class of persons, those "who are willing to work and who in past times have found abundant opportunity to work, but who now find their economic condition so uncertain, their industrial tenure so unstable, that they are frequently without employment."[14]

Along with the new view that unemployment had structural causes came a variety of proposals to remedy it. During the 1890s, when the charity agencies were swamped with requests for relief, some suggested that the government intervene by hiring the unemployed for public works projects, as was being done in Europe. Another European solution was the establishment of public employment offices and labor exchanges, which were tried but proved ineffectual in the United States. (In 1909, a private employment exchange was created by wealthy American reformers who hoped the project could finance itself by charging user fees; it quickly became insolvent.)[15] Finally, there was unemployment insurance, and the Europeans were pioneers here, too. England adopted one of the world's first compulsory unemployment insurance programs in 1911, after three years of testimony, research, and deliberation by the Royal Commission on the Poor Laws and the Relief of Distress Through Unemployment.[16]

The commission's majority report presented the position associated with William H. Beveridge, who was one of the first economists to distinguish between cyclical and frictional unemployment, the latter being what Beveridge termed an "irreducible minimum" below which unemployment never falls, even in the best of times. Beveridge attributed high frictional levels of unemployment to a "reserve of labour" made up of workers needed only for peak production periods in the seasonally unstable industries to which they were attached. He thought that a national system of labor exchanges would reduce these reserves by coordinating the seasonal labor requirements of different industries and by providing information on available jobs and workers. That is, the level of frictional unemployment could be lowered if the labor market were made more efficient. Matching jobs and workers would help to absorb what Beveridge described as the "stagnant reserve which drifts about the streets today."

But according to Beveridge, little could be done to eliminate cyclical unemployment. "Unemployment is part of the price of industrial competition," he said, and "there may be worse things in a community than unemployment. The practical reply is to be found in reducing the pain." He proposed that unemployment insurance be used to alleviate the "pain" of cyclical fluctuations, which, he said, were "in some degree inevitable."[17]

The programs developed in England and the ideas that lay behind them had a strong impact on American reformers. In 1910 Henry Seager, an economist at Columbia University, published his influential *Social Insurance,* which described the new developments in Europe and suggested similar reforms for the United States. Echoing Beveridge, Seager argued that the seasonal irregularity of employment "is the chief cause of unemployment." He proposed a system of labor exchanges for the United States and also called upon employers to stabilize employment voluntarily by planning their labor requirements, deseasonalizing their product lines ("so that the labor force most needed in the slack season can be turned into the other"), and smoothing out production by relying less on overtime. Seager wrote approvingly of the work done by Louis D. Brandeis to stabilize employment in the garment industry. Like Seager, Brandeis (who was then litigating the Eastern Rate case) had come to believe that "in the scientifically managed business, irregularity tends to disappear." The emphasis on private initiatives and good management represented the beginning of a uniquely American approach to unemployment; the Royal Commission had never placed as much emphasis on stabilizing employment through voluntary efforts.[18]

Between 1909 and 1915, two groups were active in discussing British findings and interpreting their suitability to the United States. One was the Russell Sage Foundation, headed by Paul U. Kellogg. The foundation's Committee on Women's Work (of which Seager was a member) produced several influential studies of irregular employment in industries employing large numbers of women, such as bookbinding, artificial flower-making, millinery, and the garment trades. These reports were written by Mary Van Kleeck

and Louise Odencrantz, middle-class feminists intent on demon-
strating the structural causes of women's employment problems.
Following Seager, Van Kleeck argued in 1913 that the seasonal
character of women's work could best be remedied by adopting
more rational and efficient management policies: "Laymen who
talk about the 'marvelous organization of modern industries' need
only inquire into the methods of steadying the seasons in almost
any trade which employs a large number of women to discover
proof of a lamentable lack of efficient organization."[19]

The second, and more important, group advocating labor market
reform was the American Association for Labor Legislation
(AALL), which had been created to promote workers' compensation laws. It began to shift its attention to unemployment around
1910, when the work of the Royal Commission was generating
intense interest among American reformers. By 1913 the AALL
had a membership of over 3,000 persons drawn from a wide variety
of Progressive reform endeavors. Its officers included industrial
welfare workers (Lee K. Frankel), labor leaders (Samuel Gompers),
settlement house workers (Jane Addams), and liberal employers
(Henry S. Dennison). Louis D. Brandeis was a vice-president, and
socialist mayor Victor Berger was on the administrative council.[20]

The AALL sponsored the First National Conference on Unemployment in February 1914, just as another major depression was
beginning. The conference issued several recommendations for alleviating the growing unemployment problem in the United States.
Most of these were consistent with the European approach; they
called for accurate labor market statistics, a national system of
labor exchanges, and compulsory unemployment insurance. But
one proposal—the regularization of employment by new management methods—reflected an American preference for private, voluntary measures.

The conference did little more than touch on the idea that unemployment could be reduced by stabilization techniques. AALL
secretary John B. Andrews prepared a conference report which
noted that "a few progressive employers" had taken steps to reduce
seasonal fluctuations in labor demand, but he had nothing further
to say on the subject. The only other conference participant to
discuss private employment practices was Meyer Bloomfield, who
drew attention to the Boston Employment Managers' Association

as the "one organization in this country . . . looking into this matter." By the time the AALL held its second national conference ten months later, however, the employment stabilization idea had become very popular.[21]

Local Activism

During the depression of 1914-15, groups whose purpose was to administer relief and to sponsor research promoting the new approach to unemployment sprang up in several different cities, including Boston, Philadelphia, and New York.

Boston. A branch of the AALL, the Massachusetts State Committee on Unemployment was chaired by Robert G. Valentine, and a number of its members were AALL officers. In 1914, AALL secretary John B. Andrews asked the committee to assist Juliet Poyntz, a former student of the Webbs, in her research on seasonal instability of employment. Tead and Henry S. Dennison, a member of the committee, arranged to have companies belonging to the Boston Chamber of Commerce fill out Poyntz's questionnaires, and the Chamber of Commerce published her report.

Poyntz found a close connection between levels of unemployment and seasonal fluctuations in employment among Boston firms. Her recommendations for reducing unemployment included a shorter working day, production for stock during slack seasons, and the establishment of personnel departments and intrafirm transfer systems. Said Poyntz:

> All establishments of any considerable size should maintain a special employment department required to keep careful records of employment including the number of workers of each class employed throughout the year . . . wages, hours, workers hired and discharged, etc. The policy of such a department should be directed toward maintaining regularity as far as possible in instructing other departments of the business as to their employment requirements. So far as possible, employees should be shifted from one department to another so that they may become familiar with various kinds of work necessary to the conduct of the business. . . . Employers should be educated to the necessity of maintaining an efficient organization by providing regular work.

What makes these proposals—which, in essence, involve stabilizing employment through an internal labor market—so interesting is that they came as a response not to labor shortages but to severe unemployment.[22]

Philadelphia. Mayor Blankenburg of Philadelphia convened a meeting of the city's major employers in December 1914 to discuss ways of relieving Philadelphia's unemployment crisis. One outcome of the meeting was a proposal that the city sponsor a general study which would suggest how to minimize unemployment in the future. The young Wharton School instructor appointed to conduct the study, Joseph H. Willits, produced a report entitled *Steadying Employment* several months later.

Willits first differentiated between what he termed "permanent unemployment" and unemployment arising from cyclical crises, claiming that the former was more severe than the latter. Then, in a move that was becoming characteristic of the American approach, Willits chose to ignore cyclical unemployment in the remainder of his report and to focus instead on ways of reducing permanent levels of unemployment. He encouraged Phialdelphia's employers to adopt various stabilization measures: coordinating sales and production departments, diversifying product lines, and producing for stock during slow seasons. One of his chief recommendations was that "the handling of the employment problem should not be left to foremen of different departments, but should be transferred to some high grade functionalized employment official or department." Like Juliet Poyntz, Willits established a rationale for personnel management that was based on the prevention of unemployment.[23]

New York. The New York City Mayor's Committee on Unemployment was appointed in December 1914. Chaired by Elbert H. Gary of U.S. Steel, it included prominent employers, labor leaders, and social reformers. The committee hired Mary Van Kleeck to conduct several studies of unemployment and then submitted its own report in January 1916.

The report recommended the same approach to unemployment as the groups in Boston and Philadelphia were promoting: a mix of private stabilization measures (including the establishment of personnel departments) and public measures (including labor exchanges and vocational guidance programs). Noting that the city's industries tended to be seasonally irregular and that local employers failed to retain workers during slack periods, the report emphasized that a considerable, if incalculable, amount of unemployment could be controlled through "special effort" by employers. Such stabilization would not only reduce unemployment but made good business sense as well: "The real economies resulting from a more efficient and productive labor force, which a steady working force would undoubtedly be, should be as good for business as the movement for better sanitation, good lighting, and reduction in the number of accidents proved to be." Thus, stabilization methods were presented as a profitable proposition that rational employers would be quick to adopt.

But the New York committee's ambivalence about this line of reasoning was reflected in its reference to the profitability of measures (e.g., industrial safety) which employers had adopted only after compelled to do so by legislation. Apparently, the committee was aware that some employers might not regard stabilization as a paying proposition. In fact, several passages in the report suggested that, profitable or not, steady employment was the worker's right and the employer's moral obligation:

> The public interest demands that those who have been drawn into any industry and are willing and efficient shall be reasonably certain of regular and continuous employment. The ideal which New York has a right to expect its industries to approximate, or at least strive for, is that every worker who offers his services shall be entitled to a "steady job."

The question of whether stabilization was indeed profitable was vitally important to the American labor market reform movement. If employers could be convinced that it paid to stabilize employment, then unemployment could be considerably reduced without resort to legislative intervention.[24]

The Engineers

The idea that efficient management practices might alleviate unemployment appealed to Frederick W. Taylor's followers, who were, as we have seen, more imbued with the progressive ethos of

social service than was Taylor. Eager to refute the claims of organized labor and other critics that scientific management was harmful, they became ardent advocates of the new approach to
unemployment.

A liberal Cleveland employer and an active member of the Society
for the Promotion of Scientific Management, Richard A. Feiss
argued that the provision of steady, continuous employment was
the most important factor in solving the unemployment problem.
In several talks given in 1915, Feiss recommended that companies
adopt better employment management techniques, including the
establishment of a personnel department, as a way to stabilize
employment. Feiss claimed that these ideas were creations of the
scientific management movement, but this was only partly true.
Although several firms in the Taylor fold had established personnel
departments prior to 1915, unemployment and employment stabilization did not receive any detailed attention from the efficiency
engineers until the depression.[25]

Another prominent engineer who favored the new approach to
unemployment was Morris L. Cooke, Taylor's young protegé. During the depression, Cooke served as director of Philadelphia's public works department in the reform administration of Mayor Blankenburg; it was Cooke who picked Willits to write the city's
unemployment report. In a 1915 lecture entitled "Scientific Management as a Solution of the Unemployment Problem," Cooke
maintained that "ninety percent of all the unemployment which
makes men and women suffer and which demoralizes and degrades
them can be eliminated by proper organization *within* our factory
walls." He noted that a scientifically managed firm could reduce
unemployment by smoothing out production peaks and balancing
production departments. Greater coordination and planning—the
staples of scientific management—would eliminate the "waste" of
irregular employment. Moreover, said Cooke, "the outcome will
be the same whether the employer strives for this result on account
of a more or less altruistic interest in his employees or on account
of money-making considerations which appear to afford ample
argument for it or because both of these motives actuate him."
Dressed in new garb, this was the old Taylorist credo that greater
efficiency in management would redound to the benefit of employer
and worker alike. Thus, the concept of employment stabilization

appealed to the Taylorists because it promised that major social problems could be solved through the same efficient managerial techniques then being applied to production.[26]

Slow Progress

At the AALL's Second National Conference on Unemployment, which took place in December 1914, employment stabilization now was a central focus of attention. The AALL's official program for the prevention of unemployment encouraged employers to "make every job a steady job" and explained in detail how this could be done through "regulation of output"—the various administrative techniques to stabilize employment—and through the establishment of personnel departments. These departments, said the AALL, would lower unemployment by reducing discharges, by using internal transfers to curb layoffs, and by dividing the work force into groups and "keeping higher groups continuously employed."[27]

A year after issuing this program, the AALL conducted a survey to determine the extent to which employers had adopted its recommendations. Most of the evidence was discouraging. John B. Andrews noted that only a few employers had made systematic efforts to stabilize employment; even fewer had tried to prevent layoffs with work-sharing or make-work construction projects. Andrews thought it unlikely that employers would voluntarily stabilize employment without "the financial compulsion" of an unemployment insurance law.[28]

Others were similarly pessimistic. In New York City, the Mayor's Committee on Unemployment issued a second report more than a year after the depression had ended. Like the first report, it called for employment stabilization; but it took a radical turn, suggesting that political pressure might be necessary to force employers to take action. The report noted "the value of . . . movements which through fundamental social and political changes aim to purge our industrial system of general evils which have crept into it." This was strong stuff. Ralph Easley of the National Civic Federation reacted to the report by publicly labeling its author, Henry Bruere, a "dangerous" socialist.[29]

Easley missed the point. What Bruere was proposing was hardly socialism; he was proposing reforms, some of them major, within the existing industrial system. Bruere, who later became vice-president of the Bowery Savings Bank, was no more radical than most members of the AALL, the Taylor Society, or the Boston EMA. But old ideas die slowly, and many employers, including members of the National Civic Federation, still believed that existing employment practices were the only way.

Like the engineers, Bruere and other reformers envisioned a more regulated and orderly society, one that would require some short-term restraint by employers in the interest of long-term stability and, ultimately, employer profitability. What probably annoyed Easley most was Bruere's implicit suggestion that employers must choose not between existing practices and reform, but between reform and more radical change. Robert G. Valentine put the choice clearly at a 1914 meeting of the AALL:

> In simple form the proposition is that either we must advance rapidly toward state-wide socialistic control of the bulk of individual action, or else we must make our present freedom of individual action socially legitimate by thoroughgoing organization of social responsibilities of which the most significant feature would deal with the limits of unemployment. . . . We feel that if a choice had to be made between a world where these forces [of competition] had free play and a world where they were chained up, we would choose the competitive world with all its havoc and distress, and with its hope and possibilities. But that choice we do not consider it necessary to make— we see a third course which seems to us possible and practicable. . . . In a word, employers are beginning to see that the social problems of industry must be solved and that they must contribute to the solution. If private industry is to continue to exist, it must, both as a good moral and good business proposition . . . organize through all its factors . . . to protect the competing individual and the competing group from destructive forces for which they are not in any individual way responsible.[30]

Employment Associations

John B. Andrews, like others in the labor market reform movement, was disappointed by the slow pace of change during the depression. Yet he discerned one bright spot "of great promise for steadier employment in the future." Andrews was referring to the various associations created during the depression for the purpose of encouraging local employers to practice stabilization and personnel management.

In New York City, the Mayor's Committee on Unemployment, with help from Meyer Bloomfield, established the New York Society for the Study of Employment Problems, which was made up of personnel managers, engineers, and reformers who sought the cooperation of businessmen to alleviate unemployment. Like its Boston predecessor, the society said it was trying to develop "a rational, humanized employment policy which would result in greater regularity and permanency of employment."

In Philadelphia, the group that Blankenburg and Cooke had convened in 1914 became a permanent organization called the Philadelphia Association for the Discussion of Employment Problems. Members met to talk about stabilization, personnel management, and other employment reforms. Joseph H. Willits, the association's first secretary, said the association's aim was to eliminate "the wastes experienced by both employer and employee resulting from improper selection, direction, and discharge of labor." Similar groups were formed in Newark and Detroit.[31]

Together, these groups became the nucleus of the postdepression personnel management movement. Between 1915 and 1917, members of the associations wrote articles and organized conferences to popularize personnel management and to publicize new methods for ensuring employment stability. When the first national personnel management organization was formed in 1918, these associations were chartered as local chapters. But well before that time, most of them had shifted their primary concern from unemployment to a related but somewhat different problem. As one speaker said at a conference organized by the Boston association in 1916: "We soon came up against the fact that the problem of unemployment was seriously affected by men hunting for jobs, by the shifting of the labor force. Of course, we at once drifted into the question of the turnover."[32]

III. Labor Turnover

As we saw in chapter 1, instability was a characteristic feature of the traditional system of factory employment. Labor turnover rates were continuously high throughout the late nineteenth and early twentieth centuries, and it was not uncommon for firms to have annual turnover rates in excess of 300 percent. Even during the depression year of 1914, a group of Detroit factories reported separation rates of over 100 percent.[33] But before 1910, neither employers nor social reformers voiced much concern about the phenomenon, although some writers traced tramping and vagabondage to labor market conditions. Turnover was only dimly perceived as a problem, and rarely was it linked to structural causes.[34]

After 1910, perceptions of turnover began to change as the new approach to unemployment focused attention on the relation between employment methods, unemployment, and employment instability. In fact, the first American studies of labor turnover were an outgrowth of research into the causes of unemployment. These included the Russell Sage studies as well as a series of reports, issued between 1912 and 1915 by the New York Factory Investigating Committee, containing data on separation rates in the state's seasonal industries. Further, in 1914 the U.S. Bureau of Labor Statistics launched an investigation of unemployment that soon shifted orientation and became instead a detailed, quantitative study of turnover. That same year, the first estimates of turnover cost were published by Magnus Alexander, an officer of the AALL and a General Electric executive. As with unemployment, high turnover came to be seen as something that could be controlled by a change in private employment conditions and practices. Thus, labor turnover was "discovered" not because turnover rates rose sharply but because an old set of facts was viewed in new ways.[35]

Joseph Willits' report on unemployment in Philadelphia illustrates how unemployment research dovetailed into the turnover issue. On the basis of a rigorous analysis, Willits concluded that the hiring and firing policies of local firms resulted in what he called "an industrial roulette wheel" of labor turnover. Then he pointed out several ways in which turnover contributed to unemployment. First, excessive hiring and firing created a reservoir of unemployed workers attached to a particular firm or industry; each of these unemployed workers reasoned "I will soon be rehired" and so rather than seeking work elsewhere, they remained unemployed. Second, because of the brief tenure associated with high turnover, employers felt no obligation to retain employees during a downturn; this attitude led to greater numbers of jobless workers. Finally, frequent job changes were said to "break down the self-reliance of workers," making them less industrious and hence less attractive to employers.[36]

Work Habits

Like unemployment, the turnover issue elicited a host of misgivings about the social and private costs of the drive system. As Willits' last point suggests, concern over deterioration of the work ethic often lay just below the surface in discussions of both topics. Indeed, high rates of quits and dismissals were said to promote bad working habits and to erode ambition. Said one economist, "Working is something of an acquired habit, which if interrupted, is difficult to regain again." Men who regularly quit their jobs, said another observer, "have consumption standards as deficient as their industrial skill. Their sense of values is warped." Frequently these charges were directed at a group derisively tagged "the floaters," workers who never held on to a job for very long. Between 1913 and 1915, workers with less than three months' tenure accounted for three in five quits, a phenomenon that cut across all skill levels.[37] Two basic approaches were taken to lowering turnover and shoring up the work ethic.

The first was environmental and resembled the stabilization measures recommended in the unemployment literature. It entailed reforming employment practices and providing incentives for stability ("anchors for drifting workers"). The reorganization of employment at Ford Motor in 1913 was the most widely publicized prewar case of a dual attack on turnover and working habits. Like other Detroit companies, Ford had quit and dismissal levels that were extraordinarily high by modern standards; in 1913 the separation rate was 370 percent.[38]

The reorganization affected most aspects of employment at Ford. Anything that made workers more sedulous—from welfare work to wage incentives—came to be seen as part of the solution to the turnover problem. The most famous aspect of the reorganization was a profit-sharing plan, which the company called "the greatest revolution in the matter of rewards for its workers ever known in the industrial world." The plan actually involved a wage supplement which raised a worker's pay to a minimum of five dollars per day and which was given only to those employees found to be thrifty, moral, and hard-working. To determine a worker's eligibility for the supplement, the company's new Sociological Department sent several dozen investigators to look into his living conditions, get character references from his neighbors, examine his savings account, and scrutinize his attendance and production records. Only if the worker passed all these tests did he receive the supplement. The plan thus provided several incentives for stability, including the provision that a worker who quit and was later rehired had to again be certified by the Sociological Department, a process that could take months.[39] The Sociological Department also used its investigators to deter absenteeism, which was a serious problem at Ford: one-tenth of the firm's work force was absent at some time each week during 1913. The department gave offenders moral object lessons on absenteeism and on punctuality. For example,

> A man late three times in a year without good cause is given a hearing before an impartial court. If it appears that the man was at fault he is assessed from ten to twenty-five dollars which is given to charity. Upon the next day, he is taken in an investigator's car to the house of some worthy people in need, to whom he personally hands over the stipulated amount.[40]

Another part of the Ford reorganization was aimed at foremen. Prior to 1913, the foreman had full authority to hire, supervise, pay, and dismiss workers. As a result, discharge rates were high, and wage scales at the firm's Highland Park plant were varied and confused. Under the new system, a foreman wanting to fire a worker had to check first with the personnel department, which investigated to see if a discharge was justified; if not, the personnel department transferred the worker to a different part of the plant. In addition, the introduction of a wage classification system— ostensibly designed to "prevent the favoritism of a foreman for an employee"—reduced the number of wage rates at Ford from sixty-nine to eight.[41]

The second basic approach to reducing turnover and strengthening the work ethic was simply to do a better job of screening out floaters. This gave an obvious boost to personnel management. For instance, under Ford's new system, the personnel department, rather than the foreman, had the power to recruit and select new employees. Employers were advised to avoid former railroad workers ("they're used to sitting a lot, and to taking days off or sitting on sidings, and of course, they're mobile workers") as well as former miners (who "resent supervision and are used to quitting when work is done for the day"). Some writers suggested that employers hire only married men or home-owners.[42]

This approach, in contrast to the environmental approach, viewed turnover as the manifestation of an incorrigibly defective work ethic and a progressive deterioration in an individual's work habits. A government official said that the "initial symptoms" of this condition were "carelessness in regard to his or her work . . . The next logical stage of the disease, usually evidenced after the first day of rest, is absenteeism." Then, he said, came the quit. In 1915, when the National Association of Corporation Schools asked its members for their opinions about the causes of turnover, the most common reply was "wanderlust," followed by "drink and gambling," "lack of family responsibility," "the disposition of the individuals," and finally, the tendency to be "lazy and dissolute."[43]

Exit, Voice, and Loyalty

The new studies of turnover revealed that the labor market lacked any semblance of stability. The perpetual movement of workers between jobs was deeply disturbing to those reformers seeking to create a more rational and orderly society. In their view, not only did instability contribute to unemployment and indolence, but also—and just as distressing—it was linked to worker unrest and dissatisfaction (or what many, borrowing from military jargon, began to term "low morale"). Indeed, Sumner Slichter thought that the work ethic aspects of turnover were insignificant compared with the relation between turnover and morale: "Far more important than as a *cause* of demoralization among workers is the turnover as a *symptom* of demoralization . . . a symptom of conditions which give rise to unsatisfactory conditions and relations which naturally sap the morale of the men." That is, turnover was a symptom of potential conflict and labor unrest.[44]

Beginning in mid-1912 and continuing through 1913, a series of strikes hit employers across the country, and for the first time, large numbers of unskilled workers were involved. The Lawrence textile strike of 1912 was followed by a wave of textile strikes that swept across the Northeast. New industrial firms like Studebaker and Firestone experienced brief, spontaneous walkouts. Goodyear was plagued by trouble from the IWW, which also played a role in the textile strikes. At the time that Ford Motor was devising its reorganization plan in 1913, several unions—including the AFL's Automobile Workers, the Machinists, and the IWW—were attempting to organize the company's work force. In New York and New Jersey, nearly 25 percent of all workers were involved in strikes in 1913.[45]

Discussions of turnover were often explicit about the relationship between turnover and unrest. In modern parlance, they treated "exit" as an alternative to "voice." As one economist put it, trade unions "voice their protest against bad conditions by sending a committee to see the firm. The unorganized voice their protest by 'asking for their time.' " Another economist observed that turnover rates were higher in unorganized industries, a finding that Samuel Gompers used to curry favor for the labor movement. Describing turnover as a "vast striking back of individuals in desperation, a vast disorganized protest," Gompers claimed that "organized trades have practically no labor turnover."[46]

Early supporters of personnel management noted that the same conditions that gave rise to quits and low morale in the present might lead to strikes or worse in the future. If these conditions could be identified and remedied, they reasoned, morale would improve, quits would fall, and the possibility of industrial revolt would be greatly lessened. After 1910, a handful of progressive companies with personnel departments began to conduct regular exit interviews. A Philadelphia employer active in the city's Association for the Discussion of Employment Problems said that at his firm, departing workers were interviewed before they received their back pay. The results, he said, "are illuminating. When men quit or are discharged, they have no reason for withholding information. Complaints are heard of nagging foremen, lost time in waiting for work, and other complaints bearing on shop efficiency. Those are investigated and if the fault is with us, it is remedied."[47]

Another practice initiated at this time was the collection of data on turnover for use as a "morale index," the precursor of modern attitude surveys. The personnel manager at Norton Grinding Company, a leader in employee welfare work, said that his firm viewed turnover data "as an index of the degree to which management is successful in keeping in close touch with its employees." Slichter noted that management at other companies viewed the data as "an indication of the character of its industrial relations, of the degree of discontent within the plant."[48]

High turnover rates were frequently attributed to the impersonal atmosphere of the large corporation. An early book on turnover recommended that "each member of the organization . . . be made to feel that he is really a member of the organization instead of being an appendage to a machine with only a number tag as a designation." Shop meetings, suggestion systems, and plant contests were prescribed. According to Boyd Fisher, one way to reduce turnover and labor relations problems was to develop grievance procedures: "Hear complaints," he said, and "give every man a chance to 'knock.'" Turnover was also attributed to the deadening effects of modern factory labor and particularly to scientific management, which had made work "highly repetitive" and "intolerably tedious."[49]

Thus, low turnover came to be regarded as a desideratum for the well-managed, strike-free firm, an indication that the company was sensitive to the problems of its workers and that it provided them with outlets for voicing dissatisfaction. Moreover, a low turnover rate helped to stabilize worker effort and gave management time to build a corps of loyal employees. In his 1914 study, Magnus Alexander pointed out that a transient work force heightened "the difficulty of maintaining among the employees a spirit of general contentment and of loyalty to the management. As quicksand cannot be kneaded in the hands into a solid lump, so also will it be found difficult to take hold of an ever-changing mass of employees and transform it into a homogenous, intelligent, and contented body."[50]

Turnover Cost and Employment Reform

The new concern with turnover was not attributable to any increase in separation costs associated with technological change of a firm-specific character.[51] In fact, manufacturing technology was becoming less firm-specific and idiosyncratic than it had been in the nineteenth century. The United States was developing a capital goods industry, which allowed firms to purchase identical machinery from national vendors instead of having to craft their own, as in the nineteenth century. As one manager said in 1917, all firms "can buy the same kinds of machinery if they know where to get it; or they can design the same kind. Processes cannot now be kept entirely secret."[52]

Moreover, the wide-scale introduction of a technology that de-emphasized skill and lowered training costs not only reduced separation costs for the employer by making workers more interchangeable but also made it easier, or less costly, for the worker to change jobs. Discussions of turnover often noted that the opportunity for movement from plant to plant was facilitated by the standardization of equipment and the ease with which workers could learn a new job. As economist Paul H. Douglas observed: "The very process of machinery which made work more specialized, made the worker less specialized. He was now transferable. . . . A machine-tender who has learned the general principle of caring for a machine can tend ribbon-weaving machinery as well as shoe-making. He is really an interchangeable part in the industrial mechanism."[53]

Of course, there was still some cost attached to replacing an experienced employee, even though training costs were decreasing. Generally speaking, an incumbent is always more valuable to the employer than a new worker. As a Philadelphia employer told Joseph Willits in 1915, "it is cheaper to retain the man with his experience and knowledge of the company's way of doing business than it is to engage a new man." He added, however, "The argument can be pushed too far." Indeed, Alexander found the estimated replacement costs at several firms to be positive but usually not very large. And in some instances—as when senior workers learned to cooperate in restricting output or when an incumbent worker felt entitled to better pay simply because of his tenure— other factors outweighed any benefit accruing to the employer from the worker's experience.[54]

Although turnover costs were neither large nor rising, advocates of personnel management gave much emphasis to them, in order to legitimize reforms—principally, the restriction of the foreman's discharge prerogatives and the provision of employment security— which they regarded as necessary for other reasons. To understand the need for this strategy, one must appreciate that, within most firms, there were two opposing views about the desirability of reform.[55]

On the one hand, personnel managers (and their supporters) were deeply concerned about the long-term consequences of the drive system. Employment insecurity and a failure to recognize a worker's "sense of property rights in jobs," warned Ordway Tead, "will give rise to a stronger and stronger consciousness of injustice or to unconscious suppressed desires." The foreman's drive system, said Meyer Bloomfield, was the cause of "a surprisingly large percentage of labor difficulties" that could easily be avoided by restraining foremen and by regulating their power to hire and fire. A popular account of turnover put the matter bluntly. In it, a group of employers was asked whether

> any one of you men has ever given a thought to what went on in the minds of those two thousand-odd workers you wasted last year; men who, for no legitimate reason, walked out of your factory gates for the last time on the say-so of Tom This or Mike That. . . . It's what goes on all over the country. It's the logical outcome of a rotten system. But it hits back not only at the industry that fosters it, but eventually at the whole social fabric.[56]

On the other hand, production managers and line officials were satisfied with the drive system, since it allowed for flexible adjustments to shifts in demand and was effective in holding down unit labor costs. And, indeed, Sumner Slichter thought that the drive systes *was* profitable, given a short-run perspective on what he called "the interests of employers as a class." Production managers often took this limited perspective. They were men who, as one personnel manager put it, "consider labor a commodity, to be bought and sold on the open market when trade is brisk and disposed with at will when demand subsides." They were reluctant to protect workers from dismissals, even when labor relations problems threatened, believing that liberal treatment undermined motivation and discipline.[57]

Faced with this resistance, proponents of employment reform tried to "sell" their ideas by appealing to other managers' cost-consciousness rather than to their political acumen or humanitarianism. Linking changes in the drive system to turnover cost made reform seem a more businesslike proposition and gave it an economic rationale. Replacement cost estimates were used to justify proposals that many managers would have rejected had other, less calculable, considerations been adduced. Such estimates, said Boyd Fisher, provided "figures that we can wave in front of the face of factory managers and say, 'it costs you so much for turnover and we can prove it.' It seems that there are a large number of managers who can be convinced only by combining an appeal to their altruism with an appeal to their pocketbooks." The emphasis on costs and efficiency allowed personnel managers to present themselves as hard-headed realists rather than naive dreamers whose ideas could be dismissed without a hearing. Magnus Alexander hinted at this strategem when he noted that "well-intentioned academicians in the field of industrial economics, social workers as well as professional muckrakers, usually fail to accomplish sought-for improvements. They arouse temporary attention by their sensational statements, but do not clinch the interest of responsible persons."[58]

Related to this strategy was the widespread tendency to portray the foreman as the chief cause of turnover. In a 1915 article, E. M. Hopkins, an early leader of the Boston EMA, traced labor turnover to the foreman's "lack of comprehension which allows him to discharge carelessly or on caprice." But the importance attached to the issue of the foreman's power in hiring and firing involved more than a simple attempt to reduce turnover levels; discharges never accounted for more than about 20 percent of all separations in the 1910s, a fact that reformers like Hopkins usually failed to mention. The vehemence of the attack on foremen was fueled by deeper concerns about the social consequences of the drive system. At times, however, this attack was self-serving, particularly when savings in turnover costs were used to justify a transfer of authority from foremen to personnel managers.[59]

Finally, the focus on turnover costs aligned personnel management with the new corporate emphasis on cost accounting. Under the influence of systematic management methods, firms were beginning to require that each department pay its share and justify expenses by its effect on the bottom line. In 1916, Robert Clothier, then a personnel manager at Curtis Publishing Company, suggested that turnover rates could provide "a fairly accurate measure of the efficiency and value of an employment department." Others noted that savings in turnover cost were an accounting criterion that could be used for "determining the amount of money that shall be expended on the personnel department."[60]

But supporters of employment reform sometimes gave wildly inflated estimates of turnover cost. Further, because anything that made workers more content or loyal could be shown to have some effect on turnover rates, a wide range of programs now were touted as cost-effective solutions to a purportedly costly problem. The National Association of Corporation Schools said that turnover was costing employers "between two and five billion dollars" and then declared that "the solution to the problem is, of course, education." Similarly, welfare workers now had an economic rationale for their expensive programs. W. A. Grieves, welfare director for Nash Motor, issued a study claiming that companies could reduce turnover costs by building hospitals, restaurants, banks, and bakeries for their employees.[61]

Personnel managers were not always so disingenuous; sometimes they tacked on to their discussions of turnover a disclaimer hinting that replacement costs were only the tip of the iceberg. Thus, a fictional account has a young personnel manager explaining turnover to his superiors:

> You men think these figures too startling because it's a new slant on old problems that you've accepted much as you accept the law of gravitation. Their financial menace lies in the fact that they can be duplicated at random in any manufacturing center of the country. Of course, I'm simply talking business now, and giving you what, from my point of view, is the less costly dollars-and-cents end of the turnover. "Does that mean you think there's something bigger involved than even the direct loss to the employer?" Something so big, Mr. Gray, that the calculations of simple arithmetic can't cover it. . . . There isn't a factory today that contributes more to unemployment, and the so-called 'unrest' of labor, or that spreads more bitterness and belief in the duty of antagonism toward the authority of the employer, than the existence of the unregulated turnover.[62]

But despite these disclaimers, other managers were skeptical of the cost figures thrown about by employment reformers and personnel managers. The superintendent of a large textile mill said that he considered the cost of replacing a skilled worker "inconsequential" and reported that the departure of less skilled workers resulted in "no appreciable loss." A prominent engineer, charging that turnover had become a "fetish" among personnel managers, noted that if the man to be replaced "is an unskilled or semi-skilled laborer, as so many of today's employees are, the cost of replacement is small." Moreover, as another engineer pointed out, low turnover rates sometimes *raised* labor costs because "in such cases it becomes necessary to increase the daily or hourly rates occasionally, if not regularly, which is not very pleasing to some types of managers."[63]

Overall, it is hard to say whether companies that tried to stabilize employment and to moderate the drive system were more strongly motivated by economic or by other considerations. As Sumner Slichter wrote in 1919, the decision to adopt a more liberal labor policy was ultimately a matter "of judgment rather than of cost-accounting, since the precise effects upon costs of many expenditures can not be traced." There can be no doubt, however, that the turnover issue affected qualitative judgments about the drive system and provided a common focus and a justification for the various groups that fed into personnel management.[64]

IV. Professionalism

The ultimate bond between these various groups was not their common interest in a particular industrial or social problem but their common way of looking at and solving these problems. Each of the groups comprised college-trained professionals, individuals who idealized technical competence, rational administration, and reform led by experts. Although they differed on particular techniques and theories, people as dissimilar as Morris L. Cooke, Meyer Bloomfield, Mary B. Gilson, and Clarence J. Hicks agreed in their belief that the professional manager could bring order and enlightened change to industry by virtue of his knowledge, professional ethics, and ability to evaluate rationally all sides of an issue.

At one level, the emergence of the professional in industry may be viewed as an outcome of the manufacturing firm's transformation into an increasingly large and complex business organization whose operations were the objects of systematic planning and administration. Thus, the new emphasis on professional management was part of a bureaucratic trend marked by such phenomena as an increase in the ratio of administrative to production employees and the parceling out of traditional entrepreneurial functions to staff specialists. Just as marketing and production were coming under the greater conscious control of specialized managers, so employment was an area within the firm's operations that was increasingly subject to nonmarket processes of allocation and planning, overseen by a specialist. All of these changes reflected the bureaucratic tendency to supercession of the market by internal organization and management.

But in the employment sphere, technical problems were also social problems, and industry's greater reliance on the professional was part of a wider search for social stability in a rapidly industrializing society. The roots of personnel management are to be found not only in the technical imperatives imposed by the firm's growing size and complexity—these created the empty slots in the managerial hierarchy—but also in the backgrounds of those who filled these slots. The professionals employed in industry as personnel specialists brought with them the same ideologies and techniques that were being applied to social problems outside of industry.

Thus, at another level, personnel management can be seen as a response to the same pressures that produced the era's Progressive reform movement. There were strong similarities between them. Both were made up of new middle-class professionals eager to expand their influence and control—either within the corporation or in the public sphere—in order to promote social justice and order. The Progressives sought to weaken laissez-faire social philosophies just as proponents of personnel management sought to redirect employment practices, making them less subject to market forces and more reliant on intervention. Although seeking humanitarian reforms, the Progressives absorbed and deflected pressure from below in the same way that personnel management preempted some of the concerns of organized labor. The two movements rationalized the stresses and strains of a new industrial society. Each introduced reforms that helped to avert more radical change and thus to strengthen existing institutions.[65]

These parallels aside, personnel managers and their supporters had to operate within sharper limits than did the Progressive reformer. They had to convince the employer that reform and self-restraint were in his own best interests and that change would bolster the work ethic, forestall strikes, mitigate radicalism, and improve efficiency without unduly raising worker expectations or undermining traditional authority. Here the professional ideology developed by the industrial engineers proved to be useful in advancing employment reforms.

Professionalism was a prominent issue in the engineering literature between 1890 and 1920, when engineers became deeply concerned about their autonomy and influence in the large corporations where they increasingly found themselves employed. A related dilemma was how to reconcile their allegiance to the employer with their professional pretensions and corresponding social responsibilities. Industrial engineers like Frederick W. Taylor gave more attention to these issues than did engineers in other specialties, in part because questions concerning the structure of the managerial hierarchy arose naturally in the course of the industrial engineer's work. But Taylor's interest in defining the expert's corporate role also reflected his status as an independent consulting engineer. He was obsessively concerned that his clients accept his recommendations in their entirety and respect the expertise and autonomy of his associates.[66]

Fundamental to Taylor's system was his appeal to science and professional knowledge as legitimators of the engineer's attempts to rationalize production management. Taylor claimed to have discovered an entirely new system of management in which scientific laws were substituted for traditional decision-making procedures. The authority of technical expertise became a basis for attacking not only the "rule-of-thumb" methods used by foremen and skilled workers but also the traditional powers of the firm's owners. Because it transferred initiative away from them and questioned their natural superiority, some employers regarded Taylor's system as an impetuous obstruction of their prerogatives.

Taylor's professional ideology shaped the outlook of a wide range of specialists employed by industry, including welfare workers and other engineers. Its influence was twofold. First, it provided a formula for changing traditional methods of organization and forms of authority: By virtue of his technical expertise, the trained professional could claim a directive role that reduced the authority of those above and below him in the corporate hierarchy. Second, it gave credibility to the professional's self-image as an arbiter of conflicts between management and workers: Presumably, the professional could act in the best interest of both groups because he had an invariant measure of social welfare—the science of production and human behavior. Said Taylor, "Both sides must recognize as essential the substitution of exact scientific knowledge and investigation for the old individual judgment or opinion."[67]

Taylor's emphasis on expertise as opposed to customary forms of authority also helped to legitimate efforts then under way to professionalize management by teaching it in schools of business. By linking science to management, Taylor undercut the traditional academic disdain of commerce. His system occupied a central place in the curricula of the new business schools at such universities as Dartmouth, Harvard, and Pennsylvania. These developments appealed to men like Louis D. Brandeis, who was disturbed by the power and the rank commercialism of the "titans of industry." Brandeis, author of *Business: A Profession*, believed that professional managers would introduce a different set of values into the business world, and other intellectuals shared his optimism. At a meeting of the Efficiency Society in 1912, Thomas N. Carver, a Harvard economist, could proclaim: "It is my opinion that the various schools of business administration are doing more for the labor problem than all the radical reformers put together."[68]

A Professional Model

Deeply influenced by the scientific management ideology, supporters of employment reform had similar high hopes that the professionalization of personnel management would help to humanize industry. The emphasis on professional expertise was intended to insure that the personnel manager had sufficient authority to influence other managers and was, at the same time, someone who could inject liberal values into the firm: a "big man," imbued with the liberal spirit that a university education was supposed to impart. Slichter believed that the personnel manager should be an "expert" with "exceptional insights into human nature." It was thought that the drive system could best be reformed if the professional, a man of science and class neutrality, was placed in charge of finding a private solution to industry's problems. Harlow S. Person, who introduced personnel management courses to the Tuck School of Administration in 1915, viewed the personnel manager as the catalyst whose expertise and broad vision would bring "the business conscience into alignment with the social conscience."[69]

According to this professional model of personnel management, the personnel manager was to be a third force in the firm, neither staff nor line, who would mediate between workers and management. Edward D. Jones said that the personnel manager must be an intermediary "between parties which have traditionally been opposed to each other, namely capital and management on the one side, and labor craftsmanship on the other. He must always perform the functions of a mutual interpreter and often those of a peacemaker." Professional independence would allow the personnel manager to intervene in disputes between foremen and workers, as well as to reconcile opposing interest at higher levels. If it were to play this role, the personnel department had to be independent of the manufacturing division and, to some extent, of the rest of the firm.[70]

The professionalism and the relative autonomy of the personnel department demanded by this model were also intended to permit the personnel manager to act as an advocate for the firm's employees. Jean Hoskins of Eastern Manufacturing Company said that personnel managers should be people "with an outside point of view, strong in their policies and strong in their ideals," and not "one of the reigning company executives." Only then would workers feel that the department was acting in their best interests and was "the only place in the plant where the outside point of view gets in." In what he admitted was a "fanciful" scenario, Meyer Bloomfield envisioned a day when workers would be willing to pay part of the salary of the personnel manager and would look to him as just another professional for hire, much like a lawyer or physician.[71]

Writing in 1919, Sumner Slichter noted that personnel management's "professional spirit, ideals, and standards" would "not exert a radical influence upon the membership, but their tendency will be liberalizing." An emphasis on professional values linked the movement to an agenda of priorities beyond the employer's narrow interests. A professional was responsible to the public and his peers as well as to his employer. Bloomfield argued that the "science of handling men" connoted professional responsibilities and that it was "affected with a public interest." He emphasized the elements of public service in personnel management by pointing to the growth of university courses on the subject.

The emphasis on professionalism had one unintended consequence: It brought managements closer to developing a unified view of their interests. As professionals, personnel managers shared their problems and ideas in journals, textbooks, and presentations at numerous conferences and meetings. Members of groups like the Boston EMA regularly visited one another's plants and exchanged information on their employment techniques. The previously private and isolated world of the firm became part of a community of professional concern. As a result, companies developed closer ties with one another and came to share a body of common knowledge and methods for dealing with labor problems.[72]

Nevertheless, those in the personnel management movement who were most concerned with the issue of professionalism tended to be sympathetic to trade unionism. Liberals like Bloomfield, Boyd Fisher, and Mary B. Gilson, as well as former socialists like Algie Simons and Ordway Tead, believed that professional personnel managers could introduce enlightened ideas about employee rights and collective bargaining to industry. But even though these liberals recognized the benefits of unionism, they were not convinced that unskilled immigrant workers were ready to receive them. Mary B. Gilson thought that workers had to be educated for the responsibilities of union membership and that personnel reforms "had some educational value for both management and workers in preparing the ground for unionism." Of course, the personnel management movement included conservatives who opposed unions and distrusted the professional model. They viewed reform and restraint not as an opening wedge for unionism but as a way to ensure that the unions lost their attractiveness. Change was necessary, but it should be unilateral and designed to maintain employer control.[73]

By mitigating the drive system, personnel managers of both persuasions weakened the potential appeal of trade unionism insofar as they preempted reforms demanded by skilled workers. In the case of less skilled workers, personnel management was to bring some of the benefits that the trade union had delivered to the more skilled, including allocation by rule, enhanced security, and rudimentary grievance mechanisms. But liberals like Mary Gilson (who referred to labor spies as "human termites") did not think that personnel management was undermining unions. Rather, they believed that by removing the most egregious features of the drive system, their reforms would prevent radical change from below and so foster the emergence of a more reasonable and enlightened management and more responsible, accomodative labor unions.[74]

CHAPTER 5

CRISIS AND CHANGE DURING WORLD WAR I

Most employers were slow in realizing that changes in employment methods could bolster the work ethic and serve to dampen worker unrest. They were held back by their fear of raising both costs and expectations, by their emphasis on quick results, and by their skepticism about the relationship between morale and effort. Moreover, labor was cheap and abundant, and the drive system seemed an effective mode for keeping costs and expectations in line. These conditions held until 1915. But as the tightening of labor markets induced by the war created a host of new problems and intensified old ones, employers became markedly more receptive to change.

I. The Employer's Dilemma

During the period between 1916 and 1920, the demand for labor accelerated at the same time that the supply was curtailed by wartime conscription and the cessation of European immigration. As unemployment rates fell to their lowest levels since the 1880s, employers sought for ways to overcome the unprecedented labor shortage. They made up some of the shortfall by hiring women into nontraditional occupations such as machinery and metalwork: The proportion of women in the manufacturing labor force rose from 6 percent in 1914 to a peak of almost 14 percent after the second draft in 1918. Another solution was to encourage non-European immigration. Judge Gary of the U.S. Steel Corporation favored the importation of unskilled workers from Asia and Mexico; indeed, five times as many Mexican immigrants entered the United States between 1910 and 1920 as during the preceding decade. But the largest additions to the manufacturing labor force came through internal migration. The number of farm workers dropped by nearly half a million between 1915 and 1920 as people flocked to the war production centers of the Midwest and Northeast. Companies sent recruiters to the large cities and rural areas of the South, despite the efforts of local authorities to suppress this activity. One labor agent "hired a brass band and sent it on a motor truck to visit points frequented by blacks on Saturday nights. Torch lights, promises of a month's annual leave with pay, and a little fervid oratory built up his needed force quite rapidly. It also shut down 75 square miles of farms."[1]

In mass production industries like metalworking and meatpacking, the number of black workers increased dramatically. Black employment in manufacturing rose 40 percent between 1910 and 1920, with most of the gains coming after 1915. Black workers now took the least skilled and least desirable jobs that had previously been filled by European immigrants. In the steel industry in 1920, 17 percent of all unskilled workers were black, as compared with 6 percent in 1910. While some black migrants thought they were "bound for the Promised Land," as a popular poem put it, they often found the North to be a hostile place. In one steel town, black recruits were confined in a segregated camp patroled by armed guards, and several Northern cities experienced serious race riots in 1919.[2]

Despite the tapping of new sources of supply, labor scarcity persisted in most industrial areas, much to the dismay of employers, who were accustomed to a buyer's market. Some began to call for a national labor conscription while others demanded that the U.S. Employment Service import workers from Puerto Rico. Pirating labor ("scamping") became common in major industrial cities, as employment agents scoured the streets for recruits. One B. F. Goodrich manager complained in 1920 that seven large employment agencies in Akron were scamping workers from the local rubber factories and supplying them on a daily basis to employers in over twenty states. Although the U.S. Employment Service was supposed to regulate the allocation of workers to war industries, it was unable to control the labor market. A USES official reported an incident in which a trainload of workers was brought to a War Department construction job: "But bright and early the next morning the agent of a firm which has a government contract and a plant a few miles away came over, offered the men three cents an hour advance, and took the whole trainload away."[3]

One serious consequence of the tight labor market was an erosion of effort norms and shop floor discipline. In the past, a labor surplus, as reflected in high unemployment rates even during good times, could be relied upon to maintain worker discipline and to make the foreman a credible driver. But the severe labor shortage caused by the war weakened the traditional forces for maintaining effort and discipline. The result was a deterioration in what Sumner Slichter called "capital's ability to compel production."

Labor productivity declined in various sectors of the economy (see table 5.1); even the number of bricks laid per eight-hour day by Indiana bricklayers fell from 1,100 in 1909, to 900 in 1916, to 540 in 1920. Absenteeism and tardiness soared; it was not uncommon for a firm to find up to one-fifth of its work force absent on any given day. One manager complained that thousands of men in Akron were "hanging around the pool halls," and another from Missouri said that "if you can tell me any way in which we can distribute the thousands of men that are hanging around our moving picture shows at 11 o'clock in the morning waiting to get in, you will help us to solve some of our labor shortage problem." Employers feared that they were witnessing the virtual collapse of the work ethic. When Guy Tripp of Westinghouse Electric addressed a dinner in New York in 1920, he said that "effort" at Westinghouse had fallen off by 20 to 30 percent and that "this

Table 5.1. Average Annual Rates of Change in Labor Productivity

Industry	Period	
	1899–1909	1909–1919
Manufacturing	1.1	0.8
Primary metals	3.8	−0.4
Fabricated metals	2.9	2.0
Machinery, nonelectric	1.8	0.7
Electrical machinery	1.3	0.0

SOURCE: John W. Kendrick, *Productivity Trends in the United States*, National Bureau of Economic Research Study No. 71 (Princeton, N.J.: 1961), p. 152.
NOTE: Data are rates of change in output per unit of labor input.

transcends in its vital importance all questions of strikes, wages, prices, and everything else."[4]

Despite Tripp's ordering of priorities, strikes were very much on employers' minds. A wave of labor unrest swept the country between 1916 and 1921. The ratio of strikers to all workers during these six years remained constant at the level that was later reached during the more famous strike years of 1934 and 1937. Five city-wide general strikes took place during the war; and the period immediately following the war saw a bold attempt to organize workers in the steel industry; a policemen's strike in Boston; general strikes in Chicago, New York, and Seattle; and national strikes by railway workers and coal miners. Not only labor militance but also the size of the labor movement increased rapidly, with trade union membership nearly doubling between 1915 and 1920. Unions made inroads throughout the manufacturing sector, even penetrating some of the mass production industries like autos, electrical machinery, and rubber products. Within the working classes, socialist and syndicalist influences flourished, as did curiosity about the Bolshevik revolution, an event that may have had a greater impact on American employers than on their employees.[5]

This combination of problems—labor shortages, reduced productivity, and worker unrest—led to an increase in quit rates. As usual, turnover was highest among inexperienced workers: At Firestone in 1919, the "floaters," those with less than two months' tenure, accounted for half of all quits. Turnover—which before the war was a topic of concern only to a small group of employment reformers and personnel managers—began to receive national attention and became the subject of numerous books, articles, and conferences. Yet the wartime rise in quit rates was not entirely unprecedented. Even in a relatively "good" prewar year like 1913, labor turnover approached wartime levels: The unemployment rate was about 35 percent higher, and turnover was 33 percent lower, in 1913 than in 1917-18. As is the case with other industrial relations problems, the sudden concern with turnover may partly be explained as a threshold effect: Turnover rates (as well as unemployment, strikes, and labor productivity) reached levels never before experienced. In addition, what distinguished the war from earlier periods was the extent to which strikes and labor militance had percolated down to the mass of unskilled and semiskilled workers. That these workers might someday join unions (as a few were already doing) seemed more of a possibility than ever before. To those employers who could see the handwriting on the wall, labor turnover—the "individualistic strike"—became a warning signal of future difficulties.[6]

The Personnel Boom

Faced with this breakdown in the traditional system of labor adminstration, employers now found personnel management an attractive alternative, one that promised to simultaneously relieve labor shortages, improve productivity, and promote labor peace. As one observer noted in 1919, worker unrest was "causing employers to perceive more and more clearly the necessity for a substantially liberal labor policy in order to avoid the organization of their plants." Thus, despite lingering doubts about the wisdom of tampering with tradition, a substantial minority of industrial firms rapidly established personnel departments.[7]

Between 1915 and 1920, the proportion of firms employing over 250 employees that had personnel departments increased sharply: from roughly 5 percent to about 25 percent. This development was not limited to large or technologically advanced companies.[8] When a national conference of personnel managers was held in 1918, the largest proportion of attendees came from medium-sized firms in the strike-prone metalworking industry (32 percent). Also well-represented were large steel companies (9 percent), the chemical industry (8 percent), and the motor vehicle industry (8 percent).[9] The impetus to form these new departments usually came from top management, although when General Electric workers went on strike after World War I, an investigator reported to Owen D. Young that, among other things, the strikers wanted the company to hire a "Manager of Man Power." Shortly thereafter, GE conducted an internal study which criticized management for hiring the "greatest engineers" to maintain the efficiency of its machinery, but failing to employ "specialized human nature engineers to keep its human machinery frictionless."[10]

This rapid growth in the number of personnel departments created a new occupation almost overnight: Whereas 500 persons attended a national conference of personnel managers in 1917, close to 3,000 were present at a similar conference held in 1920. The backgrounds of these new personnel managers were diverse. A few had working-class origins, having started out as skilled workers and then moved up to become foremen and superintendents. The majority, however, were college-educated. Some were relief workers, educators, and reformers, but most had previously been employed in private industry. Some came from areas requiring public relations acumen and social skills, such as sales, real estate, and law. Others came from technical fields related to personnel management such as safety and sanitation, welfare work, and production superintendence, although only a minority were engineers.

Conflict occasionally flared between personnel managers and engineers as each group sought to prevent the other from encroaching on its professional turf. In 1918, one industrial engineer—responding to a rumor that "efficiency engineers" were to be excluded from membership in a new personnel management organization—said that industrial engineers were too busy with standardization and cost studies to be interested in taking over "the hiring and firing, the job analysis, the welfare and housing problems." Throughout industry, he said, "there is a great big job for two great big men and great big salaries if they will adopt even the commonest rules of salesmanship and boost—not knock."[11]

The wartime personnel management movement had a strong professional orientation, and personnel managers were quick to form professional organizations. The first local associations had been established before the war as labor market reform groups; these were the Societies to Discuss Employment Problems, which, along with several groups affiliated with local chambers of commerce, made up the ten local associations that existed when the United States entered the war in April 1917. By mid-1920 fifty industrial cities, from Brooklyn to Peoria to Los Angeles, had personnel management groups.

The local associations served both professional and practical functions. At regular meetings and occasional conferences, members discussed personnel techniques, shared common problems, and heard lectures by visiting dignitaries like Meyer Bloomfield and Walter Bingham. At the practical level, the associations exchanged information on employment methods and local labor market conditions. During and after the war they cooperated with the USES and other government agencies to prevent "destructive labor recruiting" and to ensure the placement of discharged soldiers. With some exceptions, the local associations maintained a high degree of professionalism in their activities. The Oakland-San Francisco association was led by an economics professor from the University of California, Ira B. Cross, and meetings were held at the Berkeley Faculty Club.[12]

Given the burst of activity at the local level and the movement's professional pretensions, the creation of a national organization was only a matter of time. The first national conference of personnel managers was held in 1916. At the second conference, held in Philadelphia in 1917, a committee was formed to find a way to bring the local associations closer together, and at the 1918 conference in Rochester, a new national organization—the National Association of Employment Managers (NAEM)—was launched for the express purpose of promoting the study of employment problems, the growth of local associations, and the establishment of personnel departments. S. R. Rectanus, personnel manager at ARMCO, became the first president of the NAEM (he was replaced in 1919 by Phillip J. Reilly of Dennison Manufacturing), and other officers included such liberals as Boyd Fisher, Joseph Willits, Jane Williams of the Plimpton Press, and R. C. Booth of the Federal Board for Vocational Education, as well as personnel managers from the Norton Company, Westinghouse, and Du Pont.

Compared with the local associations, the NAEM did very little. It ran a professional placement service that included employment listings in each issue of its monthly newsletter, *Personnel*. It disseminated information on personnel management and claimed to have answered thousands of inquiries in 1919 and 1920. And it held several short conferences during 1919, including one in Chicago on the theme of foreman training.

The 1919 Cleveland convention of the NAEM (soon to be renamed the Industrial Relations Association of America) attracted over 1,000 persons, far more than had been anticipated. Many of the speakers at the conference had recently worked in Washington—an indication that members of the personnel movement had been heavily involved in the government's efforts to control the war labor market. The liberal atmosphere of the postwar recon-

struction period was evident at the conference; even a speech by
Cyrus McCormick, Jr., betrayed no outright hostility to organized
labor. But by the time of the next convention in May 1920, the
nation had turned hostile to unionism, and this change of mood
was reflected in some of the sessions, one of which was devoted to
the topic of combatting radicalism. Nevertheless, the convention
heard John R. Commons make an impassioned defense of collective
bargaining (a speech which may have contributed to his being
branded a "Parlor Red" during the Red Scare of that year), and
Sidney Hillman of the Amalgamated Clothing Workers attacking
employee representation plans.[13]

The liberal guiding lights of the personnel movement insisted
that the local and national associations adopt a neutral stance on
issues related to unionism, neither opposing nor favoring organized
labor. When a group of open-shop employers tried to take control
of Pittsburgh's personnel association shortly after the war, Boyd
Fisher mounted a campaign to stop them. He complained that the
employers had "distorted [the association] and its purposes to fit
a militant anti-union program without in any sense furthering the
legitimate aims of the employment manager." On the other hand,
responding to criticism from the left, Joseph Willits defended the
movement's reluctance to take a stand on unionism. "While this
may tend to indicate what the industrial democrats call a paternalistic policy," he said, "nevertheless such a policy is a good deal
more broad-minded and democratic than getting together chiefly
to condemn and combat unions." Neutrality was fundamental to
the liberal's conception of a professional model of personnel management, and this professionalism permitted a more open and rapid
diffusion of new employment techniques.[14]

Government

The war period was marked by the federal government's heavy
involvement in the economy, including the labor market. The government's complex apparatus for regulating the war labor market
operated at both national and industrial levels and included a vast
array of regulatory functions. The motives behind the establishment of the various war labor agencies were many but may be

reduced to one: to maintain the uninterrupted production and distribution of war material. The achievement of this overriding objective required the speedy resolution of disputes through government mediation as well as the prevention of disputes before they occurred. In the critical shipbuilding industry, the government's Emergency Fleet Corporation was guided by the dictum that "industrial disputes should be settled by a removal of the basic causes of labor unrest." Thus, by seeking to maintain and improve employment conditions, the government's war labor agencies constituted another factor contributing to the spread of new personnel methods.[15]

Among the major causes of wartime strikes were employer hostility to organized labor and the deterioration of the work environment. To prevent work stoppages, the War Labor Board and other agencies followed two major principles: The first was to allow workers to join unions without interference and to insist on some form of collective bargaining wherever possible; the second was to develop and enforce industry-wide standards for wages and working conditions. Both principles had their origins in the Ordnance Department's General Order 13, which became a model for other war labor edicts. The Ordnance Department employed a number of Taylor Society members during the war, and two of them— Morris L. Cooke and Mary Van Kleeck—drafted the order in 1917.[16]

Cooke and Van Kleeck's support for collective bargaining drew on Robert G. Valentine's idea that worker participation in industry would stimulate creativity and boost worker morale; it also reflected a wartime fascination with the ideal of industrial democracy. But neither General Order 13 nor the War Labor Board (WLB) made a clear distinction between the bargaining practiced by independent unions and that practiced by company unions and shop committees: All were supposed to promote industrial democracy. Well-meaning liberals like Cooke thought that shop committees would function like regular unions, restraining foremen and removing, as one WLB official put it, "the petty tyranny of 'bosses.'" The unions themselves remained suspicious of shop committees, knowing that most of the twelve companies which had voluntarily established their own plans by 1917 had intended them as substitutes for independent unions. Nevertheless, the WLB and other agencies like the Shipbuilding Labor Adjustment Board often ordered the opposing parties to form shop committees as a way of resolving labor disputes. One hundred and fifty-seven of these compulsory plans were introduced during and after the war. Few of them were very effective, however, and most failed to survive past the early 1920s.[17]

The second principle followed by government agencies—the development and enforcement of wage and working condition standards—was implemented in ways more acceptable to organized labor. General Order 13, addressed to all Ordnance Department contractors, required an eight-hour day, extra pay for overtime, the maintenance of existing safety and sanitation standards, and the provision of a "living wage" (a minimum wage tied to the cost of living). These standards—adopted by the War Labor Board, the Labor Department, and other branches of the War Department—represented a significant departure from the federal government's traditional laissez-faire stance toward labor legislation.[18]

But the formulation of rules and standards covering all contingencies that might lead to strikes was beyond the capability of the various adjustment boards and service sections. For this reason, the government looked to personnel management to introduce so-called best-practice employment methods. One government official expressed the hope that personnel managers would reduce labor disputes by acting as "modern industry's conscience." Thus, the industrial service groups of the War Department prodded the industries they regulated to form personnel departments. For instance, the Ordnance Department employed Boyd Fisher, Mary Van Kleeck, and Professor Edward D. Jones of the University of Michigan to direct a campaign designed to impress managers and contractors with the idea that their labor problems could best be handled through a personnel department. By mid-1918, Van Kleeck had assigned a female personnel manager to each of the department's arsenals.[19]

The Shipyards. The shipbuilding industry was the site of intense government efforts to propagate personnel management. During the prewar years, the industry had relied on a fairly primitive drive system. Wages were low, working conditions harsh, and welfare and safety programs virtually nonexistent. Until 1917, not a single shipyard in the nation utilized the services of a personnel manager. Labor relations were hostile, with most shipyard owners adamantly refusing to deal with unions.

America's entry into the war brought a rapid increase of employment in shipbuilding. The number of workers engaged in Emergency Fleet Corporation work rose from 88,000 in October 1917 to 385,000 one year later. This sudden influx of workers created a labor relations crisis. Several major strikes occurred in 1917, and the total number of strikes in the industry rose from 27 in 1916, to 101 in 1917, to 138 in 1918. Labor turnover rates were astronomical, running about 235 percent in November 1917. Roughly one in six working days was lost to absenteeism during the first nine months of 1918.[20]

To cope with this situation, the Shipbuilding Labor Adjustment Board was created in August 1917, with Henry Seager of the American Association for Labor Legislation as its first secretary. At about the same time, the Emergency Fleet Corporation formed an Industrial Service Section to improve employment methods and conditions in the yards. Under the direction of Meyer Bloomfield, the Emergency Fleet Corporation mounted an educational campaign to convince shipyard owners of the value of personnel management. Bloomfield convened several national and regional conferences of shipyard managers to discuss common employment problems and methods for implementing personnel management techniques. The government gave the shipyards extensive help in establishing and running personnel departments: For instance, it printed and distributed standard forms for such employment procedures as hiring, promotion, and discharge; and it even provided plans for the layout of employment and service buildings. In addition, the Emergency Fleet Corporation reimbursed the yards on a per-diem basis for each person they sent to one of the govenment's crash training courses in personnel management; within six months, seventy shipyard employees had completed the course. As a result of this frenetic activity, the number of personnel departments in the industry increased sharply: from none in April of 1917 to thirty-four at the close of the war.[21]

The typical shipyard personnel department was a highly centralized operation that usurped much of the foreman's power to allocate labor. It was responsible for hiring and selection and, usually, for transfers from one part of the yard to another. It promoted efforts to fill vacancies by internal transfers rather than by outside hiring. Although foremen retained the power to discharge workers, all dismissals were investigated by the personnel department. One shipyard hired a special Labor Adjuster to settle grievances between foremen and workers on the spot, and other yards initiated foreman training classes in employment methods. The personnel staff introduced new workers to their foremen and helped them to find housing. Welfare work was administered by special service bureaus within the personnel department, and workers were provided with such amenities as free medical care, restaurants, and housing.[22]

Personnel management in the yards was based on the professional model. The new personnel managers were expected to introduce and maintain high standards of employment for shipyard workers, to "discover better opportunities for them and to protect their rights." They were required to have some college education, which was presumed to give them "the ability to acquire new ideas and a scientific point of view" and "a sympathetic understanding of the problems affecting the worker."

Employers remained hostile or indifferent to the government's attempt to regulate employment conditions in the yards. Indeed, some of them charged that their workers were being "coddled" by the Emergency Fleet Corporation's programs. D. R. Kennedy, a shipyard personnel manager, said that personnel management had grown rapidly during the war only because "dire necessity has forced many reactionary employers into doing something about labor and employment." He might have added that hefty cost-plus contracts provided another incentive for employer cooperation.[23]

Personnel Courses. Shortly after it began to promote personnel management, the government also took steps to expand the supply of qualified personnel managers by offering training courses in the area. The idea originated in the Council for National Defense, but the project itself was coordinated by the Storage Committee of the War Industries Board, headed by Morris L. Cooke. Boyd Fisher and Professor Edward D. Jones were transferred from the Ordnance Department to the War Industries Board in January 1918 to begin planning the courses. The project was given top priority by the War Department and the seven other government agencies involved in the crash effort to set it up. Those involved had high hopes for the project. When Morris L. Cooke addressed its first graduating class, he noted that "the time is not far distant when the U.S. Chamber of Commerce or some other agency will list the larger industrial establishments in this country and ask them the question, 'Have you an employment department?' and social pressure will be brought to bear on those that have not these departments, because they will have become a social menace."[24]

The first government course in personnel management was offered at the University of Rochester under the supervision of Professor Meyer Jacobstein. Priority was given to those applicants sent by their employers, who had to promise to employ them in the personnel department upon graduation. Students who took the course on their own initiative were referred to a government placement service, which found jobs for them in private industry. Seven of the students in the first class came from the shipyards, two from the ordnance arsenals, two from Du Pont, and the remainder from a variety of firms including General Electric, Packard Motor, National Malleable Castings, and Passaic Cotton Mills.[25]

The program spread rapidly. By the end of the war, Harvard, Columbia, the New School, Carnegie Tech, Northwestern, Reed College, Berkeley, and several other universities were offering courses, taught by academics and experts with an interest in personnel management. Local employers served on course oversight committees. The Employment Management Division of the War Industries Board controlled instructional methods and curricula, which had been devised by Boyd Fisher, Edward D. Jones, and Brewer Whitmore, a professor at Smith. Approximately 80 percent of the curriculum was devoted to personnel department practice, 10 percent to labor economics, and the remainder to elementary statistics and industrial management. The course included lectures on the formation of a personnel department, the hiring and assignment of workers, transfer and promotion, wage payment methods, shop discipline, turnover, and welfare work.[26]

To avoid controversy, little mention was made of such subjects as trade unions or the open shop. Boyd Fisher justified this exclusion on the grounds that the courses "should emphasize the professional and technical objects of the employment manager and should permit of no alternative instruction." But some regarded this decision as a mistake. At the 1918 NAEM conference, Ethelbert Stewart of the Bureau of Labor Statistics argued that, since trade unionism was the "most puzzling thing" personnel managers would encounter, it should be included in the curriculum. "When you leave out that subject," said Stewart, "aren't you leaving out the only way that a fellow can get a milepost?" Meyer Jacobstein responded lamely by noting that instructors were pressed for time and could not cover every issue in detail. He also pointed out that the courses took no stand on unionism: "We have not taught our service men that they are going to 'bust' labor unions; and if there is any general manager who is going to put a man from our course into a job with the idea of eliminating trade unions from industry, he is mistaken."[27]

When the war ended, the government's personnel courses faced an uncertain future. Some members of the NAEM, skeptical that a competent personnel manager could be trained in six weeks, wanted to cancel them. But powerful supporters, including Bernard Baruch of the War Industries Board and Commerce Secretary William Redfield, favored their continuation. Thus, in January 1919, the government transferred responsibility to the recently created Federal Board for Vocational Education (FBVE). Boyd Fisher, retained as head of the program, broadened it by adding correspondence, part-time, and on-site training courses. Like its wartime proponents, the FBVE believed that the program could help "bring together . . . employers and employees for a mutual understanding of their problems." The FBVE gave a vocational twist to the courses by stresssing how personnel management could be used to develop "fairly well-defined paths of promotion in industry" and by training personnel managers to be a link between the schools and industry.[28]

But opposition to the program did not abate. Personnel managers complained that its graduates were less qualified than those who had come up through the ranks. Ralph G. Wells of the Boston Employment Managers' Association said that he was against the course because it led graduates to think that "because they have taken it and studied a few books they are equipped to go to the plant and handle the problem in any way." Beneath these professional concerns was a fear that course graduates would flood the market and depress the salaries of those already employed in the field; Wells noted that the course had produced a "surplus" of personnel managers.

Boyd Fisher defended the program by noting that, until its appearance, personnel managers were simply "plucked out of industry, social work, and law and told to 'go to it.'" Now, he said, they at least had some prior knowledge of their profession. Nevertheless, the program's days were numbered, especially as the government began to dismantle other war labor programs, and in July 1919 it was discontinued. Yet during its brief lifespan of fourteen months, the program had trained over 600 personnel managers. Moreover, by publicizing personnel management and encouraging war contractors to establish personnel departments, the government had given the personnel movement an important boost and strengthened its professional orientation.[29]

II. Employment Reforms: Ideal and Real

Although the early personnel textbooks painted a uniform picture of industry's new personnel departments, the structure of these departments varied considerably. Some were grafted onto existing welfare or service departments, whereas others were initiated at the same time as industrial welfare programs (which had burgeoned during the war). Smaller companies administered their employment activities through a single department. At larger firms, each major personnel activity—employment, welfare, health and safety, training—constituted a separate department within a larger unit.

The actual practices of most firms differed sharply from what was envisioned by the movement's proselytizers and textbook writers. Only a few departments, perhaps no more than fifty, approached the ideal of a fully centralized department, equal to the firm's other functional divisions, controlling both the formulation and the execution of all labor-related policy. An independent and powerful personnel department was needed to curb recalcitrant line officials and to administer programs that required intrafirm coordination. Without such authority, it had little chance of replacing the foreman's balkanized and decentralized methods with a companywide employment system. Yet most personnel departments failed to establish their independent authority and to adopt the full range of policies that were considered "best practice" at the time. To understand the reasons for this failure, we must look closely at the potential range of employment reforms.[30]

During the war personnel departments made deep raids into the foreman's territory, most commonly taking over the functions of selecting and assigning new employees. As experts in human relations, personnel managers were supposed to be more skilled than foremen in picking new workers and putting them at their ease. The vocational element in personnel management fostered the belief that one could find "the right man for the right job" by matching a worker's characteristics to the job specifications developed by the personnel department. In gauging a worker's abilities, a few personnel managers relied on sophisticated trade and intelligence tests similar to those then being used by the Army's new Committee on the Classification of Personnel. Others scrutinized application blanks to see what they might reveal about a person's hidden character: the care with which the application had been filled out, the handwriting, whether the form was smudged or folded, and so on. Katherine Blackford's theories of selection, which emphasized judging a person's mannerisms and appearance, were popular. The personnel manager at Curtis Publishing suggested the following technique: "On greeting the candidate, look at him attentively and directly and during the first part of the interview study his face carefully." This was supposed to give the personnel manager "an opportunity to discover whether his candidate's expressions betray intelligence, candor and earnestness."[31]

According to the new procedure, foremen had to requisition workers from the personnel department and were not allowed to refuse the workers sent to them. To create a good first impression and cut down on turnover, personnel managers escorted new workers around the plant, showed them their lockers, and introduced them to their foreman. At large firms like Du Pont, new workers saw a film about the firm's products and were given a handbook outlining the company's rules and regulations.[32]

Textbooks recommended that personnel departments maintain employment records and keep a list of applicants on file, to be drawn upon when the demand for labor increased. These records could also be used to screen out union members. In open-shop cities like Detroit and Lansing, the employers' association had on file the names of union members and other undesirables; personnel managers supplied the association with names and checked with it before hiring a new worker. A number of firms deliberately hired workers of different ethnic backgrounds in order to forestall unionization. In 1917, the head of the employment office at Illinois Steel's South Works said that the personnel manager "is like unto a chef, in charge of the mixture at his particular plant."[33]

In actuality, however, the hiring techniques of most personnel departments were rudimentary (see table 5.2). Only about half kept employment records; very few used tests; and maintaining a list of reserve applicants was said to be "seldom practiced." The personnel manager spent much of his time trying to convince foremen of the virtues of centralized selection. Resistant to change and resenting their loss of authority, foremen blamed production problems on the personnel department's poor judgment in selecting workers, a ploy that personnel managers called "the foreman's alibi." Personnel managers complained that they had a harder time selling their selection methods to foremen and line managers than to the firm's top executives.[34]

Table 5.2. Employment Practices in Industry, 1918–1923

	All Firms[a]	Firms with Personnel Departments[b]
Personnel department	10–15% (est.)	
Records of hiring and firing	18	50%
Use of selection tests	4	12
Job analysis	12	—
Centralized wage determination	—	38
Periodic wage increases	24	—
Plant promotion plan	15	—
Promotion by formal ratings	12	—
Vacancies posted	2	—
Personnel department has a say in dismissals		36

a. Data from Leslie H. Allen, "The Workman's Home," *Transactions of the ASME* (1918), 40:217; Paul F. Gemmill, "Methods of Promoting Industrial Employees," *Industrial Management* (April 1924), 67:240, 243, 246; Roy W. Kelly, *Hiring the Worker* (Boston, 1918), p. 32. These data probably are biased upward by the overrepresentation of advanced firms in the surveys.

b. Data from "A Survey of Personnel Activities of Member Companies," National Association of Corporation Schools (NACS) *Bulletin* (August 1920), 7:347–348; Kelly, *Hiring the Worker*, p. 32.

Standardization

Companies in which personnel managers controlled the selection process relied heavily on the vocationalist technique of job analysis, whereby personnel departments collected data on the many jobs within a company to determine the tasks involved in each (job description) and the skills required to perform it (job specification). With this information at his fingertips, a personnel manager who had no firsthand knowledge of what an anglesmith did could nevertheless describe the job to an applicant and determine whether he had the proper training to perform it. Although some personnel managers excluded foremen from the data collection process, most believed that involving foremen in the process would lessen their resentment over the loss of their hiring prerogatives.[35]

Extensive job analyses were also conducted by the government agencies that recruited and trained workers for the war effort. The Army's Committee on the Classification of Personnel, which was run by a group of vocational psychologists, had a classification division that developed job analyses for over 400 manual trades needed by the army. This information allowed inexperienced clerks to select and assign recruits to those units where their skills were most needed. The USES performed job analyses for every occupation in twenty key industries; and when the war was over, the Federal Board for Vocational Education made this information available to the public.[36]

Another reason for the great interest in job analysis was that the technique could be used to rationalize industrial wage structures, which were a hodgepodge of disparities and inequities. This was the legacy of the foreman's control over rate setting, industry's heavy use of incentive pay systems, and weak unionization. Because wage inequities were a major cause of wartime strikes and turnover, they became a central concern of the new personnel departments. Job analysis and standardized occupational nomenclature made it easier to classify jobs into groups, to standardize wages within groups, and thus to reduce the inconsistencies that might touch off disputes.[37]

A sharp departure from the anarchy of existing wage determination practices, the introduction of job classification and wage standardization signaled a recognition that wages were part of a relative structure. As one lecturer told a Harvard Business School audience in 1920, "in a plant there are a thousand variations in pay, skill, privileges, and emoluments that represent an almost infinite number of standings." These relative differences, he said, were as important to workers as their absolute wage levels.

Classification was intended to create a rate structure that was internally consistent. Although market rates might have accomplished the same purpose, they were often unavailable; more important, some semiskilled jobs were unique to a given firm. At Clothcraft Shops, a pioneer in wage standardization, the personnel manager recalled that "we carefully went over our rates, always with the idea of the relativity of rates in our plant in mind. That nebulous thing known as the 'market rate' did not govern us."[38]

Because classification and standardization involved a high degree of centralization in wage determination, the foreman's discretion in this area was greatly reduced. Usually the personnel department conducted the classification study, although foremen were sometimes asked to participate. In 1918 Westinghouse Electric set up at its East Pittsburgh plant an Occupations and Rates Committee that included several foremen. Using job analysis data, the committee divided jobs at the plant into five classes on the basis of a job's requirements for skill, executive ability, strength, and special care. Once jobs were assigned to classes, a range of hourly wage rates was determined for each class; piece and bonus rates were not allowed to exceed the range limits. A similar procedure was followed by other companies that classified wages, including Dennison Manufacuturing, Clothcraft Shops, Goodyear Tire and Rubber, International Harvester, and Sperry Gyroscope. Firms differed in the criteria they used for classification; most relied on criteria that were vague and rarely subject to careful measurement or worker review. With the notable exception of International Harvester, these classification schemes stopped short of applying objective criteria to the determination of every job wage in a plant, as in a job evaluation plan: The rate on a particular job was still indeterminate, although the range of rates was narrowed.[39]

The pressure to rationalize rate structures often came directly from the unions, who regarded classification as a way of removing various intraplant inequities, especially those produced by incentive pay. Classification enhanced a union's bargaining power by estab-

lishing standard rates for large groups of workers, thus tying these
workers together in a common wage band. Because of this politi-
cizing effect, and because classification undermined some of the
incentive effects associated with bonus and piece wages, some
employers vehemently opposed it.

Nowhere did the unions and employers fight more fiercely over
classification and standardization than in the Bridgeport munitions
industry. Many of the industry's highly skilled machinists were on
a bonus wage system which resulted in tremendous inequities (with
one local factory reporting sixteen different rates for a single occupation). Moreover, under this system, no minimum level of earnings was guaranteed; if production was delayed or if machines
broke down on a given day, a worker might be paid little or nothing.
The foreman's complete control over wage determination led to
multiple rates not only for bonus workers but also for those paid
by the piece or by the hour.

In the summer of 1917, the machinists demanded a wage increase, a classification system, a guaranteed minimum rate, and the
closed shop. After a series of delays, the matter was referred to the
Ordnance Department, which recommended a wage increase and
a classification system. But when nothing had changed by May of
1918, some 10,000 machinists went out on strike. Now their demands became more specific: They called for the standardization
of occupational titles, seven job classifications, a minimum rate in
each classification, and the right to participate in any classification
study. The strike attracted national attention, and the War Labor
Board was soon involved in trying to resolve the dispute.[40]

At hearings held in Bridgeport during the summer of 1918,
lawyers for the city's Manufacturers' Club argued the employers'
case against classification and standardization. They claimed, in
part, that occupational nomenclature could not be standardized in
an industry as "complex and varied" as machinery. But their basic
contention was that the workers' demands were inimical to the
employer's freedom to organize production and pay workers on
an individual basis; wages, they said, should be attached to individuals, not to jobs:

> We must preserve this right of the employer to assign and grade
> men as he sees fit, without attempting to fix any inflexible name or
> any inflexible rate of pay. That is, it is only by permitting this full

freedom of the employer that the employer is able to manage his establishment and secure that efficiency which ordinarily comes out of the hourly rate, when the employer can reward each individual case. In other words, we have as many hourly rates as there are human beings. Destroy this system and you will hobble . . . the organizing genius of the manufacturer.

Because the War Labor Board could not reach an agreement the case had to be decided by an arbitrator, who granted wage increases and minimum wages but rejected the demand for the classification system. Employers and national leaders of the machinists' union accepted the decision, but the workers continued to strike. They returned to work only after President Wilson threatened to revoke their draft exemptions.[41]

Elsewhere the unions had slightly more success in getting the government to extend classification and standardization, as when the War Labor Board ordered General Electric to set up a joint committee for the purpose of classifying jobs and standardizing wages in the company's Lynn and Schenectady plants. Under union pressure, the government also banned piecework on all railroads under its control and eliminated the incentive pay plan at Bethlehem Steel, Frederick W. Taylor's former client.[42] Interestingly, the government continued to be concerned with the classification issue long after the war because of union activity in its own backyard: In response to the demands of the National Federation of Federal Employees, which had been formed in 1917 to organize clerical and other workers in the federal government, Congress created a classification committee in 1919. Noting that "the government has no standard for fixing pay, no plan for relating salaries paid to the character of the work performed, [and] no system of promotion or advancement," the committee recommended that the government conduct job analyses, standardize occupational titles, and develop new job classifications and pay standards.[43]

Finally, the government spurred the adoption of more orderly and equitable pay scales *within* firms by its efforts to make wage rates more consistent *across* firms. To help monitor and control labor costs and to head off disputes, various government agencies encouraged employers to minimize interfirm wage disparities by classifying their jobs and then paying standard rates (such as the union scale for the locality or region) to everyone within the classification. This particular policy was widely resisted by employers not only on ideological grounds but also out of a recognition that regional standardization tended to level wages up, not down.[44]

Thus, despite pressure from unions and government, job analysis and wage standardization were less popular in practice than a review of the contemporary literature would suggest (see table 5.2). Except for the pioneering firms mentioned earlier, companies continued to set wages on a decentralized basis, with rate setting controlled by foremen or time-study engineers rather than personnel managers. Although the new methods would have made pay practices more orderly, and although they were considered "best practice" by the personnel textbooks of the day, most employers were wary of them. As in Bridgeport, they were worried that these methods would undermine incentives, hinder flexibility, and facilitate collective wage bargaining.[45]

Internal Promotion

The many prescriptive articles and books about personnel management that were published during the war commonly held that an internal promotion system was essential to a well-managed firm. There were several reasons for this belief. First, vocationalists in the personnel movement thought that a promotion plan provided an incentive for greater effort and for a deeper commitment to work. They emphasized the need to motivate manual workers, to "put the zest of the struggle and contest into their work, [and] the hope of better things tomorrow to take their minds off the difficulties of today."[46] Second, these policies were supposed to develop a worker's skills systematically and to act as a screening device by which "the competent and persevering employee gradually rises to the top." Third, internal promotion and hiring plans were believed to depress turnover by rewarding the worker for stability and giving him the "hope that efficiency in his present job will win him something better." Fourth, they were thought to "engender loyalty and *esprit de corps*" by reducing the foreman's allocative power and making promotions subject to definite criteria. Loyalty would increase if workers were assured that their good behavior and ability would be recognized and rewarded. But as Sumner

Slichter observed in 1919, internal promotion also enhanced the employer's control over the work force by raising the cost of separation to the employee. If the practice were widely followed, he said, it would allow "the traditional coercive policy [to] be pursued much more efficiently."[47]

Several types of promotion plans were in use during this period. The most complex, and also the most rare, were those that specified promotion ladders and advancement criteria for all jobs in an establishment. Dennison Manufacturing, for example, constructed a detailed plan by performing analyses of the skill requirements for each job in the plant and then using these data to map lines of promotion between jobs requiring similar skills. In the second type of plan, job analysis was used to classify jobs into groups, and promotion occurred within and between groups. For instance, the Ford Motor plan specified six classifications, with three incentive wage levels for each classification. Finally, the simplest and most widespread plan involved no lines or classes, although promotions were supposedly based on definite merit criteria.[48]

The new promotion plans called for a high degree of centralized control by the personnel department, which now functioned as a clearinghouse for all internal labor allocation. Foremen were regarded as too prejudiced to judge promotability and too parochial to allow a good worker to switch departments. This attitude was exemplified in the rhetorical question posed by a Westinghouse official to a group of personnel managers: "How does a foreman know what opportunities there are for advancement outside his own department, and if he *does* know, isn't it true the average foreman visualizes his company in terms of his own department and is often unwilling to impair [its efficiency] by losing a man through transfer or promotion?"[49]

After the war, a small but growing number of companies began to experiment with merit rating, a process in which the foreman was expected to participate, although the use of standardized evaluation criteria narrowed his zone of discretion. At a Boston automobile factory, foremen graded workers on forms resembling a student's report card. At the government's arsenal in Springfield, Massachusetts, each worker was rated twice a year by a rating board made up of three managers and the worker's foreman; two-thirds of the rating was based on the worker's output, and the remainder on his attendance, "application," and "habits." Eastman Kodak simply distributed to all of its employees a list of the criteria used by the personnel department in determining promotions; these included ability, knowledge, willingness to take orders, and tact. (Few of the rating plans used seniority as a criterion.) Merit criteria were also used to determine wage increases. By 1920, firms like Armour, Westinghouse, and White Motor were giving their production workers periodic merit wage increases. Because position promotions were irregular or episodic, these increases provided an incentive in lieu of promotion and served as a sop to workers passed over when someone was hired from the outside.[50]

Usually, however, the more elaborate promotion plans were accompanied by a policy of filling vacancies from within. The incentive effects of promotion were weakened if a firm turned to the external labor market to fill its vacancies. As Meyer Bloomfield pointed out, "Nothing is more discouraging to a man than to see outsiders brought in continually and promoted over the heads of tried and tested workers." And if vacancies *were* to be filled internally, a definite transfer and promotion plan eased the bureaucratic task of finding appropriate workers. But in those frequent instances where promotion lines were vague and labor allocation decentralized, promotion continued to be somewhat haphazard, and the policy of hiring from within was only minimally enforced.[51]

Firms were reluctant to implement a definite promotion plan because they thought that it would hinder allocative flexibility. As the plant manager at a large manufacturing firm put it: "Our business is not a progressive series of positions. Any good organization is always adjusting itself to new conditions. Lines of promotion are absurd." Others maintained that promotion plans created unrealistic expectations among incumbent workers: first, that a particular job would be theirs when it became vacant (an expectation which hampered the firm when it preferred to hire an outsider to fill the vacancy); and second, that a vacancy would soon open up. W. A. Grieves of Nash Motor told the 1919 NAEM convention that systematic promotion "doesn't work out in practice because you know as well as I that there are not major jobs for more than ten percent in your organization." In fact, when the Lynds surveyed six factories in Middletown over a two-year period in the early 1920s, they found that a worker's chances of being promoted to foreman ("the real step up") were only 1 out of 424.

Another reason managers were slow to introduce systematic promotion was their belief that, if advancement appeared to be automatic, workers would become "soft." One manager said:

> I am convinced that it is better for the business as well as the men themselves to keep them more or less anxious in regard to advancement. I do not want to pose as a slave driver, but it has been my experience to find that if a man is fairly sure of anything his interest in it wanes in proportion to his sureness. If that same man has nothing more than the assurance that, if in all else he is equal to a candidate from the outside he will get a better position when the chance comes, he will go at things a lot harder and accomplish more.

Firms with promotion plans considered it wise to view them as guidelines rather than as inflexible rules and definite commitments. Only a very few companies guaranteed their workers a fully internal hiring policy for above-entry-level positions.[52]

Consequently, internal promotion plans were not widespread (table 5.2), nor were merit rating and merit wage systems. The absence or ineffectual enforcement of promotion plans meant that foremen still controlled most promotions, even in firms with a personnel department: Out of a group of companies surveyed in 1923, only 3 percent gave their personnel departments a say in promotions. A personnel manager at one firm complained that "pull" still determined who would get promoted, then added, "It is a long, slow process trying to introduce modern personnel methods."[53]

Discipline and Dismissal

The new personnel departments were faced with the formidable task of finding some way to restore order and discipline to the turbulent shop floor. Because of wartime labor shortages, the threat of being sacked for insubordination, absenteeism, or slackened effort had lost its deterrent effect. A 1919 editorial in *Iron Age* complained of "a lack of initiative on the part of the skilled men to do a fair day's work, because of having no fear of dismissal."[54]

Many companies tried to solve the problem by introducing a system of monetary penalties and rewards. Thus, a worker who violated disciplinary rules could be fined, with the personnel department deducting the specified amount from his paycheck. At

Cheney Brothers, for example, a worker might have his wages cut for indiscipline or tardiness. But the docking system had a number of disadvantages. As Meyer Bloomfield noted, "At best it is a negative method, not a positive one [and] it frequently arouses the employee's resentment." Carrots, not sticks, were in order, so a number of companies began to give out rewards for good attendance and performance records. General Electric paid a bonus to any worker with fewer than six absences during the hot summer months; other firms, such as Du Pont and Yale Lock, rewarded their most punctual workers with annual wage supplements. Taking a page out of the military's book, Brighton Mills recognized good attendance records by issuing buttons made out of celluloid, bronze, silver, and gold.[55]

None of this was very new; nineteenth-century textile mills had also relied on graduated rewards and penalties. What distinguished these practices from earlier ones was that they were based on a much more methodical and equitable enforcement of a detailed and consistent set of disciplinary rules and regulations. These were often printed up in pamphlets with innocuous titles like "Information for Employees" or "Valuable Information for the Guidance of Employees." Standard Oil of New Jersey issued to every new employee a list of the company's rules and penalties for infractions, together with a statement of procedure for dismissal. These regulations were formulated by the personnel department and applied on a company-wide basis; foremen were no longer permitted to devise their own shop rules. As one observer commented, the power to establish rules was being "gathered under one authority so that they may be harmonized into a consistent policy, and may be made the definite responsibility of competent officials."[56]

Along with the centralization of policymaking came unprecedented efforts to hold foremen accountable for their disciplinary methods. Personnel departments reached deeply into the foreman's territory by eliminating or restricting his discharge privileges and by giving workers the right to appeal when they felt a foreman had treated them unfairly.

These changes were prompted by several motives. First, they were part of a search for less coercive ways of eliciting worker effort than what the personnel director at Goodyear called "the poison of fear" and "police authority." It was thought that workers would conform more readily and work harder if discipline was meted out consistently and fairly. Goodyear called this strategy "winning the worker's confidence and good will"; others referred to it as "industrial democracy" (although the term had broader connotations).[57]

Of course, more was at stake than bolstering productivity. A second motive was the desire to reduce unionism's appeal by preempting reforms—job rights and disciplinary due process—that the unions had achieved for their members. These new disciplinary systems were premised on the idea that, as in the union sector, the worker had "a right to his job which can be defeated only by his own conduct." Moreover, since unfair dismissals were a primary cause of labor disputes, some managers thought that a more careful handling of disciplinary offenses would keep the worker from becoming an "officer in the ranks of Bolshevism."

A final motive was to forestall government intervention. The War Labor Board insisted that workers be reinstated with back pay whenever an employer was found to have dismissed them because of their union activities. Although some employers chose to subvert the law, others felt compelled by the government's scrutiny of their disciplinary activities to develop new rules and standards governing dismissal.[58]

Personnel departments varied considerably in the extent to which they assumed control of worker discipline. At some firms, like Firestone, the foreman could do no more than suspend a worker from his department; the worker then went to the personnel manager for a hearing and possible transfer to another department. Others, like Jersey Standard, issued a list of offenses for which a foreman could dismiss a worker and guaranteed the right of appeal to the personnel department. Personnel managers regularly lectured foremen on the need to change their disciplinary methods: In an address to the company's 3,000 foremen, Goodyear's personnel director said, "The driver must go"; foremen at a Philadelphia firm were told, "Your system may have been good once but it won't go now."[59]

The ethos of professional neutrality found practical expression in these new disciplinary systems. Personnel managers could claim that their "broader viewpoint" put them in a position to "pass unbiased judgment on a discharged employee and give him an impartial hearing." And the personnel department *had* to be somewhat independent and neutral if workers were to trust it to define and protect their rights. Hence disciplinary reform led the personnel department to function as both union and management. One personnel manager said that his "most important duty is just this one thing: to come in close contact with employees; to gain their confidence; to hear their troubles and adjust them; to be their champion and *at the same time* the guardian of the company's interest."[60]

The personnel department's independence was also necessary to ensure that it had the authority to monitor and overrule foremen and other line officials, who were more resentful of reforms in this area than in any other. They regarded the unrestricted discharge as fundamental to maintaining effort and authority relations on the shop floor. That a worker could now appeal a discharge to the personnel manager was said to be "demoralizing to the discipline of the factory." It undermined the foreman's authority, independence, and prerogative to establish his own rules. As Bloomfield remarked: "To have a department come along and take away the last of his glory by denying him the right to hire and fire has seemed to many foremen to be the last straw."[61]

Because personnel managers were well aware that they could not succeed without the foreman's cooperation, they tended to introduce disciplinary reforms in a piecemeal fashion. According to one survey, even though most personnel managers believed that they should have the sole right to select workers, they were less willing to assert that right in the case of dismissals. George Halsey, a personnel manager at Cincinnati Milling Machine Company, warned a 1920 conference on employment management that "anybody who tries to put [a full system] in a plant that has been entirely without one should be the fellow who got knocked dead and not the foreman. Do it slowly and gradually—go into the mud puddle first and make just as little stir as you can; gradually sell your service to the foremen."[62]

But this advice may have been no more than an attempt to make a virtue of necessity, since the slow pace of change was often attributable to the personnel department's lack of authority in this area. In the steel industry, for example, personnel managers were described as "powerless" and "a futility as far as redress [of grievances involving the foreman] is concerned." Similarly, a 1918 study found personnel departments involved in discharge decisions at only about one-third of the firms surveyed, either to approve the foreman's choice (23 percent) or to make the determination independently (13 percent). In other firms, limits were imposed on the extent to which the personnel manager could overrule the foreman; rarely did he have the power to reinstate an employee. One observer concluded that "the foreman's authority is almost invariably upheld," and another said that foremen "may still be as petulant as ever about discharging."[63]

The Foreman

Since personnel management involved a transfer of authority away from the foreman and his shop floor realm, some friction between foremen and the new personnel departments was inevitable. But the conflicts inherent in this centralization process were heightened by the personnel manager's habit of attributing most of industry's labor problems to the foreman. Thus, a speaker at a 1920 personnel management conference declared: "It is high time [to] stop criticizing the radicals and agitators and lay some of the blame where it belongs—in the hands of the people who have the worker in their charge the largest number of hours per day." Such remarks were often arrogant in tone, as when foremen were called "corrupt" and "barbaric," epithets which reflected the college-educated manager's disdain for the foreman's lowly origins. Like the Progressive municipal reformer intent on "cleaning up" ward politics, the personnel manager sought to substitute his own brand of enlightened administration for the foreman's rougher, earthier style. And as in municipal reform, this meant enlarging the role of the middle-class professional at the expense of traditional, often immigrant elements.[64]

For their part, foremen were contemptuous of the "college boy" and loath to cooperate with him. When Meyer Bloomfield interviewed a group of foremen in 1920, he found that they felt robbed of initiative and responsibility in employment matters and that they were particularly resentful over losing their disciplinary prerogatives. But foremen had powerful allies in their battle with the personnel department. Production managers, plant superintendents, and other line officials often took the foreman's side in disputes with the personnel manager (a problem rarely encountered by industrial engineers). Line officials wanted to "get the goods out" and viewed personnel reforms as a hindrance to that goal. When Ordway Tead and Robert Bruere were hired to introduce modern personnel management at Leeds and Northrup in 1919, they met with steady opposition from the firm's production department. Their call for higher wages to improve morale and productivity was countered by the production manager's argument that it would be cheaper to put workers on incentive pay and to pressure foremen for greater output. Their recommendation for a foreman training class was flatly rejected by the production manager, who could see no need for one.[65]

After the war, some personnel managers began to take a more conciliatory approach to the foreman. "He has the idea that the old way is good enough," said Earl Morgan of Curtis Publishing. "He has to be sold and it is up to the employment manager to do it." One way to accomplish this goal was by involving foremen in the personnel department's activities. At Dennison's, foremen were invited on a rotating basis to work in the personnel department for three months as assistant personnel managers. They interviewed prospective employees, read books on personnel management, and visited other plants to observe their employment procedures. The personnel manager at Dennison's felt that "once they get into the [personnel] department they have to consider the company as a company and not simply as one department." At Acheson Graphite, the personnel manager spent three afternoons each week with the company's foremen, discussing topics of mutual concern.[66]

Another way of winning the foreman's support was through training classes. H. L. Gardner, personnel manager at Du Pont, said that "until we can give our foremen a thorough understanding of the principles behind our methods and gain their hearty support, we cannot consider that we have sold employment management to the foremen." Foreman training was also viewed as an indirect way to reach production officials and convince them of the need for a personnel department; Earl Morgan called this "business insurance." Most training programs instructed foremen in human relations as well as in the technical aspects of foremanship. International Harvester hired Meyer Bloomfield to give a series of evening lectures to the company's foremen on the importance of personnel management. Bloomfield thought that these classes would make foremen feel more like professionals and so increase their empathy with the personnel manager. The course at Goodyear included discussions of the firm's economic structure—how profits were made, how profitable the firm was—in the hope that foremen would pass this information along to workers and refute "what they have heard the night before from somebody on a soapbox on the corner."[67]

An additional impetus for foreman's training came from the new Federal Board for Vocational Education. When the FBVE took charge of the government's personnel management courses, it began to promote classes in foremanship. Under the Smith-Hughes Act, the FBVE was allowed to reimburse local authorities for the cost of these classes, which could be conducted in the plant and on company time provided that they remained under control of local school authorities. Various groups took advantage of federal subsidies: Private training firms advertised in business publications, promising that their courses would increase teamwork, "sympathy," and profits; Goodyear, Packard Motor, and Miller Lock packaged their training programs and made them available to other organizations; and Joseph Willits organized a class at the University of Pennsylvania's Wharton School that attracted over a thousand foremen from local firms. But in 1920 and 1921, editorials began to appear in publications like *Industrial Management,* warning that foreman training had become a "fad" and should not be regarded as a "cure-all" for industrial problems. At the same time, the personnel management movement became a target of increasing criticism; thus, by mid-1920, it was starting to lose some of its momentum and prestige. Events during the depression of 1921–22 showed just how weak industry's commitment to change had become.[68]

Looking back on the war years, one is struck by how much was accomplished in a short period of time. A substantial minority of firms had, through personnel management, introduced a more equitable employment relationship, one that encouraged workers to remain with the firm and be loyal to it. Line managers lost their exclusive right to determine corporate labor policies, and foremen gave up some of the power they wielded in their balkanized fief-doms. New company-wide rules and procedures enmeshed the employment relationship in a web of bureaucratic rationality.

Several interrelated factors contributed to this transformation. Primary among them was the threat of labor unrest. Personnel management reduced the potential for unionization by replicating within the firm some of the union's protective structures. Second, labor shortages forced firms to stabilize employment and seek alternatives to dismissal as a way of maintaining discipline. Third, extensive government regulation of private employment prac-tices—resulting from the need to control the labor market and to win labor's support for the war—spurred industry's adoption of new personnel policies. Finally, the professional orientation of the personnel movement facilitated these developments by publicizing new techniques, by bringing outside ideas into management, and by making change more acceptable to the work force.

It should be noted that having a personnel department made it much easier to administer programs requiring intrafirm coordina-tion and to place checks on line officials. Data from a 1918 survey showed that a firm with a personnel department was ten times more likely than a firm without such a department to conduct job analyses, four times more likely to have a promotion plan, and three times more likely to regulate dismissals.

Yet despite the efforts of personnel managers to persuade em-ployers and line officials of the virtues of the new approach, old attitudes and practices persisted, limiting the scope of pre-1921 employment reforms: Internal labor market arrangements affected only a minority of the work force and were unevenly applied even for this minority. That these arrangements were either restricted to particular groups or ineffectually practiced suggests that most em-ployers had a less-than-wholehearted commitment to an enduring employment realtionship.

In 1919, Joseph Willits pointed to the continued dominance of what he called the "Bourbon employer," adding that "the events of the war have justified his previous beliefs as to the essential depravity of American workmen." Willits thought that the war had hardened, rather than softened, the employer's prejudices, his conviction that liberality eroded discipline, that foremen had to be upheld in disputes with workers, that labor was a commodity. The persistence of this traditional ideology made it difficult for personnel managers to expand their influence either within or beyond the minority of firms that had initiated personnel departments by 1920.[69]

CHAPTER 6

A DIFFERENT DECADE:
MODERATION IN THE 1920s

I. Labor Markets

The 1920s are usually characterized as a "golden decade," a time of prosperity, growth, and tight labor markets. There is evidence to support this popular view: The aggregate unemployment rate for the civilian, nonfarm labor force was lower between 1923 and 1927 than it had been for any five-year period since 1900, and real annual earnings for nonfarm civilians increased 26 percent between 1920 and 1929.[1]

But these aggregate figures mask the fact that during the 1920s, the labor market in manufacturing was moving in an opposite direction (see table 6.1), and this is critical to understanding why the decade was so different from the period that preceded it. Manufacturing employment was stagnant throughout the 1920s, and stood at the same level in 1929 as it had in 1919. This understates the decline in blue-collar employment because shifts occurred in the occupational composition of the manufacturing labor force: Wage earners as a proportion of all manufacturing employees fell

Table 6.1. Employment Changes, 1920–1929

	Nonfarm	Industry	Wage Earners in Industry
1920–1923	10.4%	−3.4%	—
1923–1929	12.2	0.8	—
1925–1929	7.9	4.7	2.9%

SOURCES: S. Lebergott, *Manpower in Economic Growth* (New York, 1964), pp. 512, 514; David Weintraub, "Unemployment and Increasing Productivity," in *Technological Trends and National Policy*, Report to the National Resources Committee (Washington, D.C., 1937), p. 75.

from 92 percent in 1916 to 89 percent in 1929, with the decline in
transportation and utilities being even steeper (from 90 percent to
81 percent). Further, between 1923 and 1927, unemployment rates
in industry were *higher* than for any other five-year period since
1900, excluding depression years (see table 6.2).[2]

Earnings reflected these differential labor market patterns. Between 1920 and 1929, the earnings of manufacturing workers rose
only two-thirds as rapidly as those of other civilian nonfarm employees; and in relatively depressed industries like steel, real weekly
earnings *fell* 8.3 percent between 1923 and 1929. Moreover, most
of the increase in real earnings in manufacturing represented a
decline in consumer prices rather than an increase in nominal wage
rates. In 20 out of 26 manufacturing industries, average hourly
wage rates decreased between 1920 and 1929.[3]

Causes of Labor Market Stagnation

The term "techonological unemployment" was coined in the
1920s, when elastic credit and a pent-up demand for plant and
equipment helped to fuel a mechanization boom that resulted in
the displacement of large numbers of workers.[4] Proxy measures of
labor-displacing technological change confirm this trend. Thus,
labor productivity grew at an annual rate of 3.8 percent between
1919 and 1929, compared with a rate of 1.7 percent between 1899
and 1914. Similarly, while the annual ratio of total wages to total
value-added in manufacturing was constant between 1899 and
1914, by 1929 it had dropped to 12 percent below the 1899-1914
level. In short, as table 6.3 indicates, employment increased far less

Table 6.2. Average Annual Unemployment Rates, 1900–1927

	Civilian Nonfarm	Manufacturing and Transportation
1900–1904	10.5%	4.9%
1904–1909[a]	8.3	4.6
1909–1913	10.4	4.8
1916–1920	6.1	3.8
1923–1927	5.2	5.6

SOURCES: Lebergott, *Manpower*, p. 512; Paul H. Douglas, *Real Wages in the U.S., 1890–1926* (New York, 1930), p. 445.
a. Excluding 1908, a depression year.

Table 6.3. Index of Output and Employment in Manufacturing

	Volume of Output	Employment
1919	100	100
1923	122	96
1929	148	100

SOURCE: Leo Wolman and Gustave Peck, "Labor Groups in the Social Structure," in Wesley C. Mitchell, ed., *Recent Social Trends in the United States* (New York, 1933), p. 805.

rapidly than output during the 1920s. Finally, the decennial rate of mechanization, as measured by horsepower per wage earner in manufacturing, rose 50 percent during the 1920s, compared with a 15 percent increase during the previous decade.[5]

Technological displacement contributed to unemployment because of the slow absorption of displaced workers into expanding industries. A 1928 study by the Brookings Institution found that the technologically displaced worker did not easily find a new job: Nearly half of the unemployed workers included in the study were out of work for more than six months.[6] These findings are consistent with those of similar studies conducted at the time.[7]

Market maturity was another major cause of employment stagnation. Excess capacity and diminishing returns afflicted such older industries as steel, cotton, shoes, and the railroads. For example, employment in the cotton textile industry, which had increased steadily from 1800 to 1920, began to decline during the 1920's due to market saturation and competition from new products like rayon. Similarly, the railroad industry suffered declining growth for the first time in its history, partly as a result of competition from the new motor vehicle industry. Of course, some industries— including chemicals, oil, electrical manufacturing, and public utilities—grew rapidly and reaped high profits. But these were capital-intensive industries, whose employment growth was insufficient to spark an overall sectoral increase in employment.[8]

One attempt to measure the secular stagnation in manufacturing employment was economist Frederick C. Mills' study of the net change of employment in different manufacturing industries. Using five-year intervals for 1899–1914 and two-year intervals for 1923–29, Mills calculated what he called a "permanent separation rate": the ratio between the number of "withdrawals" (workers who withdrew or were forced to withdraw from the industry in which they had been working) and the average number employed in the industry. He found that during the 1920s, 49 out of every 1,000 workers left the industry in which they were employed, compared with 21 workers out of every 1,000 between 1899 and 1914 (table 6.4).

Migration Patterns

During the early 1920s, employers were worried that the curtailment of European immigration resulting from the war and the subsequent imposition of immigration quotas would lead to labor shortages. At a National Association of Manufacturers' symposium on immigration held in 1923, U.S. Steel, Packard Motor, American Car and Foundry, and other heavy users of unskilled labor all argued for a relaxation of quotas.[9] But this anxiety had dissipated by the middle of the decade. A 1925 editorial in *Iron Age* declared: "There can be no doubt that the country at large, whatever the various reasons, is well satisfied with the present immigration law." Don D. Lesochier, the noted labor economist, later said that it was "obvious" that the "slowing down of population growth did not produce a labor shortage or a probability of such a shortage. An increased amount of unemployment was evident in the years immediately preceding the depression of 1930."[10]

In those areas or industries where a labor surplus failed to meet demand, migration closed the gap. First, the number of Mexicans in the population more than doubled between 1920 and 1930. According to the 1930 Census, large numbers of Mexicans had settled in Detroit, Chicago, Gary, and other industrial cities, where they worked in the steel, meat-packing, and automobile industries, all heavy users of unskilled labor.[11] Second, the net migration of

Table 6.4. "Permanent Separation Rates" of Wage Earners in Manufacturing

	1899–1914	1923–1929
Coal and petroleum products	5.0%	3.2%
Iron and steel	1.5	4.0
Machinery	0.2	2.6
Textiles	1.5	4.8
Transportation	4.2	11.5

SOURCE: F. C. Mills, *Economic Tendencies in the United States* (New York, 1932), pp. 419–423.

native-born whites and blacks into the nation's major industrial centers was higher during the 1920s than in the preceding decade. The black urban population outside the South rose by 70 percent between 1920 and 1930. Blacks made up 25 percent of the labor force in the Midwest's iron foundries and metal works in the late 1920s. They also accounted for about 10 percent of the workers at Studebaker and at Ford's River Rouge plant, although some automobile manufacturers such as White Motor still refused to hire them.[12]

Effects of Labor Market Conditions

The manufacturing labor market of the 1920s was a buyer's market, in contrast to the seller's market of 1916–20. One important consequence of this change was a marked decline in labor mobility: Average monthly quit rates in manufacturing dropped from 5.4 percent in the 1919–23 period to 2.5 percent in the 1924–29 period.[13] While these data are biased and must be viewed with caution,[14] there undoubtedly was much less mobility than in the prewar period. Labor mobility was inhibited by the depressed state of the manufacturing labor market: nominal wage stability, stagnant employment, technological unemployment, and the slow absorption of the unemployed. Sumner Slichter commented in 1929 that "the most important single influence" on quit rates was "the relative abundance of men and scarcity of jobs which have existed . . . almost continuously since 1920."[15]

Workers in industries with stable or declining employment levels were reluctant to quit their jobs for fear of prolonged unemployment. And as the average age of the manufacturing labor force rose, the quit rate declined even more; older workers were less likely to quit.[16] But even younger workers in expanding industries were timorous about trying their luck, as is demonstrated by Woytinsky's comparison of the relationship between accession and separation rates in the pre- and post-1921 periods. Before 1921, monthly accession and separation rates moved together; that is, increases in separations occurred at about the same time as increases in accessions. After 1921, however, increases in separation rates lagged several months behind increases in accession rates at firms where employment was expanding. According to Woytinsky, this lag meant that "workers were already scared by the threat of unemployment and no longer changed their jobs as freely as before the war." Indeed, when the Lynds visited Middletown (Muncie, Indiana) during the mid-1920s, they found widespread fear of unemployment among the town's working-class families.[17]

Given the labor surplus, high productivity, and low unionization and quit rates, employers had little reason to be concerned with turnover. As a result, the personnel management literature of the 1920s is almost devoid of articles on the subject. One researcher found that firms were still collecting turnover data in 1927, but he noted that few attached any importance to the figures.[18] Quits were no longer viewed as indicative of poor worker morale or of bad working habits; a loose labor market solved both problems.

Another major consequence of high unemployment was a weakening of the labor movement. Union membership peaked in 1920 at over 5 million, then declined during the depression of 1921–22, leaving the unions with 3.6 million members in 1923. Membership continued to drop slowly but steadily, falling to 3.4 million in 1929, a 32 percent decrease from the 1920 level. Not all unions suffered a loss. The building trades showed a slight gain in union membership during the 1920s. But in manufacturing, where the labor market was weakest, union membership fell from 1.9 million in 1920 to less than 800,000 in 1929, a decline of nearly 60 percent.[19]

Even sharper than the decline in union membership was the reduction in strike activity: from 3,411 strikes in 1920 to 921 in 1929, a drop of more than 70 percent.[20] The proportion of the work force involved in strikes was lower in the seven-year period between 1923 and 1929 than it had been at any point since 1890. In short, unionized workers became less willing to strike.

Of course, other forces besides the labor market surplus contributed to the debilitation of the labor movement. The craft unions were still incapable of organizing the new mass production industries, despite efforts by the AFL to make itself more appealing to employers in those industries.[21] Further, the prestige that labor enjoyed during the war had disappeared by the mid-1920s, as the social climate grew more conservative: Public opinion toward organized labor turned negative; the courts were measurably more hostile, issuing a large number of decisions and injunctions unfavorable to labor; and last but not least, employers became openly belligerent, mounting a strong open-shop movement and other forms of resistance.[22]

All these factors combined to create an environment that was not conducive to liberal employment policies. Most of the problems that had justified employment reform during the war period were gone: The union threat had receded, productivity was high, turnover was low, and labor was easily available. On top of this, the new political conservatism—marked by a lack of interest in social experimentation—carried over into industry. Employers who had never fully accepted personnel management were now even less likely to be swayed by arguments about the relation between morale and efficiency. Professional personnel management could not easily survive the resurgence of "get-tough" labor policies and the waning of a wartime sense of urgency.

Thus, during the 1920s employers no longer felt the same pressure to maintain or expand their personnel programs. The number of firms with personnel departments continued to grow, but much less rapidly than during the war period (table 6.5). Within these firms, more conservative policies prevailed. Personnel departments usually continued to have responsibility for selecting employees and for administering welfare programs, but they lost much of their independent authority and their effective control over foremen. Allocative decisions were decentralized and once again left to the

Table 6.5. Coverage of Personnel Departments, 1915–1929

Company Size	1915	1920	1929
Proportion of firms employing over 250 employees with personnel departments	3–5% (est.)	25%	34%
1,000–5,000 employees	—	—	39
Over 5,000 employees	—	—	55
Labor Force			
Proportion of industrial workers employed by firms with personnel departments	—	14%	20%

SOURCES: 1915 and 1920 figures are based on calculations in S. M. Jacoby, "The Origins of Internal Labor Markets in American Manufacturing Firms, 1910–1940" (Ph.D. dissertation, University of California, Berkeley, 1981), pp. 374, 617; 1929 figures come from NICB, *Industrial Relations Programs in Small Plants* (New York, 1929), pp. 3, 20, and NICB, *Industrial Relations: Administration of Policies and Programs* (New York, 1931), p. 54.

foreman's discretion. Although these companies did not completely revert to prewar drive policies, very few of them were committed to expanding the liberal policies of the war period. As a result, personnel management lost most of its zeal for reform.

Again, this picture conflicts with the conventional view of the decade. For example, Sumner Slichter in 1929 argued that the change in the labor market had failed "to end the interest of businessmen in labor's good will," principally because of "the dread of labor trouble"[23] He noted the recent growth of sophisticated programs such as employee representation and pecuniary welfare benefits. But Slichter's optimistic meliorism applies only to those few highly visible firms—employing at most 10-15 percent of the industrial labor force—that expanded their personnel programs during the 1920s. Here memories of the war period kept personnel programs in place long after the union threat was gone. But elsewhere, even in many firms with personnel departments, there was a retrogression.

II. The Decline of the Liberal Model, 1920–1922

January 1920 marked the peak of the postwar business cycle. By March some experts were already predicting a major decline in business conditions, and a more conservative mood gripped the nation. The defeat of the steel strike the preceding fall had increased management's determination to check the spread of labor militance and unionism. The strike provided the impetus for the open-shop drive of the American Plan. By the end of 1919, organizations like the National Founders' Association, the National Association of Manufacturers, and the National Metal Trades Association had resumed their prewar advocacy of the open shop. A nationwide network of open-shop associations was in place by the fall of 1920, including 50 groups in New York, 46 in Illinois, and 23 in Michigan. Because of the Red Scare hysteria, which crested in the summer of 1920, the open-shop movement was able to draw on lingering public suspicion that organized labor was Communist-inspired. Postwar hopes for reconstruction and cooperation now gave way to calls for a "return to normalcy." Hostility to progressive reform movements became widespread.[24]

Liberals in the personnel management movement viewed these events with foreboding. Shortly before the massive Industrial Relations Association of America (IRAA) convention of May 1920, Dudley Kennedy predicted that employers would eliminate their personnel departments and return to a drive system if economic conditions took a turn for the worse. Kennedy warned that employers would "seize with avidity what they consider a long-deferred opportunity to put the screws down," saying that he had "heard hints thrown out along these lines" in his travels around the country. That summer, Sumner Slichter observed that a return "to the old drive methods" was under way in some industries. The sharp wage cuts and heavy layoffs of the following winter proved that these fears were well-founded. But the hardwriting on the wall spelled out a different message for conservatives in the personnel management movement.[25]

Several months before the depression hit, the split between conservatives and liberals in the personnel movement began to widen. Prior to 1920, the two factions had managed to maintain a working relationship, while disagreeing over such issues as neutrality in labor relations, but the emergence of a tougher attitude toward labor and the implied threat to the survival of personnel management changed that relationship. Whether motivated by fears about their own future or by genuine ideological differences, the conservatives launched a broad-based attack on their more liberal conterparts and succeeded in articulating a program for the movement that was more in tune with the times.

The most common charge leveled against the liberals was that they had gone too far in blaming the foreman for industry's labor problems and stripping him of his authority. Following a speech by Dudley Kennedy at the 1920 IRAA convention, in which he urged personnel managers to practice a mixture of restraint and reconciliation in their relations with foremen, Ralph G. Wells of the Employment Managers' Association of Boston angrily threw down the gauntlet:

> I feel that the foreman is one of the most abused men in industry today. Industrial relations men, employment managers, and all of us, are using the foreman as an alibi. We get together in a meeting of this sort and say what the foreman should do. Really, the discussion so far as the employment managers are concerned, has come

about largely because the employment managers have found it impossible to get things across. . . . An employment manager, to my
mind, ought to be a private secretary to a foreman, because a
foreman is the production man and the man we must depend upon
to get our production across.

H. W. Casler, a vice-president of the New York Telephone Company, said that much of the blame heaped upon the foreman was
undeserved and that he needed to be given more recognition and
authority. The time had come, said Casler, to "wipe out the charges
against him and start out anew with a clean slate." Others criticized
the personnel manager for having carried reform too far. Dwight
Farnham, an engineer, reported that "I have actually heard half-
baked personnel managers tell the foremen that they expected to
stamp out czarism and injustice to the workmen."[26]
   The real issue, however, was not how much sympathy the foreman deserved, but what role the personnel department should play
in the relationship between foreman and workers. One critic of
liberal peronnel management termed the issue "the bogey of over-
centralization."[27] The outlines of that issue had been set forth in a
heated debate that took place shortly before the 1920 IRAA convention, at a meeting of the Employment Managers' Association
of Boston. The debate centered on the question of whether the
personnel department should have line authority or be a staff
department. Conservatives like Ralph G. Wells argued that the
personnel department should be an auxiliary to the firm's production division, functioning as an advisory staff to line officials (that
is, foremen and production managers). In Wells' view, foremen
should be given greater discretion in allocating, disciplining, and
discharging workers, while the personnel department should simply lay down guidelines for foremen to follow and refrain from
interfering in the day-to-day management of workers.[28]
   This conception of personnel management was the opposite of
what had been the liberal tendency to restrain foremen and develop
a personnel department capable of steering a course independent
of the production division. Under the conservative model, the personnel manager no longer would be an impartial force for change
within the firm; the liberals' professional ethos would have to be
sacrificed. This new model had the virtue of preserving traditional
authority relations between foremen and workers at a time when

calls for a reassertion of authority and discipline were on the increase. Presumably those personnel managers who adopted this decentralized model would stand the best chance of weathering the oncoming depression.

The depression of 1920–1922 hit hardest in manufacturing, where unemployment rates rose to the highest levels since the 1880s: 21 percent in 1921 and 15.4 percent in 1922. Prices and wage rates collapsed. Despite the employment reforms of the war period, most companies evidenced no commitment to an enduring relationship with their employees. Little was done to cushion workers from the shock of job loss.[29] A few firms like McElwain Shoe and Dennison Manufacturing engaged in work-sharing or provided other relief programs like company gardens, and some paid layoff compensation "as a means of ensuring continuity of employment." But a survey by the Russell Sage Foundation turned up few other instances of work-sharing or dismissal pay, which it termed "unusual relief arrangements." The American Association for Labor Legislation reported that most employers offered no relief of any sort to laid-off workers and noted that employment stabilization was equally rare.[30]

The depression revealed that a company didn't need a personnel department to maintain morale or keep turnover rates low. The fear of job loss took care of that. The pressure of unemployment, said economist Paul H. Douglas, "force[d] the workman to produce more, to be steadier at work, and to be more docile." By June 1920, articles lauding the increase in labor productivity began to appear in the business press. In July, a survey of manufacturers in New York City found that over half felt that the "efficiency" of labor had increased. Another 10 percent saw no change in efficiency but sensed "a better spirit among the employees." In October the National City Bank of New York announced that it had received reports from "all lines of manufacturing" that labor efficiency was increasing. The National Association of Corporation Schools said that workers were "assuming a more satisfactory attitude toward production and that unrest and radicalism is [sic] dying out."[31]

The depression had a variety of observable effects. First, turnover rates sank: in 1921, the median quit rate in manufacturing dropped to one-fourth of its 1920 level. Second, labor productivity quickly improved. For example, output per man-day in the Akron tire industry rose from 1.4 in 1920 to 2.8 in mid-1921; a motor factory reported an output per man-hour increase of 160 percent during the twelve months after April 1920. Finally, labor militance decreased sharply. The number of strikes fell from 3,411 in 1920 to 1,112 in 1922, and the unions lost over a million members.[32]

Motivated by the need to trim costs, the desire to "put the screws down," and the realization that a personnel department was superfluous when unemployment was high, many employers made deep cuts in their personnel departments. "Employers Cut Off Personnel Work," read a headline in the *New York Times* during January 1921. One employer reported that, with unemployment on the increase, "people are now more willing to work hard and do it more cheerfully than heretofore. Therefore, personnel departments as such are not so great."[33] A large electric company that had built up a personnel department of over one hundred persons fired everyone except a few clerks, who were retained to record hirings and dismissals. Another company said it was "less inclined to experiment now compared to previously. Previously when in doubt we may have said, 'Try and see.' Now when in doubt, if an expense in involved, we are inclined to say, 'Don't try.' "[34]

Although these moves were touted as cost-cutting necessities, they owed more to the desire to restore old-fashioned discipline. In 1928, long after the dust had settled, W. J. Donald of the American Management Association commented: "More personnel men lost their jobs because they were given and used too much authority, because they usurped the prerogatives of the line organizations and consequently interfered with normal disciplinary procedure, than because of business depression." As a General Motors executive put it in 1921, it was "time for the discontinuance of many industrial relations activities, which may possibly be termed wartime exigencies, and the getting down to absolute essentials."[35]

Those personnel departments that survived the depression adopted the conservative model of personnel management, which returned power to the foreman. A 1923 survey of personnel departments found a marked trend toward both decentralized "control" and decentralized "execution" of employment policy.[36] Personnel departments also lost their status as independent divisions, on an equal footing with the firm's other departments. Shortly after

Arthur H. Young's departure from International Harvester in 1922, the industrial relations department he had headed was made subsidiary to the firm's production division. President Cyrus McCormick, Jr., said, "We have found we can progress far more quickly, far more soundly, if the Industrial Relations department is considered not as standing alongside the manufacturing department, but as part of it."[37] When Ordway Tead surveyed personnel administration in 1923, he estimated that at only a handful of companies did the personnel manager still hold a major administrative post. Charles Piez, a moderate employer, summed up these developments by noting that the depression was

> bound to reconstruct many of the positions developed during the past five years, and bound to bring us back to a period when business principles, tinged with sympathy and consideration for our employees, will supercede many of the altruistic sophistries which the unusual conditions of the past five years have injected into the conduct of business.[38]

Personnel managers initially downplayed the depression's impact on their movement. An editorial in the January 1921 issue of the IRAA's bulletin said that there was "an undertone of optimism that increases in volume daily" and that personnel management had a great future. In April 1921 another editorial claimed that relatively few firms had discontinued their personnel activities. But the gravity of the situation could no longer be ignored when the IRAA was forced to postpone its May 1921 convention because of "existing industrial conditions." A year earlier it had attracted 3,000 persons to its Chicago convention. Moreover, its membership dropped from over 2,000 members to under 1,400, a decline of 30 percent in less than a year.[39]

Personnel managers who still held their jobs fell in with the more conservative mood. In September 1921, the Employment Managers' Association of Boston—which had been the birthplace of Bloomfield's neutral, professional approach to personnel management—was absorbed into the open-shop Associated Industries of Massachusetts at what the *Boston Globe* described as a "love feast." Mary B. Gilson recalled:

> Personnel workers in general were in line with the conventional attitude or else they were discreetly noncommittal. . . . There was

no overt evidence of challenging the fundamental ideas of the employers' groups. One was considered merely contentious, and perhaps exhibitionist, if the shortsighted and unconstructive viewpoints of the American Planners were questioned.[40]

In short, the liberal conception of the personnel manager as a neutral force for reform in industry was thoroughly discredited.

Ordway Tead and Henry Metcalf's personnel management textbook—a synthesis of the liberal, professional approach—received generally negative reviews when it was published in 1921. *Automotive Industries* dismissed it as being of no value because it was "too theoretical." Even Henry S. Dennison, usually sympathetic to liberal positions, felt that the text would "repel" businessmen because of its "occasional hints of a desire to shatter the sorry scheme of things entire." Progressivism and professionalism were now viewed as archaic or worse. Arthur H. Young, who became one of the proponents of the conservative model, predicted in 1921 that "those employment managers who have looked upon their jobs as more or less professional will find that they have no more jobs left."[41]

III. Dissemination of the Conservative Model

Although antiprofessional, the new model of personnel management was still more progressive than having no personnel department at all. It received strong backing from a number of large and relatively enlightened industrial companies, which used their influence within a network of closely linked management organizations to disseminate the model and to marshall approval for it.

The SCC and Its Principles

The top executives of ten of America's leading corporations founded the Special Conference Committee (SCC) in 1919 to coordinate labor relations and personnel policies. The SCC had close philosophical, financial, and personal ties to the Rockefeller interests: Alfred C. Bedford, president of Standard Oil of New Jersey, initiated the committee; Clarence J. Hicks was its chairman from

1919 to 1933, during which time he also headed the personnel department at Jersey Standard; and the SCC was headquartered in the offices of Raymond Fosdick, a Rockefeller attorney in New York. In addition to Jersey Standard, member firms included Bethlehem Steel, Du Pont, General Electric, General Motors, Goodyear, International Harvester, Irving National Bank, U.S. Rubber, and Westinghouse. Because its very existence raised sensitive legal and political questions, the committee operated in secret, with no funds, no telephone, and no stationery in its own name.[42]

In 1920 the members of the SCC adopted what they called "a simple set of principles" that embodied their shared philosophy of labor relations and personnel management. Opposition to unions and to collective bargaining was fundamental. But in contrast to the open-shop drive of the American Plan, the SCC's approach to combating unionism was relatively sophisticated, drawing on the Rockefeller-Hicks philosophy of industrial relations, which stressed the putative harmony of interests between capital and labor. The SCC believed, as Rockefeller once wrote, that "the only solidarity natural in industry is the solidarity which unites all those in the same business establishment."[43] In 1920 it said,

> the lessons of the war have reinforced previous experience that the human element in industry is a factor of greatest importance. Progress depends upon cooperation and in industry cooperation must be based on the acceptance by employers and employees of some practical application of the principle that capital and labor are dependent.[44]

Employee representation was the main vehicle for the "practical application" of the SCC's philosophy. The committee developed its own version of employee representation, the Joint Conference Plan, modeled after the company union which Hicks had introduced at Jersey Standard in 1918. By 1929, eight of the ten members of the SCC had instituted employee representation plans. These plans, said Hicks, were an attempt "to organize identity of interest where it exists in order to reduce the area of conflict."[45]

The second component of the SCC's program comprised the so-called new or pecuniary welfare work—pensions, paid vacations, group insurance, and the like—which helped to "establish a mutual interest between management and employees" and allowed workers "to share in the distribution of profit." One advantage of this "new" welfare work was that it minimized the resentment bred by more traditional welfare programs, which Clarence Hicks had long argued were best left to organizations like the YMCA. "Care must be taken," said the SCC, "to avoid paternalism." The SCC was also aware that the new welfare work boosted the public image of its members: Through welfare benefits, it said "forward-looking corporations have won an improved position before the bar of public opinion."[46]

The final component of the SCC's program was employment management, which was regarded as necessary to "ensure consistent policy." The SCC endorsed such techniques as record-keeping, transfer systems, and orientation sessions for new employees. But it took a more moderate approach to employment reform than had been popular during the war. It was against wage classification, believing that "wages should be related primarily to performance." It also opposed "any guarantee of remunerative employment" and all forms of unemployment insurance. Lastly, the SCC disapproved of the professional, centralized model of personnel management, believing instead that power should be returned to the foreman in order to preserve authority and discipline on the shop floor. However, realizing that decentralization might mean a return to the prewar situation, the SCC supported foremen's training programs as a way of minimizing that risk.[47]

The SCC promoted this three-point program through its close ties to organizations like the YMCA. During the 1920s, the YMCA held annual Human Relations in Industry conferences at Silver Bay, which always attracted several hundred people, including prominent employers, personnel managers, and even the occasional union leader (in keeping with the YMCA's "neutrality zone" policy). The SCC's corporatist philosophy, with its emphasis on a community of interest between workers and management, permeated the Silver Bay meetings. Employee representation and the new welfare work were the principal topics of discussion. Clarence Hicks, a former YMCA official, and Arthur H. Young, now an advisor to the Rockefeller interests, chaired the conference organizing committees. But more important than the YMCA as an outlet for the SCC's ideas was the newly formed American Management Association.[48]

Genesis and Influence of the AMA

By the end of 1920, the board of directors of the Industrial Relations Association of America was dominated by conservatives. Whether by design or accident, the organization's top positions were taken over by members of the SCC: J. M. Larkin (Bethlehem), Arthur H. Young (International Harvester), and Cyrus S. Ching (U.S. Rubber). Other board members included Ralph G. Wells, E. A. Shay, and C. M. Culver, all of whom were active in open-shop employers' associations. After the new officers took over, the tone of the IRAA's newsletter, *Personnel,* shifted. Now each issue carried at least one article attacking radicalism, Bolshevism, or the closed shop. In a sharp departure from previous editorial neutrality, the "Creed of the Employers' Association of Northern New Jersey," an open-shop group, was printed in the newsletter. Yet the conservatives had inherited an organization that was in serious financial difficulty; *Personnel* ceased publication in October 1921.[49]

The National Association of Corporation Training, successor to the NACS, was also in dire straits, since the New York Edison Company, which had supported the organization since 1913, was no longer willing to subsidize it. By 1921, the NACT's Executive Committee, like the IRAA's, included several members from firms belonging to the SCC. So it came as no surprise when a meeting was held at the Executives' Club in New York in February 1922 to discuss a merger of the NACT and the IRAA. Three of the nine members of the merger committee were representatives of SCC firms. A formal merger took place in May 1922 and the new organization was named the National Personnel Association (NPA).[50]

The NPA's first and only convention was held in November at Pittsburgh, a center of open-shop activity. The NPA's conservatism deeply disturbed many former members of the IRAA. In April 1922, Boyd Fisher wrote to Morris L. Cooke to complain about the group, which he said was trying to "disband the IRAA and start absolutely fresh." Fisher was especially concerned about the attempt to cast personnel management in an antiprofessional mold. "The spirit of a great many men has weakened during the last year," he wrote, "and many such as Cy Ching, Ralph Wells and the people in the associated industries [open-shop organizations] assert that personnel work is not a profession but a business position." Fisher called for renewed emphasis on the professional approach, whereby the personnel manager would act as the workers' advocate and serve as an independent check on line management. The industrial relations man, he said, has "certain obligations to the workers with whom he comes in contact," and "an independent duty to them."[51]

Cooke, a leading exponent of professionalism in engineering, had recently attempted to organize a group to counteract the propaganda of the open-shop movement. In his reply he expressed agreement with Fisher and suggested that personnel managers be subject to licensing, just like registered nurses and accountants. Cooke closed by encouraging Fisher to preserve the professional orientation of the old IRAA: "I believe that it is well not futile to get up a national association along lines comparable with those that controlled the last organization."[52]

Fringe groups like the Personnel Research Federation and Cooke's Taylor Society functioned as repositories for the more liberal tendencies in personnel management throughout the 1920s.[53] But what Cooke, Fisher, and other liberals failed to realize in the early years of the decade was that the spirit of accommodation and restraint that had previously informed the personnel management movement was irretrievably lost. The conservative model would dominate personnel management for the rest of the decade.

A year after the NPA's founding, its directors decided to substitute the word "Management" for "Personnel" in the organization's name. This change epitomized the effort to promote a more decentralized form of employment management. According to the *American Management Review's* first editorial, the new name was intended to "emphasize the final responsibility of the line organization in the personnel job"; that is, to emphasize that the personnel department was subsidiary to production executives and line officials. The word "personnel" was dropped, said the editorial, because "in many quarters it is regarded as highbrow." The American Management Association's first meeting at the Bankers' Club in New York in March 1923 resulted in a declaration explaining how the AMA conceived of the new relationship between staff and line:

> The responsibility for *doing* in business rests upon the line organization. Its individuals are in the closest contact with persons or the human agencies of commerce and industry. Therefore the line organization must deal directly and at first hand with personnel work.[54]

The personnel manager's task was merely to "study human management problems and recommend solutions for them." He supplied the "tools" that others used in carrying out "the general policy of adequate attention to the human side of management." Production managers and the foreman, who was called "a teacher and a diplomat," were to have complete autonomy in the daily management of employees.[55]

Throughout the 1920s the AMA was the leading exponent of the SCC's conservative, decentralized model of personnel management. (The SCC considered the AMA to be "the organization best qualified to give nationwide impetus to sound industrial relations policies.") Through such publicists as Edward S. Cowdrick, W.J. Donald, Sam Lewisohn, and Arthur H. Young, the AMA pushed the idea that the foreman was again to be the center of the employment relationship. He was to have more say in selection and dismissal; labor allocation and discipline were his prerogatives. Personnel management was supposed to serve an advisory function, "like a research chemist," said Donald. The personnel manager should never intrude into the foreman's realm except in an advisory capacity. "Instead of building castles in the air about independent industrial relations departments owing allegiance to nobody," wrote Lewisohn, "let personnel men realize that theirs is a staff function. They will be most valuable when they get others to put into effect their ideas."[56]

This decentralization gave the foreman considerably more discretion and authority than he had had under the wartime model of personnel management. As a Conference Board study noted in 1930, "many progressive companies [today] thrust on the foreman as much responsibility as he can carry and . . . return to him in large measure those managerial functions held by the small-shop foreman of a half century ago." Personnel departments in these companies often did little more than administer benefit and employee representation plans. To reflect this change, the name "Industrial Relations" Department was discarded in favor of "Personnel Service," "Labor Service," or simply "Service" Department.[57]

Decentralization also slowed the pace of employment reform, making it more difficult to control foremen, set up internal promotion plans, and provide for employment security. For these reasons, liberals like Mary B. Gilson castigated the AMA, saying that it was "responsible for turning the clock back a considerable distance in regard to the development of centralization in the selection and training of workers as well as in safeguarding discharges, because of their blind zeal in defending what they called the foreman's 'rights.'"[58]

Others criticized the AMA for compromising the professional standards of the pre-1921 employment management associations. Morris L. Cooke said the AMA was "essentially a mutual aid organization and not a professional society" and attacked its policy of holding meetings open to members only. In addition, Cooke opposed the AMA's periodic attempts in the late 1920s to merge with the Taylor Society, on the grounds that the AMA lacked professionalism and was "essentially anti-labor union."[59]

Despite these criticisms, the personnel strategy promoted by the SCC and the AMA had some features that were intended to curb the worst abuses of the drive system. One such feature was foremen's training, designed to make foremen more effective and enlightened managers. By 1928, there were reported to be over 900 foreman training courses in the United States. The courses taught the foreman how to use human relations techniques to make himself "both big brother and boss to his people."[60] Foremen were told that they were a "door of communication" and that they had to be "mentally capable of representing management to the men and men to the management." They were instructed on how to give orders and when it was appropriate to give "snappy answers" to a worker's question.[61] They also received training in technical matters related to production management. The mix of technical and personnel topics varied, although by the end of the decade some critics charged that the programs gave too much emphasis to technical subjects at the expense of leadership training.[62]

The YMCA was heavily involved in both foremen's training and in foremen's clubs during the 1920s. This involvement reflected its traditional emphasis on the aristocracy of the working class as well as the influence within the YMCA of the SCC-AMA approach. The foreman training courses, organized by local Y secretaries, sought to develop "teamwork," "cooperation," and "a new social order in industry," and to inculcate spiritual values, especially those that emphasized a unity of interest in industry. The owner of a hat company told a 1924 Silver Bay session on foremanship that the YMCA's programs created "a spirit of friendliness in which recognition of worth finds expression with all working for the family."[63] The foremen's clubs, part of the YMCA's efforts to develop Christian leaders of men, sponsored a mix of technical, inspirational, and popular programs designed to give foremen "a broadened knowledge and viewpoint," and to "provide an opportunity for exchange of ideas." Foremen who belonged to the clubs were encouraged to participate in community betterment activities and to attend the YMCA's foreman training classes held at Silver Bay. Some of the foremen's clubs in Ohio broke away from the YMCA in 1925 to form their own organization, the National Association of Foremen (NAF). Both YMCA and NAF clubs were carefully controlled by top management and were usually headed by a local personnel manager or plant superintendent.[64]

A second potential source of restraint on the foreman was the company union, or employee representation plan. Most such plans had been hastily introduced between 1918 and 1920 to counter the union threat and then eliminated as the threat receded after 1921, leaving a core of about 400 companies—most of them very large—that had representation plans in 1928.[65] Even many of these plans atrophied in the late 1920s. In those few firms where company unions remained active, the personnel department usually exerted careful control over them, making sure they did not fade out for lack of worker interest. As the SCC noted in its 1929 report:

> No representation plan is good enough to run itself . . . The plans which have had the highest measure of success are those in which responsible executives have taken active and continuing interest and to which they have furnished enlightened guidance. Employee rep-

resentation, in fact, furnishes an effective means through which management can exercise its normal function of leadership over the working force.[66]

The well-known shortcomings of employee representation were attributable to management's fear of giving the company union too much independence. The workers who represented their fellow employees were often very conservative men, in part because eligibility to vote in company union elections was based on seniority and citizenship. But just to be sure, companies rarely allowed representatives to meet on their own and imposed restrictions on the topics that could be discussed at meetings between the representatives and management. As a result, important issues were generally ignored. Instead, company unions concerned themselves with such trivial or uncontroversial matters as plant safety and sanitation, details of welfare plans, and the purchase of candy for Christmas parties.[67]

Most employee representation plans included a grievance procedure that was supposed to offer aggrieved workers a means of protesting when their supervisors violated company rules or treated them unfairly. But in only a few exceptional companies were employee representatives aggressive and top managers willing to overrule supervisors when a grievance was deemed legitimate. More often, reality failed to correspond to theory—not surprising, in light of the new emphasis on the foreman's independence—and the grievance system was fraught with problems both in design and in operation.[68] For one thing, representatives were often unwilling to press the grievances of their fellow employees. For another, some companies required that workers initially take their grievances up with their foreman, a practice that made them reluctant to voice any complaints, even though the foreman's decision could be appealed to a higher level. Moreover, higher levels of the grievance procedure were internal to management, terminating with the president of the company or some other top official. (Outside arbitration was almost never used, although some plans provided for it.) Managements were unwilling to overrule their foremen, many of whom were hostile to the representation plan. To placate them, some companies went so far as to promise line managers that no provision in the representation plan would be allowed to encroach on their powers. Given all these flaws in the grievance system, the foreman was rarely challenged. Even at liberal Jersey Standard, fewer than 2 percent of the matters discussed in joint conferences between 1919 and 1926 involved actions by foremen, such as promotions or discharges.[69]

Thus, the restraints on the foreman included in the AMA-SCC model were often ineffectual in practice. However well-intentioned the training courses, they could not make the foreman change his behavior. Grievance procedures were faulty. Personnel departments lacked authority to monitor the enforcement of rules intended to ensure fair treatment on the job. Moreover, the decentralized model meant that fewer rules were laid down for foremen to follow. As one study found in 1927: "Where there were any statements of policy at all, their nature was often general warnings against the unwisdom of 'firing men in anger,' statements of the need for 'patience in breaking-in new men' or for foremen to be 'decent' in their treatment of workers."[70]

Yet in the conservative 1920s, the AMA seemed relatively progressive with its call for "adequate recognition to the most important factor—the human factor."[71] The companies in the AMA-SCC group constituted a progressive minority compared with other firms. For the roughly 10 percent of the industrial work force employed by them (table 6.6), they were comparatively attractive places to work, as contemporary observers like Slichter and Leiserson were quick to point out.[72] But elsewhere, personnel departments and programs were either moribund or nonexistent, a fact often overlooked.

Table 6.6. Personnel Management, 1928–1929

	Proportion of Firms (employing over 250 workers)	Estimated Proportion of Industrial Labor Force (all firms)
Personnel department	34%	20%
"New" welfare work	15–25	10–15
Employee representation	9–19	5–10
Foremen's training programs	9–19	5–10

SOURCES: NICB, *Industrial Relations in Small Plants*, pp. 3, 16, 20; NICB, *Collective Bargaining Through Employee Representation* (New York, 1933), p. 16; BLS, *Handbook of Labor Statistics*, Bulletin No. 1865 (Washington, D.C., 1975), p. 105; NICB, *Industrial Relations: Administration of Policies and Programs* (New York, 1931), pp. 43, 70.

Outside the Progressive Minority

During the 1920s, some companies had personnel departments but little else: no foreman's training programs, no employee representation plans, and no other innovative personnel policies. These firms, which employed from 5 to 10 percent of the industrial labor force, let their personnel programs lapse after 1920. The only activities engaged in by their personnel departments were recruitment and selection. One study found that "many personnel departments are what one executive described as 'mere fronts.' The term is especially applicable where such departments are definitely ordered not to interfere with 'production' and where the personnel staff is given to understand that its function is not an integral part of the administration." At these firms, said economist Leo Wolman, "there was a reversion to older methods," even to a drive system. For example, in the automobile industry, the most common worker complaints during the 1920s were speed-ups, accidents, and foreman favoritism. After Ford Motor cut its work week in 1926, it began "pressing [employees] to do work better and faster."[73]

Another group, the vast majority, comprised companies that had no personnel department. Most of these firms were small or medium-sized, but some were large (table 6.5). Although there were fewer companies without personnel departments in 1929 than a decade earlier, the size of this group shrank more slowly than before. One researcher found that the hesitancy to install a personnel department was "usually based on a fear of robbing sub-executives [i.e., foremen] of important prerogatives. This hesitancy coincides with the loyalty always shown the supervisory force and with the lack of regard for the self-respect of workers." Autocratic methods and arbitrary practices persisted, encouraged to some extent by labor market conditions. In some companies, the researcher observed "the callousness so characteristic of many controlling executives. The general manager who paid lip service to the obligation for treating men 'decently,' but who felt there was nothing for a man to do when he had a grudge (to which the foreman would not listen) except to 'stick around for a while and finally quit,' is one example."[74] These attitudes were a throwback to what one employer said some twenty years earlier, "If a man is dissatisfied, it is his privilege to quit."[75] Much had changed during those two decades, but not at these companies.

The interests of many of the small and medium-sized firms in this group were represented by the National Association of Manufacturers, which continued to advocate the open shop and to oppose the progressive approach to labor relations. At the urging of a few of its more moderate members, the NAM created an Industrial Relations committee in 1923 to look into employee representation, personnel management, and the "new" welfare work. But the committee's proposals held no appeal for the majority of NAM's members and were ignored.[76] Although nearly one-half of the industrial labor force worked in small firms in 1929, only a tiny proportion of these firms had innovative personnel policies (table 6.7).

Large firms tended to be more advanced, but there were numerous exceptions; in 1929 only half of the firms employing over a thousand workers had a personnel department. For example, one California company which in 1927 employed 28,000 workers neither had nor believed in a personnel department. The company's foremen had full authority to hire, promote, and dismiss workers. There was no company policy on transfers and promotions, and no coordination between departments. A top manager explained: "The policy of management in this organization is that every foreman is a personnel executive and that all are co-workers so they need no personnel or 'Santa Claus' department

Table 6.7. Personnel Policies, by Plant Size, 1929

	Small (Under 250 employees)	Large (Over 250 employees)
Personnel department	2.5%	34%
Centralized discharge	4.4	24
Internal promotion and transfer system	4.0	24
Employee representation	2.5	9
Group pension plan	0.2	2
Mutual benefit association	4.5	30

SOURCE: NICB, *Industrial Relations Programs in Small Plants*, pp. 16, 20.

to hand out goodies to them."[77] Size was an important, but by no means the only, determinant of corporate employment policy.

Correlates of Personnel Policy

During its earlier phase of expansion, personnel management was not related in any obvious way to particular industrial characteristics such as technical sophistication or profitability. Most wartime industries had been buoyed by high demand and hefty cost-plus contracts. After 1920, however, some industries declined, while other, more dynamic, "new" industries emerged to take the lead. The decade's progressive minority of companies often came from such industries as electrical machinery, scientific instruments, chemicals, public utilities, and food products, whose high and stable profit levels assured them of sufficient funds to finance personnel programs. Companies outside the progressive minority were more likely to be from relatively low-profit industries such as machinery, steel, textiles, and meat packing.[78]

Profitability, which was related to technical sophistication, was not the only determining factor other than size. Companies in the progressive minority also tended to come from industries with relatively stable seasonal and cyclical product demand. Among the industries with the smallest swings in production and employment during the 1920s were public utilities, chemicals, department stores, and producers of consumer nondurables like soap, sugar, and dates. The assurance of a continuous derived demand for labor permitted firms to institute employment policies that were based on the presumption of a continuing employment relationship. Firms that were not on the technological cutting edge but were relatively stable, such as producers of consumer nondurables, were the decade's heaviest users of employment stabilization techniques and constituted the tiny group that guaranteed employment to their workers. Medium-sized, low-technology but stable firms like Columbia Conserve, Dennison Manufacturing, and Hills Brothers had more advanced personnel policies and offered their workers greater job security than firms that were larger and possessed more market power but either were less stable (e.g., auto producers), less profitable (e.g., textile mills), or both (e.g., steel mills).[79]

Finally, ownership patterns were important. One study found that companies with "pioneer" personnel programs tended to be privately owned or tightly controlled. One quarter of these companies had no important public shareholders, and another 25 percent were controlled by a minority block of owners. Under these conditions, such well-known liberal employers as Henry S. Dennison, Morris Leeds, Horace Cheney, and William P. Hapgood could exercise their preferences over those of more conservative managers and shareholders.[80]

IV. Personnel Management in Practice

The uneven development of personnel management led to divergent employment policies. The employment relationship was rendered more transitory and inequitable by some measures and less so by others. On the one hand, companies in the progressive minority gave their workers more security through seniority regulations and the "new" welfare work. On the other hand, foremen again were key figures in a variety of allocative decisions. As a 1930 Conference Board study noted: "In recent years the pendulum has swung back, and the tendency has been to restore to the foreman and other line officials actual administration of all matters directly affecting their subordinates."[81] Companies with personnel departments differed in the degree of autonomy they allowed their foremen. At U.S. Steel, the foreman was granted control over most aspects of employment and wage administration, while at relatively progressive firms like Westinghouse and General Electric, there were checks on the foreman's discretion. But even here, foremen continued to wield considerable power over work assignments, promotions, and dismissals. As one student of the electrical manufacturing industry put it, workers in the 1920s "lived in a halfway house between arbitrary rule and systematic policy."[82]

The foreman's return to power was clearly manifested in areas such as layoffs. The Conference Board found that, during the brief recession of 1927, most layoff decisions were made by foremen and other line managers; only one-third of the 169 large firms surveyed said that their personnel managers were involved in such decisions (table 6.8). Similarly, the proportion of firms that allowed the personnel department a say, either advisory or final, in discharge decisions fell from 36 percent in 1918 to 24 percent in 1929, despite the growth after 1918 in the number of personnel departments.[83] In short, the importance of the personnel department declined during the 1920s.

The decentralization of authority made it difficult to expand programs that required the foreman's cooperation, such as internal promotion systems. The proportion of firms with explicit promotion plans remained roughly constant throughout the decade (table 6.9). True, the lack of an explicit plan does not mean that no promotions occurred. For example, of the blacks hired as unskilled laborers by the steel industry during the war, 4 percent had risen to skilled positions by 1928. Nonetheless, promotion decisions tended to be haphazard and fraught with favoritism. Eighty-five percent of firms surveyed in 1929 reported that they used no formal system to rate workers for promotion but rather relied on "personal observations," which can be translated to mean that workers were promoted at the foreman's discretion. One semiskilled worker said that the personnel department at his firm was "a joke" and that workers got their promotions through "pull." As a result, most black workers did not fare as well as those in the steel industry. Only two out of some four thousand blacks at Ford's River Rouge

Table 6.8. Person Responsible for Layoffs in Large Firms, 1927

Personnel manager	4%
Personnel and line managers	31
Line managers	65

SOURCE: NICB, *Lay-Off and Its Prevention* (New York, 1930), p. 53.

Table 6.9. Proportion of Firms with Promotion Plans, 1918–1929

	1918	1924	1929
All firms	20%	26%	17%
Large firms	—	—	24

SOURCES: Roy W. Kelly, *Hiring the Worker* (Boston, 1918), p. 32; Paul F. Gemmill, "Methods of Promoting Industrial Employees," *Industrial Management* (April 1924), 67:240–241; W. D. Scott, R. C. Clothier, and W. R. Spriegel, *Personnel Management*, 6th ed. (New York, 1961), p. 584; NICB, *Industrial Relations in Small Plants*, p. 20. Note that these plans did not necessarily cover all or even most workers in an establishment.

plant were employed as skilled workers in 1929. Moreover, where promotion systems did exist, they often did not produce an internal labor market. Information on job openings was not disseminated on a plant-wide basis: fewer than 3 percent of firms surveyed in 1924 relied on vacancy lists to inform workers of job openings in other departments. Companies were reluctant to restrict themselves to hiring from within.[84]

Wage determination also remained the foreman's prerogative in most companies. At International Harvester's McCormick plant, 90 percent of all wage rates continued to be set by foremen, despite the existence of a job evaluation plan. Elsewhere, formal plans to standardize wages were still a rarity. During the 1920s, only a handful of companies introduced classification and evaluation techniques to rationalize their rate structures. In fact, industry moved in the opposite direction by converting a growing number of jobs to incentive pay. By 1928, 53 percent of all manufacturing workers were on piecework, and 39 percent on some kind of incentive pay.[85] Ironically, Morris L. Cooke, a former disciple of Frederick Taylor, was worried about the consequences of this development. In a letter written in 1928 to an AFL official, Cooke said: "The manufacturers of this country are pushing into this area with a rapidity which we hardly realize. Perhaps the labor movement may wake up before it is too late and move for the adoption of policies and practices which will allow it to retain some measure of control."[86]

Decentralized wage determination and the tendency to rely on incentive pay produced complex rate structures that were riddled with inequities. In consequence, skill differentials within industry widened. An International Labor Organization study of industrial relations found wider differentials in the United States than in other industrialized nations. The failure to continue the wartime experiments in wage standardization gave unions a potent organizing issue in later years.[87]

New Directions in Security

Companies in the progressive minority made some advances in three areas related to job security: recognition of seniority, the "new" welfare work, and employment stabilization. But the assumption on which these advances were based—that employment is to be an enduring relationship—was still not deeply rooted in management thinking. Consequently, whenever the goal of providing security conflicted with other corporate objectives, such as short-run profitability or allocative flexibility, it was the former which suffered.

Seniority. A greater adherence to the principle that seniority should be a factor in layoff decisions was evidence that large firms were willing to protect the job rights of their incumbent employees. In 1927, 40 percent of the large firms surveyed by the Conference Board reported that they made seniority a primary factor in determining layoffs (but not for all of their employees.) In contrast, during the severe recession of 1921–22, the Special Conference Committee had come out in favor of using merit as the primary criterion in layoff decisions.[88]

Yet the commitment to seniority remained weak. Sixty-one percent of the firms surveyed during the 1927 recession gave no preference to senior workers when rehiring; 14 percent went so far as to erase all accumulated seniority when a laid-off worker was rehired, no matter how short the layoff, a practice which adversely affected pension and other benefits tied to seniority. Even those firms where seniority was a primary factor in layoff decisions had highly restrictive rules as to where and when it applied. To make things easier for the employer, most seniority systems were departmental rather than plant-wide and carried no transfer rights. That is, if a department reduced operations, a worker could not move to another department in the plant and take the job of a less senior worker. Morover, at many firms, seniority became more important than efficiency or ability only after a worker had been with the company for more than five—and, in some cases, more than ten or twelve—years. That is, the use of seniority as the governing factor in layoffs was itself a seniority benefit.[89]

Welfare Benefits. Another area in which efforts were made to strengthen the bond between firms and their employees was the "new" welfare work, which included such quasi-pecuniary programs as profit-sharing and stock ownership plans, group insurance, pensions, and paid vacations. Some firms had introduced these programs piecemeal before and during the war. But as the new welfare work became more popular during the 1920s, they were implemented *en bloc*. Personnel departments busied themselves administering these programs, which did not depend on the foreman's cooperation for their expansion or success.

Most of the programs had an eligibility rule known as the "continuous service" provision: A worker had to be continuously employed for a certain period before he was eligible to receive benefits. Because of this linkage between benefits and tenure, the programs were advertised during the war as a way to reduce labor turnover. But due to high entry costs and restrictive eligibility rules, they often failed to reach those groups with the highest turnover rates, particularly young and unskilled workers. For example, most of those participating in employee stock ownership plans were managerial employees (despite claims that the plans promoted "people's capitalism"). Similarily, at U.S. Steel, unskilled and semiskilled workers accounted for over 75 percent of the firm's employees but for only 20 percent of those receiving pension benefits. By the 1920s, most managers were prepared to admit that the programs had little effect on turnover.[90] As Arthur H. Young noted in 1925: "The employee is exceedingly rare who thinks of his pension until he has been with the company many years and reached an advanced age. You know as well as I do that turnover among long service employees is quite small."[91]

Although the programs did not reduce turnover, employers believed that they reduced the likelihood of labor disturbances and promoted "loyalty" and "cooperation." Because of the continuous-service provision, a worker with a break in his service record—such as might be caused by a suspension, by participation in a strike, or by other forms of "disloyal" behavior—could not receive welfare benefits. Thus, the worker paid dearly for any union activity. The practice of tying benefits to an unbroken service record was aimed at skilled workers, the group most likely both to belong to unions and to qualify for welfare benefits. The strategy sometimes worked. For example, in 1919 the Studebaker Company introduced a program consisting of pension, paid vacation, and stock ownership plans. When a strike occurred in Detroit in 1920, the firm's skilled body painters and trimmers refused to participate for fear they would lose their new benefits.[92] An economics professor at Northwestern noted that the new welfare work was "likely to arouse the suspicion of the employees that the employer is endeavoring to shackle them. They are likely to feel that he simply wishes to protect himself against any possibility of group action on their part."[93]

Unlike the "old" welfare work, these programs used financial incentives to promote desired behavior and so avoided the charge of paternalism. To discourage employees from purchasing leisure-intensive products like automobiles, pension and savings plans were sometimes tied to home building programs. Employers believed that, by teaching workers lessons about deferred gratification and the economic importance of capital, stock purchase and profit-sharing plans would "counteract radical tendencies." The older, more paternalistic programs did not disappear during the 1920s, but they were scaled back. Between 1925 and 1930, the welfare activities most commonly eliminated were eating facilities, employee magazines, social organizations, athletics, and company picnics.[94]

The new welfare work had other objectives as well. Employee stock ownership supplanted profit-sharing during the 1920s because it helped a firm to raise capital without diluting management control. More important, influential management groups like the SCC continued to stess that, if workers were forced to seek security from their employers rather than through political activity, the danger of America's becoming a welfare state would diminish. Arthur H. Young told a management conference in 1927 that the new welfare work was the result of "a sense of social responsibility rather than business urgency" and that because of it, "employees are shut off from whatever advantages might come to them through widespread social legislation."[95]

But one should not make too much of these programs.[96] The new welfare work did little to relieve popular pressure for social legislation because it affected so few workers. During the 1920s, benefit programs were rarely found outside of the progressive minority and covered no more than every seventh industrial worker in 1929 (see table 6.10).[97] Moreover, because of stringent eligibility provisions, the number of workers who actually received benefits under these programs was far smaller. International Harvester's paid vacation plan was so restrictive that not a single production worker at the firm's plant in Fort Wayne in the early 1930s qualified

Table 6.10. The New Welfare Work, 1929

Program	Proportion of Large Firms with Program
Profit-sharing	5%
Employee stock ownership	17
Health and accident insurance	15
Group pension plan	2
Mutual benefit association	30
Paid vacation for wage earners	25

SOURCE: NICB, *Industrial Relations Programs in Small Plants*, p. 16.

Table 6.11. Employer Expenditures on Welfare Programs as a Proportion of Total Annual Payroll, 1918–1929

1918	1924	1927	1929
2.0	1.5	1.0	2.0

SOURCES: A. L. Whitney, "Administration and Costs of Industrial Betterment for Employees," *Monthly Labor Review* (March 1918), 6:199; AMA, *Cost Finding for Personnel Activities* (New York, 1924), p. 6; Robert W. Dunn, *The Americanization of Labor* (New York, 1927), p. 197; NICB, *Industrial Relations Programs in Small Plants*, p. 40.

for it. Pension plan eligibility rules were especially strict. One expert estimated that no more than 5–10 percent of the workers at companies with a pension plan would ever qualify. As a result, in 1930 fewer than 2 percent of all retired workers received an industrial pension.[98]

Finally, welfare benefits were meager. Mutual benefit associations, which protected against accidents and illness, had benefit rates ranging from five to six dollars per week, paid out for a limited number of weeks. Group life insurance, which was enthusiastically marketed by the insurance companies during the 1920s, paid such small amounts to beneficiaries that even the Conference Board said that they were "inadequate for the support of a family, or even of an individual for a considerable period." Most pensions were so small that some workers refused to retire.[99] Companies apparently paid for the new welfare work by disbanding older programs rather than spending additional money; welfare expenditures as a proportion of company payrolls remained constant (and low) between 1918 and 1929 (table 6.11). In conclusion, despite the high-minded rhetoric that accompanied it, few companies spent enough on the new welfare work for it to have had a widespread effect on worker loyalty or economic security.

Employment Stabilization. During the depression of 1920–22, employment stabilization was promoted by the same groups that had previously pressed for it. The American Association for Labor Legislation called for employment stabilization in its "Practical Program to Prevent Unemployment." Stabilization was strongly endorsed in a report on President Harding's 1921 Conference on Unemployment, chaired by Commerce Secretary Hoover; much of the report was written by members of the Taylor Society. They were also largely responsible for another influential study, *Waste in Industry* (1921), which was published under the auspices of the Federated American Engineering Societies, and which tied unemployment to poor management practices and urged employers to adopt stabilization techniques.[100]

After the depression, stabilization became popular with other relatively liberal management groups like the American Management Association, which saw it as an alternative to a political solution of the unemployment problem. The AMA's publications carried numerous articles on stabilization. In 1925, Sam Lewisohn and Ernest G. Draper, founders and guiding lights of the AMA, wrote a book on the topic in collaboration with two Wisconsin economists, John R. Commons and Don D. Lescohier—*Can Business Prevent Unemployment?*[101]

These publications emphasized reducing seasonal fluctuations in demand through such techniques as product and market diversification, advertising, and sales planning. Cyclical unemployment received less attention, although various methods for reducing the impact of the business cycle were discussed, including training for transfers, demand forecasts, and production for inventory. Techniques for sales and production planning became more sohpisticated and popular during the 1920s, with organizations like Babson's Statistics Organization providing economic forecasts to hundreds of clients.[102]

The names of the few dozen companies that were successful at stabilization appeared and reappeared in literature on the subject: Columbia Conserve, Dennison Manufacturing, Dutchess Bleacheries, Eastman Kodak, Hills Brothers, Leeds and Northrup, Procter and Gamble, and the Walworth Company. All had taken steps to insulate themselves and their employees from fluctuation in seasonal—and, in a few cases, cyclical—demand. All were also leaders in the use of personnel management practices. They shared certain other features. Most produced consumer nondurables, goods for which demand was stable and predictable across seasons and cycles. Often these were standardized products like soap and canned goods that could be produced for inventory without risk of technological or stylistic obsolescence. Packard Motor, well known for its stabilization program, was the only major automobile producer in the 1920s that refused to adopt the new marketing strategy of annual model changes. Others made precision products that required a large input of highly skilled workers, who were relatively costly to recruit and replace.[103]

As a result of stabilization, several of these firms were able to offer their workers unemployment insurance, usually in the form of a guarantee of a minimum number of weeks of employment or pay per year. The plan introduced at Procter and Gamble in 1923 was typical: It guaranteed at least forty-eight weeks of work or pay to all workers who had more than six months' tenure and who participated in the firm's stock purchase plan. Other companies—such as Leeds & Northrup, Dennison, and S. C. Johnson—provided unemployment insurance in the form of reserves to be paid out to eligible workers who became unemployed through no fault of their own.[104]

Representing a major change from the insecurity and uncertainty of industrial employment, stabilization and unemployment insurance were said to be "the most powerful weapon against the agitator that can be imagined." John R. Commons thought that stabilization demonstrated how "Capitalism can cure itself, for it is not the blind force that socialists supposed; and not the helpless plaything of supply and demand, but it is Management."[105]

Yet employment stabilization and unemployment insurance remained uncommon during the 1920s. Surveying personnel practices in 1929, Henry Bruere wrote that "stability is in many lines of industry the exception rather than the normal state of employment." Fifteen employment or wage guarantee plans were in operation in 1920; by 1929 their number had increased, but only to 35. Unemployment reserve plans were equally rare; there were about a dozen such plans in 1929.[106] Thus, little stabilization had been achieved by the end of the decade. Smoothing out production cycles simply was not feasible in many industries. Most producers of durable goods were subject to large swings in seasonal and cyclical demand. Style changes and storage costs made production for stock unprofitable in these industries.

In addition, certain factors peculiar to the 1920s created barriers to stabilization. The 1921 deflation, when wholesale prices fell by almost 40 percent, caught many distributors with excess stock on hand; they were anxious to avoid a repeat of this situation. After 1921, as prices stabilized or declined, many distributors engaged in widespread hand-to-mouth buying, leaving manufacturers with two options: either to produce at a relatively even rate and accumulate off-season stocks, or to have on hand sufficient surplus equipment to permit producing on a seasonal peak basis.[107]

They chose the latter course, for several reasons. First, with prices declining, the cost of accumulating stocks appeared to be relatively greater than the cost of idle equipment. Second, the decade's high investment levels had led to excess capacity in various industries. According to one measure, industrial capacity utilization rates fell below 90 percent in seven of the nine years after 1920. With surplus capital already available, manufacturers were inclined to produce at uneven rates. Finally, high rates of labor-displacing technological change created a labor surplus that was available for hire when production rose to peak rates. An Australian visiting the United States in 1928 observed: "Because of the ease with which labour can be obtained and discarded, there is little necessity for the employer to stabilize his rates of production over the year."[108]

As a result of this choice, production and employment became more seasonally unstable during the latter half of the 1920s, especially in durable and semi-durable manufacturing industries, including automobiles, steel, and furniture (see table 6.12). This increase in seasonal instability may also have contributed to heightened cyclical sensitivity. The small size of inventories meant that any cyclical reduction in demand would immediately be translated into a decline in production, rather than being buffered by stocks.

The worker would have found seasonal instability less of a problem if he had had some assurance of being rehired after a seasonal layoff. But the practice of systematically rehiring workers by their seniority was still unusual. When Ford Motor shut down to prepare for its annual model changes during the 1920s, it laid workers off strictly on the basis of their ability, although the layoff might be

Table 6.12. Changes in the Seasonality of Production and Employment,
1919–1930

Industry	Period	Measure	Average Deviation[a]	Range[b]
Automobiles	1919–24	Employment	3.8	15
	1925–30		4.1	18
Cotton goods	1919–24	Employment	1.6	—
	1925–30		2.0	—
Furniture	1919–24	Employment	1.6	—
	1925–30		3.1	—
Steel ingots	1920–25	Output	6.4	25
	1926–31		7.5	31

SOURCE: Simon Kuznets, *Seasonal Variations in Industry and Trade* (New York, 1933), pp. 210, 311, 399.
a. The average deviation of a seasonal index from 100.
b. The difference between the highest and lowest months in the index.

postponed "if [the foreman] happened to like you, or if you sucked around him and did him favors." When production started up again, there was no seniority in rehiring. A former worker was often rehired at the starting rate, even though he had been earning more before the layoff.[109] One auto worker recalled:

> The annual layoff during the model change was always a menace to the security of the workers. Along about June or July it started. The bosses would pick the men off a few at a time . . . In October and November we began to trickle back into the plants. Again the bosses had the full say as to who was rehired first. Years of service with the company meant nothing . . . generally speaking, the first laid-off worker had no assurance of any kind that he would be called back at any specific time.[110]

One expects that these workers would have received a compensating wage differential for their employment instability, as some construction workers did. In a world of perfect information and mobility, such compensating variations would hold. But in the real world, any such offset was of a weak and partial character. As Slichter observed in 1926, workers were "guided too much by daily or hourly earnings and too little by annual income." Differentials, he said, were "inadequate."[111]

Of course, there were some exceptions to the general rule of inadequate offsets. In 1921, the Ladies Garment Workers (ILGWU) was able to negotiate a guarantee from Cleveland's garment man-

ufacturers of forty weeks of work per year at two-thirds of minimum weekly wages. Elsewhere in the highly seasonal apparel industry, there were twenty-two joint unemployment insurance
plans, negotiated primarily by locals of the Clothing Workers
(ACWA). In 1928, these plans covered 60,000 workers, a number
roughly four to five times greater than the number covered by
private, nonunion plans. Through unions, workers were able to
force some sharing of the burden of instability. The seasonality of
employment in the men's clothing and rubber tire industries was
exactly the same between 1923 and 1931. Both industries were
highly unstable, and employers in both faced various economic
barriers to stabilization. But because of unions, a clothing worker
was more likely to be compensated for seasonal income losses than
was his counterpart in the nonunion tire industry.[112]

Thus, the 1920s were qualitatively different from the period that
preceded them. Change now occurred more slowly, or not at all.
As a result, in most manufacturing firms in 1929, even those that
had personnel departments, employment continued to be somewhat transitory. Layoffs came without notice, seniority was often
ignored, dismissals were unregulated, and rehires were haphazard,
if they occurred at all. Although companies in the progressive
minority were more likely to provide stability and security to their
workers, this was done only within very narrow limits.

There is no doubt, however, that the progressive minority pursued a different path during the 1920s than other manufacturing
firms. By tying the worker more closely to his employer, these
companies had begun to realize some of the incentive effects of an
internal labor market. Policies such as seniority rules, internal
promotion, and the new welfare work encouraged workers to
remain with the firm and be loyal to it. As observers like Sumner
Slichter realized, these policies—by improving morale at the same
time as they raised the cost of dismissal—could stabilize effort
norms and enhance the employer's control in a gently coercive
fashion.

Given their potential, it is surprising that these policies were
pursued by so few employers; even companies in the progressive
minority adopted them in a halfhearted and contradictory fashion.
Part of the explanation for this reticence lies in factors external to

the firm. As we have seen, the weak labor market and the decline of manufacturing unionism sharply reduced the pressure to adopt new policies. But change was also inhibited by management's own reluctance to make labor a fixed factor, or to do anything that might interfere with the foreman's prerogatives. It was cheaper and less disruptive to control worker effort by a combination of close supervision, traditional allocative practices, and a plethora of wage incentive plans. The upshot is that the quasi-permanent employment relationship with which we are familiar was largely a post-1929 development.

CHAPTER 7

THE RESPONSE TO DEPRESSION

I. Old Wine, New Bottles, 1929–1931

The eighteen months following the stock market crash of October 1929 marked a period both painfully similar to and radically different from previous depressions in the United States. As before, neither government nor industry had a clear picture of the severity of the situation. Adequate unemployment statistics were unavailable, and no one knew exactly how many workers were unemployed. Trying to reassure the public, President Hoover manipulated the employment statistics for January 1930 to show an upturn that had never occurred. But this pronouncement was challenged by Frances Perkins, Mary Van Kleeck, and others; and later in the year the government was forced to ask the Metropolitan Life Insurance Company to conduct a national survey of unemployment.[1]

The American worker was no better prepared for job loss in 1930 than he had been in 1921. In Philadelphia, 60 percent of the unemployed had no savings at all; the rest had only enough to last them, on average, six weeks. Most of the available relief came from private sources, and by late 1930 many of these charitable funds were exhausted. Local governments struggled with varying degrees of success to fill the gap, but most municipal relief programs were bankrupt by the fall of 1931.[2]

As in the depressions of 1914–1915 and 1920–1922, it was initially hoped that unemployment could be controlled if industry adopted employment stabilization measures, including the by-now traditional techniques of inventory production, maintenance and repair work, production planning, diversification, and sales research. Even though stabilization had been accepted by only a handful of firms during the 1920s, and even though it had not proved capable of alleviating cyclical unemployment, the concept nevertheless aroused widespread enthusiasm and attracted an impressive array of support. Advocates included long-time adherents from the Taylor Society and the American Association for Labor Legislation (AALL), as well as new converts from organized labor.

In January 1930, at the instigation of his Commissioner of Labor, Frances Perkins, Governor Roosevelt of New York appointed a Commission on Reducing Unemployment Through Stabilizing Industry. Henry Bruere, an old friend of Perkins, chaired the commission, which also included John Sullivan of the State Federation of Labor and Ernest G. Draper, who was influential in liberal management circles and ran a firm that was famous for having successfully stabilized employment during the 1920s.[3]

The commission held hearings throughout the state to determine what industry was doing to reduce unemployment. Questionnaires were sent to hundreds of firms asking them if and how they were regularizing employment. The commission's report of November 1930 approvingly cited numerous firms that were using employment stabilization techniques (many of them from the same group that had been touted as exemplars of stabilization during the 1920s) and recommended that others be encouraged to emulate them. It cautioned that stabilization would solve only seasonal unemployment problems, noting—rather gingerly—that public unemployment insurance might be a necessity. But it failed to emphasize sufficiently that stabilization would be of limited benefit, at best, in reducing joblessness in New York.[4] As a result, the report was considered to be an endorsement of the technique as a way to eradicate all forms of unemployment.[5]

The influence of the New York commission was felt throughout the nation. During the fall of 1930, local stabilization committees were formed in Baltimore, Cincinnati, Indianapolis, Rochester, Detroit, and Philadelphia. These groups encouraged employment stabilization as well as work-sharing and coordinated relief efforts. At its November convention, the AFL urged other states to follow New York and establish stabilization commissions. The President's Emergency Committee for Employment, launched by Hoover in the fall of 1930, vigorously supported employment stabilization and asked the Taylor Society for information on how the technique could be used to fight unemployment.[6]

In fact, nearly every major management organization flirted with the idea during the winter of 1930–31. The Personnel Research Federation and the U.S. Chamber of Commerce held conferences on stabilization, and it was discussed at meetings of the American Management Association (AMA) and the National Metal Trades Association. A group of liberal employers, including Henry S. Dennison, Morris Leeds, and A. Lincoln Filene, funded studies of stabilization at two universities and financed the publication of a book, *Reducing Seasonal Employment* (1931).[7]

Despite the great interest and the mountains of material generated by the concept of stabilization, the practice did not spread very far beyond the firms that had experimented with it during the 1920s. General Electric tried to incorporate stabilization techniques into its unemployment insurance plan of 1930, as did the firms participating in the Rochester plan of 1931.[8] But few other examples can be found. Advocates could cite the names of no more than two hundred firms that made intensive efforts to stabilize employment, and most of these were predepression plans touching only a tiny portion of the labor force. A 1930 survey of New England employers found that only 5 percent rotated their work force or manufactured for stock.[9] One economist, estimating that stabilization plans affected less than 1 percent of the labor force in 1932, commented: "the cold facts of experience are that, despite the many years' talk of stabilization, these programs have so far made insignificant progress."[10] Evidence from the automobile industry, as well as from my own calculations for the manufacturing sector, show that employment was *more* seasonally unstable from 1930 to 1933 than it had been during the 1920s.[11]

Employment stabilization was popular with politicians, managers, and trade unionists because it promised to alleviate the unemployment crisis without resort to extensive government regulation and spending. But employers seldom adopted its techniques, finding it cheaper and easier to shift the burden of seasonal instability onto their employees. Paul H. Douglas, a student and proponent of employment stabilization, admitted in 1930 that the only effective way to deter seasonal instability was through an

unemployment insurance law that would penalize irregular
employers.[12]

Further, the supporters of stabilization misgauged the severity
of the depression. By the fall of 1931, when unemployment was
reaching catastrophic levels, few people could continue to believe
that a reduction in seasonal unemployment would significantly
affect the total volume of joblessness, or create new jobs. Glenn A.
Bowers warned managers in 1931 that employment stabilization
was "not the mystic gate through which industry might pass to rid
itself of the doldrums."[13]

As during the depression of 1920–1922, considerable attention
was also given to private unemployment insurance plans, which
took the form either of an annual wage or employment guarantee,
or of a reserve fund that paid out benefits to a firm's unemployed
workers. Only those companies from seasonally stable industries
offered such plans; these same companies were also likely to have
taken steps to further stabilize employment. Because this was a
private and voluntary approach to unemployment, the plans were
promoted by the same individuals and groups that urged stabilization in 1930–31, ranging from the Taylor Society to the U.S.
Chamber of Commerce, the Conference Board, and the National
Association of Manufacturers. The Taylorists viewed private unemployment insurance as "good management practice"; other
management groups simply hoped that it would stave off demands
for the government to provide jobless benefits.[14]

Except for the ones achieved through collective bargaining, these
plans gave coverage to relatively few workers, and their mortality
rate was high. Only a few new plans were introduced during the
first years of the depression, the best known being General Electric's
and that of fourteen firms in Rochester, New York.[15]

Despite the publicity it received, private insurance could not
begin to cope with the massive unemployment produced by the
depression. Of the nineteen plans initiated by 1933, seven were
discontinued, and another seven either reduced their benefit
amounts or shortened the length of time during which workers
could receive benefits. Such well-known providers as Dennison
Manufacturing and Leeds & Northrup were forced to suspend
payments in 1932. Several of the firms participating in the Roch-

ester plan were unable to pay any benefits, and even General Electric, one of the nation's largest and most profitable firms, was forced in 1932 to cut its benefit amounts. A Princeton economist estimated that no more than 32,000 workers were covered by company plans in mid-1933.[16]

It is easy to understand why many plans did not survive past 1932. But it is less clear why so few employers were willing to experiment, especially during 1929-1930, when attention was focused on the issue and unemployment had not yet risen to overwhelming levels. Perhaps employers realized that a private plan could not remain solvent for very long. Another explanation, offered by J. Douglas Brown in 1933, was that employers lacked "a sense of obligation . . . and recognition of future needs."[17] That is, they still viewed employment as a transitory relation, to be maintained only during good times. Moreover, those who did practice labor retention preferred to have the cost borne by their employees, as under work-sharing schemes.

There was also considerable interest in dismissal compensation during the first two years of the depression, and a small number of firms adopted new plans. In 1932, the Bureau of Labor Statistics found that 8 percent of a group of industrial firms offered dismissal compensation. Liberal groups like the Taylor Society and New York's stabilization commission backed dismissal compensation. Management publicists made much of the few plans that were in operation.[18]

But a careful examination of these plans shows that almost none gave severance pay to blue-collar workers. Instead they were limited to salaried white-collar employees. At Bethlehem Steel, for example, dismissal compensation was intended only for salaried employees, although a few "meritorious" wage earners could receive it.[19] Goodyear was an exception, but it gave severance pay only "to the employee we are trying to get rid of, either because of inefficiency or old age."[20] If one views dismissal compensation as a form of liquidated job rights, very few blue-collar workers had those rights before 1933. As one personnel manager said in 1931, dismissal compensation was "a nice idea, but there's no justification for it."[21]

Thus, the initial response to the depression resembled previous experience in several ways. But the depression also brought some significant departures from past practice. Employers, especially larger firms, made greater efforts to provide relief and to maintain wage rates than they ever had before, although these efforts were by no means universal or long-lasting.

Work-Sharing

One such notable change was work-sharing, which had been tried as an alternative to layoffs in previous depressions (chiefly in unionized establishments) but which was not widely implemented until after 1929. In order to reduce the number of layoffs, firms either shortened daily or weekly work hours or rotated shifts, thus maximizing the number of employed workers but reducing average earnings.

It is difficult to estimate exactly how widespread the practice was. Data from a government survey show that, whereas 15 percent of establishments had part-time employment in September 1929, the proportion had climbed to 42 percent by January 1931. Average weekly hours in manufacturing dropped from 44 in 1929 to 38 in 1933. Of course, some establishments laid workers off and then cut the hours of remaining force without attempting any work-sharing, although they may have called it such. And many, if not most, of the firms that practiced work-sharing introduced it at the same time as they laid off inessential workers. At Bethlehem Steel, available work was shared only among "efficient and loyal workers"; the rest were laid off.[22] One should bear this in mind when noting that studies conducted in 1933 which specifically asked whether companies practiced work-sharing drew an affirmative response of 76–83 percent.[23]

Work-sharing received mixed reviews from organized labor. Unions that had traditionally relied on it, such as the printing and needle trades, were its strongest supporters. Some AFL leaders backed it in the belief that it might lead to a permanent reduction in the work week when prosperity returned. But other unions denounced it as an expedient device that amounted to no more than a "sharing of the misery."[24]

The Hoover administration and employer groups vigorously promoted work-sharing. The President's Emergency Committee on Employment (PECE) declared in 1930 that "distribution of work was recognized as the most practical step that can be taken [to reduce unemployment]." The President's Organization on Unemployment Relief, successor to the PECE, in 1931 said: "It is the duty of workers and employers to assist those who are out of work by agreeing to an adjustment of working time so that work . . . may be more widely and equitably distributed among a larger number."[25] In August 1932, President Hoover helped to launch a national Share-the-Work Movement, headed by Walter Teagle of Standard Oil of New Jersey. The movement received enthusiastic support from groups like the Special Conference Committee and the U.S. Chamber of Commerce. Regional work-sharing organizations, spearheaded by employers, soon appeared on the West Coast and in New England.[26]

The administration and private groups argued that sharing work would increase purchasing power since many workers were earning more than they needed. Moreover, the alternative to work-sharing was relief, and proponents claimed that industry could provide this more effectively than could the government or charitable organizations. The first argument is dubious in that many employed workers already lived close to the margin. The second argument points more closely to the true raison d'etre of the movement, as can be seen from the experience of the giant firms that made up the Special Conference Committee (SCC).[27]

The SCC was deeply worried in 1931 that "radical legislation," such as the unemployment insurance bill then being considered in Wisconsin, might soon be enacted unless industry took decisive steps to reduce unemployment. At the time, nearly all the firms belonging to the SCC were on short hours, which they termed work-sharing.[28] J. M. Larkin, director of industrial relations for Bethlehem Steel and an SCC member, pointed out that work-sharing was supported by his company because "each employee has demonstrated to him that his job is his greatest hold on economic security. Even though . . . the number of working days has afforded barely a subsistence wage, yet I wish to emphasize that it has represented far more in total dollars than would obtain under any form of employment insurance."[29] That is, employers hoped that work-sharing would ease demands for unemployment insurance and other public measures which were ideologically repugnant and which could prove costly. A virtue of work-sharing was that the relief burden was shouldered entirely by employed workers.

A desire to avoid costly state intervention was not the only reason why employers supported the work-sharing movement. Some embraced it as a panacea that could end the depression, just as some had viewed the employment stabilization movement that preceded it.[30] Others, which had to cut their hours—either because of reduced demand or because they were trying to avoid wage cuts—made a virtue of necessity by calling this work-sharing. Thus, not all the firms engaging in the practice were motivated by the SCC's political acumen. Moreover, few firms adopted work-sharing out of any unconditional commitment to their employees; they reserved the right to judge who was efficient, needy, or loyal enough to receive work.

During the fall of 1932, when the depression was at its worst, the AFL voted to seek congressional assistance in enacting the five-day week and the six-hour day. This action represented both a retreat from the AFL's traditional voluntarist philosophy and an attempt to force the administration and industry to prove their support for work-sharing. Shortly after the AFL convention, Senator Hugo Black introduced a bill in Congress that would have denied channels of interstate commerce to firms that were not on the thirty-hour week. Although a few employers supported the bill, most strongly opposed it. The steel industry argued that it was impractical; the National Association of Manufacturers (NAM) claimed that it was unconstitutional. The bill was never enacted, although regulation of working hours was to become a cornerstone of Roosevelt's recovery efforts.[31]

In another departure from past practice, private firms provided a variety of relief programs for their employees. Relief had been a rarity in 1921, but now—no doubt spurred by the gravity of the situation—industry acted more generously. Some companies, such as Inland Steel, established relief funds and matched worker contributions. Endicott-Johnson Shoe prepared hot meals for its unemployed workers. Bethlehem Steel, along with many other firms, provided gardens in which unemployed workers could grow vegetables. Usually the relief was offered only to current or former employees. However, the firms belonging to the SCC donated money to and worked together with community relief organizations.[32]

But even though these programs were relatively inexpensive and made for good public relations, relatively few firms offered them. According to a Conference Board survey, only one-third of a group of very large firms provided unemployment relief between 1930 and 1933.[33] One of the most egregious examples of corporate abdication of responsibility to its employees and the community was Ford Motor Company. At Ford in 1931, some workers were on short-time, and others had been laid off. Since neither group could make ends meet, they had to turn to Detroit's public relief agencies for assistance. The city paid out $800,000 to Ford workers each month yet received no taxes (or other funds) from the company, which lay just outside the city's limits. A local resident dubbed Detroit "Henry Ford's silent partner."[34]

In striking contrast to the situation in 1921, personnel departments were relatively immune to closures, at least initially. There were cutbacks (at 40 percent of firms surveyed by one study early in 1931), but this was a far cry from the wholesale elimination that had occurred a decade earlier. Although their claims may be somewhat exaggerated, knowledgeable observers like Whiting Williams and E. S. Cowdrick said they saw no evidence of any extensive junking of personnel departments in 1930 and 1931.[35] One might conclude from this that these departments had been fully accepted by their companies. But there are other, more compelling explanations. First, because many of these departments were no longer involved in line activities, they posed little threat to the autonomy of operating managers when decisions were made about how to conduct production and work force retrenchments. Second, some companies (often the same ones engaged in relief work) tried to maintain the welfare programs they had introduced during the 1920s, and their personnel departments usually had the responsibility for administering these activities.[36] Third, and most important, the depression's effects were felt only gradually in certain industries; the full force of disaster did not hit until the fall of 1931.

Wage Rigidity

The most dramatic and notable deviation from past depressions was the rigidity of hourly wage rates. In November 1929, shortly after the stock market crashed, President Hoover held a White House conference with major employers from key industries; he later met separately with union leaders. The President asked both groups to pledge that they would not initiate wage reductions, on the new theory that this would maintain purchasing power and contribute more to prosperity than a classical deflation. After the meeting, various business leaders made pronouncements opposing wage cuts as inimical "to the interests not only of wage earners, but also of business." But companies which tried to hold their wage rates steady were fighting a losing battle. They were forced to find other ways to pare their labor costs—by cutting workers, hours, or the effort wage—and each of these policies undercut consumer purchasing power and the logic of wage rate stabilization.[37]

For most of 1930 there seems to have been no reduction in the hourly wage rates of major industries. As working hours were reduced, however, average weekly earnings began to plummet.[38] Despite this drop in earnings, government and industry declared themselves pleased with the results of Hoover's wage maintenance policy. Even the AFL reported in September 1930 that employer attitudes had changed, and there was now "a widespread appreciation of the necessity of high wages to create purchasing power."[39]

But the average firm was able to forestall wage reductions for only about eleven months after the 1929 downturn. By the fall of 1930, evidence that smaller firms were cutting rates was trickling in. Thirteen out of nineteen central labor union councils reported wage cutting in their areas.[40] During early 1931, the mounting pressure of unemployment and losses had forced a number of prominent firms to cut wages. By the middle of 1931, the NAM, representing smaller firms, began to call openly for wage reductions. The building trade unions were reported to be secretly shading their rates.[41] On the whole, however, unionized workers were better able to postpone cuts than were the unorganized. Moreover, some large firms, especially those in less competitive industries, maintained their rates well into 1931. At Special Conference Committee meetings in 1931, members queried each other about their wage policies and their intentions with respect to rate cuts.[42]

The dam finally burst in the fall of 1931, when both the average number of workers receiving wage cuts and the average size of firms cutting rates rose sharply.[43] When U.S. Steel cut its rates in September 1931, the automobile, textile, and rubber tire industries quickly followed suit. Ford Motor, after making numerous promises not to cut rates, announced sweeping reductions of 20–40 percent in October 1931.[44]

Not all firms made across-the-board reductions. Rather, at the behest of top management, companies in the automobile, tire, and other industries made selective cuts, giving concessions to key groups (usually skilled workers) and seriously upsetting customary wage differentials. Though done to minimize the risk of labor disturbances, this move left less skilled workers feeling that wage cuts had been carried out inequitably, a charge that would return to haunt management in later years.[45]

President Green of the AFL urged workers to strike rather than submit to wage cuts. Sporadic strikes were mounted in 1931 and 1932. While representing an increase over the very low level of activity recorded in 1930, these strikes were still relatively limited—both in number and size—compared with figures for most pre-depression years. The labor movement was weak and demoralized. Powerful unions in the coal and apparel industries were in ruins by the end of 1932.[46] Writing in 1932, Louis Adamic found the AFL to be

> ineffectual, flabby, afflicted with the dull pains of moral and physical decline. The big industrialists and conservative politicians are no longer worried by it. Indeed, the intelligent ones see in it the best obstacle—temporary at least—to the emergence of a militant and formidable labor movement . . . The ten year decline of the whole organization, I think, has already gone too far to be rejuvenated by anybody.[47]

II. Broken Promises, 1931–1932

The wage-rate reductions of the fall and winter of 1931–32 symbolized more than the failure of Hoover's economic policies. They signalled that the depression had finally sapped the strength of industry's giants, which were now forced to speed up the pace of retrenchment, cutbacks, and layoffs.

In addition, the wage cuts represented the first of a string of broken promises. Large, liberal firms had promised not to cut rates, implying that they would take care of their workers through work-sharing, relief, and welfare. The violation of these implicit understandings had a levelling effect on industry. Those firms whose personnel policies had made them part of the progressive minority during the 1920s no longer looked quite so outstanding, especially to their employees, who in the future would be more inclined to go outside the firm in seeking economic security.

One such broken promise involved work-sharing. Firms that had assured work to their "loyal and efficient" employees were forced to step up layoffs after 1930 as average weekly earnings dipped below the subsistence level. Yet few companies, even those in the progressive minority, were well-prepared for layoffs. As late as 1935, only 21 percent of surveyed industrial firms reported that they had definite procedures for layoffs.[48] Consequently, as in the 1920s, foremen had considerable control over the discharge process (see table 7.2), a situation which resulted in numerous inequities. According to an article in the May 1936 issue of *Fortune* magazine, "steel workers are filled with stories of money lost to foremen after a better-than-usual pay, and never repaid or expected, of minor officials who have small business interests that the men patronize in the hope of getting more work."[49]

Even in firms with definite layoff procedures, foremen had considerable power. Because they were allowed to exercise discretion in weighing such factors as need and seniority, the worker never knew exactly what to expect. Moreover, only a minority of firms surveyed in 1932 (18 percent) reported that seniority was a factor in layoffs; over half of the surveyed group based layoffs strictly on the worker's "efficiency."[50] For instance, one Ford Motor official said in 1931, "ability is the rule."[51] Thus, foremen were left with considerable room to play favorites.

Because the foreman's power was still intact, the economic pressure of falling prices and profits led to a resurgence of the drive system in some industries and to its intensification in others. One of the most frequent complaints of a group of workers interviewed by an industrial psychologist in 1930 was "the nature of supervision."[52] Drive methods were endemic to certain industries, such as auto manufacturing. A Chrysler employee testified in 1933 that, during the previous two years, speed-ups had become "the worst weed in our wheat field." He said that the demand for "more and more production" from fewer and fewer men had turned the plant into "a race track." The situation was the same at General Motors, where workers who complained were told by their foreman, "If you can't keep up, we'll get a man that will."[53] The increase in speed made work especially difficult for older workers, and their problems were compounded by the practice of ignoring seniority in allocative decisions.

Some companies not only ignored seniority but even followed a policy of getting rid of older workers, partly because of a widespread belief that men over the age of forty or forty-five were inefficient and slow. The dismissal of older workers created a serious morale problem, but managements had more pressing concerns during the depression. At one steel mill where older men with good service records (many of them immigrants who could not read English) were being dismissed, the company justified the dismissals on the grounds that a state safety law prohibited workers unable to read English from operating cranes. To make matters worse, men over the age of forty who had been laid off by one company found it very difficult to get new jobs in the steel, auto, and other industries. A few companies made things easier for them by offering pensions or dismissal compensation, but most had no such plans.[54]

Liberal groups like the Taylor Society and the AALL condemned the practice. The AALL claimed that age discrimination in hiring and layoff was "a major factor contributing to the exceptional distress of the present recession."[55] While data on age distributions in industry are an unreliable guide, they do suggest that the practice of dismissing older workers was not uncommon. For example, in 1932, 27 percent of Indianapolis' population, but only 19 percent of the workers employed at the city's major industrial firms, were between the ages of forty-five and sixty-four. Similarly, national data show that the average age of workers in the manufacturing sector declined between 1930 and 1940. Once again, industry was sowing the seeds of discontent.[56]

Some of the biggest broken promises involved welfare programs created by those companies that constituted the liberal minority of the 1920s. During the depression many of these firms discontinued their newer pecuniary benefit programs as well as such traditional welfare services as company outings and magazines (see table 7.1).[57]

Other plans were scaled back but not wholly discontinued. Hence the data in table 7.1 underestimate the shrinkage of welfare capitalism. A common practice in reducing the cost of welfare programs was to shift funding to a contributory basis, where previously the employer had absorbed the entire cost. The proportion of noncontributory pension and health and life insurance plans fell sharply between 1929 and 1932. Numerous pension plans turned out to be actuarially unsound because of employer underfunding, a fact that pensioners discovered when their benefits were cut. Fewer than half of all pension plans in 1932 offered any guarantee of payment.[58]

Employee stock ownership plans had been touted during the 1920s as an example of workers' capitalism and the harbinger of an "economic revolution." But these plans fell on very hard times when the stock market crashed. One of their supposed benefits was the company's guarantee to repurchase its stock if an employee needed money. Yet nearly two-thirds of the firms surveyed by the Conference Board in 1931 reported that they had made no mandatory promise to repurchase the stock at its original price. This

Table 7.1. Welfare Work During the Depression

	Discontinued Plans, 1930–32[a,b] (proportion of active plans in 1934–1935)	Active Plans, 1935[b] (proportion of all industrial firms)
Stock ownership plan	108% (L)	6%
Health and accident insurance	8	31
Mutual benefit association	9	26
Paid vacations	70 (L)	12
Pension plan	15	6
Company outings	48 (L)	n.a.
Employee magazines	69	n.a.

SOURCES: a) National Industrial Conference Board (NICB), *Effect of the Depression on Industrial Relations Programs* (New York, 1934), pp. 4–8; NICB, "Company Pension Plans and the Social Security Act," Studies in Personnel Policy No. 16 (1939), p. 25. b) NICB, *What Employers Are Doing for Employees* (New York, 1936), pp. 11–22.
NOTE: L = firms employing an average of 2300 workers.

left employee shareholders, who had sometimes been coerced into buying stock, with virtually worthless or illiquid investments.[59] Profit-sharing plans, another form of workers' capitalism, were also scaled back or left in a moribund state by the depression.[60]

Company unions, the pinnacle of welfare capitalism, were eliminated entirely by a substantial minority of firms during the depression. Eighty-six employee representation plans, covering 300,000 workers and accounting for roughly 20 percent of the plans in existence, were discontinued between 1929 and 1932.[61] Other company unions lost their funding or became inactive. At Goodyear, the Industrial Assembly did almost nothing in the five years after 1929; fewer than six votes were taken by the assembly during that period.[62] In 1931 International Harvester first considered discontinuing its works councils to save money, then decided to retain them but to reduce its financial support for council activities. At the time, council meetings had degenerated into lengthy discussions of trivial topics such as the company's sale of mason jars to employees. But the councils were still useful to management. When wage rates were reduced in 1931 and 1932, management tried to soften employee opposition by submitting the cuts to the works council for ratification.[63]

These developments inevitably had an effect on personnel departments; there simply was less for them to do as the depression wore on. Their principal areas of responsibility—including the administration of welfare benefits, representation plans, and relief work—had either shrunk or disappeared. Hiring was sporadic or nonexistent; even employee record-keeping had been curtailed at many firms. Line management still protested every time the personnel department sought to involve itself in daily employment decisions.[64]

Although a few personnel departments (only about 5 percent of those in existence in 1929) were eliminated entirely during the depression,[65] most were downgraded in size and responsibility. They had come to be regarded as an extravagance. According to a 1932 survey of New York employers, over half thought that personnel work either was "inessential" or "could readily be dispensed with."[66] To prevent further cutbacks, personnel managers advised each other to set high standards and make their work more scientific, a formula that had failed to work in 1921. Yet the cutbacks were less severe than they had been a decade earlier, partly because personnel departments had carved out for themselves a niche of essentiality, as administrators of extra-work programs. Their higher survival rate did not reflect any wholehearted acceptance of personnel work by top management. In most firms, personnel departments were still "down there."[67]

In later years, employers tried to account for the startling success of unionism. Many blamed themselves for failing to give their personnel departments sufficient authority before 1933. As one employer said in 1939:

> The mistake that has been made by management in the past was that of relegating labor matters to a secondary place . . . Had we faced the facts and placed labor relations on a plane level with that of production and distribution, and had we at the same time assigned labor relations policy to an executive comparable in rank with those handling production and distribution, we would probably not have had many of the troubles from which we have suffered during recent years.[68]

Supporters of personnel management were all too aware of the events taking place in 1931 and 1932. Early in 1933 William M. Leiserson gloomily wrote that the "depression had undone fifteen years or so of good personnel work." Leiserson thought that corporate concern for "human beings" and the "human factor" was eroding under pressure of the business collapse. He warned that "labor is going to look to legislation and not to personnel management for a solution of the unemployment problem."[69]

Leiserson's analysis was correct, but his perspective was limited. True, many workers were disillusioned by management's broken promises with respect to employment security. Others were probably dismayed by the quick slide from benign to sometimes brutal employment conditions. But it is important to bear in mind that these regressions occurred only in the minority of firms which had something to renege on. In 1929, no more than 20 percent of the industrial labor force worked in firms that had personnel departments; 15 percent at most were employed by companies offering welfare benefits, and only a fraction of these workers ever received them; and fewer than 10 percent were covered by an employee representation plan.[70]

Thus, on the eve of the New Deal, industry was poorly prepared for what lay ahead.[71] The vast majority of companies had no direct experience with personnel management, collective bargaining, or employee representation. In better shape were the firms that constituted the progressive minority of the 1920s but even their advantage was relative. Few of them had ever treated personnel policy as a matter of primary importance. Moreover, they were at a disadvantage for having raised and then disappointed the expectations of their employees. Finally, neither the progressive minority nor the vast majority of companies (except for those covered by the Railway Labor Act of 1926) had dealt with government regulation of industrial relations since 1918.

III. NIRA and the Formulation of a Strategy, 1933–1935

Passage of the National Industrial Recovery Act (NIRA) in 1933 set in motion a chain of events similar to those of the World War I period. The pace of employment reform quickened. Personnel management experienced a spurt of growth. Government regulation and trade union membership both increased sharply. Only labor market conditions separated the two periods. In contrast to the war period, millions remained unemployed, and turnover rates were extraordinarily low during the mid-1930s.[72]

To boost purchasing power and reduce unemployment, the NIRA called for the establishment of minimum wage and maximum hours standards in every industry. Private trade associations were encouraged to submit to the National Recovery Administration labor codes detailing precise employment standards for their industry.[73] In its famous section 7(a), the Act also provided that employees "shall have the right to organize and bargain collectively through representatives of their own choosing, and shall be free from the interference, restraint or coercion of employers . . . in the designation of such representatives or in self-organization or in other concerted activities for the purpose of collective bargaining . . ." Organized labor saw the section as giving congressional sanction and protection to collective organization and bargaining; thus, it represented a major victory. Employers, although not happy with the language of 7(a), nevertheless interpreted it to mean that new company unions could be formed and that those already in existence could be continued.[74]

Workers, and the unions that sought to represent them, lost no time in pressing for the right to bargain. A burst of organizing and an upsurge in work stoppages occurred immediately after passage of the Act. Strikes in the latter half of 1933 approached levels not seen since 1921. Workers formed unions, sometimes spontaneously, and struck to demand employer recognition. Unions that had sickened after 1929, including those of the miners and clothing workers, quickly revived. New federal labor unions, directly chartered by the AFL, began to appear in industries where they had previously been rare, including rubber tires, electrical manufacturing, automobiles, and petroleum refining. Between June and October 1933, the AFL and its member unions issued charters to 3,537 federal labor union locals.[75]

The year 1934 was marked by even greater upheaval: there were dramatic and violent strikes by auto parts workers in Toledo, longshoremen in San Francisco, and truckers in Minneapolis. By the end of 1934, total union membership stood at over 3.5 million, a gain that nearly equaled the loss of membership between 1923 and 1933. By mid-1935, an additional 800,000 workers had become union members. Even before the formation of the Committee for Industrial Organization (CIO) in November 1935, the proportion of organized workers in industrial unions steadily increased, from 17 percent in 1929 to 27 percent in 1933 to 33 percent in 1934.[76]

The NIRA was barely a month old when the trend of strike activity turned sharply upwards. Yet the Act provided no machinery for handling labor disputes. To fill this gap, President Roosevelt appointed a National Labor Board (NLB), headed by William M. Leiserson, in August 1933. The NLB conducted representation elections and held hearings to determine if an employer had discriminated against union members or supporters. But because it lacked enforcement powers, the board was eventually overwhelmed by employer refusals to comply with its orders. Thus, in July 1934, it was replaced by the first National Labor Relations Board, which had slightly more authority. In addition, the President created special labor boards during 1934 in the automobile, steel, and petroleum industries.[77]

Managements were, as noted earlier, unprepared for these events. They needed personnel specialists to aid them in code creation and compliance, experts who could interpret 7(a) and minimize the chance that they would be forced to appear before one of the labor boards.[78] They needed new strategies to mollify employees and contain the union threat. The NIRA had turned the employer's world upside-down. As one manager observed in 1934: "At the present time no established, reputable and legitimate business can afford to be careless and thoughtless in its relationships with employees . . . the need for fact and reason and for conscious, intelligent labor planning on the part of management is greater than at any time in the past."[79]

As a result of these exigencies, the proportion of industrial firms with personnel departments, especially very large firms, increased dramatically between 1933 and 1935 (see table 7.2). For example, the twelve giant companies that made up the SCC expanded and upgraded their personnel departments in 1933 and 1934.[80] As E. S. Cowdrick, secretary of the SCC, said in 1934: "Whatever doubt yet remained as to the importance of personnel administration in the managerial program has been brushed aside in the rapid march of recent events."[81] Outside these citadels of industry, there was also a rush of activity, although it was frequently disorganized and poorly planned. Some companies were slow to accept their new personnel departments; others still saw no need for such departments. Those firms that had been pioneers during the 1920s adapted most easily to the new situation.[82]

Edward A. Filene made a national study of employer reaction to the NIRA in the early months of 1934. He found that employers, especially in large firms, were obsessed with "a general fear" that union power threatened their "safety."[83] At the same time, it was widely believed that the threat posed by unionism was temporary and controllable. Managements thought that the impulse to unionize could be squelched if they moved quickly to adopt personnel policies that would reduce worker grievances to a minimum. In a bulletin issued to all his managers in 1934, one employer noted that "any labor disturbance or unrest" at the firm would be viewed as evidence that management had failed "to fairly administer the company's labor policies."[84] At least through 1935, managements were confident that if they took the initiative and mounted a major effort, they could preserve their nonunion status and even avoid Labor Board charges. A former Labor Board official who was sympathetic to management said in 1935:

> There is only one basic cause for labor troubles and that is poor administration of personnel. No employer who has developed and maintained an intelligent program of personnel administration has ever been hailed before the labor board. Further than that, such employers do not have labor troubles nor do they have to worry about the so-called labor agitator. Their battle is won before they start.[85]

The "intelligent program" that personnel managers devised was a three-pronged strategy consisting of company unions, foreman training programs, and various employment reforms. Different companies used different mixes of these common responses, but rarely was any part of this strategy effectively carried out in the absence of a personnel department.

There was another, less benign, response to the upsurge of unionism: resort to violence and intimidation, which cut across all strata of industry. To deter unions and avert strikes, companies used or were prepared to use espionage, tear gas, guns, hired goons, and strikebreakers. Following a complete investigation of these practices, the La Follette Committee reported that the list of corporations using espionage "reads like a blue book of American industry."[86] Even relatively liberal firms were included on the list. In the mid-1930s these firms expanded their ammunition supplies along with less lethal union deterrents, such as pension coverage. This may seem contradictory. But most employers and operating officials were pragmatic and undisturbed by philosophical inconsistency. More important, they still lacked confidence in the personnel strategy and were ready to introduce force in the event that persuasion failed.

Company Unions

As noted, passage of the NIRA brought an immediate increase in the number of employee representation plans. Of the plans in existence in 1935, nearly two-thirds were established after the NIRA was enacted. In 1935 there were between 600 and 700

company unions, covering from two to three million workers.[87]
Like their predecessors, these new company unions tended to be
concentrated in large firms. But now they were found in a more
diverse group of industries than before, including automobiles,
chemicals, rubber products, and steel. Whereas none of the automobile firms had representation plans before 1933, virtually all
had them by 1934. The number of steel industry plans grew twelve-
fold between 1933 and 1934.[88]

Another departure from the 1920s was the weaker relationship
between personnel management and company unionism, especially
at smaller firms. Among small companies with company unions in
1935, only about one-third had personnel departments, a much
lower proportion than in 1929. The drop was less sharp for large
firms.[89]

These changes reflect the expedient nature of many of the new
company unions, which were introduced without any management
planning or support. Often they were hastily created in the face of
an impending strike. A Bureau of Labor Statistics study found that
the effectiveness of a company union (as measured by the speed
and success of grievance resolution) was closely related to the
presence of a personnel department.[90] In the absence of a personnel
department, there was no full-time official to administer the representation plan and see to it that supervisors took the plan seriously. Workers in these firms were reluctant to raise grievances for
"fear of the reaction of foremen."[91]

But not all of the new company unions were artifices. Some
resulted from expansion by companies that had experimented earlier with employee representation. In 1933, AT&T, General Electric, Goodyear, and Jersey Standard each increased the number of
plans they offered. Passage of the NIRA forced them to revitalize
plans that by 1932 had often become moribund. Other companies
that had no prior experience with representation plans rushed to
start company unions in 1933 and were even willing to grant these
unions a measure of independence. This group included General
Motors and Goodrich, as well as U.S. Steel, which in 1933 hired
Arthur H. Young to oversee its new plan.[92] Managers from both
groups of companies were concerned that other, more haphazard,
plans would undermine their efforts to make employee representation appear legitimate, especially to Congress.[93] A Jersey Stan-

dard official thought that there would be a "shock to the prestige of representation caused by the blow-up of those [plans] which are ill-conceived."[94]

That the new and revitalized company unions were more active and democratic than most of those in existence before the NIRA was partly attributable to Labor Board pressure. For example, because of Labor Board influence, fewer restrictions were placed on employee voting eligibility, and meetings of worker representatives could be held with no managers present (provided that the meetings dealt with "non-joint" issues). The major impetus for change, however, came from external union pressure.[95]

As a result of this pressure, after 1932 company unions came to resemble independent unions more closely. First, provisions to arbitrate disagreements between management and the company union were widely adopted. Second, company unions were consulted on wage matters and even allowed to decide on the distribution of a given wage increase, issues that had been sacrosanct to management during the 1920s.[96] Third, to compete better with outside unions, the number of employee representatives was increased. Goodyear tripled the size of its Industrial Assembly in 1935. Finally, it became commonplace for managements and company unions to sign written, fixed-term agreements.[97]

But despite these changes, employee representation remained an inadequate method for collective bargaining. Managements continued to set the rules of the game and refused to let liberalization go very far. Arbitration clauses existed but were almost never invoked. Wages were discussed but only after the company had already announced what it was going to do. Because workers still feared reprisal from supervisors, grievances tended to be limited to issues like safety and other physical working conditions. Even at Goodyear, a firm with a long history of enlightened company unionism, worker representatives at one subsidiary were "afraid to do anything."[98]

The revitalization of company unions was, by and large, a case of too little too late. Company unions fared poorly in representation elections supervised by the NIRA's various labor boards. Between August 1933 and September 1935, independent unions received 67 percent of the votes cast, with only 29 percent going to company unions—a poor showing for employee representation.[99]

Foreman Training

In what proved to be a short-sighted move, numerous foreman training activities were eliminated between 1930 and 1933. Firms did not give high priority to programs designed to expose foremen to the managerial outlook or to technical material. Well over half of all foreman training courses and close to 90 percent of foremen's clubs were discontinued during the early years of the depression. On top of this, many firms demoted some foremen back to the ranks as a cost-cutting measure. These actions left most managements poorly prepared to mobilize their foremen to meet the challenges of the post-NIRA period.[100]

Immediately after passage of the NIRA, groups such as Industrial Relations Counselors and the SCC began to urge their clients and member firms to initiate or revive programs directed at foremen. Early in 1934, bellwether firms like Goodyear, General Motors, and International Harvester launched a variety of foreman training activities.[101]

The most common activity was a training class held after work on company premises. In contrast to foreman training of the 1920s, which had dealt primarily with technical subjects, these classes emphasized "human relations" and personnel management techniques, covered such topics as selection and discipline methods and the new labor laws, and included lectures on leadership, motivation, and "tact."[102] In addition, some firms experimented with the conference method of training, in which foremen were exposed to subject material through guided group discussions. This method was popular because it permitted foremen to let off steam within the confines of a carefully controlled situation.[103]

Both types of training were given a boost by the federal government. In 1934 and again in 1936, Congress passed vocational education bills that earmarked funds for trade and industry training. These funds were distributed to the states, which spent them on foreman training programs for private industry.[104] In California, for example, the state's Bureau of Trade and Industrial Education solicited clients from industry to participate in state-run foreman training classes and conferences, held not only at the workplace but also in local schools and universities. As in private programs, the emphasis was on human relations topics. Many of the California companies participating in the program were staunchly opposed to unions. The Los Angeles Merchants and Manufacturers Association, a bastion of antiunion sentiment, sponsored the coordination of the state's foreman conference program. While the programs did not specifically explain how to discourage labor unions, this was clearly one of their functions, at least in the eyes of industry. Hence the federal government ended up subsidizing a subtle form of union avoidance.[105]

Foremen's clubs—which sought to promote a sense of cohesion and loyalty to management through social activities and lectures—also made a comeback after 1933. The YMCA, which was deeply distrusted by organized labor during the 1930s, jumped on the bandwagon and stepped up support for its foremen's clubs after 1933. These clubs were affiliated with the YMCA's new national organization, the National Council of Foremen's Clubs, launched in 1934. Membership was concentrated in the Midwest and totaled between ten and fifteen thousand during the 1930s.[106]

One reason for the revival of foreman's training was industry's plan to use foremen as its first line of defense against unionism. The foreman's task was to "sell" workers on the company by convincing them of the truth of whatever propaganda—on the company union, corporate policies, or benefit programs—the personnel department wished to promote. Training programs coached foremen on factual details as well as on effective methods of presentation. At the end of 1933, International Harvester's personnel manager told the firm's plant managers:

> Organized forces are making determined efforts to gain followers and frequently twist facts to further their efforts. It is therefore necessary for us to put the facts squarely before our men to show them a true picture . . . This can only be done by frank and formal discussion and it is first necessary to enlighten the foremen and other key men to fortify them to intelligently explain and argue if called upon.[107]

The foreman's personality was enlisted in the fight. It was hoped that human relations training would make the foreman a more trusted and sympathetic supervisor, and so deter unionism. A management conference was told that, "foremen who enjoy the confidence and friendship of their men are probably the best preventive [against labor troubles] a manufacturer can have." Moreover, as the worker's confidante, a foreman could detect "misunderstandings or incipient unrest," as a 1934 company memo put it.[108] But one personnel manager warned that this sudden solicitude might "awaken the suspicion that we have not been giving employees a square deal all along."[109]

Personnel managers viewed the foreman not only as a line of defense against but also as a primary cause of labor unrest. By teaching foremen modern personnel techniques, firms hoped to minimize the risk that workers would turn to a union because of the "unfairness or stupidity or ignorance of a single supervisor."[110] Of course, the best way to curb the foreman's misuse of his prerogatives would have been to take them away from him. Yet few personnel departments were able or willing to do this, at least initially. Instead, large firms such as General Motors let their foremen retain considerable power, hoping that training programs would teach them how to wield that power wisely. Given past history, this hope had little chance of being realized, at least in the short run.[111]

Some firms realized early on that their foremen's loyalty could not be taken for granted, especially in light of the demotions and cutbacks of 1930–32. Since the foreman's effectiveness as a first line of defense would be vitiated if the foreman himself were antagonistic to management, a second purpose of the training programs was to bolster the foreman's loyalty to the company. For instance, foremen's clubs and conferences regularly featured presentations by top management officials who tried to make the foremen feel a part of management, often by feeding them tidbits of information about confidential corporate plans.

In retrospect, it is doubtful that foreman training was a successful deterrent to rank-and-file unionism in the 1930s. First, the programs were slow in getting off the ground. In 1935 the proportion of firms offering training programs was lower than it had been in 1929. Further, except for an occasional foremen's club at a small or medium-sized firm, the programs were limited to large firms. The ratio of foremen to production workers in manufacturing did not rise between 1930 and 1940, although one would expect an increase if training programs had been widely implemented.[112] Finally, line management from the top down was infected, as one personnel manager complained in 1935, "by tradition and prejudice."[113] A ten-week course would do little to make a foreman less leery of "human relations." In a few exceptional firms, an active personnel department had, over the years, tempered and transformed line management's outlook. But these firms were the ones least in need of foreman training.

Reforming Employment

The heart of the personnel management strategy was the restructuring of employment procedures and policies. Most of the reforms introduced after 1933 were borrowed from a stock of partially implemented innovations that had been devised during the World War I period. As before, activity in this area was a response to the surge of interest in unionism and an attempt to cope with the government's new regulatory intervention in the labor market. Veteran personnel managers were aware of these parallels to the past and of the role that employment reform could play in deterring unionism. Early in 1940, one manager remarked that these reforms were "not new or original ideas. For example, one only has to review the publications of the AMA during the 1920s to discover a full discussion of most of the personnel practices which are now receiving wider acceptance. In the handful of companies which practiced sound personnel management during the 1920s, one never hears today of serious labor difficulties."[114]

In a break from earlier trends, allocative procedures were centralized and made subject to definite rules and procedures. Personnel departments sought to wrest control of hiring, transfer, promotion, and dismissal from the foremen. As a result, allocative decisions were increasingly made on a companywide rather than a departmental basis (see table 7.2).

Personnel departments focused a great deal of attention on dismissal practices. The lack of definite procedures in this area was a longstanding worker grievance that had been intensified by several years of depression. Moreover, many of the cases that came before the labor boards involved charges of discriminatory dismissal for union activity and employers realized that these cases could easily become union organizing issues and bring them unwanted public-

Table 7.2. Employment Practices in Industry, 1929–1963

	1929	1935–36	1939–40	1946–48	1957–63
Personnel Department (L)	34%	46%		61%	81%
1,000–5,000 employees	39	62		73	
5,000 +	55	81		88	
Employee rulebooks (A)	—	13	16%	30	43 (L)
Centralized selection (A)	32	40	42	63	
(L)	42	53	55		
Dismissal					
Foreman sole authority (A)		55		24	
Personnel department involved (A)		7	17	31	
(L)	24	38			
Allocation, Wages					
Centralized transfer and promotion (L)	24	42			
Promotion charts (A)			19	25	28
Merit rating (A)		11	16	31	
(L)	14	16			42
Job evaluation (A)				55	72
Seniority, Security					
Layoff results in loss of all seniority (A)	14	3	2	1	0.5 (L)
Seniority rules (A)			50	83	
Pension plans (A)	2	6	8	23	73 (L)
Number of wage or employment guarantee plans	35	79	138	196	
Paid vacation plans	25 (L)	12	47		

SOURCES: 1929: National Industrial Conference Board (NICB), *Layoffs and Its Prevention* (New York, 1930), p. 56; NICB, *Industrial Relations Programs in Small Plants* (New York, 1929), pp. 16, 20; NICB, *Industrial Relations: Administration of Policies and Programs* (New York, 1931), p. 54. 1935: NICB, *What Employers Are Doing for Employees* (New York, 1936), pp. 23, 33, 60–65; NICB, *Personnel Practices Governing Factory and Office Administration* (New York, 1937), pp. 73–74, 78. 1940: NICB, "Personnel Policies in Factory and Office," Studies in Personnel Policy No. 23 (1940), p. 15; NICB, "Personnel Activities in American Business," Studies in Personnel Policy No. 20 (1940), pp. 19–29. 1946–48: NICB, "Personnel Practices in Factory and Office," Studies in Personnel Policy No. 88 (1948), p. 13; NICB, "Personnel Activities in American Business (Revised)," Studies in Personnel Policy No. 86 (1947), pp. 16–36; W. D. Scott, R. C. Clothier, and W. R. Spriegel, *Personnel Management* (New York, 1961), p. 583. 1957–63: *Ibid.*, p. 583; NICB, "Personnel Practices in Factory and Office: Manufacturing," Studies in Personnel Policy No. 194 (1964), pp. 17, 52, 111, 139; H. E. Steele and H. Fisher, Jr., "A Study of the Effects of Unionism in Southern Plants," *Monthly Labor Review* (March 1964), 87:260. Data on employment guarantee plans from Office of War Mobilization and Reconversion and Office of Temporary Controls, *Guaranteed Wages,* Report to the President by the Advisory Board (Washington, D.C., 1947), p. 293.
NOTE: A: proportion of all industrial firms; L: proportion of industrial firms with more than 250 employees.

ity. They were also liable to lose their Blue Eagle, although this in itself hardly was a serious penalty.[115]

On the other hand, the labor boards might exonerate an employer who could prove that a dismissal was motivated not by antiunion sentiment but by the worker's violation of an established rule or some other "objective factor."[116] Thus, disciplinary rules proliferated, and efforts to keep detailed service records were initiated. Foreman training programs included careful discussions of the new company rules, section 7(a), and, later, the Wagner Act.[117]

However, merely promulgating rules and keeping records were insufficient protections from unionism and the law because there was no guarantee that foremen would go along with the new policies. In recognition of this problem, personnel departments stepped up their involvement in day-to-day disciplinary and discharge practices (table 7.2). In 1934, General Motors, Chrysler, and International Harvester established review procedures, to be carried out jointly by the personnel department and the foremen, to determine if dismissals were likely to bring the company before the Automobile Labor Board.[118] GM warned its foremen that dismissal had to "rest upon clear and explicit cause and must be reasonable."[119]

As it became more difficult to dismiss workers for union activity, efforts were made to ensure that the hiring process screened out those workers who might become union supporters. Selection was once again centralized (table 7.2), and foremen were forbidden to do their own hiring. At Goodyear, General Motors, and other large firms, personnel departments made it a standard procedure to check an applicant's background carefully before hiring. On the theory that "birds of a feather flock together," Goodyear even went so far as to inquire into the applicant's neighborhood and the employers of all persons living or boarding with him. In describing these practices, the head of the firm's personnel department noted that "we do not have to hire certain individuals, but once we get them in we usually have difficulty in getting rid of them. So the main purpose [of the new procedures] is to cover the ground pretty thoroughly before they are actually hired."[120]

To build employee morale, large companies restored some of the welfare benefits that had been cut before 1934. Some programs, like profit-sharing and stock ownership, were never rebuilt. But others, including pensions and health insurance, experienced rapid growth between 1933 and 1935.[121]

Reducing wage inequities was another step taken to improve morale. ARMCO, General Electric, Kimberly-Clark, and several other large firms adopted job classification and evaluation plans during this period. These methods, which had first been tried during the war, were intended to enhance the firm's control over its rate structure and to improve its relations with employees. Wage determination was made more impersonal, fair, and consistent by attaching rates to jobs rather than to individuals. No doubt some firms adopted job evaluation in anticipation of having to defend their differentials to a union. But the technique did not become widespread until after 1935, when the threat of unionization had grown more intense.[122]

Actual or anticipated union demands—in this case, for seniority-based layoffs and rehires—led some large companies to adopt definite layoff procedures that gave heavier weight to seniority but left management a high degree of discretion. But because unions were still somewhat weak, many companies failed to take action on this issue. An exception was the automobile industry, where fledgling federal labor unions were able to apply political pressure and thus have some of their demands met.[123]

Prior to the formation of the Automobile Labor Board (ALB), none of the automobile manufacturers had formulated either definite layoff procedures or rules governing the weight of seniority in layoff decisions. A 1934 government survey of the industry found "inequitable" layoff and rehire practices, including extensive discrimination against older workers.[124] Since its formation in 1933, the Automobile Workers' Union had called for a seniority-based layoff system but was unable to get employers to concede to this or any other of its demands. When it threatened to strike in 1934, the government intervened and set up the ALB, one of whose functions was to resolve the seniority issue. Two months later, the ALB issued a set of rules to govern layoffs and rehires in the auto industry. A compromise that gave some weight to seniority, as well as to need and merit, the rules also defined how seniority was to be measured and applied.

The careful recordkeeping required to determine layoff order under the new rules led to the expansion of the industry's personnel departments and the centralization of the layoff process, which had previously been controlled by foremen. After the NIRA was declared unconstitutional in 1935, the auto industry continued to apply these rules until the union was able to negotiate contracts that tied security more tightly to seniority. Thus, according to historian Sidney Fine, the ALB "introduced the concept of job tenure by rule in the automobile industry."[125]

The greater emphasis on employment security represented a major change in personnel policy. Indeed, opinion polls showed that job security was the primary concern of workers during and after the depression. After 1933, some companies took new steps to alleviate the concern of their workers. First, a small but growing number of firms offered their employees guarantees of annual employment or income (table 7.2). Second, workers were allowed to retain their seniority for longer periods after layoff, a step implying greater employer commitment to an enduring employment relationship (table 7.2). Third, the number of firms offering dismissal compensation to their hourly workers increased slightly, a development that may have been sparked by the negotiation in 1934 of severance pay plans for unionized railway workers.[126]

In a dramatic break from the past, the government began to pressure private employers to provide more job security to their employees. The nation's first compulsory unemployment insurance law was adopted in Wisconsin in 1932. Under this law, employers who provided guarantees of income or employment to their workers were completely exempted from the unemployment insurance tax. As a result, close to 100 Wisconsin companies adopted guarantee plans between 1933 and the end of 1935, when the law was changed.[127] At the federal level, the NIRA's hours codes were intended to compel work-sharing. President Roosevelt announced in 1933 that the legislation would force companies to "hire more men to do the existing work by reducing the work-hours of each man's week." At first there was some doubt as to whether the codes would have any effect. Nevertheless, an economist hired by the automobile industry, which had complained bitterly about the inflexibility of the codes, found that the hours standards were responsible for higher employment levels in the industry after 1933 than otherwise would have been expected.[128]

Roosevelt and the ALB, at the urging of the unions, also tried to force employers in the automobile industry to do something about reducing the seasonal instability of employment. A combination of political pressure and fear of publicity led the industry's trade association to announce that, beginning in 1935, member firms would introduce new car models in the fall rather than in January. This change created more stable employment by encouraging demand during a season when sales were normally low. Thus, external compulsion achieved an objective that proponents of employment stabilization had been seeking for twenty years.[129]

The decisions of the various labor boards also gave legitimacy and quasi-legal standing to the concept of job rights, which had its origins in trade union practices. The boards' standard remedy for workers who had lost their jobs because of proven employer discrimination was to order them reinstated to their previous positions. Although these reinstatement orders were not enforceable, they nevertheless represented a historic challenge to the contractual or "at will" doctrine of employment. Similarly, in certain discrimination cases the boards recognized the employer's right to discipline workers but supported the concept that discipline ought to be corrective; that is, a wayward worker should be given a chance to improve himself and retain his job before the employer applied the ultimate sanction of dismissal. These principles eventually found their way into the Wagner Act, labor arbitration, and corporate personnel policies.[130]

But despite the flurry of activity touched off by government and union pressure, the reforms instituted in the NIRA's wake did not reach far beyond industry's progressive minority. Most companies continued to be characterized by an absence of rules and restraint. In 1935, over half of all firms still allowed their foremen to be the sole arbiters of dismissal; over three in five lacked dismissal rules; and four in five had no definite procedure for layoffs. Seniority was not widely recognized as an allocative determinant, nor were most workers protected by other devices that assured their job security, such as employment guarantees, rehiring rules, or stabilization policies.[131] Although personnel managers called for company-wide promotion policies, explicit career ladders were rare, and there were numerous complaints that foremen continued to block interdepartmental promotions.[132]

Thus, in many firms, even large ones, line management and

tradition continued to control employment policy in 1935. Although personnel departments were trying to change the situation, most of them were too new or too weak to succeed. They lacked both the authority to enforce their policies and the support of management's highest echelons. One manager complained in 1934 of the "blind, stubborn adherence to tradition for its own sake," and another disparaged "the executive who would say, 'who are you down there in the personnel department, to tell me how I should run the business?' " He continued, "I am wondering if that fear and that attitude has not been the reason for keeping some personnel departments 'down there.' "[133] Small firms—those employing less than one thousand workers—took their cues from the larger companies that were pacesetters in their industry. Consequently, the majority of these firms had not yet established personnel departments by 1935 (table 7.2).

But more than time and tradition were working against the newly organized personnel departments. Until passage of the Wagner Act in mid-1935, the external pressures of unionism and government were simply too weak to convince employers that the personnel management strategy would be advantageous to them. In the view of operating managers the benefits of the strategy did not justify its cost. Because of this short-sighted view, internal transformation often came only after it was already too late to halt unionization.

In the years following the Wagner Act, managements were anxious to find scapegoats to blame for the remarkable success of unions in industry. Some accused the new National Labor Relations Board, and even the entire administration, of pro-labor bias.[134] Others put the responsibility on the foreman's shoulders, with one executive claiming that over 60 percent of strikes were attributable to line management's failure "to carry out commitments already made by management."[135] But blaming the foreman disingenuously overlooked the fact that top management had given him the authority he was now accused of misusing. It would have been more honest if management had acknowledged its own role in bringing about unionization: Too many firms moved too slowly during the 1920s and 1930s in the direction that personnel managers had charted as early as the World War I period. A few prominent managers recognized their own responsibility. One said in 1937:

> A number of so-called progressive employers have, over a period of
> twenty years, voluntarily done a great many of these things to their

lasting credit. The point is that not enough employers have done it. It has often been said that it is the 10 percent that are holding back. It may be more accurate to say it has been the 10 percent who have taken the lead. It would not take very long to list the companies in these United States who have taken the lead and have been progressive and done these things voluntarily, and done them in the hope and expectation that we would have been saved some of these developments of the past three years.[136]

CHAPTER 8

ANOTHER GREAT TRANSFORMATION, 1936–1945

I. Before the War: The Unions Grieve and Management Moves

Close to five million workers joined unions between 1936 and 1939. Much of that gain occurred during 1937, a watershed year for organized labor. In 1940, on the eve of World War II, the unions could boast that more than one out of every three manufacturing workers was a union member. Buoyed by an economic upturn between 1934 and 1937—during which time industrial employment rose by over 20 percent—and by passage of the Wagner Act, the new Committee for Industrial Organization (CIO) overcame years of resistance to unionism in such heavy industries as steel, transportation equipment, rubber, and electrical manufacturing.[1]

In the wake of the Wagner Act, employers launched a determined counter-offensive. They refused to cooperate with the new National Labor Relations Board and mounted numerous legal challenges to the Act, claiming that it was unconstitutional. They conducted an extensive propaganda campaign to convince employees and the public that, by eliminating company unions, the Act would "destroy harmonious relations between workers and management," as a Bethlehem Steel newsletter put it.[2]

Roosevelt's reelection and the 1937 Supreme Court decision upholding the Act defused the public campaign to overturn the Act and drove some employers to despair: "The America we have known is dead," declared one.[3] But these events had little effect on the other, less visible, side of industry's offensive.

The strategy of using employment reforms to deter unionism was given new life. Companies that had adopted this strategy rather hesitantly during the NIRA period now pursued it wholeheartedly. For example, one month after passage of the Wagner Act, General Motors held an urgent meeting of its top managers to discuss a "program to reduce employee grievances." Plant managers were to make an immediate check of their foremen's abilities as "labor handlers"; hiring was to be centralized; the "irritations" caused by unsatisfactory wage differentials were to be reduced; and promotion from within was to be given more emphasis.[4] In companies that had introduced personnel management at an early date, trends toward the centralization and standardization of employment were intensified. As a result, in 1937 personnel managers were said to be "rising to a place of new importance in the management function."[5]

Companies which prior to 1935 had disregarded the personnel strategy now appeared to embrace it. In a report issued early in 1937, the National Association of Manufacturers (NAM)—whose membership consisted chiefly of smaller firms—recommended the adoption of a variety of employment reforms designed to prevent "labor difficulties." This recommendation represented a departure from the NAM's previously belligerent stance and a reversal of its tendency to ignore personnel management. C. E. French of Industrial Relations Counselors observed that companies which "previously had given little thought to industrial relations have found it most necessary since passage of the Act to make changes in their methods and in their whole approach."[6]

But some firms moved so slowly, even after 1935, that few changes were made before the unions moved in and expanded whatever rules, job security measures, and standardized procedures were in place. Occasionally, a company did not even have a personnel department until after a union had organized its workers.[7] More commonly, however, unionization occurred after the firm had already implemented a range of employment reforms. In such cases, unions adapted to the status quo and used preexisting policies as a basis for formulating new demands, sometimes incorporating the firm's personnel policies into the collective agreement. Developments in the unionized sector were closely watched and imitated by firms that had managed to avoid unionization.

The Quest for Security

The most important innovations emanating from the unionized sector related to job security. Two officials from the steelworkers' union could claim in 1941 that the CIO unions had "introduced a new doctrine into American industry . . . namely, once management has hired an employee who makes good . . . it must continue to give employment or preference for employment to that employee."[8] The vigor with which unions championed the issue was a reflection of the times, of forces beyond the employer's control. Because of the havoc wreaked by the depression, workers were more interested than ever before in protecting their jobs, as is evidenced by the increase in union agreements containing layoff provisions, which nearly doubled in proportion between the 1920s and 1930s.[9]

Yet security was by no means an entirely new issue. Instead, the 1930s provided the first opportunity for many industrial workers to communicate effectively with employers, who had previously been deaf to their concerns. A majority of companies in 1935 still adhered to the tenets of the drive system: that the foreman's authority was absolute, that too many rules hindered flexibility, and that security was detrimental to motivation. True, a number of progressive employers had tried to follow a different philosophy during the 1920s. But they lost their workers' trust when, at the height of the depression, they reneged on implicit promises to provide employment security.

Seniority. One important union-sector innovation was the application of seniority criteria to layoff, rehire, and promotion decisions. Managers were not opposed to seniority per se. As noted, some firms had used it as an allocative criterion before the depression. But few had adopted the rigid and all-encompassing approach that the unions now demanded. Opposition to seniority stemmed from the belief that it would reduce efficiency by making ability a less important factor in allocative decisions, especially promotions. Production managers also expressed concern that the unions' approach would make it more difficult to adjust the work force smoothly to changes in the level or composition of demand.[10] Seniority appealed to workers because it enhanced job security.

Older workers viewed it as protection against the discrimination that some companies had practiced when making layoffs. Younger workers as well were determined to prevent the recurrence of what they had witnessed during the early 1930s. One young electrical worker said, "I seen these guys getting laid off—fifty, sixty years old. . . . I said, 'I'm going to be old someday. I want security.' "[11] Workers of all ages found seniority attractive because it established the claims of current job holders to future job opportunities. Under seniority rules, preference in promotion and rehiring was given to current and former employees, as against outsiders.

Another attractive feature of seniority, in the eyes of workers, was that it deeply undercut the foreman's power to reward and punish, to be capricious or abusive. The introduction of seniority rules served to establish a logical and orderly procedure for distributing job opportunities. Union officials favored these rules because they prevented foremen from discriminating against the union's supporters. Although the Wagner Act had outlawed discrimination, distrust of management on this issue remained strong. In 1938, the Rubber Workers charged that a firm's retention of seventeen junior workers on an exempt (from layoff) list was "little more than a subterfuge for favoritism and discrimination," despite the fact that the company employed over 8,000 workers.[12]

The seniority principle was widely established at an early date, at least with respect to layoffs (see table 8.1). By 1938 it was not unusual for unionized firms to list on large bulletin boards the names of active and laid-off workers, ranked by seniority.[13] But union seniority systems sank much deeper roots between 1938 and 1950: they were expanded to apply both to larger groupings of jobs (thus leading to plant-wide and company-wide seniority districts) and to a larger number of allocative decisions (including promotions, rehires, job assignments, and transfers).

The extension of seniority to new areas of decision making is attributable in part to the growth in labor's bargaining power during and after World War II. It is also attributable to the ordinary process of institutionalization as management learned that its dire predictions did not come to pass and as both parties grew more familiar with the sometimes highly technical problems posed by seniority rules. The federal government hastened these developments by giving special protection to the seniority rights of return-

Table 8.1. The Application of Seniority in Union and Nonunion Firms, 1938–1954

	1938[a]		1948–1954	
	Union	Nonunion	Union	Nonunion
Seniority Used For:				
Layoffs	95%	50%	99[d]	85[d]
Rehires	—	—	81[b]	—
Promotions	—	—	73[b]	—
Seniority Governs:				
Layoffs	69	8	73[b]	11[c]
Promotions	—	—	38[b]	5[c]

SOURCES: a) NICB, "Curtailment, Layoff Policy and Seniority," Studies in Personnel Policy No. 5 (1938), pp. 7–9. b) "Survey of Contracts Under Taft-Hartley Act," Labor Relations Reference Manual (Washington, D.C., 1948), 22:5; U.S. Bureau of Labor Statistics, "Analysis of Layoff, Recall and Worksharing Procedures in Union Contracts," Bulletin No. 1209 (Washington, D.C., 1957), p. 30. Data refer to proportion of collective bargaining agreements. c) NICB, "Seniority Systems in Nonunionized Companies," Studies in Personnel Policy No. 110 (1950), p. 5. d) H. Ellsworth Steele, William R. Myles, and Sherwood C. McIntyre, "Personnel Practices in the South," Industrial and Labor Relations Review (January 1956), 9:248.

ing veterans, although this preference undercut the seniority claims of women working in war plants.[14]

Nonunion firms also relied more heavily on seniority after 1935, largely as a defensive measure. A 1950 study of seniority reported that "a great number of nonunionized firms are constantly aware of the implied threat of unionization if their personnel procedures are mishandled. Their attitude is that as long as they keep their house in order, they can remain unorganized."[15] In addition to these so-called threat effects, the existence of a personnel department made it more likely that a nonunion firm would follow seniority rules. Some personnel managers were happy to introduce seniority systems, since the centralization of allocative authority implicit in such a system increased their own power.[16]

But seniority was more narrowly and flexibly applied in nonunion firms, which continued to give strong emphasis to merit and to managerial discretion. As the data in table 8.1 indicate, at the end of World War II a unionized firm was about seven times as likely as a nonunion firm to base promotions and layoffs on seniority. This is not to say that nonunion firms made decisions arbitrarily. In fact, their allocative procedures were only slightly less rule-bound than those in the unionized sector. Formal procedures helped to insure supervisor consistency and fairness, thus serving as another guard against union inroads.[17] For example, the proportion of nonunion firms with definite layoff procedures rose rapidly after 1935, from 50 percent in 1938 to over 80 percent in 1950.[18]

Layoffs. The use of layoffs (as opposed to reductions in hours or work-sharing) as an adjustment mechanism was one area in which nonunion firms did *not* imitate the union sector. Starting with somewhat similar policies in the late 1930s, the two sectors grew markedly different over time. The nonunion sector's initial preference for adjustments in hours grew stronger, probably because it wanted to avoid becoming entangled in the complex bumping procedures that became standard practice in unionized firms, while the more dynamic union sector showed a striking shift away from work-sharing and toward layoffs (see table 8.2).[19]

To be precise, the preferred union policy in the late 1930s was to share work until everyone was working less than some minimum (usually from 24 to 32 hours per week) and then to begin making layoffs in reverse order of seniority.[20] Perhaps because it was highly egalitarian and thus in keeping with union traditions and the spirit of the times, work-sharing was strongly supported by workers and unions during the late 1930s. A survey taken during the recession of 1938 found that 97 percent of the workers at a large manufacturing firm favored some form of work-sharing.[21] Union leaders liked it because it helped to maintain unity in the ranks at a critical juncture in the unions' development.

Table 8.2. Adjustment Policies in Union and Nonunion Firms, 1938–1954

	1938[a]		1950–1954	
	Union	Nonunion	Union[b]	Nonunion[c]
Hours reduction first	60%	53%	30%	64%
Only	18	26	24	—
Then layoff	42	27	6	—
Layoff first	32	35	64	25
Only	10	11	—	—
Then cut hours	22	24	—	—
Both or no fixed policy	8	12	6	11

Sources: a) NICB, "Curtailment, Layoff Policy and Seniority," Studies in Personnel Policy No. 5 (1938), p. 5. b) U.S. Bureau of Labor Statistics, "Analysis of Layoff, Recall and Worksharing Procedures in Union Contracts," Bulletin No. 1209 (Washington, D.C., 1957), p. 36. c) NICB, "Seniority Systems in Nonunionized Companies," Studies in Personnel Policy No. 110 (1950), p. 37.

But memories of the early 1930s, when employers had cut hours below the subsistence level, made workers reluctant to support a policy of unlimited work-sharing. Moreover senior workers were less inhibited than before about opposing the policy because stop-gap jobs were now available from the WPA, making it easier for younger workers to survive while on layoff. Leaders of the new CIO unions worried that the combination of shift rotation and low incomes produced by unlimited work-sharing would deprive the union of a stable core of dues-paying members. Hence the two-stage procedure of work-sharing followed by layoffs was adopted by unions in the automobile, rubber, steel, and electrical industries.[22]

The shift away from this two-stage procedure took place gradually over the next twenty years. One important factor in the shift was the availability of unemployment insurance, although benefits were quite meager until well after World War II. As late as 1954, both unions and managements expressed concern about the inadequacy of unemployment benefits. Not until benefits were liberalized and supplemented by private plans (the SUB plans negotiated in the late 1950s) did major unions finally support straight layoffs.[23]

The increasingly high level of welfare or "fringe" benefits after World War II, especially in unionized firms, provided an incentive for employers to agree to union demands for straight layoffs. Because benefits were a fixed cost to be paid regardless of how many hours an employee worked, it made economic sense for companies to favor layoffs during downturns.[24]

While these economic factors are important, they do not tell the whole story. The shift to straight layoffs can also be explained by the unionized sector's growing acceptance of seniority as an equitable principle of distribution. After the war, unionized workers were more likely than nonunion workers to be affected by seniority in a variety of ways, from promotions to parking privileges. They became accustomed to regarding seniority as fair, even though it slighted need and merit. According to a survey of manual workers conducted in the late 1950s, current and former union members were twice as likely to favor seniority layoffs as were those who had never belonged to a union, whatever the worker's own seniority.[25]

Finally, as historian Ronald Schatz has pointed out, a new and younger generation entered the factories during and after World War II. They had only dim memories of the depression and of the egalitarian spirit that had supported work-sharing. The times had changed too. The prosperous postwar years were a less favorable spawning ground for egalitarianism than were the 1930s. It is also possible that the spread of seniority itself fostered values inimical to work-sharing. Not without justification did some prewar union leaders regard a seniority system as "an undesirable encouragement of a selfish, individualistic philosophy contrary to the ideals of solidarity and the best interests of the union as a whole."[26]

Guarantees. The continuing problem of unstable seasonal employment prompted another union initiative: guaranteed wage or employment plans to compensate workers for seasonal income losses. First broached by the auto workers in 1934 and supported by a number of the new CIO unions, this idea gained renewed attention at the end of the decade. In a 1938 pamphlet, the steelworkers called upon employers in the industry to stabilize employment using both traditional techniques and industry-wide planning.[27]

The number of guarantee plans rose rapidly between 1935 and 1940, although they still covered only a small fraction of the labor force (see table 7.2). Two-thirds of the firms with guarantee plans were unionized; CIO unions were more likely to be involved than AFL unions, which tended to be leery of the idea, in part because seasonality had traditionally been a justification for high craft wages. The increase in the number of plans was attributable not only to union pressure, but also to provisions in the 1938 Fair Labor Standards Act (FLSA) exempting an employer from the Act's overtime provisions if he offered a wage guarantee plan.[28]

But most large employers resisted demands to provide guarantee plans. Only 10 percent of the plans were found in establishments employing more than 1,000 workers. As during the 1920s, many of the companies offering the guarantees were either retail establishments or small producers of consumer nondurables.[29] A partial exception was General Motors, which in 1939 introduced (without notifying the union) an "income security plan," which was not a guarantee but a wage advance plan for senior workers. They could receive a wage advance during seasonal or other slowdowns but had to pay the money back when hours returned to normal or overtime levels.[30]

This is not to say that most large companies ignored union pressure for guarantees. Instead of instituting costly annual wage plans, however, employers again displayed great interest in employment stabilization techniques. Management publications in the late 1930s and early 1940s carried a plethora of material on the subject, much of it spurred by the employers' hope that successful stabilization would attenuate union demands for guarantees.[31]

Certain aspects of the government's new active labor market policy were designed to encourage private employment stabilization. The experience rating provisions in state unemployment insurance laws penalized unstable employers, although contemporary studies found that relatively few firms undertook appreciable stabilization efforts in response to the provisions. Further, the overtime provisions of the FLSA, like the NIRA's hours codes, were intended to provide an incentive for smoothing out production cycles.[32]

Nonetheless, the evidence suggests that the seasonal instability of industrial employment did not decline during the late 1930s, at least at the aggregate level. Either employers were saying much and doing little, or they had no chance to take action before defense preparations made the issue moot. With industry operating at full capacity after 1940, both sides temporarily lost interest in guarantee plans. General Motors quietly dropped its income security plan in 1942.[33]

Promotions. Unions also tried to improve the security of their members by pressuring firms to change their promotion methods. One union official in 1941 complained that most unions, "particularly those in the mass production and other industries, have found little if any systematic plan for advancement or promotion of workers to better-paying positions."[34] Unions sought more uniform and formalized promotion policies that would deter abuses by foremen and open jobs up to members. They insisted that heavier weight be given to seniority in promotions and that post-and-bid systems for internal vacancies be introduced. They also demanded that companies create or more carefully define internal lines of promotion.[35]

Some managements rushed to improve their promotion methods in anticipation of union demands. Both General Motors and Westinghouse announced new internal promotion policies shortly after

passage of the Wagner Act. These firms—as well as others like
RCA, Kimberly-Clark and L-O-F Glass—began pressuring their
foremen to promote from within whenever possible. Personnel
managers thought that an internal promotion plan, if applied fairly,
would make unions less rigid in their demands for promotions
based on seniority.[36] But formalization took place very slowly in
this area, in part because of continued resistance from foremen. A
1939 study by Princeton's Industrial Relations Section found that
definite promotion lines were still "rare" and that companies which
"usually have been the leaders in industrial relations progress have
not been greatly concerned with this aspect of employment management relations."[37]

Management's Defense

Innovations in employment policy after 1935 did not flow exclusively from organized labor. In nonunion firms, management
took the initiative in several areas, both to forestall unionization
and to secure managerial prerogatives in case a union gained entry.
In unionized firms, management fought to prevent union encroach-
ment into areas that it had reserved for itself. Intensive efforts were
made on the ideological front to win the loyalty of the labor force,
whether unionized or not.

One innovation initiated by management had to do with the
formulation and announcement of corporate employment policies.
At least until the mid-1930s, many companies resembled the employer who "flatly refused to put his labor policies in writing on
the grounds that if he did so he and his executives would be
committed to making them effective."[38] But after 1935 there was
a sudden outpouring of company handbooks and policy statements
(table 7.2). The reluctance to put policies in writing ebbed as
companies became aware of the many advantages that a "web of
rules" provided.[39]

First, definite policies helped personnel departments to control
foremen; standardizing employment procedures throughout the
organization made it less likely that independent supervisors would
commit acts that opened the doors to union organizers. Second, in
unionized firms, policy statements and rulebooks enhanced the

foreman's authority in disputes with union stewards and workers, giving management a better chance of winning in grievance arbitration and maintaining its prerogatives. Finally, policy statements served an ideological function since they helped to show that the company, rather than the union, was the source of benign employment practices. This made any current or future collective bargaining agreement appear somewhat superfluous and certainly less impressive.[40]

Industry's complex and irrational wage structures—the legacy of years of decentralized and uncoordinated wage setting by plant managers and foremen—were a major grievance among many workers. The steel industry was a notorious example. In the late 1930s, Carnegie-Illinois had 15,000 separate wage classifications; American Steel and Wire had over 100,000.[41] The inequities that inevitably accompanied this diversity made a tempting target for union organizers. Before the steelworkers' union won their first contract, their research department

> functioned almost exclusively as an agency to ferret out wage inequalities. . . . Quickly they were sent out to organizers, who found the material very good agitational dynamite. Loudspeakers blared at the mill gates, "How about your mill? Is a millwright in the blooming mill worth eighteen cents more than a millwright in the electric furnace department? No! No! A thousand times No! Join the union and bring justice to all workers."[42]

To prevent such inequities from becoming "agitational dynamite," managements hastened to adopt job evaluation plans after 1935. The plans depersonalized wage payment, forced companies to compare their rates with those prevailing in their area or industry, and thus made for greater consistency of rates. Adjusting inequities was also a cheaper way to boost worker morale than paying across-the-board rate increases.[43] Liberal management groups like the AMA and Industrial Relations Counselors strongly urged their members to adopt job evaluation. So did the conservative National Metal Trades Association, which developed a standard evaluation plan for use by its members.[44]

There were other reasons for this haste. Unions, particularly the new CIO unions, were trying to narrow skill differentials while pushing all rates upward. Job evaluation gave management a device to maintain preferred differentials and contain union wage pressures. The prospect of having to bargain over wage differentials led many firms preemptively to adopt job evaluation in case they were unionized. According to one study, half of the plans in existence in 1946 had been implemented before 1941, usually without any union involvement in the process of rate rationalization.[45]

Union leaders often denounced job evaluation as a "management tool." One survey found that two out of every three union officials were opposed to it.[46] They argued that inequities could better be removed through collective bargaining and that job evaluation was intended to bypass the union's function in this area. There was also some dissatisfaction with management's claim that job evaluation should be the sole determinant of a job's worth. But, as we shall see, during World War II job evaluation was supported by a significant minority of unions, many of them CIO unions that were able to introduce job evaluation jointly with management, rather than having it presented to them as a fait accompli.[47]

As with job evaluation, the post-1935 growth of merit rating was an attempt by managements to retain control of the employment process. Because merit rating plans used standardized criteria to rate worker performance and attitudes on the job, they constituted a defensible alternative to union demands that pay and allocative decisions be based strictly on seniority (see table 7.2). Merit rating, again like job evaluation, was portrayed as a highly technical, quasi-scientific solution to a myriad of management's problems.[48]

At nonunion firms, merit rating was seen as a tactical necessity. Thompson Products was in the midst of an organizing drive when it introduced a rating plan in 1939. The firm distrusted its foremen and thought the plan would reduce worker charges of discrimination. As the company told its foremen, the plan would also be "of untold value *if* at some future date" stricter seniority rules were demanded.[49]

Unionized firms had similar motives for introducing merit rating. First, it forced foremen to be more fair and consistent, thus weakening the basis for union demands to give greater weight to seniority. Second, it provided hard data to justify departures from seniority, thus giving managements a better chance to win grievance disputes.[50]

With very few exceptions, unions strongly opposed merit rating.

In their view, not only did it undermine seniority principles, but also it reserved too much power to foremen, under the guise of objective and impersonal performance ratings (a point that some managers were willing to concede).[51] But nothing angered unions so much as the inclusion of subjective, attitudinal factors in merit rating plans. Some plans permitted discrimination against union activists by allowing foremen to rate the worker's "loyalty" and "enthusiasm" and by attempting to plumb worker attitudes toward unions. Thus, one plan asked the foreman to comment on the worker's "reaction to shop life and his effect on the general morale (is he actively or passively antagonistic?)" and to indicate whether the worker was someone who "follows others" or helps to "mold opinions of small group[s]?"[52]

Selling the Company

Companies experimented with other techniques to determine how workers felt toward management, unions, and related issues. Sophisticated attitude testing programs were begun in the late 1930s at Armstrong Cork, Sears Roebuck, Westinghouse, and other firms. At Sears, a "morale score" was computed on the basis of employee responses to questions about attitudes toward the company.[53] Companies hoped that the survey results would help them to identify, before any union did, departments where morale was low and issues that were festering. Personnel managers thought that test results would prove to top management that the personnel strategy was producing "the desired employee attitudes."[54]

A larger number of companies tried to mold employee attitudes by means of extensive information and public relations campaigns. Workers were subjected to an endless barrage of pamphlets, magazines, monthly letters, and films. Managements acted as if they were engaged in a propaganda war not merely against hostile worker attitudes but against ideological threats to the foundations of capitalism. By 1940, one out of every six workers received information from his employer on "the American economic system."[55]

After 1935, the restoration and expansion of welfare benefits was the most expensive of the employer activities designed to promote worker loyalty. During this period the number of workers covered by pension, profit-sharing, paid vacation, and health insurance plans grew steadily. The proportion of firms with these plans in 1940 far exceeded levels reached a decade earlier. Employers used the plans either to deter unions (as when International Harvester twice sweetened its profit-sharing plan in the midst of CIO drives) or to weaken workers' loyalty to them. Most companies steadfastly refused to bargain over welfare benefits, in the hope of convincing employees that they owed neither their benefits nor their security to a union.[56]

Despite the apparent failure of company unionism, the other half of welfare capitalism's legacy from the 1920s, Industrial Relations Counselors and other management groups stepped up their efforts in behalf of these plans. Although the New Deal diminished the hope that private efforts might stave off government welfare programs, employers did not give up the fight. Rather, as a Jersey Standard executive said in 1935, they were "supplementing the government schemes for economic security with definite cooperative benefits to make their employees have enough stake as capitalists to insure their continued support of this system."[57] Far from displacing private efforts, government entry into the pension field established minimum standards of protection and stimulated interest in the subject on the part of worker and employer alike. A 1939 study found that, following passage of the Social Security Act in 1935, twice as many companies adopted pension plans as abandoned them. As management publications were fond of pointing out, for a very small outlay a firm could earn its employees' gratitude by supplementing the inadequate pension provided by the government.[58]

Personnel Management

As the foregoing suggests, personnel management served somewhat different functions in unionized and in nonunion firms. In nonunion companies, its function was preventive. Companies that avoided unionization were widely credited with having "good" personnel administration. Even the most traditional employers were now willing to grant that the personnel department constituted a "necessary evil" and "good insurance."[59]

The continuing irony in personnel management was that it best served the purpose of thwarting unionism by introducing the same reforms the unions sought. "Meet the situation more than half way," said a personnel expert in 1937, "rather than wait till the resounding thump of a labor organizer's fist splits the panel of your office door."[60] While most executives were not enamored of the unions' rigid approach to job security and other matters, they were willing to "meet the situation more than half way" in order to preserve their nonunion status. Opposition to unionism was not only a matter of economics; it stemmed from the desire to preserve management's freedom, or at least the illusion of it.

The function of personnel management in unionized firms was at first ambiguous. At some companies, it was hoped that, with the aid of enlightened personnel policies and belligerent legal tactics, the unions might soon be dislodged. At others, the feeling was one of defeat, reinforced by the prevailing wisdom that a firm got what it deserved and that unionization was a sign that past personnel techniques had failed. A third position accepted unions as a permanent feature of the environment but held that an active personnel department could contain their impact; this view had become dominant by the end of the war.[61]

According to the consensus view, the union-management relationship was an armed truce, and personnel management should be used to defend managerial prerogatives and to compete for worker loyalty. The union's base of support could eventually be eroded if company-initiated employment reforms were used to remove the sources of worker discontent. After the war, one executive recalled:

> Personnel programs were inaugurated during the thirties because many managements saw in them a device for preventing unionization. When the unions organized anyway, as they usually did, enthusiasm for personnel management in these companies often reached a pretty low ebb. In some companies when unions organized the employees faster than the companies could organize personnel departments, management often reasoned that since personnel management seemed to obviate the need for unions, a liberal use of personnel techniques would keep the union weak and docile.[62]

In one respect the spread of labor unions had a similar impact on unionized and on nonunion firms: It elevated the status and authority of the personnel department. The personnel function in larger firms was finally taken out of the manufacturing division and given a status equal to that of other major departments.[63] Even chief executives accepted the need for a personnel department and for a less traditional approach to labor. The personnel manager, said one somewhat partisan observer, "is no longer the lone crusader."[64]

This period witnessed the creation of a network of local and national organizations—not unlike that which had existed during World War I—partly in response to the widespread demand for information on the latest developments in government regulation and on the technical aspects of personnel management. The American Management Association was the most active of the national organizations. Although it had lost close to half its members between 1930 and 1935, the AMA quickly rebuilt itself afterward, and began sponsoring conferences around the country and publishing a variety of materials.[65]

The AMA had close ties to the major corporations that made up the Special Conference Committee, which funneled financial and other support to the AMA. After the SCC was exposed by the La Follette Committee in 1937, resources were shifted to its sister organization, Industrial Relations Counselors. Clarence J. Hicks, who served on the boards of all three organizations, was instrumental in channeling Jersey Standard money through IRC to help establish industrial relations centers at a number of major private universities. The universities expanded their selection of personnel courses and began to offer conferences and to issue publications of their own.[66]

Other groups with roots in the World War I period revived themselves in the late 1930s. The Conference Board, which had a stronger research orientation than the AMA, gave greater emphasis to personnel management after 1935. The Personnel Research Federation enjoyed a new respectability, as did the Taylor Society, which now called itself the Society for the Advancement of Management. Members of all of these organizations still gathered at the YMCA's annual Silver Bay Industrial Conferences. These organizational links and common sources of information helped to create a consensus among managments about how best to approach the related problems of unionism and government regulation.[67]

Personnel managers and their academic supporters again became interested in establishing a professional basis for personnel management. At the same time, the pre-1921 conception of personnel management as an impartial third force within the firm experienced a resurgence. The personnel manager at Swift wrote in 1940 that the "good personnel man must be absolutely sincere in his determination to be fair to both management and employees. . . . He carries no brief for either. It will be impossible for him to be impartial in his judgement if he has any axes to grind."[68]

But personnel managers in unionized firms found it increasingly difficult to maintain this image, since union leaders were quick to disparage their claims to neutrality. One union official told a conference of personnel managers: "Whereas you gentlemen present yourselves to the workers as specialists and as technicians and as detached professionals, they sort of chew at the end of their cigars, or spit after they have swallowed a little tobacco from the end of their cigarettes, and say, 'Yes, but who is paying you?' "[69]

Personnel managers in nonunion firms found it somewhat easier to present themselves as guarantors of the employee's rights, whose professional neutrality permitted them to intervene in disputes between foremen and workers. A few firms allowed workers to appeal grievances involving foremen directly to the personnel manager, although formal nonunion grievance systems did not flourish until the war. Nevertheless, a professional stance made it easier for the personnel manager "to build up a close and confidential relationship with the employees so that they will discuss many of their grievances with him informally."[70]

Marginal Men

The personnel department's willingness to hear grievances about line management was bound to cause conflict, as it had during World War I. Moreover, though he still had important duties to perform, the foreman was being stripped of his authority and prerogatives as decisions in a number of areas—hiring, promotions, wage determination, dismissal—were centralized or made subject to strict rules and procedures.[71] In 1938, Lawrence Appley of the AMA summarized the events of the preceding three years:

> Specialists suddenly sprang into action. Special surveys were conducted and in each case the center of the attack seemed to be the foreman or supervisor, simply because he was in a position where all the activities of the organization were coordinated for the workers. . . . One by one his responsibilities were taken away from him.[72]

Foremen complained that they were bypassed by the personnel department, kept in the dark about the company's plans and problems, and taken for granted by top management.[73]

The foreman in a unionized company had an especially rough time. Management rarely consulted him during contract negotiations and sometimes even failed to provide him with a copy of the collective bargaining agreement. And the union crimped his prestige and authority even more than did the personnel department. Shop stewards challenged his every move. They frequently short-circuited him in the grievance procedure, correctly perceiving him to be powerless. Managements went along with this, because they had little faith in the foreman's ability.[74] One economist observed that, because of unions, foremen "no longer controlled the employment of the men who worked under them; even if they did recommend the discharge of an incompetent worker, the union usually could get him reinstated . . . In general, they were pretty well kicked around by both sides."[75] To make matters worse, foremen watched as the wages and working conditions of unionized production workers improved while their own employment conditions stagnated. Production workers were given job security, but many foremen were only temporary gang bosses.[76]

Most managements did not recognize the gravity of the situation until foremen in the Detroit automotive firm of Kelsey-Hayes Wheel formed a union in 1938, the United Foremen and Supervisors, which spread to Chrysler in 1939, shortly after Chrysler had signed a collective bargaining agreement with its production workers. Shunned by the UAW, the union affiliated with the CIO. Later, however, the CIO disowned it. Then the NLRB refused to hear its petitions, and some of its members were fired. Given this united front of opposition from labor, management, and government, it is little wonder that the union dissolved in 1940. But it set a precedent for the larger foremen's unions of World War II, and it shook managements out of their complacency. Though shorn of many of his responsibilities the foreman was still essential to the maintenance of discipline on the shop floor. He also remained a key link in the effort to contain the effects of rank-and-file unionism. Top managers worried that a unionized foreman might prove ineffectual because of divided loyalties.[77]

After 1937, foremen's training programs were aimed at getting the foreman to accept the loss of his prerogatives and at the same time to feel that he was still a part of management. At courses and conferences, the details of new corporate employment policies were spelled out to him, and the logic behind them explained.[78] A more interesting development was the reemergence of the National Association of Foremen (NAF), an organization of foremen's clubs. Moribund during the early 1930s, it was revived around 1936 with financial and other assistance from midwestern employers, notably in the automobile industry. By 1937 it claimed 20,000 members.[79]

Unlike the YMCA's National Council of Foremen's Clubs, the NAF was openly opposed to foremen's unions. At its 1937 convention (hosted by Chrysler), it adopted a resolution that any club that was affiliated with a foremen's union would be expelled from the organization. In contrast to the YMCA's clubs, most of the NAF's clubs were made up of foremen and supervisors from a single firm, an arrangement that made for tighter management control and discouraged the development of union proclivities. To give foremen a management viewpoint, the NAF devised its own foreman training programs and published an attractive magazine, *The National Foreman* (later called *Supervision*).[80]

Government and the Small Exception

Thus, between the Wagner Act and World War II, employment policy and management structures underwent a remarkable transformation that cut across all types of industries and organizations, with the important exception of small and medium-sized firms (those employing less than a thousand workers). Although these firms often took their cues in the personnel area from their larger brethren, they tended to be more conservative and informal. As late as 1940 one personnel consultant noted that the majority of smaller firms still regarded personnel management as "a luxury."[81]

Nevertheless, as a result of union organization and the pressures of trying to cope with government regulations, some small companies created personnel departments and formalized their employment practices during this period. The new NLRB forced firms, whether large or small, to pay close attention to their employment practices and to adopt uniform procedures. In response to the Wagner Act, the National Association of Manufacturers encouraged its relatively small member firms to keep careful employee records and to hire full-time personnel managers.[82] The complex rules and data-gathering requirements of unemployment insurance, social security, and minimum wage laws also made imperative the centralization of the personnel function. For example, the Fair Labor Standards Act required firms to keep records of the wages and hours of all their employees. Thus, the spread of government regulation hastened the erosion of decentralized systems of labor administration in all firms, regardless of size. This effect was especially marked during World War II.[83]

II. World War II—The Pattern is Set

The advent of war brought another round of expansion in the number of personnel departments, particularly at small and medium-sized companies (table 7.2). Smaller firms needed experts who could cope with a strengthened labor movement and an expanded array of government regulations. During the war, as practical knowledge of personnel management became a more valuable commodity, the emphasis shifted: The question was no longer *whether* to have a personnel department but how to operate that department.[84]

In larger firms, the status of the personnel department reached an all-time high. A 1945 survey found that, in seven out of eight large manufacturing firms, the personnel department was an independent unit whose head reported directly to the company's president, just like any other division. Personnel departments grew in size as well as status; the ratio of staff personnel positions to number of employees increased as new positions were created to meet the special needs of the war-time labor force, with its larger proportions of migrants and women. But the expansion also indicated top management's high regard for personnel management and the policy of self-restraint.[85]

Employment policies began to move more rapidly in the direction set during the preceding period. Foremen were forced to defer to the personnel department and to follow company-wide procedures. Allocative practices and wage setting became enmeshed in increasingly rigid rules. Finally, employment security and other ties that bound a worker to his current employer were strengthened. The motive forces behind all these developments were the continued growth of unions and of government regulation, and the new need to conserve scarce labor.

Unions added over five million members to their rolls during the war; this figure represents roughly two out of every three production workers in manufacturing in 1945. But numbers alone do not tell the whole story. On the eve of the war, the unions had still not succeeded in penetrating such industry giants as Westinghouse, Ford, and the Little Steel companies (including Bethlehem, Inland, and Republic). The contracts that had been signed frequently lacked any provisions for union security. This situation changed after 1940. First, continued employer resistance to strikes became more costly as profits from defense production began to mount in 1941. Second, the desire to avoid wartime strikes led the government to support collective bargaining more vigorously. The National War Labor Board (NWLB), formed in 1942, compelled employers to negotiate with and grant membership security to the unions. As a result, unions in 1945 were not only larger but also more powerful and firmly entrenched. [86]

Government's impact on the labor market extended far beyond collective bargaining. During the war the nation came close to having a command labor market, as the President and agencies like the War Manpower Commission made important decisions affecting pay and labor allocation within and between firms. Government intervention resulted in more standardized employment conditions across industry. The government gave its imprimatur to the personnel practices established by major companies and unions; indeed, the dissemination of these practices was an explicit policy of the NWLB. The U.S. Employment Service trained personnel managers for private industry; as during World War I, this government activity brought modern personnel techniques and philosophies to new (aircraft) and still backward (shipbuilding) defense industries.[87]

Labor shortages provided another reminder of World War I. The scramble to attract and retain war workers further boosted the power of the personnel department. Now that labor was a scarce resource, employment was suddenly too important to be left to the foreman; his remaining administrative duties were reduced. The foreman's job was made even more difficult by an increase in problems on the shop floor. As in 1917, employers complained that labor shortages "discourage submissiveness on the part of labor." Quits and absenteeism rose, and labor productivity sank. But foremen were no longer free to discipline workers, in part because of management pressure to conserve labor.[88]

Internal Labor Markets: Widening and Deepening

As labor became scarcer during the war, informal methods of hiring proved inadequate to handle the demands of rapidly expanding companies. Consequently, recruitment and hiring became the most centralized and standardized of personnel activities. Few large firms continued to permit foremen to hire on their own (table 7.2). Instead, workers were carefully recruited and then put through a bureaucratic rigmarole of application forms, interviews, and employment tests. To a much greater extent than during World War I, the army's intelligence and psychological testing spilled over into private industry. By 1947, about one-fifth of all industrial firms relied on employment tests.[89]

Further constraints on recruitment and hiring were imposed by federal agencies seeking to allocate war workers to the industries where they were most needed. For instance, the War Manpower Commission (WMC) was empowered to penalize firms for labor pirating, while the U.S. Employment Service stipulated that certain employers had to employ its referrals. In areas where labor was especially scarce, the WMC set up "stabilization plans" to regulate hiring and prevent labor hoarding.[90]

Union pressure also played a role in the centralization of recruitment and hiring. One management study found that over half of all new employees had acquired some grievance against their employer by the time they started working. Consequently, personnel departments were reluctant to entrust foremen with the important task of hiring workers and giving them a good first impression of the company. New workers were treated to elaborate initiation rites, including movies, speeches, and other activities intended to arouse their gratitude and loyalty.[91]

Training and Promotion. To cope with its labor shortage problems, industry was forced to embark on a massive training program during the war. Conventional training methods were simply no longer adequate to increase the supply of skilled labor as rapidly as necessary. Moreover, training had to be provided to millions of new recruits—women and migrants from rural areas—who never before had worked in factories.

The standard solution to all these problems was a process that combined manpower planning, job simplification, and training by progression from one simplified job to another. Manpower planning allowed firms to identify their projected labor and training requirements. The government was heavily involved in this as well as other aspects of industry's training program. Shortly after its inception, the WMC asked all firms to aid in the orderly deployment of labor by preparing "Manning Table" plans, which outlined their current and future manpower needs. To facilitate training and the transfer of labor to areas where it was most needed, firms were asked to describe their jobs in standard terms taken from the recently compiled *Dictionary of Occupational Titles*. This requirement forced firms to conduct extensive job analyses and to create a rational structure of well-defined but rigid job titles.[92]

Next, jobs were simplified by means of industrial engineering techniques. Skilled jobs were broken down into a set of simpler tasks that could be learned quickly. In 1940 the WMC set up the Training Within Industry program, which offered training courses to foremen. One of these courses, Job Methods, taught almost a quarter of a million foremen how to perform job simplification analyses.[93]

The final stage in the process was the establishment of an internal promotion system whereby workers advanced along a chain of progressively more complex jobs. Alternatively, families of jobs requiring similar skills were identified; a logical promotion line was then formed out of existing jobs. Both the WMC and the Training Within Industry (TWI) program helped employers to set up job ladders. C. R. Dooley, head of TWI, echoed the early vocationalists when he remarked, "Jobs are not static. . . . One job leads to a better one, and, step by step, the employee receives his training and advances in skill. The job is a rung on the ladder of progress—this is the efficient way as well as the American way. Upgrading is a method that leads workers upward."[94]

Similarly, the War Labor Board's wage control rules encouraged employers to adopt formal promotion policies since board approval was not required for any wage increase resulting from a bona fide promotion. Firms could prove the legitimacy of a promotion by showing the board "an orderly and definite procedure for rising between classification adjustments," in the form of either promotion ladders or job classification charts. In addition, by allowing automatic length-of-service wage increases up to some ceiling rate (despite the wage freeze), the board turned the practice of tying wage increases to seniority into an industrial norm. By 1943, three out of five firms were paying wage increases for so-called in-grade progression.[95]

Unions also hastened the spread of internal promotion systems during the war. Because of their new bargaining power, they could negotiate limits on management's discretion to determine who was eligible to fill job vacancies. Promotion ladders narrowed the eligible group down to everyone in the classification below the vacancy; seniority provisions narrowed the choice further. Opportunities for union members were enhanced by the adoption of post-and-bid systems that gave insiders the first crack at vacancies. These vacancy posting systems were associated with unionism but not with the presence or absence of a personnel department (see table 8.3). Finally, as seniority was institutionalized, unions found that promotion ladders aided in the specification of bumping units showing which jobs were open to those choosing to displace less senior workers in lieu of layoffs.[96]

Of course, these developments did not always proceed smoothly. Some foremen continued to play favorites, causing one Detroit worker to complain in 1945 that "upgrading is a racket; it's not

Table 8.3. Job Posting in Industry, 1952 (proportion of firms posting jobs)

	Unionized Firms	Nonunion Firms
Has personnel department	43%	5%
Has no personnel department	38	7

SOURCE: H. Ellsworth Steele, William R. Myles and Sherwood McIntyre, "Personnel Practices in the South," *Industrial and Labor Relations Review* (January 1956), 9:248–250.

what you know, but who you know."[97] Foremen opposed job posting, which eroded their autonomy by breaking down departmental barriers. Nevertheless, the war did much to forge a distinctively American pattern of internal career ladders composed of rigidly defined jobs.

Wage Determination. Many companies—especially smaller firms that wanted to get control of their rate structure in preparation for collective bargaining—continued to adopt job evaluation plans unilaterally (i.e., without consulting unions). Yet during the war, managements and unions often cooperated voluntarily and instituted job evaluation on a joint basis, despite warnings from managers that the union should be consulted only after the evaluation had been conducted. Here again, the War Labor Board's wage stabilization rules provided an incentive for adopting a particular personnel practice.[98]

The board was concerned by the large number of grievances filed to reduce inequities in intraplant rate structures. Accordingly, it allowed wage increases to reduce imbalances but usually asked that the increases be justified by reference to an evaluation plan. This requirement provided two routes around the wage freeze. First, as board officials conceded, the introduction of an evaluation plan raised total wages because rates below the evaluation standard were increased, whereas those above were not cut.[99] Second, once a plan was in place, unions and managers could use it to justify additional inequity requests before the board. For example, in 1941 the board ordered the booming California aircraft industry to adopt a multi-employer evaluation plan. The board later rejected several industry requests for a general rate increase. But repeated use of the inequities provision "allowed the whole wage scale to be jacked up gradually to higher levels. . . . [This] resulted in an average wage increase of more than 15 cents an hour" between 1943 and 1945.[100]

In some cases (including the iron ore, steel, cotton textile, lumber, and shipbuilding industries, as well as in individual firms), the board ordered the parties to negotiate and adopt an evaluation plan so as to relieve tensions produced by inequities. The steel plan was the result of union demands in 1943 to eliminate interplant and intraplant rate inequities, the issue in nearly half of the grievances filed at U.S. Steel in 1942. The board turned down the union's demand to equalize interplant pay but ordered over ninety companies to negotiate a plan with the union to rationalize their internal rate structures.[101]

As job evaluation and internal promotion plans became more prevalent, new emphasis was given to the consistency of the individual firm's wage structure. Wage systems were made commensurate with the status and opportunity structure within the firm; correspondingly less attention was given to external labor market developments. Shortly after the war, one economist reported: "Where job evaluation has established occupational wage differentials, the criterion is governing in spite of differences in market rates or occupational differentials otherwise prevailing in the locality."[102]

In addition to job evaluation, the NWLB triggered a dramatic expansion of pecuniary welfare benefits. Firms were allowed to adopt "reasonable" group insurance, pension, profit-sharing and vacation plans without NWLB approval (table 8.4). They used these fringe benefits to bolster worker loyalty and to mitigate the effect of the wartime wage freeze. For unions, welfare benefits were a way to expand the scope of bargaining now that wage level issues were moot. There was also considerable worker demand for these benefits, even after the war.[103]

Table 8.4. Welfare Benefits for Hourly Workers in Manufacturing, 1940–1946 (proportion of firms)

	1940	1946
Health insurance	36%	68%
Hospitalization insurance	33	64
Profit-sharing plan	7	12
Pension plan	8	23

SOURCE: National Industrial Conference Board (NICB), "Personnel Activities in American Business," Studies in Personnel Policy (SPP) No. 20 (New York, 1940), p. 24; NICB, "Personnel Activities in American Business (Revised)," SPP No. 86 (New York, 1947), pp. 22–23.

Yet most employers still were opposed to bargaining with unions over the administration and size of these benefit plans, claiming them as a managerial prerogative. After the war some employers urged that fringe benefits be excluded by law as an issue for collective bargaining. This last-ditch effort to preserve the corporatist thrust behind pecuniary welfare work was defeated by union pressure and, ultimately, by the Supreme Court's 1949 *Inland Steel* decision, which brought such benefits under the scope of bargaining.[104]

Employment Security: Guarantees and Dismissals. In 1943, the steelworkers's union (USWA) revived the employment stabilization issue by demanding annual wage guarantees from the steel companies. It was a strange time to launch such a campaign: War workers were employed year-round, and most of them were working overtime. But as the war had reached a turning point and victory began to seem likely, fears of a postwar depression were kindled. According to various surveys conducted in 1944, workers ranked regularity of wages as more important than any other issue except the maintenance of high wage rates. Annual wage plans increased the worker's feeling of security. There were other reasons for the campaign: Union bargaining power was high, as were company profit levels. The USWA told industry employers in 1944 that they easily could stabilize employment and afford to pay an annual wage.[105]

Although the NWLB rejected the union's demand as "unworkable," the issue did not die down.[106] After the war the USWA continued to press for an annual wage plan, and now it was joined by several other powerful CIO unions, including the UAW and the Packinghouse Workers. Walter Reuther called the annual wage an "economic necessity" that would assure workers of a steady job. Saying that management was doing "too little to advance regularized employment," the research director for the Textile Workers warned in 1946: "Labor will not continue indifferent to the current practice of making workers shoulder the costs and risks of irregular employment. It will call for government action unless significant progress is made."[107]

Employers were slow to accept union demands, arguing that guaranteed wage or employment plans were too restrictive and impractical. While the number of plans increased between 1943 and 1950, no more than a quarter of a million workers were covered by 1950. But because of union strength after the war, managements could not continue to ignore the issue. The consensus was that, to counter union demands for guarantee plans, management would have to try harder to stabilize employment.[108] Employee handbooks began to promise that the company would provide "security of job and income" (Armstrong Cork), "stability of employment" (Kodak), and "stability of earnings and continuity of employment" (Jersey Standard). Although these promises were not legally enforceable, like a union contract, there is some evidence that companies tried to be true to their word. Seasonal variations in manufacturing employment were considerably smaller after the war than they had been at any time since 1919. This historic decline in seasonality may have smoothed the way to industry's acceptance of SUB plans in the late 1950s.[109]

The unions had their greatest impact on employment security through their regulation of discipline and dismissal. Disciplinary procedures and the creation of a grievance system were usually among the first items that a newly organized union wanted to discuss with management. By 1940, both of the major contracts in the auto and steel industries provided for a multi-step grievance system ending in arbitration. During the war, the practice of grievance arbitration received a boost from the NWLB, which "insisted, as a matter of paramount importance, upon arbitration as the final step of grievance procedure."[110] Moreover, the unions' wartime no-strike pledge forced them to rely more heavily on the grievance procedure. Anxious to avoid wildcat strikes and overwhelmed by the disciplinary problems arising from labor shortages and an inexperienced work force, management often capitulated to union demands in this area. At the end of the war, 85 percent of collective bargaining agreements included provisions for grievance arbitration.[111]

As a result of union pressure and the growth of a body of arbitration norms, management's disciplinary practices became subject to various due process restrictions, including the worker's right to have prior knowledge of rules and penalties, to introduce evidence into disciplinary hearings, and to appeal a decision. Managements were forced to develop elaborate disciplinary rules and to involve the unions in this developmental process.[112]

The most significant effect of union activity was widespread acceptance of the principle that a worker could be dismissed only for just cause, and only after he had exercised his rights to due process. Along with the arbitrator's ability to reinstate an unfairly dismissed worker, the just cause principle undermined the key element of the drive system—the foreman's freedom to dismiss a worker at will. Right after the war, one researcher found the steelworkers' union taking the position that the foreman "must be able to give valid and almost statistical proof of cause before he fires a man" and recognizing that "to the traditional foreman such a requirement seems like an insufferable invasion of his rights, if not a death blow to his executive standing."[113]

Centralization and the Foreman

By the end of the war, most companies no longer gave their foremen unchecked authority to dismiss workers. A 1945 study reported that in only 11 percent of the firms surveyed did foremen retain this power. Personnel and plant managers became more involved in the dismissal process (table 7.2). As during World War I, personnel departments offered the foreman the rather dubious comfort that his prestige would be enhanced because workers would now "think of him not as the person who holds a figurative whip over them but as the friend who advises them of violations."[114] The reasons for the foreman's loss of power included not only union pressure but also labor shortages and management's distrust of the foreman's ability to administer discipline fairly. Many wartime foremen were inexperienced, having recently been promoted from the ranks. In 1943, 42 percent of General Motor's foremen had held their posts for less than one year.[115]

As a result of these checks from above, the union steward often had more power than the foreman to regulate shop floor discipline. To bolster the foreman while at the same time maintaining their own centralized control, personnel departments decided to offer him more training in "human relations." During the war, Dale Carnegie-style programs for foremen proliferated. Using sophisticated behavioral techniques like sociodrama, sociometry, and role-playing, these courses trained foremen to be gentle persuaders so that they would be better able to maintain discipline and to compete with the union steward for the worker's loyalty.[116] The aftermath of one human relations training program conducted at General Electric during the war is described as follows: "Throughout the week, the foreman makes it a point to engage employees in conversation on some general subject of mutual interest. Usually it does not take long to discover whether a worker has something bothering him . . . After these conversations, the foreman writes a brief report. These reports are sent to the superintendent's office each night."[117]

The government mounted its own foreman training programs during the war. For instance, the TWI program—developed by academic proponents of the human relations approach to management, including Fritz Roethlisberger of the Harvard Business School—taught foremen to "work with people" and to "treat people as individuals." TWI boasted that this course, which was given to half a million foremen in private industry, raised war production by reducing the number of grievances filed.[118]

Large nonunion companies ardently believed that their nonunion status was linked to the quality of supervision in their plants. They were likely to offer foreman training programs and to have highly centralized disciplinary systems. Both were intended to reduce worker grievances about unfair discipline and dismissal. During the war a few nonunion firms adopted formal multistep grievance procedures that were very similar to those found in unionized firms, except that they usually terminated with the personnel manager or company president (so-called open door procedures) rather than with an outside arbitrator.[119] Since these nonunion complaint systems allowed the worker to jump steps in the procedure by going directly to the personnel department if the grievance involved his foreman, they provided a way for companies to keep tabs on their foremen. At the same time, they gave disgruntled employees some outlet, other than organizing or quitting, for expressing dissatisfaction.[120]

Of course, centralization extended far beyond the area of discipline and dismissal. Personnel departments during the war were deeply involved in a range of activities that once had been the foreman's prerogative, including hiring, wage setting, and promotions. Organization charts, new layers of management, and company rules and legalisms proliferated. Even firms employing no more than a few hundred workers tended to centralize most aspects of employment.[121] Personnel managers were aware of the dangers involved in this radical pruning of the foreman's responsibilities. But they felt that centralization was made necessary by the exigencies of war—government regulation, labor shortages, inexperienced workers and foremen—and by the need to prevent further union inroads. At best, said one personnel manager, all that could be done was somehow to bring foremen "closer" to the personnel department.[122]

Not surprisingly, foremen were demoralized by these developments. Three in five of some 900 foremen surveyed at the end of the war reported that they felt left out of management and did no more than follow orders. Another survey of eight major industries found a majority of foremen complaining of having responsibility but no corresponding authority. Others, especially older foremen, said they were handicapped by restrictions on their activities emanating from the personnel department. Those from unionized companies were annoyed at being "shortcircuited" by management during grievance procedures.[123]

Foremen were troubled by other issues, chief among them job security. They feared (quite accurately, as it turned out) that they would be laid off or returned to the ranks when war orders were cut back or cancelled. Unions were reluctant to credit the seniority records of demoted foremen for the time they had served in management. Pay was another major problem. It was not unusual for hourly workers to put in so much overtime that they earned considerably more than their salaried foremen. Finally, many foremen in unionized companies had recently been promoted from the ranks, where they had enjoyed the protection of a collective bargaining agreement and a grievance procedure. As part of management, however, foremen had few definite policies to protect them and only rarely had access to any sort of grievance system.[124]

Several foremen's unions were established during the war. The largest was the Foreman's Association of America (FAA), which was formed at Ford Motor in 1941 and which then spread to other companies including Packard and Chrysler. By 1944 the FAA had 33,000 members, most of them concentrated around Detroit. Though only a minority of foremen ever joined these unions, managements were nevertheless deeply worried by supervisory unionism and were determined to check its growth.[125] They responded to the threat in three ways.[126]

The first response was to improve the pay and perquisites of foremen. Pay differentials over hourly workers were widened, and fringe benefits upgraded. Other trivial changes were made to bolster the foreman's status. He was given a desk, telephone, and special parking space, and was allowed to represent management when announcements were made or special awards handed out.[127]

Second, companies spent more on formal programs intended to increase the foreman's familiarity and identification with management. Private training courses and conferences were expanded, even though foremen were by now "very critical of the ridiculous training programs which management has purchased or developed for them." In addition, the number of foremen's clubs was increased. Because of fears that the clubs might become a vehicle for union organization, however, the YMCA opened up its foremen's clubs to all levels of management so as to dilute their identity.[128]

A third response was to give foremen more power and authority by decentralizing personnel activities. Reducing the personnel department's involvement in line activities became more feasible toward the end of the war and during demobilization, when labor shortages eased and government regulation was relaxed. After the war some companies, usually small ones, gave their foremen more authority to hire and dismiss. Elsewhere, the most common form of decentralization was to give foremen the right to reject employees selected by the personnel department.[129]

Except for these modest responses, little else was done. There was no widespread return of power to the foreman, such as had occurred after World War I (table 7.2). Management advisory groups like the AMA and Industrial Relations Counselors were opposed to decentralization. Companies that claimed to have decentralized actually took very limited steps in this direction. So-called decentralization might entail no more than, for example, keeping the foreman apprised of personnel decisions and policies and thus giving him the feeling rather than the substance of power.[130]

One reason for the limited extent of decentralization was that the threat of supervisory unionism began to recede even before the war was over. Then in 1947 Congress passed the Taft-Hartley Act, which excluded foremen's unions from the protection of the National Labor Relations Act. One manager noted in 1948 that employers felt that Taft-Hartley had "solved" their "foreman problem."[131]

But a more important factor was managements' perception that unions were now deeply entrenched and would not quickly lose strength as they had in 1921. The end of the war unleashed a wave of strikes, and a bitter struggle for power began in unionized firms across the nation. Management was concerned as never before with defining and defending its rights, especially in the personnel area where the unions had made their deepest incursions. Management rights clauses, which outlined areas in which unions would not be allowed to encroach, were for the first time widely inserted into collective bargaining agreements. Decentralization would have given foremen much of the responsibility for holding the unions at bay, and management did not believe that its foremen had either the inclination or the ability to bear this responsibility.[132]

Finally, decentralization would have meant rolling back some of the employment reforms of the preceding ten years. These reforms depended on centralized control to ensure fairness and uniformity. In the case of job security measures, they were linked to a plant-wide system of labor allocation. Union strength precluded any such policy of reversion.

This is not to say, however, that personnel departments were immune to postwar cutbacks. As war contracts ended, pressure to trim personnel budgets grew. Cutbacks were most common at smaller firms that had created personnel departments as expedients to deal with war labor problems. Special wartime welfare programs were eliminated, as were some new aspects of personnel management, such as employee counseling and testing, that were "suspected by top management and the budgeters as being a luxury and a 'newfangled' idea."[133]

As after World War I, personnel managers searched for new ways to justify their budgets. One approach was to develop seemingly objective numerical measures—for instance, data on trends in labor turnover and absenteeism, attitude testing results—that would demonstrate the benefits of personnel department activities. Another way to protect budgets was to foster professionalization. After the war, personnel managers experienced a sudden burst of professional consciousness and manifested great interest in developing professional associations and codes of ethics. New journals and organizations lent an air of objective professionalism to personnel management, as did contacts with university researchers.[134]

These developments would have pleased earlier advocates of a scientific, neutral approach to personnel management. But professionalism now had a more restricted meaning than it had had for liberals in the early days of personnel management. Few postwar personnel managers conceived of themselves as neutral forces for change within the firm. Rather, professionalism had become a device to secure higher pay and greater prestige within the corporate hierarchy. Personnel managers thought of themselves as a part of management, and management was not the independent profession that Brandeis and the Taylorists had hoped it might prove to be.

Thus, the ten-year period following the Wagner Act was a time of accelerated diffusion and institutionalization of the internal labor market: Wages, promotion, and tenure were more tightly tied together. Job evaluation was linked to promotion ladders, seniority principles were strengthened, and job and relative wage structures became more rigid. Employment was made considerably more rulebound and more secure. However, this process did produce one casualty. The once powerful foreman was now described as management's "marginal" or "forgotten" man, terms that symbolized industry's forty-year transition from the drive system to the employment bureaucracy of the internal labor market.[135]

CONCLUSIONS

At the end of World War II, the field of labor economics was in a state of intellectual ferment as scholars weighed the consequences of industry's new employment system. Nearly everyone agreed that a transformation had occurred, although some questioned whether the change was for the better. Sumner Slichter, for example, said in 1947 that union pressure had "converted millions of jobs which previously had been held on a day-to-day basis into lasting connections," but a year later he warned that the surge of unionism meant that the United States was "gradually shifting from a capitalistic community to a laboristic one."[1] Others feared that, in the quest for security, too much had been relinquished: Labor market flexibility, economic efficiency, and even individual freedom were said to have declined. Clark Kerr viewed the spread of internal labor markets as part of a general trend "from the largely open to the partially closed society," with "fraternity triumph[ing] over liberty as 'no trespassing' signs are posted in more and more job markets."[2]

Fueling these concerns was a belief that the unions had succeeded almost too well in advancing labor's interests. In the political arena, where they had become a powerful force, unions were seeking to expand programs—national unemployment insurance, higher minimum wages, full employment laws—which augmented the gains already made through collective bargaining. In the workplace, union members were protected by a host of employment security plans that nonunion companies matched to the extent they felt necessary. These plans, it was argued, had rigidified the labor market and immobilized the labor force: Workers could no longer afford to leave their jobs. Terming this state of affairs "a new industrial feudalism," critics claimed that golden handcuffs now chained workers to their jobs.[3]

Indeed, turnover rates had fallen considerably from the very high levels that existed before 1920. While it is impossible to chart accurately the post-1920 drop in mobility, the data show that by the end of World War II, the hypermobility of the pre-1920 period had disappeared from all except the very lowest strata of the manufacturing labor market. Paralleling the decline in labor turnover was a downward trend in geographic mobility among manual workers. In short, between 1920 and 1950 workers became more attached not only to their workplaces but also to the communities in which they lived.[4]

This drop in mobility was one of the most important consequences of the employment system that had become widespread for manufacturing workers. Seniority rules and internal promotion policies gave workers a reason to remain with their employers. Grievance systems and nonunion complaint procedures provided an alternative to quitting and reduced the probability of being fired. Of course, a heavier use of layoffs counterbalanced the decline in dismissals, but because of rehiring commitments and because seniority was retained over a long period, workers on layoff were less likely to change jobs.[5]

Granting that the claims of a new industrial feudalism have some substance, it should also be pointed out that the decline in mobility had sources wider than the change in employment practices. One key factor was the passage of restrictive immigration laws that took effect in 1921, 1924, and 1929. The laws checked what had once been a huge backflow by making it more difficult for an emigrating alien to re-enter the United States at some future time. During the 1920s and 1930s, emigration fell to less than half of its previous levels. Workers who might have returned to their native countries instead sank down roots, started families, and committed themselves to particular employers and communities. Since the laws also led to a sharp decline in immigration levels, fewer newcomers entered the labor force after 1920. Newcomers are, by definition, persons without strong ties to a particular place, hence potentially mobile. Conversely, the decline in immigration meant that the children of earlier waves of immigrants now made up a larger proportion of the manufacturing labor force. Presumably this second generation chose to remain in the communities where their parents had finally settled. In other words, changes in the composition of the labor force resulted in a decline in geographic mobility, which in turn contributed to the drop in job mobility.[6]

The decline in geographic mobility also helped to create (though much later than is commonly supposed) stable, working-class communities centered on the workplace. Two points should be noted here. First, this phenomenon undoubtedly eased the task of organizing labor unions during the 1930s, and so indirectly fostered lower levels of job mobility. Second, it suggests that workers' ardent pursuit of job security after 1930 stemmed not only from a fear of unemployment but from an urge to protect these new forms of communal stability. Thus, changes in the workplace and in the community were mutually reinforcing.

As mentioned earlier, some postwar economists felt that the reduced flow of human resources through the labor market would undermine economic efficiency. But recent economic research suggests that this concern was groundless. According to the theories of labor retention based on turnover that developed during the 1960s and 1970s, the long-term decline in labor market fluidity was not necessarily undesirable: The immobilization produced by internal labor markets was said to be allocatively efficient because it reduced an employer's separation costs. However, these newer theories go too far in the opposite direction, overemphasizing the role played by efficiency incentives in the formation of internal labor markets.[7]

The historical record indicates that the employment reforms introduced during World War I and after 1933 were attibutable not so much to competitive market forces as to the growing power of the unions and the ascendance of the personnel department over other branches of management. These factors—along with the severity of the depression and changes in the composition of the labor force—led to changes in what Robert Solow has termed "social conventions or principles of appropriate behavior" and pushed firms to adopt policies that decasualized employment and curbed the excesses of the drive system.[8]

With the benefit of forty years' hindsight, we may observe that these policies often enhanced efficiency by reducing turnover and increasing morale, or by stimulating programs to upgrade the work force. But this effect was by no means obvious to the managers of firms in transition, who were skeptical that internal labor market arrangements would lower costs. Efficiency incentives were neither strong enough nor obvious enough to produce the modern internal labor market.

Economists in the late 1940s and early 1950s were also concerned about the social consequences of industry's new employment system, fearing that stable, long-term employment relationships might erode the worker's "initiative and self-reliance." Clark Kerr argued that, without labor turnover, a society would be "without independence of spirit, self-reliance [and] competitive urge." Here Kerr was defending the values of nineteenth-century liberalism—limited commitments, freedom of movement—against what he saw as the encroachments of an increasingly bureaucratic world. Curiously enough, recent Marxist critiques have voiced similar concerns: The autonomous artisan has everywhere been replaced by the modern worker, caught in a seamless web of bureaucratic domination, that stretches from the workplace to the state.[9] Both Kerr and the Marxists have overstated their case and romanticized the past. Yet it is undeniable that certain values—notably a kind of footloose independence—*were* lost in the shift away from a market-oriented employment system. At the same time, however, the shift has allowed other values to flourish, including equity, security, and a greater equality of outcomes, particularly between white- and blue-collar employees.

The Collar Line

The white-collar employee of the nineteenth and early twentieth centuries worked in a world that was physically and socially separate from the world of the manual worker. Differences within the white-collar group—between executive and clerk—were differences of degree rather than kind: Male white-collar employees of whatever level shared perquisites, aspirations, and a work culture distinct from the manual worker's. Although the collar line (the income and status gap between white- and blue-collar employees) was less marked in the United States than in England or Germany, it nonetheless existed: Regardless of rank, salaried employees in the United States enjoyed a variety of privileges that were unavailable to those on the other side of the collar line. These included shorter working hours, the absence of nightwork, paid vacations and other benefits, and job security.[10]

The employer had a gentlemen's agreement with his top salaried employees that they would not be dismissed except for disloyalty or (under extraordinary circumstances) poor performance. In fact, until the 1910s, American courts interpreted payment of a monthly or yearly salary as evidence that the employer had made an implicit employment commitment for the period of compensation, meaning that the salaried employee could not be dismissed at will. In other ways, too, the white-collar man was treated like a gentleman: He was trusted to perform without close supervision; his failures were ascribed to poor judgment (rather than inadequacy) and were not necessarily punished; and discipline, when meted out, was usually mild. Dismissal was a last resort and could often be avoided by transferring the employee to an unimportant sinecure. Even low-level salaried employees enjoyed status privileges and had a degree of job security that manual workers lacked.[11]

One clear effect of the employment reforms discussed in this book (and a latent function of trade union activities) was to erase some of the distinctions between salaried and hourly employees, especially in the area of job security. By the early 1950s, the blue-collar worker could say, with William Whyte's Organization Man, that "his relationship with The Organization is to be for keeps" because if he was "loyal to the company . . . the company would be loyal" to him. Though still far from being treated like a gentleman, the blue-collar worker was accorded somewhat more consideration: His loyalty was carefully cultivated and, if unionized, he could be dismissed only for cause. Moreover, survey data show that benefits previously reserved to salaried employees—paid vacations, pension plans, paid sick leave—had by the mid-1950s been extended to include a majority of blue-collar workers. Thus, the collar line was permanently blurred, although important and systematic differences remained.[12]

Underlying this change was the development of a more positive managerial image of the worker. Traditionally, managers had portrayed the manual worker as greedy, depraved, lazy, and unreliable—a creature barely recognizable as human, much less a gentleman. But after 1915 the same forces that impelled employment reform—enlightened personnel management, union pressure, and government labor standards—also produced a change in this image, albeit a painfully slow one. Indeed, in a content analysis of various management publications, Reinhard Bendix found that not until the late 1930s and early 1940s did managers become fully aware of the blue-collar worker as a "human being," possessing a personality, attitudes, dignity, and rights.[13]

Patterns and Personnel Management

A number of other major points emerge from this study. First, the growth of internal labor markets in large firms was erratic, occurring chiefly during World War I and the Great Depression. Yet most of the innovations that constitute the internal labor market were available by 1915, if not earlier. The implication is that large firms implemented these reforms only when prodded by various external forces, chiefly the threat of unionization. Labor scarcity and government regulation of the labor market also were important: They spurred internal labor market growth during World War I and reinforced established practices during World War II.

A different growth pattern was found at small and medium-sized firms. Although some of these firms were part of the progressive minority, most did not adopt internal labor market arrangements until after the mid-1930s. They tended to act only when the threat of unionization was immediate, and sometimes not until after their workers had been organized. They also waited until clear patterns and standards had been established, either by their larger counterparts during the 1930s or by the government during the war.

This erratic growth reflected the low priority assigned to employment policy by most manufacturing firms. Closely related to this was the dominance of the production division in management. Line managers, some of whom began their careers as foremen, regarded the policies proposed by personnel departments as bureaucratic encumbrances that interfered with operating efficiency. Fair treatment, job protection, and the assurance of a continued employment relationship were considered inessential to the firm's mission, which was to produce at the lowest cost with the greatest degree of flexibility. For line managers, a worker either "cut the mustard" or he was out; incentive plans were thought sufficient to motivate even the least skilled worker. The threat of unionization could best be dealt with by a combination of decent pay, careful hiring, and coercion, if necessary.

Personnel managers were inclined to see things differently for several reasons. First, they were influenced by their personal backgrounds. In its early years, personnel management counted among its ranks socialists, settlement house workers, and others with a reformist orientation. (Even today the field attracts those who want to "work with people," including former union officials and relatively large numbers of women.)[14] Second, and more fundamental, the personnel manager's responsibility within the managerial hierarchy was to create and maintain stable labor relations, and this meant making long-term investments in employee good will. To amortize these investments, a personnel manager was willing to give up short-run output and efficiency in favor of long-run stability and predictability.

Achieving stable labor relations meant replicating within the firm many of the unions' protective structures. Indeed, personnel managers can be viewed as mere conduits for union threat effects in that many of their ideas were borrowed from the unions and their influence often rested on the imminence of labor unrest. But industrial relations would have taken a very different course had this managerial specialty never developed. The establishment of a personnel function introduced competition within management between the goals of the personnel department and the objectives of the firm's other divisions. As a result, managements became aware of various trade-offs—such as that between employee morale and the flexibility allowed by the drive system—that were less apparent when employment policy was subordinated to production objectives. Personnel management's roots, its quasi-professional status, and its ties to outside institutions like the universities all lent legitimacy to the new values that it brought to management. In the absence of these effects, internal labor markets would have developed more slowly, and unions would have been both more popular and more adversarial.

These effects were, however, variable. In most firms, the personnel manager had substantial status and influence only during two

crisis periods—World War I, and the years from 1933 to 1945—
when companies confronted challenges from unions and government that their traditional employment systems were unable to
resolve. They responded to those pressures by giving greater resources and power to their personnel managers, who in turn favored policies that heightened the organization's ability to cope
with uncertainty. This shift resulted in a proliferation of rules,
standard operating procedures, and hierarchical checks on first-
line supervisors.

Despite these many parallels, the two crisis periods ended very
differently. After 1920, union and government pressure faded
away, and industry's new bureaucratic employment structures were
partially dismantled. But when the second period ended in 1945,
the new employment policies remained intact because, in what
could be seen as a defeat for management, the pressure exerted by
labor and government failed to abate. But this pressure no longer
constituted a crisis for those companies that had adopted the personnel strategy. This strategy helped to check the spread of unionism and provided a corps of sophisticated personnel managers who
were able to moderate the impact of government's regulatory
interventions.[15]

Unions and Management

The influence that unions had on personnel policy can be seen
in the close association between periods of rapid internal labor
market growth and periods during which union bargaining power
was on the rise. Since unions give voice to their members' desires,
this association suggests that workers had a strong interest in the
bureaucratic features of the internal labor market, whereas management frequently eschewed them. Often it was the unions, not
management, that pushed most strongly for job ladders, wage
classification, allocative rules, and guarantees of an enduring employment relationship.

But the differences between unions and management were not
unbridgeable as is evidenced by the extensive imitation and adap-
tation that occurred on both sides. On the one had, personnel
managers borrowed freely from the stock of employment proce-

dures and principles that the unions had built up since 1870. On the other hand, in many of the companies organized after 1933, unions had to adapt to the status quo already established by the personnel department.[16] Moreover, unions and personnel managers had some mutual interests: in restraining foremen, in maintaining order and stability, and in establishing formal rules and procedures. Although most managements never full accepted unions, they came to accept many of the unions' goals, and this provided a basis for accommodation and bargaining over the shape of the internal labor market in unionized firms.

In the years after World War II, developments in the unionized sector were watched closely and imitated by nonunion companies. These firms have since proved that they can provide the same range of employment policies and safeguards as are found in unionized firms, and today these policies are diffused throughout the nonunion sector. Moreover, these days personnel innovations emanate from the nonunion sector at least as often as from the unionized sector, although this reflects the unions' loss of dynamism as much as it does any new management strategy. This situation raises an important question: If union threat effects rather than efficiency incentives were a prime force behind the adoption of internal labor market policies, does a continued dwindling of the power of organized labor mean a return to older and less benign employment practices?

The answer to this question is, probably not. First, despite some deregulation, the government continues to set standards that create or reinforce internal labor markets. Hiring and allocative practices are regulated by EEO laws; minimum wages and pensions are protected; social welfare and macroeconomic policies provide incentives for stable, long-term employment relationships; and even the employer's right to dismiss an employee at will has been called into question by recent court decisions. Moreover, the marked increase in the number of government rules over the last twenty years has, as during earlier periods, centralized and rigidified the administration of employment.

Second, past experience and the continued professionalization of management have changed managerial attitudes and beliefs. Modern managers have a relatively benign image of the worker, and they no longer doubt that the personnel strategy can reduce costs. In part this change in attitude can be traced to a wide acceptance of the motivational tenets of personnel management: that a satisfied and secure work force is more productive. Further, firms have adapted their training and administrative techniques to the existence of an internal labor market. These sunk costs prevent any quick transition to an alternative employment system.

Third, today's workers have higher standards than their forebears because the achievements of previous generations have created industrial customs, or shared norms of fair treatment. Workers now expect a "good" employer to treat them equitably, to make allocative decisions by rule, to reward seniority, and to provide advancement opportunities and employment security. These expectations not only put pressure on government to maintain its activities, but also impose constraints on employer personnel policies. Firms without internal labor markets, in an economy where most firms have them, must recruit their workers from segments of the labor force that have lower expectations and standards: that is, from among the least-skilled and least-educated workers, such as immigrants.

This is not to say that internal labor markets are immune to change. In response to pressures created by new technologies and intensified competition, industrial employers have recently begun seeking more flexible forms of work organization. They are questioning long-established allocative practices—rigid job titles, strict lines of progression—which were appropriate to mass training and production during World War II but have since become outmoded. The process has not been free of tension, however: During the war, when many unions first became heavily involved in the joint administration of the internal labor market, they built their regulatory systems around the practices now under question. Consequently, a seemingly simple proposal to revamp occupational nomenclature can have complex and unforeseen effects on seniority rules and on employment security.

A more serious strain is imposed by the recent wave of plant closings, which threaten the job security of workers throughout the manufacturing sector. Some of the displaced have been forced to seek work in marginal sectors offering less stable employment and more ambiguous futures; those who have kept their jobs wonder anxiously if they will be next. Plant closures expose the limitations of the internal labor market as an employment security mechanism; in the final analysis, workers do not own their jobs. But unlike some recent observers, I do not see these structural adjustments as portents of a weakening employment relationship and a return to more casual labor markets. Instead, I believe that the basic practices which make up the internal labor market are likely to persist, not because they are carved in microeconomic stone, but because over the years they have become embedded in a structure of law, managerial principles, and employee expectations.

Finally, it is important to realize that there are areas of the labor market where the unions have not reached, where the law is not enforced, and where managements and workers expect little of each other. Here, in what has been called the peripheral or secondary sector, one is unlikely to find internal labor market arrangements. Jobs in this sector are unstable and tenuous, and elements of a drive system still exist. How best to reduce differences between these jobs and those in the primary sector has been a vexing public policy issue for the past twenty years.

Although a historical study is an imperfect guide for public policy analysis, the transformation that occurred in American industry between 1900 and 1945 can be regarded as a successful attempt to expand the labor market's supply of good jobs. What the experience shows is that jobs can be upgraded through legislation, through trade union pressure, and through changes in managerial philosophy and values. This conclusion reminds us that our current employment structures are not the inevitable result of a free labor market, but instead were often formed in reaction to it.

Notes

Introduction

1. Stanley Aronowitz, *False Promises: The Shaping of American Working Class Consciousness* (New York, 1973), p. 26.

2. See, for example, Richard E. Walton, "Innovative Restructuring of Work," in Jerome M. Rosow, ed., *The Worker and the Job: Coping with Change* (Englewood Cliffs, N.J., 1974); David A. Whitsett, "Where Are Your Unenriched Jobs?" *Harvard Business Review* (January–February 1975), vol. 53; J. R. Hackman and G. R. Oldham, *Work Redesign* (Reading, Mass., 1980).

3. See, for example, Harry Braverman, *Labor and Monopoly Capital: The Degradation of Work in the Twentieth Century* (New York, 1974); Dan Clawson, *Bureaucracy and the Labor Process: The Transformation of U.S. Industry, 1860–1920* (New York, 1980).

4. Ivar Berg, Marcia Freedman, and Michael Freeman, *Managers and Work Reform: A Limited Engagement* (New York, 1978), pp. 64–74. Also see George Strauss, "Workers: Attitudes and Adjustments," in Rosow, ed., *Worker and the Job*, pp. 73–98; Patricia Voydanoff, "The Relationship Between Perceived Job Characteristics and Job Satisfaction Among Occupational Status Groups," *Sociology of Work and Occupations* (May 1978), 5:179–182; Robert P. Quinn, Graham L. Staines, and Margaret R. McCullough, "Job Satisfaction: Is There a Trend?" Manpower Research Monograph No. 30, U.S. Department of Labor (Washington, D.C. 1974).

5. Paul Andrisani, Eileen Appelbaum, Ross Koppel, and Robert Miljus, "Work Attitudes and Work Experience," R&D Monograph No. 60, U.S. Department of Labor (Washington, D.C., 1979), pp. 32–35.

6. Reinhard Bendix, *Work and Authority in Industry: Ideologies of Management in the Course of Industrialization* (New York, 1956), pp. 288–289.

7. Talcott Parsons, *The Social System* (Glencoe, Ill., 1951), p. 508. Also see William H. Starbuck, "Organizational Growth and Development," in J. G. March, ed., *Handbook of Organizations* (Chicago, 1965), pp. 477–479; D. S. Pugh et al., "The Context of Organization Structures," *Administrative Science Quarterly* (March 1969), 14:115–126; Clark Kerr, John Dunlop, Frederick Harbison, and Charles Myers, *Industrialism and Industrial Man* (Cambridge, Mass., 1960).

8. See, for example, Richard Edwards, *Contested Terrain: The Transformation of the Workplace in the Twentieth Century* (New York, 1979); David M. Gordon,

Richard Edwards, and Michael Reich, *Segmented Work, Divided Workers: The Historical Transformation of Labor in the United States* (Cambridge, 1982).

These perspectives have analogues in two historical models of the period covered by this book: the organizational synthesis, with its focus on the imperatives of bureaucracy; and corporate liberalism, which argues that reform was conceived and directed by large corporations to benefit themselves. Louis Galambos, "The Emerging Organizational Synthesis in Modern American History," *Business History Review* (Autumn 1970), 44:279–290; James Weinstein, *The Corporate Ideal in the Liberal State, 1900–1918* (Boston, 1968).

9. Richard C. Edwards, "The Social Relations of Production in the Firm and Labor Market Structure," in Edwards, Reich, and Gordon, eds., *Labor Market Segmentation* (Lexington, Mass., 1975), p. 8.

10. Michael Burawoy, "Contemporary Currents in Marxist Theory", *The American Sociologist* (February 1978), 13:50–64.

11. Karl Polanyi, *The Great Transformation: The Political and Economic Origins of Our Time* (1944; reprint, Boston, 1957), p. 132.

12. For a discussion of some consequences of these differences, see Ronald Dore, *British Factory—Japanese Factory: The Origins of National Diversity in Industrial Relations* (Berkeley, Calif., 1973).

13. John R. Commons, *The Legal Foundations of Capitalism* (New York, 1924), p. 311.

14. Commons, *Legal Foundations*, 72. Commons noted that "if the corporation has 10,000 employees it loses only one ten-thousandth part of its working force if it chooses to not-employ the man, and cannot find an alternative man. But the man loses 100 percent of his job if he chooses to not-work and cannot find an alternative employer . . . from the quantitative concept of the will as a choosing between actual alternatives in a world of limited opportunities, the right of the one is greater—or perhaps 10,000 times greater—than the right of the other."

15. *Ibid.*, pp. 59, 303–304, 307. Also see Philip Selznick, *Law, Society and Industrial Justice* (New York, 1969); and Sanford Jacoby, "The Duration of Indefinite Employment Contracts in the United States and England: An Historical Analysis," *Comparative Labor Law* (Winter 1982), 5:85–128.

16. Alfred D. Chandler, Jr., *The Visible Hand: The Managerial Revolution in American Business* (Cambridge, Mass., 1977), p. 497. One notable exception to the business history approach is Daniel Nelson, *Workers and Managers: Origins of the New Factory System in the United States, 1880–1920* (Madison, Wis., 1975).

17. Lloyd Reynolds, *The Structure of Labor Markets* (New York, 1951); Clark Kerr, "The Balkanization of Labor Markets," in E. Wight Bakke, ed., *Labor Mobility and Economic Opportunity* (Cambridge, Mass., 1954); Richard A. Lester, "Hiring Practices and Labor Competition," Industrial Relations Sections, Princeton University, Research Report No. 88 (1954); John T. Dunlop, "The Task of Contemporary Wage Theory," in George W. Taylor and Frank Pierson, eds., *New Concepts in Wage Determination* (New York, 1957).

18. Walter Y. Oi, "Labor as a Quasi-Fixed Factor," *Journal of Political Econ-*

omy (December 1962), vol. 70; Peter Doeringer and Michael J. Piore, *Internal Labor Markets and Manpower Analysis* (Lexington, Mass., 1971); Arthur Alexander, "Income, Experience, and Internal Labor Markets," *Quarterly Journal of Economics* (February 1974), vol. 88; Oliver E. Williamson, Michael L. Wachter, and Jeffrey Harris, "Understanding the Employment Relation: The Analysis of Idiosyncratic Exchange," *Bell Journal of Economics* (Autumn 1975), vol. 6.

19. For example, wages are not nearly as rigid in Japan and the United Kingdom as they are in the United States. Also, internal labor markets in the United Kingdom are less structured, and in Japan more structured, than they are in the United States. Robert J. Gordon, "Why U.S. Wage and Employment Behavior Differs from that in Japan," *Economic Journal* (March 1982), 92:13–44; Dore, *British Factory*, chaps. 10 and 11.

20. John Eatwell, *Whatever Happened to Britain?: The Economics of Decline* (London, 1982).

21. For a much broader elaboration of this theme, see Robert Wiebe, *The Search for Order, 1877–1920* (New York, 1967).

1. The Way It Was: Factory Labor Before 1915

1. Samuel Batchelder, *Introduction and Early Progress of the Cotton Manufacture in the United States* (Boston, 1863), passim; Stephen Marglin, "What Do Bosses Do? The Origins and Functions of Hierarchy in Capitalist Production," *Review of Radical Political Economics* (Summer 1974), 6:33–60; Caroline F. Ware, *The Early New England Cotton Manufacture* (Boston, 1931), pp. 23, 50–51, 263–266; Howard M. Gitelman, "The Waltham System and the Coming of the Irish," *Labor History* (Fall 1967), 8:227–253; Hannah Josephson, *The Golden Threads: New England's Mill Girls* (New York, 1949), pp. 220–221; Thomas Dublin, *Women at Work: The Transformation of Work and Community in Lowell, Massachusetts, 1826–1860* (New York, 1979).

2. Carroll D. Wright, "The Factory System of the United States," U.S. Bureau of the Census, *Report of the United States at the Tenth Census* (Washington, D.C., 1883), p. 548; Victor S. Clark, *History of Manufactures in the United States* (Washington, D.C., 1929), 3:15–16, 76–80, 473; Daniel Nelson, *Managers and Workers: Origins of the New Factory System in the United States, 1880–1920* (Madison, Wis., 1975), p. 4.

3. The authority of the foreman and the skilled worker, said Frederick W. Taylor, come from "knowledge handed down to them by word of mouth. . . . This mass of rule-of-thumb or traditional knowledge may be said to be the principal asset or possession of every tradesman." *The Principles of Scientific Management* (New York, 1912), pp. 31–32.

4. Dan Clawson, *Bureaucracy and the Labor Process: The Transformation of U.S. Industry, 1860–1920* (New York, 1980), pp. 75–83, 115; John Buttrick, "The Inside Contract System," *Journal of Economic History* (September 1952), 12:205–221; Nelson, *Managers and Workers*, pp. 31, 38.

5. David Montgomery, "Workers' Control of Machine Production in the Nineteenth Century," *Labor History*, (Fall 1976), 17:488–489; Clawson, *Bureaucracy*, pp. 130–166.

6. George S. Gibb, *The Whitesmiths of Taunton: A History of Reed and Barton, 1824–1843* (Cambridge, Mass., 1943), pp. 282–286; Clawson, *Bureaucracy*, pp. 126–130; Nelson, *Managers and Workers*, p. 40; Montgomery, "Workers' Control," p. 491.

7. Alexander Hamilton Church, "The Twelve Principles of Efficiency: The Eleventh Principle—Written Standard Practice Instructions," *The Engineering Magazine* (June 1911), 41:445; Gibb, *Whitesmiths*, p. 184; Ordway Tead, "The Importance of Being a Foreman," *Industrial Management*, (June 1917), 53:353.

8. David Brody, *Steelworkers in America: The Nonunion Era* (New York, 1969), p. 85; "The Characteristics of a Foreman," *The Engineering Magazine* (February 1909), 36:847; Evelyn H. Knowlton, *Pepperell's Progress: History of a Cotton Textile Company, 1844–1945* (Cambridge, Mass., 1948), pp. 159–161.

9. Joseph H. Willits, "Steadying Employment," *The Annals* (May 1916), vol. 65, suppl., p. 72; H. Keith Trask, "The Problem of the Minor Executive," *The Engineering Magazine* (January 1910), 38:501; "Fall River, Lowell, and Lawrence," Massachusetts Bureau of the Statistics of Labor, *Thirteenth Annual Report* (Boston, 1882), p. 381.

10. Brody, *Steelworkers*, p. 120; Virginia Yans-McLaughlin, *Family and Community: Italian Immigrants in Buffalo, 1880-1930* (1977; reprint, Urbana, Ill., 1982), p. 43; Arthur Hanko, "Reducing Foreign Labor Turnover," *Industrial Management* (May 1921), 61:351.

11. Fred H. Rindge, Jr., "From Boss to Foreman," *Industrial Management* (July 1917), 53:508–509; C. J. Morrison, "Short-Sighted Methods in Dealing With Labor," *The Engineering Magazine* (January 1914), 46:568.

12. Charles E. Fouhy, "Relations Between the Employment Manager and the Foreman," *Industrial Management* (October 1919), 58:336; Henry Eilbirt, "The Development of Personnel Management in the United States," *Business History Review* (Autumn 1959), 33:346; Willits, "Steadying," p. 72.

13. "Detroit's Great Growth Due to Its Open Shop Policy," *Iron Trade Review* (July 15, 1915), 57:143–145; Clarence E. Bonnett, *Employer's Associations in the United States* (New York, 1922), p. 80; Edwin E. Witte, *The Government in Labor Disputes* (New York, 1932), pp. 211–218.

14. Charlotte Erickson, *American Industry and the European Immigrant, 1860–1885* (Cambridge, Mass., 1957), pp. 17–28, 67–87; Brody, *Steelworkers*, p. 109; Don D. Lescohier, "Working Conditions," in J. R. Commons et al., *History of Labor in the United States* (New York, 1935), 3:188; Isaac A. Hourwich, *Immigration and Labor* (New York, 1912), pp. 93–101; Harry Jerome, *Migration and Business Cycles* (New York, 1926).

15. Yans-McLaughlin, *Italian Immigrants*, pp. 59–64, 72–73; William I. Thomas and Florian Znaniecki, *The Polish Peasant in Europe and America*, abridged by Eli Zaretsky (1918; reprint, Urbana, Ill., 1984), pp. 139–255.

16. Sumner H. Slichter, *The Turnover of Factory Labor* (1919; reprint, New York, 1921), p. 319; Dwight T. Farnham, "Adjusting the Employment Department to the Rest of the Plant," *Industrial Management* (September 1919), 58:202; Commission of Inquiry, Interchurch World Movement, *Report on the Steel Strike of 1919* (New York, 1920), p. 139; Nelson, *Managers and Workers*, pp. 44–45;

John P. Frey and John R. Commons, "Conciliation in the Stove Industry," U.S. Bureau of Labor Statistics (BLS) Bulletin No. 62 (Washington, D.C., 1906), p. 128.

17. John R. Commons, "Labor Conditions in Meat Packing and the Recent Strike," *Quarterly Journal of Economics* (November 1904), 19:8; Nelson, *Managers and Workers*, p. 43; Slichter, *Turnover*, p. 202.

18. Lloyd Ulman, *The Rise of the National Trade Union* (Cambridge, Mass., 1955), p. 549.

19. Philip Klein, *The Burden of Unemployment* (New York, 1923), pp. 13–37; Paul F. Brissenden and Emil Frankel, *Labor Turnover in Industry: A Statistical Analysis* (New York, 1922), pp. 80–81; Slichter, *Turnover*, p. 184; *Industrial Relations* (also known as *Bloomfield's Labor Digest*) (May 12, 1923), 15:1530.

20. Alexander Keyssar, "Men Out of Work: A Social History of Unemployment in Massachusetts, 1870–1916" (Ph.D. dissertation, Harvard University, 1977), pp. 43, 72, 76–77, 79, 107; Robert A. Gordon, *Business Fluctuations* (New York, 1961), p. 251.

21. Paul H. Douglas, "Can Management Prevent Unemployment?" *American Labor Legislation Review* (September 1930), 20:273; Mary Van Kleeck, "The Effect of Unemployment on the Wage Scale," *The Annals* (September 1915), 61:97–98; Irene O. Andrews, "The Relation of Irregular Employment to the Living Wage for Women," *American Labor Legislation Review* (June 1915), 5:319–374; Massachusetts Commission on Minimum Wage Boards, *Report* (Boston, 1912), passim; U.S. Bureau of the Census, *Census of Manufactures: 1909* (Washington, D.C., 1912), pt. 1, pp. 37–54; "Fall River," p. 306.

22. Slichter, *Turnover*, pp. 126–127, 129.

23. Keyssar, "Out of Work," p. 129; "How to Meet Hard Times: A Program for the Prevention and Relief of Abnormal Unemployment," Mayor's Committee on Unemployment, City of New York (New York, 1917), p. 24; "Guaranteed Wages: Report to the President by the Advisory Board," Office of War Mobilization and Reconversion and Office of Temporary Controls (Washington, D.C., 1947), app. C, pp. 290, 293.

24. Keyssar, "Out of Work," p. 153; Morrison, "Short-Sighted," p. 568.

25. *Industrial Relations* (December 11, 1920), 5:484.

26. At its pre-Wagner Act peak in 1920, the proportion of nonagricultural employees who belonged to unions was 18.5 percent. Leo Wolman, *Ebb and Flow in Trade Unions* (New York, 1936), pp. 172–193.

27. F. W. Hilbert, "Trade-Union Agreements in the Iron Molders' Union," in Jacob H. Hollander and George E. Barnett, *Studies in American Trade Unionism* (London, 1906), pp. 221–260; Bruno Ramirez, *When Workers Fight: The Politics of Industrial Relations in the Progressive Era, 1898–1916* (Westport, Conn., 1978), pp. 17–48; Brody, *Steelworkers*, p. 52.

28. James M. Motley, *Apprenticeship in American Trade Unions* (Baltimore, 1907); Paul H. Douglas, *American Apprenticeship and Industrial Education* (New York, 1921), p. 74; "Testimony of Samuel Gompers," in U.S. Industrial Commission, *Report on the Relations and Conditions of Capital and Labor* (Washington, D.C., 1901), 7:620.

29. Sumner H. Slichter, *Union Policies and Industrial Management* (Washington, D.C., 1941), p. 63; "Gompers," p. 603; Sanford M. Jacoby and Daniel J. B. Mitchell, "Development of Contractual Features of the Union-Management Relationship," *Labor Law Journal* (August 1982), 33:515; Howard T. Lewis, "The Economic Basis of the Fight for the Closed Shop," *Journal of Political Economy* (November 1912), 20:928–952; D. P. Smelser, *Unemployment and American Trade Unions* (Baltimore, 1919), pp. 57–74.

30. Sidney and Beatrice Webb, *Industrial Democracy* (1897; reprint, London, 1920), pp. 279–323; David A. McCabe, *The Standard Rate in American Trade Unions* (Baltimore, 1912), pp. 101–111; William H. Buckler, "The Minimum Wage in the Machinists' Union," in Hollander and Barnett, *Studies*, pp. 111–151.

31. Ulman, *National Trade Union*, pp. 483–484.

32. Montgomery, "Workers' Control," p. 496.

33. "Regulation and Restriction of Output," Eleventh Special Report of the U.S. Commissioner of Labor (Washington, D.C., 1904); Slichter, *Union Policies*, pp. 166–167; Montgomery, "Workers' Control," p. 491; G. G. Groat, *An Introduction to the Study of Organized Labor in America* (1916; reprint, New York, 1926), pp. 358–365. Unions also practiced output limitation as a way to stave off unemployment. Smelser, *Unemployment*, pp. 46–50.

34. Ulman, *National Trade Union*, pp. 542–543; Frey and Commons, "Stove Industry," pp. 128, 157; Commons, "Meat Packing," p. 17.

35. Quoted in Bernard L. Elbaum, "Industrial Relations and Uneven Development: Wage Structure and Industrial Organization in the British and U.S. Iron and Steel Industries, 1870–1970" (Ph.D. dissertation, Harvard University, 1982), p. 171.

36. Keyssar, "Out of Work," p. 107; Mayor's Committee, "Hard Times," p. 24; Commons, "Meat Packing," p. 15; Smelser, *Unemployment*, pp. 109–129.

37. Selig Perlman, *A History of Trade Unionism in the United States* (New York, 1923), pp. 181–182.

38. Slichter, *Union Policies*, p. 104; "Gompers," p. 832.

39. Dan Mater, "The Development and Operation of the Railroad Seniority System," *Journal of Business* (October 1940), 13:6–29; Robert K. Burns, "Daily Newspapers," in Harry A. Millis, ed., *How Collective Bargaining Works* (New York, 1942), p. 86.

40. David E. Feller, "A General Theory of the Collective Bargaining Agreement," *California Law Review* (May 1974), 61:728–731; "Restriction of Output," p. 21; "Collective Bargaining Agreement of the Milk Wagon Drivers' Union, Local 753, International Brotherhood of Teamsters, Chicago, Illinois, May 1924," in Slichter Papers, Littauer Library, Harvard University.

41. Julius H. Cohen, "The Revised Protocol in the Dress and Waist Industry," *The Annals* (January 1917), 69:191; Earl Dean Howard, *The Hart, Schaffner and Marx Agreement* (Chicago, 1920); Harry A. Millis and Royal E. Montgomery, *Organized Labor* (New York, 1945), pp. 708–709.

42. Waldo E. Fisher, "Anthracite," in Millis, *Collective Bargaining*, pp. 288–295; Millis and Montgomery, *Labor*, pp. 712–714.

43. McCallum quoted in Richard Edwards, *Contested Terrain: The Transformation of the Workplace in the Twentieth Century* (New York, 1979), p. 31; Slichter, *Turnover*, p. 387; Keyssar, "Out of Work," p. 153.

44. Montgomery, "Workers' Control," p. 489; Perlman, *History*, pp. 98–99, 116; Brody, *Steelworkers*, pp. 138–139.

45. "Restriction of Output," pp. 22, 29; Montgomery, "Workers' Control," p. 499. Also see Stanley B. Mathewson, *Restriction of Output Among Unorganized Workers* (New York, 1931).

46. Brissenden and Frankel, *Labor Turnover*, pp. 41, 48; Slichter, *Turnover*, pp. 57–69; William B. Wilson, "Labor Program of the Department of Labor," BLS Bulletin No. 247 (1918), p. 166. At a large metalworking plant, the number of quits rose from 581 in 1914, a depressed year, to 3,035 in 1916. The plant's proportion of quits due to "dissatisfaction" rose from 27 percent in 1914 to 34 percent in 1915, the beginning of the recovery; by 1916, these accounted for 64 percent of all quits. Slichter, *Turnover*, p. 180.

47. Stanley Lebergott, *Manpower in Economic Growth: The American Record Since 1800* (New York, 1964), p. 28; Hourwich, *Immigration*, p. 503; Walter Fogel, "Immigrants and the Labor Market: Historical Perspectives and Current Issues," in D. G. Papademetriou and M. J. Miller, eds., *The Unavoidable Issue: U.S. Immigration Policy in the 1980s* (Philadelphia, 1983), p. 73.

48. Ulman, *National Trade Union*, p. 9; Jerome, *Migration*, p. 106; Federated American Engineering Societies, *Waste in Industry* (New York, 1921), p. 300; Brody, *Steelworkers*, pp. 105–106.

49. Yans-McLaughlin, *Italian Immigrants*, pp. 26–30, 49, 78; Brody, *Steelworkers*, pp. 97–98; Stephen Hickey, "The Shaping of the German Labor Movement: Miners in the Ruhr," in Richard J. Evans, ed., *Society and Politics in Wilhelmine Germany* (New York, 1978), pp. 215–240.

50. Herbert Gutman, *Work, Culture and Society in Industrializing America* (New York, 1976), p. 28; Massachusetts Bureau of Statistics of Labor, *Tenth Annual Report* (Boston, 1978), cited in Daniel T. Rodgers, *The Work Ethic in Industrializing America, 1850–1920* (Chicago, 1978), p. 162; Slichter, *Turnover*, p. 184.

51. Gutman, *Work, Culture and Society*, pp. 38–40; H. A. Worman, "How to Secure Factory Workers," in Clarence M. Wooley et al., *Employer and Employee* (New York, 1907), p. 57; A. J. Portenar, "Centralized Labor Responsibility from a Labor Union Standpoint," *The Annals* (May 1917), 71:193.

52. Ulman, *National Trade Union*, pp. 57–59; E. J. Hobsbawm, "The Tramping Artisan," in his *Labouring Men: Studies in the History of Labour* (London, 1964), p. 34; John Davidson, *The Bargain Theory of Wages* (New York, 1898), p. 178; Smelser, *Unemployment*, pp. 75–108.

53. Ware, *Cotton Manufacture*, pp. 224–226; Norman Ware, *The Industrial Worker, 1840–1860* (Boston, 1924), p. 149; Ray Ginger, "Labor in a Massachusetts Cotton Mill: 1853–1860," *Business History Review* (March 1954), 28:84, 87.

54. Thomas R. Navin, *The Whitin Machine Works Since 1831: A Textile*

Machinery Company in an Industrial Village (Cambridge, Mass., 1950), pp. 160–161; Howard M. Gitelman, *Workingmen of Waltham: Mobility in American Urban Industrial Development, 1850–1890* (Baltimore, 1974), p. 71.

55. Rodgers, *Work Ethic*, p. 164. In an 1853 case involving a weaver who quit without giving prior notice, a Maine court said that, "The only valuable protection which the manufacturer can provide against such liability to loss and against what are in these days denominated 'strikes,' is to make an agreement with his laborers that if they willfully leave their machines and his employment without notice, all or a certain amount of wages that may be due to them shall be forfeited." *Harmon v. Salmon Falls Mfg. Co.*, 35 Me. 450 (1853).

56. Ann P. Bartel, "The Migration Decision: What Role Does Job Mobility Play?" *American Economic Review* (December 1979), 69:775–776.

57. Stephan Thernstrom, *The Other Bostonians: Poverty and Progress in the American Metropolis, 1880–1970* (Cambridge, Mass., 1973), pp. 17–23.

58. Richard J. Hopkins, "Occupational and Geographic Mobility in Atlanta, 1870–1890," *Journal of Southern History* (May 1968), 34:200–213; Thernstrom, *Bostonians*, p. 222; Clyde and Sally Griffen, *Natives and Newcomers: The Ordering of Opportunity in Mid-Nineteenth Century Poughkeepsie* (Cambridge, Mass., 1978); James P. Allen, "Changes in the American Propensity to Migrate," *Annals of the Association of American Geographers* (December 1977), 67:584–585.

59. Thernstrom, *Bostonians*, pp. 220, 289–302.

60. Slichter, *Union Policies*, p. 100; Thernstrom, *Bostonians*, p. 42.

61. Sanford M. Jacoby, "The Duration of Indefinite Employment Contracts in the United States and England: An Historical Analysis," *Comparative Labor Law* (Winter 1982), 5:85–128; Brody, *Steelworkers*, p. 78.

2. Systematic Management and Welfare Work

1. Sumner H. Slichter, "The Management of Labor," *Journal of Political Economy* (December 1919), 27:827.

2. Stanley Lebergott, *Manpower in Economic Growth* (New York, 1964), p. 510. General Electric's plants in Schenectady and Lynn each employed more than 10,000 workers in 1910, while Ford's giant Highland Park plant had 19,000 employees. Daniel Nelson, *Managers and Workers: Origins of the New Factory System in the United States, 1880–1920* (Madison, Wis. 1975), pp. 7–9: Victor S. Clark, *History of Manufactures in the United States* (Washington, D.C., 1929), 3:160–164.

3. There were exceptions to these general trends: Industries where production technology still was dependent on human skill (e.g., clothing manufacture) or where production technology was of a unit or small batch nature (e.g., machine tools) failed to significantly increase production speed, and their concentration ratios remained low. Also, there were a few industries, like agricultural implements, where increased size and concentration preceded continuous flow technology. Alfred D. Chandler Jr., *The Visible Hand: The Managerial Revolution in American Business* (Cambridge, Mass., 1977), pp. 280–281, 338–365; David A.

Hounshell, "From the American System to Mass Production: The Development of Manufacturing Technology in the United States, 1850–1920" (Ph.D. dissertation, University of Delaware, 1978).

4. Leland H. Jenks, "Early Phases of the Management Movement," *Administrative Science Quarterly* (December 1960), 5:421–447; Edwin T. Layton, Jr., *The Revolt of the Engineers* (Cleveland, 1971), p. 3; David F. Noble, *America By Design: Science, Technology, and the Rise of Corporate Capitalism* (New York, 1977), pp. 33–49.

5. Tregoing quoted in Joseph A. Litterer, "Systematic Management: The Search for Order and Integration," *Business History Review* (Winter 1961), 35:473. Also see Litterer, "Systematic Management: Design for Organizational Recoupling in American Manufacturing Firms," *Business History Review* (Winter 1963), 37:372.

6. Henry Towne, "The Engineer as Economist," *Transactions of the American Society of Mechanical Engineers* (ASME) (1886), 7:428; Henry Metcalfe, "The Shop-Order System of Accounts," *ASME Transactions* (1886), 7:441–447. Also see L. F. Urwick, *The Golden Book of Management* (London, 1956), pp. 25–26.

7. Nelson, *Managers and Workers,* p. 54; David Brody, *Steelworkers in America: The Nonunion Era* (New York, 1969), p. 19. Also see Horace L. Arnold, *The Complete Cost Keeper* (1889; reprint, New York, 1912).

8. Marc J. Epstein, *The Effect of Scientific Management on the Development of Standard Cost Systems* (New York, 1978); Brody, *Steelworkers,* pp. 18–19; F. E. Webner, "Obtaining Actual Knowledge of the Cost of Production," *The Engineering Magazine* (October 1908), vol. 36; "Cost-Methods that Give the Business Executive Control of His Business," *The Engineering Magazine (June 1912),* vol. 43.

9. Litterer, "Recoupling," pp. 382, 387; Charles DeLano Hine, *Modern Organization* (New York, 1912); Harrington Emerson, *Efficiency as a Basis for Operations and Wages* (New York, 1911).

10. Frank Richards, "Is Anything the Matter with Piece Work?" *ASME Transactions* (1903–1904), 25:70; Daniel T. Rodgers, *The Work Ethic in Industrializating America, 1850–1920* (Chicago, 1978), p. 50; Litterer, "Search for Order," pp. 462–465.

11. Frederick A. Halsey, "The Premium Plan of Paying for Labor," *ASME Transactions* (1891), vol. 12; Frederick W. Taylor, "A Piece Rate System: A Step Toward Partial Solution of the Labor Problem," *ASME Transactions* (1895), vol. 16; Taylor, *Shop Management* (New York, 1911), pp. 38–43; C. Bertrand Thompson, "Wages and Wage Systems as Incentives," in Thompson, ed., *Scientific Management: A Collection of the More Significant Articles Describing the Taylor System of Management* (Cambridge, Mass. 1914). Also see Daniel Nelson, *Frederick W. Taylor and the Rise of Scientific Management* (Madison, Wis., 1980).

12. Samuel Haber, *Efficiency and Uplift: Scientific Management in the Progressive Era, 1890–1920* (Chicago, 1964), pp. 1–50; "Taylor's Testimony Before the Special House Committee," in Frederick W. Taylor, *Scientific Management* (New York, 1947), p. 30; Taylor, "Piece Rate," pp. 892–893; Taylor, *Shop*

Management, pp. 28–29, 187–196; Milton Nadworny, *Scientific Management and the Unions, 1900–1932* (Cambridge, Mass., 1955), pp. 21–22, 78–79.

13. David A. McCabe, *The Standard Rate in American Trade Unions* (Baltimore, 1912), pp. 226–232; Nadworny, *Scientific Management*, pp. 26–33, 48–66, 78–79, 102–103; John R. Commons, "Labor's Attitude Toward Efficiency," *American Economic Review* (September 1911), 1:469.

14. Harrington Emerson, *The Twelve Principles of Efficiency* (New York, 1912); Taylor, *Shop Management*, pp. 110–121; Nelson, *Workers and Managers*, pp. 70–74; "The Foreman's Place in Scientific Management," in Thompson, *Scientific Management*, pp. 395–404; Frank G. Gilbreth, *Primer of Scientific Management*, 2d. ed. (New York, 1918), p. 10; A. Hamilton Church, *The Science and Practice of Management* (New York, 1914); Lee Galloway, *Organization and Management* (New York, 1913).

15. Taylor, *Shop Management*, pp. 96, 110, 122; Frank Barkley Copley, *Frederick W. Taylor: Father of Scientific Management* (New York, 1923), 1:272, 456; Hugh G. J. Aitken, *Taylorism at Watertown Arsenal* (Cambridge, Mass., 1960), p. 133.

16. For a different view see Nelson, *Managers and Workers*, p. 78; and Jenks, "Early Phases," p. 430.

17. Henry Eilbirt, "The Development of Personnel Management in the United States," *Business History Review* (Autumn 1959), 33:346; Fred W. Climer, "Cutting Labor Cost in Seasonal Business," *Manufacturing Industries* (May 1927), vol. 13.

18. Taylor, *Shop Management*, pp. 110–122; Henry P. Kendall, "Comment on 'The Present State of the Art of Scientific Management,'" *ASME Transactions* (1912), 34:1208.

19. "The Present State of the Art of Industrial Management: Majority Report," *ASME Transactions* (1912), 34:1134; Edwin F. Gay, "Scientific Management," lecture delivered to the Committee on Industrial Relations, Boston Chamber of Commerce, December 14, 1912, Boston Chamber of Commerce Papers, Baker Library, Harvard University, File 332–47; George D. Babcock, *The Taylor System in Franklin Management* (New York, 1918), p. 80.

20. Robert F. Hoxie, *Scientific Management and Labor* (New York, 1915), pp. 31–32, 120–121; Walter M. McFarland, "The Basic Cause of Increased Efficiency," *The Engineering Magazine* (December 1908), vol. 36; "Present State," passim; Kendall, "Comment," p. 1208.

21. Paul Monroe, "Profit-Sharing in the United States," *American Journal of Sociology* (May 1896), 1:685–709; Henry R. Towne, "Gain Sharing," *ASME Transactions* (1889), vol. 10; "Welfare Work for Employees in Industrial Establishments in the United States," U.S. Bureau of Labor Statistics Bulletin No. 250 (1919), p. 8.

22. Some of these themes are developed in John and Barbara Ehrenreich, "The Professional-Managerial Class," in Pat Walker, ed., *Between Labor and Capital* (Boston, 1979); and Christopher Lasch, *Haven in a Heartless World: The Family Besieged* (New York, 1977). Lasch is morbidly pessimistic, however, about the coherence between social reform and social reproduction.

23. Stuart Brandes, *American Welfare Capitalism, 1880–1940* (Chicago, 1976), pp. 35, 140; "Welfare Work," pp. 62, 70; John R. Commons, *Industrial Government* (New York, 1921), pp. 1–2; R. T. Solensten, "The Labor Policy of the White Motor Company," *Industrial Management* (April 1920), 59:331; Heidi Hartmann, "Capitalism and Women's Work in the Home, 1900–1930" (Ph.D. dissertation, Yale University, 1975).

24. Charles U. Carpenter, "The Working of a Labor Department in Industrial Establishments," *The Engineering Magazine* (April 1903), 25:3.

25. Brandes, *Welfare Capitalism*, p. 56; P. F. O'Shea, *Employees' Magazines for Factories, Offices, and Business Organizations* (New York, 1920); Ordway Tead and Henry Metcalf, *Personnel Administration* (New York, 1920), pp. 189–198.

26. Mary B. Gilson, "The Relation of Home Conditions to Industrial Efficiency," *The Annals* (May 1916), 65:278–279; Brandes, *Welfare Capitalism*, pp. 112–114.

27. Frank B. Miller and Mary Ann Coghill, "Sex and the Personnel Manager," *Industrial and Labor Relations Review* (October 1964), 18:32–44; Mary B. Gilson, *What's Past Is Prologue: Reflections on My Industrial Experience* (New York 1940), p. 213; Mary E. Richmond, "Friendly Visiting," American Unitarian Association, *Social Service Bulletin* (n.d.) no. 7, p. 11; James Leiby, *A History of Social Welfare and Social Work in the United States* (New York, 1978), p. 130.

28. Gilson, "Home Conditions," p. 285; Gilson, *What's Past*, p. 138; National Association of Corporation Schools, *Third Annual Proceedings* (1915), pp. 689–691.

29. Stephen J. Scheinberg, "The Development of Corporation Labor Policy, 1900–1940" (Ph.D. dissertation, University of Wisconsin, 1966), pp. 77, 212; "Testimony of Henry Ford," U.S. Senate, Commission on Industrial Relations, *Final Report and Testimony* (1916), 8:7629; Brandes, *Welfare Capitalism*, pp. 138–139; "Twenty British Quaker Employers," *The Survey* (November 23, 1918), vol. 40.

30. Nelson, *Managers and Workers*, p. 102; Brandes, *Welfare Capitalism*, p. 111; Robert Ozanne, *A Century of Labor-Management Relations at McCormick and International Harvester* (Madison, Wis., 1967), pp. 33, 50.

31. Commission on Industrial Relations, 1:343; Ozanne, *Century*, pp. 36–40, 83; Brody *Steelworkers*, pp. 89–90. One interpretation of pecuniary welfare programs is that they were a public relations ploy on the part of the newly formed trusts to ensure their image in the public eye as "good trusts." The person who launched these programs at International Harvester and U.S. Steel was George Perkins, who represented the Morgan interests at each firm and was a prominent member of the Progressive Party's right wing. Perkins, who thrust the distinction between a "good" and a "bad" trust on Theodore Roosevelt, recommended welfare work whenever either firm was threatened with an investigation of its monopolistic practices. John Garraty, *Right-Hand Man: The Life of George W. Perkins* (New York, 1960), pp. 222–226; Ozanne, pp. 73–74, 80–82.

32. The period when pecuniary welfare work first proliferated at International Harvester (1906–1912) was marked by recurring skilled labor shortages. Robert

Ozanne, *Wages in Practice and Theory: McCormick and International Harvester, 1860–1960* (Madison, Wis., 1968), p. 37.

33. Charles H. Whitaker, *The Joke About Housing* (Boston, 1920), p. 9; Brody, *Steelworkers*, p. 87; Leslie H. Allen, "The Problem of Industrial Housing," *Industrial Management* (December 1917), 54:400; James R. Adams, "A Common-Sense Attack on Labor Turnover," *Industrial Management* (November 1921), 62:301; C. A. Lippincott, "Community Conditions Affecting Labor Stability," Industrial Relations Association of America (IRAA), *Proceedings* (1920), pt. 1, p. 60; "Caring for the Unskilled Laborer," *Iron Age* (February 19, 1914), 93:504.

34. An important study of company towns is Margaret Crawford, "The Design of Company Towns in the United States, 1900–1930" (Ph.D. dissertation, University of California, Los Angeles, 1985).

35. The remaining 25 percent could not be classified. "Welfare Work," p. 119.

36. Edward Berkowitz and Kim McQuaid, "Businessman and Bureaucrat: The Evolution of the American Social Welfare System, 1900–1940," *Journal of Economic History* (March 1978), 38:120.

37. Taylor, *Shop Management*, p. 37; Daniel Nelson and Stuart Campbell, "Taylorism Versus Welfare Work in American Industry," *Business History Review* (Spring 1972), 46:5; Haber, *Efficiency and Uplift*, p. 22; Scheinberg, "Corporation Labor Policy," p. 74.

38. Sumner H. Slichter, *The Turnover of Factory Labor* (New York, 1921), p. 402; Clarence E. Bonnett, *Employers' Associations in the United States* (New York, 1922), p. 550; Brandes, *Welfare Capitalism*, p. 139; Young Men's Christian Association (YMCA), *Summary of the Industrial Conference on Human Relations and Betterment in Industry* (1920), p. 21.

39. G. D. Crain, "Health, Service and Welfare Work," *American Industries* (March 1917), 17:8; Otto P. Geier, "Human Relations Department from the Standpoint of the Industrial Physician," *Industrial Management* (June 1919), 57:502; Robert S. Quinby, "Organization and Functions of a Service Department," *American Industries* (July 1919), 19:29; Harold Ley, "Employee Welfare Work That Pays," *American Industries* (March 1922), 22:33; Brody, *Steelworkers*, p. 178; Robert C. Clothier, "The Function of the Employment Department" in BLS Bulletin No. 196 (1916), p. 9.

40. C. Howard Hopkins, *History of the Young Men's Christian Association in America* (New York, 1951), pp. 227, 231, 233, 456; Clarence J. Hicks, *My Life in Industrial Relations* (New York, 1941), pp. 18–29.

41. John J. McCook, "The Work of the YMCA Among Railroad Men," in International Committee of YMCAs, *The Jubilee of Work for Young Men in North America* (New York, 1901), p. 145; Galen Fisher, *Public Affairs and the YMCA* (New York, 1948), p. 72; Hopkins, *History*, pp. 235, 476; Paul McBride, *Culture Clash: Immigrants and Reformers, 1880–1920* (Saratoga, Calif., 1975), p. 68.

42. "Brief Historical Sketch of the Industrial Service of the YMCA," pamphlet, n.d., YMCA Historical Library, New York City; Hopkins, *History*, pp. 233, 475.

43. *Service*, Magazine of the YMCA Industrial Service Department, October and December 1918, YMCA Historical Library; Whiting Williams, *What's on*

the Worker's Mind: By One Who Put on Overalls to Find Out (New York, 1921),
p. 194; "Report of the Industrial Committee of the YMCA," September 1905,
December 1906, and May 1907, YMCA Historical Library; Hopkins, *History*,
p. 567; "Report of a Conference Held Under the Auspices of the Committee on
Work in War Industries of the National War Work Council of the YMCA,"
March 1918, YMCA Historical Library.

44. "The Yellow Pine Manufacturers Association and the YMCA," pamphlet,
c. 1914, in Industrial Service Committee Box, YMCA Historical Library; Fred H.
Rindge, Jr., "Improving the Welfare of Miners," *Presbyterian Advance* (September
2, 1926); "Report of the Industrial Committee," September 1905, YMCA Historical Library.

45. Charles Towson in National Association of Corporation Schools, *Second
Annual Proceedings* (1914), pp. 304, 491; Owen Pence, *The YMCA and Social
Need* (New York, 1946), p. 325; McBride, *Culture Clash*, p. 74.

46. "Report of a Conference," pp. 15, 35; McBride, *Culture Clash*, p. 74.

47. Gilson, *What's Past*, p. ix; Arthur Mann, *Yankee Reformers in the Urban
Age* (Cambridge, Mass., 1954), pp. 84–85; Haber, *Efficiency and Uplift*, pp. 111–
113.

48. Scheinberg, "Corporation Labor Policy," p. 70; Ozanne, *Century*, pp. 32–
33, 132, 165, 169; Allen G. Davis, *Spearheads for Reform: The Social Settlements
and the Progressive Movement, 1890–1914* (New York, 1967), p. 13; George
Martin, *Madam Secretary: Frances Perkins* (Boston, 1976), pp. 123, 130–131;
New York Times Oral History Project, *The Reminiscences of Henry Bruere* (New
York, 1972), pp. 11–14; Mary Van Kleeck, "The Professionalization of Social
Work," *The Annals* (May 1922), vol. 101.

49. Brandes, *Welfare Capitalism*, pp. 21–23; Scheinberg, "Corporation Labor
Policy," pp. 65–66; Nelson, *Managers and Workers*, pp. 109–111; William H.
Tolman, *Social Engineering* (New York, 1909); James Weinstein, *The Corporate
Ideal in the Liberal State, 1900–1918* (Boston, 1968), pp. 1–33; Marguerite
Green, *The National Civic Federation and the American Labor Movement* (Wash-
ington, D.C., 1956); Gertrude Beeks, "The New Profession," *National Civic
Federation Review* (February 1905), vol. 1.

50. Scheinberg, "Corporation Labor Policy," p. 70; Hopkins, *History*, pp.
233, 539–543; YMCA, *Summary of the Industrial Conference on Human Relations and Betterment in Industry* (1919), p. 7; E. G. Wilson, "The Social Significance of the YMCA's Industrial Conference," *Service* (October 1927), vol. 3.

51. Ozanne, *Century*, pp. 34–45; Fred H. Colvin, *Labor Turnover, Loyalty
and Output* (New York, 1919), p. 108; Frank J. Bruno, *Trends in Social Work*
(New York, 1948), pp. 141–144; Roy Lubove, *The Progressives in the Slums:
Tenement House Reform in New York City* (Cambridge, Mass., 1962); Lubove,
The Professional Altruist: The Emergence of Social Work as a Career (Cambridge,
Mass., 1965).

52. L. A. Boettiger, *Employee Welfare Work: A Critical and Historical Study*
(New York, 1923), p. 128; Otto P. Geier, "An Employees' Service Department,"
American Industries (November 1916), 17:4; "Welfare Work," p. 119.

53. Nelson, *Managers and Workers*, p. 109; Scheinberg, "Corporation Labor

Policy," p. 19; John H. Patterson, "Altruism and Sympathy as Factors in Works Administration," *The Engineering Magazine* (January 1901), vol. 20; Samuel Crowther, *John H. Patterson: Pioneer in Industrial Welfare* (Garden City, N.Y., 1923), pp. 190–206; Lena Harvey Tracy, *How My Heart Sang: The Story of Pioneer Industrial Welfare Work* (New York, 1950), pp. 138–150.

54. Daniel Nelson, "The New Factory System and the Unions: The NCR Company Dispute of 1901," *Labor History* (Winter 1974), 15:168, 170–176; Tracy, *My Heart*, p. 164.

55. Carpenter, "Labor Department," pp. 4, 6–8; "NCR Factory as Seen by English Experts of the Mosely Industrial and Educational Commissions," pamphlet, Dayton, 1904, pp. 40–42; H. A. Worman, "How to Secure Factory Workers," in Clarence M. Wooley et al., *Employer and Employee* (New York, 1907), pp. 53, 57; "A Brief Exhibit of Some Training Schools of the NCR Company," pamphlet, Dayton, Ohio, 1904.

56. Carpenter, "Labor Department," p. 4; Ozanne, *Century*, p. 33; Nelson, "New Factory System," p. 177.

57. Don D. Lescohier, "Working Conditions," in John R. Commons et al., *History of Labor in the United States* (New York, 1935), 3:320; Ozanne, *Century*, p. 174; Slichter, *Turnover*, pp. 431–434.

3. Vocational Guidance

1. Marvin Lazerson, *Origins of the Urban School: Public Education in Massachusetts, 1870–1915* (Cambridge, Mass., 1971), p. 80. Also see Charles A. Bennett, *History of Manual and Industrial Education* (Peoria, Ill., 1937), chs. 10 and 11; "Manual Training: Compiled from the Sixty-Fourth Annual Report of the Superintendent of Public Instruction of the State of Michigan," pamphlet (Lansing, 1900); and Marvin Lazerson and W. Norton Grubb, *American Education and Vocationalism: A Documentary History* (New York, 1974), pp. 2–15.

2. Lazerson, *Origins*, ch. 2 and pp. 53–56, 117–119, 131–133; James B. Gilbert, *Work Without Salvation: America's Intellectuals and Industrial Alienation, 1880–1910* (Baltimore, 1977), ch. 8: Connecticut Bureau of Labor Statistics, *Eleventh Annual Report* (Hartford, 1895), pp. 211–256. Manual training was offered in settlement houses in addition to public schools. For instance, Hull House in Chicago held classes in metalwork, woodcarving, cooking, and dressmaking. Ruskin's hope that manual training would slow the degradation of industrial life was popular among American settlement workers. Ellen Starr, an associate of Jane Addams, spent fifteen months in England learning bookbinding— a thoroughly impractical but ancient skill—so that she could teach it to the young people at Hull House. Allan F. Davis, *Spearheads for Reform: The Social Settlements and the Progressive Movement, 1890–1914* (New York, 1967), pp. 4, 12, 47–48.

3. Paul H. Douglas, *American Apprenticeship and Industrial Education* (New York, 1921), p. 215; National Association of Corporation Schools (NACS), *First Annual Proceedings* (1913), p. 120; NACS *Bulletin* (May 1916), 3:12; National Society for the Promotion of Industrial Education, *Bulletin No. 13* (Boston, 1911).

4. John Van Liew Morris, *Employee Training: A Study of Education and Training Departments in Various Corporations* (New York, 1921), pp. 30, 212; NACS, *First Annual Proceedings* (1913), p. 131; Douglas, *American Apprenticeship*, pp. 225–226. Out of 1,585 apprentices trained in NACS member firms, less than 60 percent remained with the firms after completing their training. Hence, contrary to the thrust of the modern economic literature on human capital investment, companies like General Electric were willing to spend considerable sums on general (as opposed to firm-specific) training. But despite their turnover problems, large companies had an ambivalent attitude toward public vocational education. A 1913 study found that of the companies belonging to the NACS, only 5 percent believed that the public schools could adequately train boys for work in their shops. Also, although some NACS members worried that the unions might get control of the vocational education movement, the NACS did not get actively involved in it. However, the NACS did maintain a committee on relations with the public schools which sought to "influence courses of established institutions more favorably toward industry." Thomas E. Donnelley, "Some Problems of Apprenticeship Schools," NACS, *First Annual Proceedings* (1913), p. 131; E. J. Mehren, "The NACS—A Factor in Alleviating Industrial Unrest," NACS *Bulletin* (May 1914), 1:9; Roy W. Kelly, *Training Industrial Workers* (New York, 1920), p. 134; Charles M. Ripley, *Life in a Large Manufacturing Plant* (Schenectady, N.Y., 1919).

5. Magnus W. Alexander, "The Cost of Labor Turnover," in U.S. Bureau of Labor Statistics *Bulletin* (1917) no. 227, p. 26. Also see Lawrence Cremin, *The Transformation of the School* (New York, 1961), pp. 34–36.

6. NACS, *Second Annual Proceedings* (1914), pp. 350–351; A. F. Bardwell, "Reasons for the Shortage of Skilled Mechanics and How Manufacturers Can Overcome the Deficiency," in NACS, *First Annual Proceedings* (1913), p. 125; NACS *Bulletin* (May 1914), 6:7.

7. National Association of Manufacturers, "Report of the Committee on Industrial Education," in *Proceedings of the Tenth Annual Convention* (1905), p. 143; Lazerson and Grubb, *Education and Vocationalism*, pp. 18–19; Clarence A. Bonnett, *Employers' Associations in the United States* (New York, 1922), pp. 300–301.

8. "Report of the Massachusetts Commission on Industrial and Technical Education (1906)," reprinted in Lazerson and Grubb, *Education and Vocationalism*, pp. 69–75; Douglas, *American Apprenticeship*, p. 123.

9. National Education Association, "Report of the Committee on the Place of Industries in Public Education (1910)" reprinted in Lazerson and Grubb, *Education and Vocationalism*, pp. 16, 83; Raymond Callahan, *Education and the Cult of Efficiency* (Chicago, 1962); William P. Sears, *The Roots of Vocational Education* (New York, 1931).

10. Edward Krug, *The Shaping of the American High School* (New York, 1964); Robert and Helen Lynd, *Middletown: A Study in Contemporary American Culture* (New York, 1929), pp. 181–187.

11. John Dewey, *Democracy and Education: An Introduction to the Philosophy of Education* (New York, 1916), p. 317; Charles Eliot, "Industrial Education

as an Essential Factor in Our National Prosperity," in National Society for the Promotion of Industrial Education, *Bulletin No. 5* (1908), p. 13.

12. Leonard Ayres, *Laggards in Our Schools* (New York, 1908), quoted in Sol Cohen, "The Industrial Education Movement, 1906–1917," *American Quarterly* (Spring 1968), 20:99; Eliot, "Industrial Education," p. 12; Dewey, *Democracy and Education*, p. 318. Dewey attacked the Cooley Bill, first drafted in 1912, which would have created a dual system of academic and vocational schools in Illinois. The fight against the bill was successful in part because of intense lobbying by the Chicago Federation of Labor. Grubb and Lazerson, *Education and Vocationalism*, p. 37.

13. "Massachusetts Commission," in *Education and Vocationalism*, pp. 76, 78–79. Also see Paul Osterman, "Education and Labor Markets at the Turn of the Century," *Politics and Society* (1979), 9:106–107.

14. Davis, *Spearheads*, p. 52; John M. Brewer, *History of Vocational Guidance: Origins and Early Development* (New York, 1942), p. 57.

15. Davis, *Spearheads*, pp. 7, 50, 53; John M. Brewer, *The Vocational Guidance Movement: Its Problems and Possibilities* (New York, 1918), p. 23; Brewer, *History of Vocational Guidance*, p. 57; W. Richard Stephens, *Social Reform and the Origins of Vocational Guidance* (Washington, D.C., 1970), p. 17.

16. Robert A. Woods and Albert J. Kennedy, *The Settlement Horizon* (New York, 1952); Davis, *Spearheads*, chs. 8 and 9.

17. Phillip S. Foner, *The AFL in the Progressive Era, 1910–1915* (New York, 1980), pp. 226–246; Hamilton Holt, "Arbitration of Industrial Disputes," in *Transactions of the Efficiency Society* (1912), vol. 1; Davis, *Spearheads*, pp. 104, 109.

Several early enthusiasts of grievance arbitration in the union sector later became active supporters of the personnel management movement, a link that is discussed in S. M. Jacoby, "Progressive Discipline in American Industry: Origins, Development, and Consequences," in David Lipsky, ed., *Advances in Industrial and Labor Relations* (Greenwich, Conn., 1985), vol. 3.

18. Arthur Mann, *Yankee Reformers in the Urban Age* (Cambridge, Mass., 1954), pp. 125–129, 130, 139; Stephens, *Social Reform*, p. 46; Brewer, *History of Vocational Guidance*, pp. 55, 302; Howard V. Davis, *Frank Parsons: Prophet, Innovator, Counselor* (Carbondale, Ill., 1969), pp. 3–47; "Professor Frank Parsons," *Vocational Guidance Magazine* (October 1925), 4:24–25. In the 1895 Boston mayoral election, Parsons was supported by the Socialist, Prohibition, and Populist parties but received a mere 1 percent of the vote.

19. Mann, *Yankee Reformers*, pp. 133, 137; Frank Parsons, "Compulsory Arbitration," *American Fabian* (March 1897), vol. 3; Frank Parsons, *Choosing a Vocation* (Boston, 1909), p. 50; Frank Parsons, *The Story of New Zealand* (Philadelphia, 1904); Frank Parsons, *Our Country's Need* (Boston, 1894), p. 2.

20. Brewer, *History of Vocational Guidance*, pp. 55–58; Davis, *Spearheads*, p. 53.

21. Meyer Bloomfield, *The Vocational Guidance of Youth* (Boston, 1911), pp. 29–30; Brewer, *History of Vocational Guidance*, p. 59.

22. Parsons, *Our Country's Need*, pp. 15, 69. On reform Darwinism, see

Richard Hofstadter, *Social Darwinism in American Thought* (New York, 1944), and Richard F. Boller, Jr., *American Thought in Transition: The Impact of Evolutionary Naturalism* (Chicago, 1970).

23. The NSPIE was an umbrella organization that brought together educators and businessmen to press for increased public funding of vocational education. Several of the NSPIE's founders came from Boston, including Henry Pritchett of MIT, Magnus Alexander of General Electric's training school at Lynn, and Robert Woods, a Boston settlement house worker. See Berenice Fisher, *Industrial Education: American Ideals and Institutions* (Madison, Wis., 1967), p. 130.

24. Lazerson, *Origins*, p. 159; Brewer, *History of Vocational Guidance*, pp. 59–60; Parsons, *Choosing*, pp. 91–94; Davis, *Parsons*, pp. 110–132.

25. Parsons, *Choosing*, pp. 4, 26–45, 114–119; Brewer, *History of Vocational Guidance*, p. 304.

26. *Ibid.*, pp. 65–88, 307; Parsons, *Choosing*, pp. 62–64, 122, 165.

27. *Ibid.*, p. 161.

28. Lazerson, *Origins*, pp. 158–159; Brewer, *History of Vocational Guidance*, pp. 66–68; Meyer Bloomfield, "Vocational Guidance," in National Society for the Study of Education, *Eleventh Yearbook*, Part 1 (1912), pp. 109–110; Stratton D. Brooks, "Vocational Guidance in the Boston Schools," in Meyer Bloomfield, ed., *Readings in Vocational Guidance* (Boston, 1915), p. 85.

29. "Industrial Education," *Twenty-fifth Report of the U.S. Commissioner of Labor* (Washington, D.C., 1910), p. 438; Bloomfield, "Vocational Guidance," pp. 111, 113; Brooks, "Boston," p. 83; Paul Hanus, "Vocational Guidance and Public Education," *The School Review* (January 1911), 19:51–56; Brewer, *History of Vocational Guidance*, p. 314.

30. Meyer Bloomfield, *Youth, School, and Vocation* (Boston, 1915), p. 91; Bloomfield, *Guidance of Youth*, p. 86.

31. "Industrial Education," pp. 411, 438; Brewer, *Guidance Movement*, pp. 10–11, 32; Brewer, *History of Vocational Guidance*, pp. 72, 139; Truman L. Kelley, *Educational Guidance* (New York, 1914), p. 171.

32. "Vocational Guidance," Report of the Commitee on High Schools and Training Schools of the New York Board of Education (1914), reprinted in Bloomfield, *Readings*, pp. 289, 295; Edward L. Thorndike, "The Permanence of Interests and Their Relation to Abilities," *Popular Science Monthly* (1912), 81:449–456. Also see Harry D. Kitson, *The Psychology of Vocational Adjustment* (Philadelphia, 1925), pp. 186–225; John C. Burnham, "Psychiatry, Psychology, and the Progressive Movement," *American Quarterly* (Winter 1960), 12:464–465; Matthew Hale, Jr., *Human Science and Social Order: Hugo Munsterberg and the Origins of Applied Psychology* (Philadelphia, 1980), pp. 152–158.

33. Bloomfield, *Guidance of Youth*, pp. 3–4, 94.

34. *Ibid.*, pp. 7–8; Bloomfield, "Vocational Guidance," p. 114.

35. Brewer, *Guidance Movement*, p. 189; "Massachusetts Commission," in *Education and Vocationalism*, p. 78.

36. Bloomfield, *Youth and Vocation*, p. 175. Also see Meyer Bloomfield, "The School and the Start of Life," U.S. Bureau of Education *Bulletin No. 4* (1914), reprinted in Bloomfield, *Readings*, pp. 679–720; Meyer Bloomfield, "Lessons

Europe Has for Us," in U.S. Bureau of Education, *Vocational Guidance: Papers Presented at the Organization Meeting of the Vocational Guidance Association, 1913* (Washington, D.C., 1914), p. 31.

37. Owen Lovejoy, "Vocational Guidance and Child Labor," in *Guidance Association: 1913*, pp. 13, 15.

38. Sophonisba P. Breckenridge, "Guidance by the Development of Placement and Follow-up Work," in *Guidance Association: 1913*, pp. 62–63; Bloomfield, *Youth, School and Vocation*, p. 169; Bloomfield, *Guidance of Youth*, p. 47.

39. Bloomfield, *Guidance of Youth*, pp. 13–14, 16, 23; Douglas, *American Apprenticeship*, pp. 107–108. Also see W. Norton Grubb, "Historical Evaluation of the Family: Family and State Institutions," section 3, part B, Childhood and Government Project, Earl Warren Legal Institute, University of California, Working Paper No. 7 (Berkeley, 1976), p. 72.

40. Brewer, *Guidance Movement*, p. 261; Bloomfield, *Youth, School and Vocation*, pp. 68–86; Frank M. Leavitt, "How Shall We Study the Industries for the Purposes of Vocational Guidance?" in *Guidance Association: 1913*, p. 80.

41. Charles W. Eliot, "The Value During Education of the Life-Career Motive," Address to the National Education Association (1910), reprinted in Bloomfield, *Readings*, pp. 2, 4.

42. Jesse B. Davis, *Vocational and Moral Guidance* (Boston, 1914), p. 127; Brewer, *Guidance Movement*, p. 4.

43. Bloomfield, *Youth, School, and Vocation*, pp. 21, 174; Douglas, *American Apprenticeship*, p. 108.

44. Lovejoy, "Child Labor," p. 15.

45. Bloomfield, "Vocational Guidance," p. 113; F. E. Spaulding, "Problems of Vocational Guidance," Address to the Cincinnati Department of Superintendence (1915), in Bloomfield, *Readings*, p. 73; Brewer, *Guidance Movement*, p. 117. Also see New York City, "Vocational Guidance," in Bloomfield, *Readings*, p. 324.

46. Brewer, *History of Vocational Guidance*, pp. 69–70; Ralph G. Wells, "The Work Program of the Employment Managers' Association of Boston," *The Annals* (May 1916), 65:111; Frederick J. Allen, "Editorial," *Vocational Guidance Journal* (December 1925), 4:132; Bloomfield, *Youth, School and Vocation*, p. 48. Note that several of Allen's pamphlets are reproduced in Bloomfield, *Readings*, pp. 515–541.

Others followed in Bloomfield's footsteps: Roy W. Kelly, who headed the Vocation Bureau after it moved to Harvard, left the bureau in 1917 to take charge of the Pacific Coast Bureau of Employment Research. While in San Francisco, Kelly founded the city's first personnel management association, the San Francisco Personnel Club. Karen Louise Jorgenson-Esmaili, "Schooling and the Early Human Relations Movement; with Special Reference to the Foreman's Conference, 1919–1939" (Ph.D. dissertation, University of California, Berkeley, 1979), pp. 54–61.

47. Meyer Bloomfield, "Introduction," in Roy W. Kelly, *Hiring the Worker* (Boston, 1918), p. 2; Kelly, *Training*, p. 117.

48. A. Lincoln Filene, "Remarks," in *Proceedings of the Employment Man-*

agers' Association of Boston, U.S. Bureau of Labor Statistics, Bulletin No. 202 (1916), p. 12; Meyer Bloomfield, "The Aim and Work of Employment Managers' Associations," in *Proceedings of the Employment Managers' Conference, Minneapolis*, U.S. Bureau of Labor Statistics, Bulletin No. 196 (1916), pp. 42–44.

49. Meyer Bloomfield, in U.S. Senate, *Final Report and Testimony of the Commission on Industrial Relations* (Washington, D.C., 1916) 1:393; Ida May Wilson, "The Employment Manager and Applied Vocational Guidance," *The Annals* (January 1919), 81:145.

50. The proceedings of the first three national conferences of employment managers (Minneapolis, Philadelphia, and Rochester) are contained in the Bureau of Labor Statistics' Bulletin Nos. 196, 227, and 247. Also see Brewer, *History of Vocational Guidance*, p. 186.

51. Kelly, *Hiring*, p. 9

52. Charles A. Prosser, "The New Apprenticeship as a Factor in Reducing Labor Turnover," in *Proceedings . . . Minneapolis*, pp. 45–52; John S. Keir, "The Establishment of Permanent Contacts with the Source of Labor Supply," *The Annals* (May 1916), 65:163; H. L. Gardner, "The Employment Department: Its Functions and Scope," in *Proceedings . . . Boston*, pp. 49–55; National Association of Corporation Schools, *Second Annual Proceedings* (1914), p. 757; Meyer Bloomfield, "The New Profession of Handling Men, *The Annals* (September 1915), 61:125; "Report of the Committee on Vocational Guidance," in NACS, *Third Annual Proceedings* (1915), 334, 365.

53. Henry C. Metcalf in "Report of the Committee on Vocational Guidance," p. 330; W. D. Scott, "Psychology of Business: Increasing Human Efficiency," *System* (March 1910), 17:254; Kelly, *Hiring*, pp. 6–7, 57–58; H. L. Gardner, "Psychological Tests," in *Proceedings . . . Boston*, p. 27; H. L. Gardner, "The Selection Problems of Cheney Brothers," in *Proceedings . . . Philadelphia*, U.S. Bureau of Labor Statistics, Bulletin No. 227 (1917), pp. 120–125; Burtis Breese, "Vocational Guidance Analyzed," NACS *Bulletin* (April 1916); Loren Baritz, *The Servants of Power: A History of the Use of Social Science in American Industry* (Middletown, Conn., 1960), ch. 7.

54. "Vocational Survey of Minneapolis," U.S. Bureau of Labor Statistics, Bulletin No. 199 (1915); Anne David, "Occupations and Industries Open to Children Between the Ages of 14 and 16 Years of Age," in Bloomfield, *Readings*, pp. 542–556; Ernest M. Hopkins, "A Functionalized Employment Department as a Factor in Industrial Efficiency," *The Annals* (September 1914), 61:115; Bloomfield, "New Profession," p. 126; NACS, *Second Annual*, pp. 334, 363; P. J. Nilsen, "Job Analysis," in *Proceedings . . . Rochester*, U.S. Bureau of Labor Statistics, Bulletin No. 247 (1919), pp. 132–134; Phillip J. Reilly, "Job Analysis," in *Proceedings . . . Boston*, pp. 26–27.

55. Kelly, *Hiring*, pp. 151–157; Bloomfield, *Youth, School, and Vocation*, pp. 179–200; W. C. Swallow, "Records and Filing Systems for Employment Departments," in *Proceedings . . . Boston*, pp. 32–37; Meyer Bloomfield, "Job Guidance," in *Transactions of the Efficiency Society* (1912), 1:339; Meyer Bloomfield, "Medical Inspection at the Start of Life," in Bloomfield, *Readings*, pp. 704–710; U.S. Senate, *Commission on Industrial Relations*, 10:9699–10006 and 2:1392–

1410; Arthur Williams, "The Instruction of New Employees in Methods of Service," *The Annals* (May 1916), 65:236.

56. Boyd Fisher, "How to Reduce Labor Turnover," *The Annals* (May 1917), 71:139.

57. Kelly, *Hiring*, pp. 131–136; NACS, *Third Annual Proceedings* (1915), p. 336; NACS, *Fourth Annual Proceedings* (1916), p. 304; *Employment Management: Its Rise and Scope*, Federal Board for Vocational Education, Bulletin No. 50 (1920), p. 10; Richard T. Crane, "Bringing Men Into the Game," *System* (September 1909), vol. 16; T. J. Zimmerman, "How They Hold Their Men," *System* (August 1910), 18:150–152.

58. P. J. Reilly, "Planning Promotion for Employees and the Effect in Reducing Labor Turnover," *The Annals* (May 1917), 71:139; Sumner H. Slichter, *The Turnover of Factory Labor* (New York, 1921), p. 189.

59. Katherine Stone, "The Origins of Job Structures in the Steel Industry," in Richard C. Edwards, Michael Reich, and David M. Gordon, eds., *Labor Market Segmentation* (Lexington, Mass., 1975), pp. 24–84.

60. David M. Gordon, Richard Edwards, and Michael Reich, *Segmented Work, Divided Workers: The Historical Transformation of Labor in the United States* (Cambridge, Mass., 1982), ch. 5; William Lazonick, "Technological Change and the Control of Work," in Howard F. Gospel and Craig R. Littler, eds., *Managerial Strategies and Industrial Relations* (London, 1983), pp. 126–127; Jeremy Brecher et al., "Uncovering the Hidden History of the American Workplace," *Review of Radical Political Economics* (Winter 1978), 10:1–23. Also see Robert E. Cole, *Work, Mobility, and Participation* (Berkeley, Calif., 1979), pp. 105–107.

61. Harry Jerome, *Mechanization in Industry* (New York, 1934), p. 401; Lynds, *Middletown*, p. 401; U.S. Employment Service, "Job Specifications for the Automobile Manufacturing Industry" (Washington, D.C., 1935); Slichter, *Turnover*, p. 135; Leo Wolman and Gustav Peck, "Labor Groups in the Social Structure," in Report of the President's Committee on Social Trends, *Recent Social Trends in the United States* (New York, 1933), p. 906.

62. Jerome, *Mechanization*, p. 295.

63. Isaac A. Hourwich, *Immigration and Labor* (New York, 1912), pp. 246–249; John H. Ashworth, *The Helper and American Trade Unions* (Baltimore, 1915).

64. G. M. Basford, "Training Men With Reference to Promotion," NACS *Bulletin* (October 1915), 2:25; Reilly, "Promotion," p. 136; Kelly, *Hiring*, p. 136; NACS, *Third Annual Proceedings* (1915), p. 408; Mary B. Gilson, in NACS, *Sixth Annual Proceedings* (1918), pp. 382–383.

65. Charles Fouhy, "Relations Between the Employment Manager and Foreman," *Industrial Management* (October 1919), 58:336.

4. Problems, Problem-Solvers, and a New Profession

1. For an overview, see Daniel T. Rodgers, *The Work Ethic in Industrializing America, 1850–1920* (Chicago, 1978).

2. Henry C. Metcalf, "Report of the Committee on Vocational Guidance,"

National Association of Corporation Schools (NACS), *Fourth Annual Proceedings* (1916), pp. 278, 343; Lee Frankel and Alexander Fleisher, *The Human Factor in Industry* (New York, 1920), p. 16.

3. John Dewey, *Democracy and Education: An Introduction to the Philosophy of Education* (1916; reprint, New York, 1944), pp. 262–266; Don D. Leschohier, *The Labor Market* (New York, 1919), p. 90.

4. Robert F. Hoxie, *Scientific Management and Labor* (New York, 1915); Milton Nadworny, *Scientific Management and the Unions, 1900–1932* (Cambridge, Mass., 1955); Metcalf, "Report," p. 297.

5. Joseph W. Roe, "How the College Can Train Managers," *The Engineering Magazine* (July 1916), vol. 51; Fred H. Rindge, Jr., "Can the Human Side of Engineering Be Taught?" *Industrial Management* (November 1916) vol. 52; J. W. Roe, "Industrial Service Work in Engineering Schools," *ASME Transactions* (1914), vol. 36; "The College Man and the Industrial Worker," pamphlet (n.d.), YMCA Historical Library, New York.

6. Harrington Emerson, "The Scientific Selection of Employees," *Transactions of the Efficiency Society* (1912), vol. 1; David Noble, *America By Design: Science, Technology and the Rise of Corporate Capitalism* (New York, 1977), pp. 275, 297; Frank and Lillian M. Gilbreth, "The Three Position Plan of Promotion," *The Annals* (May 1916), 65:289–296; paper delivered by F. C. Blanchard to the Efficiency Society, typescript, 1915, in John Carmody Papers, Roosevelt Presidential Library, Hyde Park, Box 2. Lillian Gilbreth's husband was Frank M. Gilbreth, an engineer and associate of Emerson's. Their home life is described in Frank B. Gilbreth, Jr., and Ernestine Gilbreth Carey, *Cheaper by the Dozen* (New York, 1948).

Another member of the Efficiency Society's board of directors was H. F. J. Porter, an independently wealthy engineer who became a staunch advocate of employee welfare work. In 1905, he opened an office in New York City to devote himself to "improving conditions in factories." He was involved with the controversial Pittsburgh Survey studies of industrial life and working conditions and set up one of the earliest employee representation plans at Nernst Lamp Works of Pittsburgh. "Biography of the Secretary, H. F. J. Porter," *Transactions of the Efficiency Society* (1912), 1:33–38; H. F. J. Porter, "Discussion," *ASME Transactions* (1919), 41:193; H. F. J. Porter, "Technical Education and the Higher Industrial Life," address delivered at Clarkson School of Technology, Potsdam, New York, pamphlet, 1902.

7. Ordway Tead, *Instincts in Industry* (Boston, 1918), p. 54; Robert W. Bruere, "Can We Eliminate Labor Unrest?" *The Annals* (January 1919), 81:97. Some of these ideas also are found in Helen Marot, *The Creative Process in Industry* (New York, 1918).

8. Associates of the bureau included Herbert Croley, Mary Van Kleeck, and Heber Blankenhorn. Marshall Olds, *Analysis of the Interchurch World Movement Report on the Steel Strike* (New York, 1923), pp. 396, 417–431; Bureau of Industrial Research (BIR), *American Company Shop Committee Plans* (Washington, D.C., 1919); BIR, *Workers' Education* (New York, 1921); Commission of Inquiry, Interchurch World Movement, *Report on the Steel Strike of 1919* (New

York, 1920), pp. 1, 6; Robert K. Murray, *Red Scare: A Study in National Hysteria, 1919–1920* (Minneapolis, 1955), p. 155; Daniel Nelson, "A Newly Appreciated Art: The Development of Personnel Work at Leeds & Northrup," *Business History Review* (Winter 1970), 44:526–530.

9. R. B. Wolf, "Use of Nonfinancial Incentives in Industry," *ASME Journal* (December 1918), 40:1035–1038; R. B. Wolf, "Control and Consent," *Bulletin of the Taylor Society* (March 1917), 3:5–20; R. B. Wolf, "Making Men Like Their Jobs," *System* (January 1919), 35:34–35; Ordway Tead and Henry C. Metcalf, *Personnel Administration* (New York, 1920), p. 204. A biography of Wolf is in YMCA, "Summary of the Industrial Conference on Human Relations and Betterment in Industry" (New York, 1920), p. 35.

10. Robert G. Valentine, "Scientific Management and Organized Labor" [1914] and "The Progressive Relation Between Efficiency and Consent" [1915], both reprinted in *Bulletin of the Taylor Society* (December 1923), 8:225–236; Nadworny, *Scientific Management*, pp. 18–20. Several months after delivering his first paper to the Society for the Promotion of Scientific Management, Valentine was picked to present the viewpoint of scientific management as part of the study Robert F. Hoxie conducted for the U.S. Commission on Industrial Relations.

11. "Fitch Directing Courses," *Personnel* (March 1921), 3:3; Meyer Bloomfield, "Men Management: A New Profession in the Making," *Bulletin of the Taylor Society* (August 1921), vol. 6; Harlow S. Person in YMCA, "Summary," pp. 30–32. In a letter to Morris L. Cooke of the Taylor Society, Mary Van Kleeck noted these consolidating tendencies: "Social workers, starting with an interest in the individual, enlarged the field of their activities to give attention to institutions and organizations as a social problem, while the engineers, starting with an interest in administration and structural organization, are coming to see that the welfare of the individual is the test of management. In other words, it seems to me that the two groups are moving toward each other." Mary Van Kleeck to Morris L. Cooke, Cooke Papers, Roosevelt Presidential Library, Box 16.

12. Gompers quoted in Phillip S. Foner, *History of the Labor Movement in the United States* (New York, 1975), 2:240.

13. Leah H. Feder, *Unemployment Relief in Periods of Depression* (New York, 1936), p. 87; John Garraty, *Unemployment in History: Economic Thought and Public Policy* (New York, 1978), p. 108.

14. Davis R. Dewey, "Irregularity of Employment," American Economic Association Publication No. 9, October and December 1894, p. 56; Joseph Dorfman, *The Economic Mind in American Civilization* (New York, 1949), 3:379.

15. Dewey, "Irregularity," p. 54; Dorfman, *Economic Mind*, pp. 222–223; Garraty, *Unemployment*, p. 120; Paul T. Ringenbach, *Tramps and Reformers, 1873–1916* (Westport, Conn., 1973), p. 148; Shelby Harrison, *Public Employment Offices* (New York, 1924); H. Hodges, "Progress of the Public Employment Bureaus," *The Annals* (January 1917), vol. 69; William M. Leiserson, *The Theory of Public Employment Offices and the Principles of Their Practical Administration* (New York, 1914).

16. B. B. Gilbert, *The Evolution of National Insurance in Great Britain: The Origins of the Welfare State* (London, 1966), ch. 5; Daniel Nelson, *Unemployment Insurance: The American Experience, 1915–1935* (Madison, Wis., 1969), p. 10.

17. William H. Beveridge, *Unemployment: A Problem of Industry* (London, 1910), pp. 76–78, 193, 202–207, 218–220, 230–235. The commission's minority report contained the somewhat different position associated with Sidney and Beatrice Webb, who thought that cyclical unemployment could be mitigated by what they called "the regularization of the national aggregate demand." On measures to deal with seasonal and frictional unemployment, however, they did not differ greatly from Beveridge. B. B. Gilbert, "Winston Churchill versus the Webbs: The Origins of British Unemployment Insurance," *American Historical Review* (April 1966), vol. 71; Sidney and Beatrice Webb, *The Prevention of Destitution* (London, 1911); Sidney Webb, ed., *Seasonal Trades* (London, 1914); J. J. Astor, A. L. Bowley, W. T. Layton et al., *Is Unemployment Inevitable?* (London, 1924).

18. Henry Seager, *Social Insurance: A Program of Social Reform* (New York, 1910), ch. 4. One influential proponent of Beveridge's ideas in the United States was William M. Leiserson, a former student of John R. Commons. See J. Michael Eisner, *William Morris Leiserson: A Biography* (Madison, Wis., 1967), pp. 11, 30–33; New York Commission on Employer's Liability, *Report of the Committee on Unemployment*, appendix 1 (Albany, 1911).

19. Mary Van Kleeck, *Artificial Flower Makers* (New York, 1913), p. 56; Van Kleeck, *Women in the Bookbinding Trade* (New York, 1913), p. 113. Also see Louise C. Odencrantz, "The Irregularity of Employment of Women," *The Survey* (May 1, 1909), and Odencrantz, *Italian Women in Industry* (New York, 1919). It is interesting to note that the world's first studies of labor turnover were conducted by German reformers associated with the Verein für Sozialpolitik, including feminists such as Marie Bernays. Bernays, like Van Kleeck, was concerned with the instability of women's employment. See Marie Bernays, "Auslese und Anpassung der Arbeiterschaft der geschlossenen Grossindustrie," in Verein für Sozialpolitik, *Schriften* (1910), 133:125–182; Paul H. Douglas, "Labor Turnover," in *Encyclopaedia of the Social Sciences* (New York, 1932), pp. 709–713.

20. Nelson, *Unemployment Insurance*, p. 13; "Proceedings of Business Meetings," *American Labor Legislation Review* (March 1914), 4:144–146.

21. John B. Andrews, "Introductory Note," and Meyer Bloomfield, "General Discussion," in *American Labor Legislation Review* (May 1914), 4:211–213, 350–352.

22. Robert G. Valentine, "What the Awakened Employer Is Thinking on Unemployment," *American Labor Legislation Review* (June 1915), 5:425, 427; "Seasonal Employment and Unemployment," Boston Chamber of Commerce Papers, Baker Library, Harvard University, File 332–53; "Seasonal Irregularity in Industry in Boston, Massachusetts," Report of the Committee on Industrial Relations, Boston Chamber of Commerce, Boston, 1914, in Boston Chamber of Commerce Papers, File 332–53. Poyntz later taught at Barnard and became an activist in the Ladies' Garment Workers.

23. Joseph H. Willits, "Steadying Employment," *The Annals* (May 1916), 65:iv, 63–91; Morris L. Cooke, "Responsibility and Opportunity of the City in the Prevention of Unemployment," *American Labor Legislation Review* (June 1915), 5:433–436.

24. "Report of the Mayor's Committee on Unemployment of the City of New

York," New York, January 1916, pp. 56–62; Feder, *Unemployment Relief,* p. 241.

25. Richard A. Feiss, "Scientific Management Applied to the Steadying of Employment and Its Effect in an Industrial Establishment," *The Annals* (September 1915), 61:103–111; Feiss, "Personal Relationship as a Basis of Scientific Management," *The Annals* (May 1916), 65:27–56; Herman Feldman, "The New Emphasis in the Problem of Reducing Unemployment," *Bulletin of the Taylor Society* (October 1922), 7:176–177.

26. Morris L. Cooke, "Scientific Management as a Solution of the Unemployment Problem," *The Annals* (September 1915), 61:147, 149.

27. John B. Andrews, "A Practical Program for the Prevention of Unemployment in America," *American Labor Legislation Review* (November 1915), 5:585–587.

28. "Unemployment Survey," *American Labor Legislation Review* (November 1915), 5:587. Henry Bruere thought that the efforts of the AALL and the Massachusetts State Committee on Unemployment ultimately accomplished little except that they "served to bring forcibly to the attention of the business groups some sense of responsibility for thinking at least constructively about the unemployment problem." *New York Times* Oral History Project, *The Reminiscences of Henry Bruere* (New York, 1972), p. 122.

29. "How to Meet Hard Times: A Program for the Prevention and Relief of Abnormal Unemployment," Report of the Mayor's Committee on Unemployment, City of New York (New York, 1917), pp. 7–8, 20; Ringenbach, *Tramps,* p. 173.

30. Valentine, "Awakened Employer," pp. 423, 425–426.

31. Joseph H. Willits, "Philadelphia Association Has Interesting History," *Personnel* (April 1919), 1:7; Willits, "Steadying," p. 76; Mayor's Committee (1916), p. 56; M. C. Rorty, "Broader Aspects of the Employment Problem," and Willits, "The Philadelphia Association," *Industrial Management* (February 1917), 52:723–725.

32. Ethelbert Stewart, "Informal Address," U.S. Bureau of Labor Statistics Bulletin No. 202 (Washington, D.C., 1916), p. 8.

33. U.S. Employment Service Bulletin, July 31, 1918, p. 2; Paul Brissenden and Emil Frankel, *Labor Turnover in Industry: A Statistical Analysis* (New York, 1922), p. 91; Sumner H. Slichter, *The Turnover of Factory Labor* (New York, 1921), pp. 30–33, 56–69.

34. Concern over tramps—homeless, unemployed men—heightened during the 1890s as a result of the publicity and controversy surrounding Coxey's Army of unemployed workers. As with labor turnover, tramping was attributed to various causes, both personal (a defective work ethic) and systemic (the alienation produced by modern factory work). In the latter view, the tramp was a "proletarian hero who refused to be crushed or shaped into a cog in the industrial mechanism." James Gilbert, *Work Without Salvation: America's Intellectuals and Industrial Alienation, 1880–1910* (Baltimore, 1977), pp. 24–26; Ringenbach, *Tramps,* passim; Feder, *Unemployment Relief,* p. 87; Alice Solenberger, *One Thousand Homeless Men: A Study of Original Records* (New York, 1911), p. 2.

35. Magnus W. Alexander, "Waste in Hiring and Discharging Men," *Iron Age* (1914), 94:1032–1033; Alexander, "Cost of Hiring and Firing Men," *The Engineering Magazine* (1915), 48:733–736; Alexander, "Hiring and Firing: Its Economic Waste and How to Avoid It," *The Annals* (May 1916), 65:128–144; W. A. Grieves, "The Handling of Men," *Efficiency Society Bulletin* (April 30, 1915), vol. 1; Irene O. Andrews, "The Relation of Irregular Employment to the Living Wage for Women," *American Labor Legislation Review* (June 1915), 5:319.

Similarly, it wasn't until the 1910s that the association between tramping and labor market conditions gained acceptance. Henry Bruere, then a New York City government official, said that the city first became aware of the onset of the 1913 depression when there was an increase in the number of applicants at municipal lodging houses. Concern for the homeless, he said, "led to the discussion of the jobless men and this in turn gave rise to the consideration of general unemployment conditions." Bruere, "America's Unemployment Problem," *The Annals* (September 1915), 61:13; Solenberger, *Homeless Men*, pp. 139, 149.

36. Willits, "Steadying," pp. 63–91.

37. Paul H. Douglas, "Absenteeism in Labor," *Political Science Quarterly* (December 1919), 34:599; Don D. Lescohier, *The Labor Market* (New York, 1919), p. 120; Peter A. Speek, "The Psychology of Floating Workers," *The Annals* (January 1917), 69:73; Boyd Fisher, "How to Reduce Labor Turnover," *The Annals* (May 1917), 71:17.

38. Lescohier, *Labor Market*, p. 115; Slichter, *Turnover*, pp. 33, 336; Brissenden and Frankel, *Labor Turnover*, p. 47.

39. Harry F. Porter, "Giving the Men a Chance: What It's Doing for Ford," in *Handling Men* (Chicago, 1917), p. 171; Samuel M. Levin, "Ford Profit Sharing, 1914–1920," *The Personnel Journal* (August 1927), 6:76; U.S. Senate, *Final Report and Testimony of the Commission on Industrial Relations* (Washington, 1916), 8:7678; Horace L. Arnold and Fay L. Faurote, *Ford Methods and the Ford Shops* (New York, 1919), pp. 96–106.

40. George Bundy, "Work of the Employment Department of the Ford Motor Company," U.S. Bureau of Labor Statistics Bulletin No. 196 (1916), pp. 63–67; Levin, "Profit Sharing," p. 78; Stephen Meyer, "From Welfare Capitalism to the American Plan: The First World War and Automobile Workers at Ford," unpublished paper delivered to the American Historical Association, San Francisco, 1978, pp. 5–9.

41. John Lee, "The So-Called Profit Sharing System in the Ford Plant," *The Annals* (May 1916), 65:300.

42. H. A. Haring, "Three Classes of Labor to Avoid," *Industrial Management* (December 1921) 62:370–373; Oscar Roder, "Employment Plans and Methods," *Industrial Management* (July 1917), 53:560; Leslie H. Allen, "The Workman's Home: Its Influence Upon Production in the Factory and Labor Turnover," *ASME Transactions* (1918), 40:220.

43. Emil Frankel, "Labor Absenteeism," *Journal of Political Economy* (May 1921), 29:487; NACS, *Third Annual Proceedings* (1915), pp. 673–677.

44. Slichter, *Turnover*, p. 158; NACS, *Ninth Annual Proceedings* (1921), p. 638.

45. David Montgomery, "The New Unionism and the Transformation of Workers' Consciousness in America, 1909–1922," *Journal of Social History* (Summer 1974), 7:512–513; Paul Litchfield, *Industrial Voyage: My Life as an Industrial Lieutenant* (Garden City, N.Y., 1954), p. 133; Meyer, "Workers at Ford," p. 7.

46. W. B. Wilson, "Labor Program of the Department of Labor," U.S. Bureau of Labor Statistics Bulletin No. 247 (1918), p. 166; Samuel Gompers, "Union Labor and the Enlightened Employer," *Industrial Management* (April 1921), 61:237; William M. Leiserson, "Collective Bargaining and Its Effect on Production," *The Annals* (September 1920), 91:47; Lescohier, *Labor Market*, p. 89.

47. John M. Williams, "An Actual Account of What We Have Done to Reduce Our Labor Turnover," U.S. Bureau of Labor Statistics Bulletin No. 227 (1917), p. 188; F. C. Henderschott and E. W. Weakly, *The Employee Department and Employee Relations* (Chicago, 1918), p. 53: Lescohier, *Labor Market*, p. 90.

48. E. H. Fish, "Employment Methods as Followed by the Norton Company," *ASME Journal* (July 1918), 40:558; Sumner H. Slichter, "The Scope and Nature of the Labor Turnover Problem," *Quarterly Journal of Economics* (November 1919), 34:336. Also see Walter D. Scott and Robert C. Clothier, *Personnel Management* (Chicago, 1923), pp. 469, 485.

49. Fred H. Colvin, *Labor Turnover, Loyalty, and Output* (New York, 1919), pp. 6–8, 11: Fisher, "Reducing Turnover," pp. 29–32; NACS, *Eighth Annual Proceedings* (1920), p. 426; Slichter, *Turnover*, pp. 188, 214; Boris Emmet, "The Turnover of Labor," Federal Board for Vocational Education Bulletin No. 46 (1919), pp. 44–55; R. B. Wolf, "Securing the Initiative of the Workman," *American Economic Review* (March 1919), 9:120–121.

50. Magnus W. Alexander, "Cost of Labor Turnover," in U.S. Bureau of Labor Statistics Bulletin No. 227 (1917), p. 27.

As during World War I, turnover continues to be viewed as an index of employee morale. A recent study of work attitudes termed quit rates a "behavior-oriented indicator of increasing worker discontent." And, as in the past, low morale still is attributed to what one government study called "the harmful effects of Taylorism." Sounding much like earlier vocationalists, the study said that job satisfaction could be increased by providing workers with "career mobility" in the face of "diminishing opportunities to be one's own boss." G. Staines and R. Quinn, "American Workers Evaluate the Quality of Their Jobs," *Monthly Labor Review* (January 1979), 102:4; James O'Toole et al., *Work in America: Report of a Special Task Force to the Secretary of HEW* (Cambridge, Mass., 1973), pp. 17–22.

51. Briefly, economists distinguish between skills that are generally useful in a variety of firms and those that are specific to a single organization. An employer will bear or share the cost of training employees in firm-specific skills, after which he has an incentive to recoup his training costs by reducing employee turnover. Hence, if it can be shown that workers' skills became relatively more firm-specific sometime during the past, one would have an explanation for the rise of employer concern with turnover. See Gary Becker, *Human Capital* (New York, 1964).

52. E. M. Hopkins, "Advantages of Centralized Employment," *The Annals* (May 1917), 71:2.

53. Paul H. Douglas, *American Apprenticeship and Industrial Education* (New York, 1921), p. 124; Anne Bezanson, Miriam Hussey, Joseph H. Willits, and Leda F. White, "Four Years of Labor Mobility: A Study of Labor Turnover in a Group of Selected Plants in Philadelphia," *The Annals*, (May 1925), Vol. 119, suppl., p. 75.

54. Willits, "Steadying," p. 67.

55. Alexander claimed that the highest turnover rates and turnover costs were associated with the new class of semiskilled operatives. He argued that because they worked with expensive equipment and machinery, greater damages were incurred by inexperienced semiskilled trainees, hence greater training costs. However, other studies found results different from Alexander's. In addition, employers increasingly were relying on vestibule training with superannuated equipment, a technique that alleviated any damage costs. Slichter, *Turnover,* p. 69; U.S. Training Service, "Training Employees for Better Production," *Training Bulletin* (1918), Vol. 4.

56. Ordway Tead, *Instincts in Industry* (Boston, 1918), p. 70; Joseph H. Willits, "The Labor Turnover and the Humanizing of Industry," *The Annals* (September 1915), 61:132–133; Lillian Erskine and Treadwell Cleveland, Jr., "New Men for Old," *Everybody's* (April 1917), 36:425.

57. Slichter, *Turnover,* p. 427; Dudley R. Kennedy, "The Future of Industrial Relations," *Industrial Management* (March 1920), 59:228.

58. Alexander, "Cost of Labor Turnover," p. 15; Boyd Fisher, "Determining Cost of Turnover of Labor," U.S. Bureau of Labor Statistics Bulletin No. 227 (1917), pp. 65–66.

59. Ernest M. Hopkins, "A Functionalized Employment Department as a Factor in Industrial Efficiency," *The Annals* (September 1915), 61:116–117; Henry S. Dennison, "Methods of Reducing the Labor Turnover," U.S. Bureau of Labor Statistics Bulletin No. 202 (1916), p. 58; Meyer Bloomfield, "The New Profession of Handling Men," *The Annals* (September 1915), 61:122.

60. C. Bertrand Thompson, "Making Each Department Pay Its Own Share," *System* (February 1915), vol. 27; Robert C. Clothier, "The Employment Work of the Employment Department of the Curtis Publishing Company," *The Annals* (May 1916), 65:109; Clothier, "The Function of the Employment Department," U.S. Bureau of Labor Statistics Bulletin No. 196 (1916), p. 11; A. B. Nevins, "How We Make It Easy to Apply the Ounce of Prevention in Management," *Factory* (June 1924), 32:938; NACS, *Seventh Annual Proceedings* (1919), p. 328.

Not until the 1920s was it recognized that turnover levels were an inaccurate measure of employee morale and of the personnel department's effectiveness. In 1928 Morris Leeds, the liberal Philadelphia employer, said that turnover "should be more carefully studied as an index of satisfactory labor relations. It is, in my judgment, being used for that purpose on the unwarrantable assumption that it does precisely indicate the value of various labor policies." Quoted in Herman Feldman, "A Survey of Research in the Field of Industrial Relations," Preliminary

Report of the Advisory Committee on Industrial Relations of the Social Science Research Council, New York, June 1928, p. 149.

61. Leon I. Thomas, "The High Cost of Labor That Comes and Goes," in *Handling Men*, p. 99; Frankel and Fleisher, *Human Factor*, p. 261; W. A. Grieves, "The Handling of Men," *100%* (1915), 4:5–15.

Boyd Fisher urged other reformers to convince companies that turnover was costing them "millions" of dollars. "The thorough-going remedies for turnover are so expensive," said Fisher, "that until even the most skeptical managers are convinced, we shall not get far with our corrective measures." Fisher, "Reduce Turnover," p. 17.

62. Erskine and Cleveland, "New Men," p. 426; NACS, *Seventh Annual Proceedings* (1918), p. 328.

63. Emmet, "Turnover," p. 14; Harry W. Kimball, "Some Reasons for Labor Turnover," *Industrial Management* (April 1919), 57:324; Colvin, *Loyalty and Output*, p. 37.

These criticisms had an effect. When a major new personnel management textbook was published in 1923, it carefully downplayed replacement cost and stressed instead such immeasurable aspects of turnover as "interest and morale." Turnover costs, said the authors, "are difficult of measurement. It is hard to set a value upon them. . . . But we are not as concerned with turnover in itself as we are with the causes for labor turnover. It is apparent that management is interested in labor turnover not so much from the point of view of the cost of replacing the men who leave, as it is interested in labor turnover from the point of view of lessened interest and effectiveness throughout the organization." Scott and Clothier, *Personnel Management*, pp. 448–449.

64. Slichter, *Turnover*, p. 427.

65. There is a large and growing body of scholarship that analyzes the rise of a new middle class and its role in furthering Progressive reform activity. Works that I found helpful include Samuel Haber, *Efficiency and Uplift: Scientific Management in the Progressive Era* (Chicago, 1964); Magali S. Larson, *The Rise of Professionalism: A Sociological Analysis* (Berkeley, Calif., 1977); Robert H. Wiebe, *The Search for Order, 1877–1920* (New York, 1967); Christopher Lasch, *Haven in a Heartless World: The Family Besieged* (New York, 1977).

66. Monte Calvert, *The Mechanical Engineer In America, 1830–1910: Professional Cultures in Conflict* (Baltimore, 1967), pp. 63–85; Noble, *America by Design*, pp. 33–49; Edwin T. Layton, Jr., *The Revolt of the Engineers* (Cleveland, 1971), pp. 57–69; Haber, *Efficiency*, p. 3; Henry Towne, "The General Principles of Organization Applied to an Individual Manufacturing Establishment," *Efficiency Society Transactions* (1912), vol. 1; Kenneth E. Trombley, *The Life and Times of a Happy Liberal: A Biography of Morris L. Cooke* (New York, 1954), pp. 47–70.

67. Frederick W. Taylor, *Shop Management* (New York, 1911), pp. 31, 110.

68. Daniel Nelson, *Frederick W. Taylor and the Rise of Scientific Management* (Madison, Wis., 1980), pp. 188–189; Lecture Notes of Henry H. Farquhar, 1916–1924, Baker Library, Harvard University Graduate School of Business Adminis-

tration; Melvin T. Copeland, *And Mark an Era: The Story of the Harvard Business School* (Boston, 1958), pp. 26, 159; Louis D. Brandeis, *Business: A Profession* (Boston, 1914); T. N. Carver, "The Redistribution of Human Talent," *Efficiency Society Transactions* (1912), 1:363; Elliot Goodwin, "Is There is Profession of Business and Can We Really Train for It?" *Efficiency Society Transactions* (June 1916), 5:292-298.

69. Harlow S. Person, "University Schools of Business and the Training of Employment Executives," in U.S. Bureau of Labor Statistics Bulletin No. 196 (1916), pp. 32-33; Slichter, *Turnover*, pp. 409-410.

Some sense of what the professional in industry meant to contemporary observers can be seen in the following description of a labor manager: "he should be something of the philosopher, of the sociologist, of the poet in that he is the firm's representative who must see first the man in the employee . . . This new kind of labor manager has brought something vital into industry which before had been missing . . . the atmosphere of his office is hardly that of the factory; it bears the mark of the professor's study . . . the labor manager is first of all a gentleman." John R. Commons, *Industrial Government* (New York, 1921), pp. 238-240.

70. Glenn Frank, *The Politics of Industry: A Footnote to the Social Unrest* (New York, 1919), pp. 42-92; Edward D. Jones, "Employment Management," in Daniel Bloomfield, ed., *Selected Articles on Employment Management* (New York, 1919), p. 126; Valentine, "Efficiency and Consent," p. 226.

71. Jean Hoskins, in Proceedings of the National Association of Employment Managers (Cleveland, 1919), p. 37; Meyer Bloomfield, "Problems of Industrial Management," U.S. Bureau of Labor Statistics Bulletin No. 247 (1918), p. 157.

72. Sumner H. Slichter, "The Management of Labor," *Journal of Political Economy* (December 1919), 27:831-832; Meyer Bloomfield, "A New Profession in American Industry," in D. Bloomfield, *Articles*, pp. 115, 117-118.

73. Mary B. Gilson, *What's Past is Prologue: Reflections on My Industrial Experience* (New York, 1940), pp. 51, 121.

There is little record of what the unions thought of personnel management. On the one hand there were those who readily agreed with one union official's characterization of the personnel manager as "a benevolent despot." On the other hand, when Sidney Hillman of the clothing workers addressed a personnel management conference in 1920, he applauded the fact that personnel managers were undercutting the influence of corporate production departments, and he expressed the hope that the shift would continue in the future. A. J. Portenar, "Centralized Labor Responsibility From a Labor Union Standpoint," *The Annals* (May 1917), 71:194; Sidney Hillman, "Organized Labor in Industry," Proceedings of the Industrial Relations Association of America, Part 1 (1920), pp. 98-102.

74. Gilson, who had worked with the Women's Trade Union League, rationalized the seeming contradiction of being pro-union yet working for an open shop employer (Joseph & Feiss) by arguing that while unions were a force for industrial democracy, at *her* company, there was no pressing need for unionization: "The morale of the shop was good. The workers were making good wages." More

revealing of her attitude was her comment that she "wanted to be free to carry out our experiments without interference from the trade unions." Gilson, *Past Is Prologue*, pp. 160–161.

5. Crisis and Change During World War I

1. Stanley Lebergott, *Manpower in Economic Growth* (New York, 1964), pp. 512, 515; "Changes in the Employment of Women in Industry," National Association for Corporation Training (NACT) *Bulletin* (February 1921), 8:60–61; U.S. Department of Commerce, Bureau of the Census, *Historical Statistics of the United States*, pt. 1 (Washington, D.C., 1975), p. 107; Hope T. Eldridge and Dorothy S. Thomas, *Population Redistribution and Economic Growth in the U.S., 1870–1950* (Philadelphia, 1958), 3:251, table A1-11; Emmett J. Scott, *Negro Migration During the War* (1920, reprint, New York, 1969), pp. 36–37; Gordon S. Watkins, *Labor Problems and Labor Adminstration During the World War* (Urbana, Ill., 1920), pp. 55–74; Paul S. Taylor, *Mexican Labor in the United States: Bethlehem, Pennsylvania* (Berkeley, Calif., 1931).

2. Sterling D. Spero and Abram L. Harris, *The Black Worker: The Negro and the Labor Movement* (New York, 1931), pp. 151-153; Charles T. Clayton, "Destructive Labor Recruiting," Bureau of Labor Statistics Bulletin No. 247 (1918), p. 56; David Brody, *Steelworkers in America: The Nonunion Era* (New York, 1969), pp. 186–187; George Haynes, "Negroes Move North," *The Survey* (January 4, 1919), vol. 41.

3. Roy W. Kelly, "Labor Factors in Our Shipping Program," *Industrial Management* (February 1918), 54:210; Industrial Relations Association of America (IRAA), *Proceedings* (1920), pt. 2, p. 553; "U.S. Training Service Organized," *Iron Age* (January 19, 1919), vol. 103; J. B. Densmore, "Lessons of the War in Shifting Labor," *The Annals* (January 1919), 81:82; U.S. Federal Board for Vocational Education (FBVE), *Third Annual Report* (1919), pp. 29–31.

4. Sumner H. Slichter, "Industrial Morale" [1920], reprinted in *Potentials of the American Economy: Selected Essays of Sumner H. Slichter* (Cambridge, Mass., 1961), p. 169; Paul H. Douglas, "Personnel Problems and the Business Cycle," *Adminstration* (July 1922), 4:17; Robert Ozanne, *Wages in Practice and Theory* (Madison, Wis., 1968), p. 111; National Association of Corporation Schools (NACS), *Eighth Annual Proceedings* (1920), pp. 540, 547–549, 555–556; "Shortage of Labor," in IRAA, *Proceedings* (1920), pt. 2, pp. 539–555; Guy Tripp, quoted in *Iron Trade Review* (January 19, 1920), 66:369; Paul H. Douglas, "Absenteeism in Labor," *Political Science Quarterly* (December 1919), 34:591–608.

5. Alexander M. Bing, *Wartime Strikes and Their Adjustment* (New York, 1921), pp. 28–30, 291–296; David Montgomery, "The New Unionism and the Transformation of Workers' Consciousness in America, 1909–1922," *Journal of Social History* (Summer 1974), 7:514; David Brody, *Labor in Crisis: The Steel Strike of 1919* (Philadelphia, 1965); Jeremy Brecher, *Strike!* (Greenwich, Conn., 1972), pp. 133–180; Leo Wolman, *Ebb and Flow in Trade Unionism* (New York, 1936), pp. 172–193.

6. NACS, *Eighth Annual Proceedings* (1920), p. 427; Paul F. Brissenden and Emil Frankel, *Labor Turnover in Industry: A Statistical Analysis* (New York, 1922), pp. 80–81; Lebergott, *Manpower*, p. 512.

7. Sumner H. Slichter, "The Management of Labor," *Journal of Political Economy* (December 1919), 27:838-839. Twelve years after the war, the Conference Board summarized the logic behind this "union substitution" strategy by noting that "most employers viewed with misgiving this expansion of labor union membership and influence during the war period . . . Employers holding such views naturally undertook to provide for their workers conditions as desirable as they could hope to secure through affiliation with a labor union, or even more attractive." National Industrial Conference Board (NICB), *Industrial Relations: Administration of Policies and Programs* (New York, 1931), p. 19.

8. The methodology used to arrive at these figures is described in Sanford M. Jacoby, "The Origins of Internal Labor Markets in American Manufacturing Firms," (Ph.D. dissertation, University of California, Berkeley, 1981), p. 617. The data are from IRAA *Proceedings* (1920), pt. 1, p. 122, and pt. 2, pp. 179–180; Robert F. Lovett, "Tendencies in Personnel Practice," in Bureau of Personnel Research, Carnegie Institute of Technology, *Service Bulletin* (February 1923), 5:11–12; Edward D. Jones, "Employment Management: Its Rise and Scope," FBVE Bulletin No. 50 (1920), p. 15; NICB, *Industrial Relations Programs in Small Plants* (New York, 1929), p. 2.

9. My tabulation of attendees at the 1918 conference includes only representatives of manufacturing firms. If a company sent more than one representative, they were included, since they often came from different plants. See Bureau of Labor Statistics Bulletin No. 247 (1918), pp. 228–249.

10. Josephine Young Case and Everett Needham Case, *Owen D. Young and American Enterprise* (Boston, 1982), pp. 193–195.

11. "Success," *Personnel* (June 1920), 2:1; "High Spots in the Lives of National Association Directors," *Personnel* (August 1920), 2:1–2, 6; Louise C. Odencrantz, "Personnel Work in America," *Personnel Administration* (August 1922), 10:11; Dwight Farnham, "The Industrial Engineer and the Employment Manager," Society of Industrial Engineers *Bulletin* (1918), 1:7–8.

12. W. H. Lange, "The American Management Association and Its Predecessors," American Management Association, Special Paper No. 17 (New York, 1928), p. 28; "Local Associations," *Personnel* (February 1919), 1:8; Roy W. Kelly, *Hiring the Worker* (New York, 1918), pp. 5–9; "High Spots in Local Association Work," *Personnel* (1919), vol. 1, various issues; "Brief Notes About Local Association Work," *Personnel* (1920), vol. 2, various issues: Ralph G. Wells, "The Work Program of the Employment Managers' Association of Boston," *The Annals,* (May 1916), 65:113–116; Joseph H. Willits, "Development of Employment Managers' Associations," "*Monthly Labor Review* (September 1917), 5:85–86; Bureau of Labor Statistics Bulletin No. 247 (1918), pp. 203–204.

13. *Personnel* (November 1919), 1:1; (January 1919), 1:2; (October 1920), 2:1; (March 1921), 3:1; Bureau of Labor Statistics Bulletin No. 196 (1916), p. 82; No. 227 (1918), p. 6; No. 247 (1918), pp. 141–145, 191–196; National Association of Employment Managers (NAEM) *Proceedings* (1919), pp. 135–

140; Sidney Hillman, "Organized Labor in Industry," and John R. Commons, "Management and Unionism," in IRAA *Proceedings* (1920), pt. 1, pp. 98–102, 125–130, pt. 2, pp. 519–535, 537–556; Robert K. Murray, *Red Scare: A Study in National Hysteria, 1919–1920* (Minneapolis, 1955), p. 170.

14. Boyd Fisher to Walter V. Bingham, February 12, 1919, Bingham Papers, Carnegie Mellon University, Box 2; Bloomfield in Bureau of Labor Statistics Bulletin No. 196 (1916), pp. 74–75; Willits, "Development," p. 86.

15. Paul H. Douglas and F. E. Wolfe, "Labor Administration in the Shipbuilding Industry During War Time," *Journal of Political Economy* (March 1919), 27:149, 393; Bing, *Wartime Strikes,* chs. 13–15.

16. "National War Labor Board," Bureau of Labor Statistics Bulletin No. 287 (1922), pp. 52–63; Bing, *Wartime Strikes,* pp. 175–178; Don D. Lescohier, "Working Conditions," in John R. Commons et al., *History of Labor in the United States* (New York, 1935), 3:321–323; "The Opportunities and Obligations of the Taylor Society," *Bulletin of the Taylor Society* (February 1919), 4:1.

17. "National War Labor Board," pp. 37–41, 138–149; "Characteristics of Company Unions, 1935," Bureau of Labor Statistics Bulletin No. 634 (1937), pp. 10–20; NICB, "Works Councils in the United States," Research Rpt. No. 21 (1919), pp. 75–93; NICB, "Experience with Works Councils in the United States," Research Rpt. No. 50 (1922), pp. 15–52; Robert Ozanne, *A Century of Labor-Management Relations at McCormick and International Harvester* (Madison, Wis., 1967), chs. 5 and 6; Stuart Brandes, *American Welfare Capitalism, 1880–1940* (Chicago, 1976), pp. 119–134; Gerald G. Eggert, *Steelmasters and Labor Reform, 1886–1923* (Pittsburgh, 1981), pp. 103–125.

18. Robert D. Cuff, "The Politics of Labor Administration during World War I," *Labor History* (Fall 1980), 21:546–569; "National War Labor Board," pp. 64–87; Bing, *Wartime Strikes,* pp. 161, 175, 185, 191.

19. Jones, "Employment Management," p. 15; Paul H. Douglas, "Plant Administration of Labor," *Journal of Political Economy* (March 1919), 27:546–547; Douglas, "War Time Courses in Employment Management," *School and Society* (June 7, 1919), 9:692.

Working conditions of women employed in war industries received special attention from the Women in Industry Service of the Department of Labor, headed by Van Kleeck and Clara Tead, as well as the Women's Service Section of the U.S. Railroad Administration. These agencies sought to preserve and improve laws regulating women's work, and they encouraged employers to provide adequate health, sanitation, and safety facilities. Bureau of Industrial Research, *How the Government Handled Its Labor Problems During the War* (Washington, D.C., 1919), pp. 6–8; Maurine Greenwald, "The Technical and the Human: Managing Women Workers," unpublished paper, Department of History, University of Pittsburgh, 1978.

20. Bing, *Wartime Strikes,* pp. 20–24; Douglas and Wolfe, "Shipbuilding," pp. 372, 384, 387; Kelly, "Labor Factors," p. 211.

21. L. C. Marshall, "The War Labor Program and the Administrators," *Journal of Political Economy* (May 1918), vol. 26; Douglas and Wolfe, "Shipbuilding," pp. 166–177, 373–374; Bing, *Wartime Strikes,* pp. 22, 298; Roy W. Kelly, *Hiring*

the Worker (New York, 1918), p. 212; U.S. Shipping Board, Emergency Fleet Corporation, *Handbook on Employment Management in the Shipyard* (Washington, D.C., 1918); "Report of the Conference on Shipyard Employment Managers," Industrial Service Department, U.S. Shipping Board, Emergency Fleet Corporation, Washington, D.C., November 1917.

22. Roy W. Kelly and Frederick J. Allen, *The Shipbuilding Industry* (Boston, 1918), pp. 10, 235–241; Meyer Bloomfield, "A New Profession in American Industry," in Daniel Bloomfield, ed., *Selected Articles on Employment Management* (New York, 1919), pp. 117–118; Harry Tukey, "Foreman Training Classes of the Submarine Boat Corporation," NACS *Bulletin* (January 1920), 7:10–15; Henry Moskowitz, "Development of a Successful Personnel Department in the Submarine Boat Corporation," NACS *Bulletin* (April 1920), 7:175–178.

23. Douglas and Wolfe, "Shipbuilding," pp. 389–390; D. R. Kennedy, "Horse Sense in Human Relations," *Industrial Management* (November 1919), 57:68.

24. Meyer Jacobstein, "Government Course for Training Employment Managers," Bureau of Labor Statistics Bulletin No. 247 (1918), p. 19; Morris L. Cooke, "The Present Labor Situation," *ibid.*, pp. 63–64; Edward D. Jones, "Uncle Sam to Train Employment Managers," *American Industries* (September 1918), 19:11; Douglas, "Courses," p. 692; Jones, "Employment Management," p. 15. In addition to the Ordnance Department and the War Industries Board, other agencies involved ranged from the Department of Labor to the Quartermaster General's Office.

25. Mary Gilson, *What's Past Is Prologue* (New York, 1940), p. 167; Douglas, "Courses," p. 693; Jones, "Employment Management," p. 12; FBVE, *Third Annual Report* (Washington, D.C., 1919), p. 80; "Presentation of Diplomas to Graduates of War Emergency Courses in Employment Management," Bureau of Labor Statistics Bulletin No. 247 (1918), p. 27; Boyd Fisher, "Horse Sense in Human Relations: A Discussion," *Industrial Management* (April 1919), 55:324.

26. Douglas, "Plant Administration," p. 549; Jacobstein, "Government Course," pp. 21, 23; Roy W. Kelly, "War Emergency Courses in Employment Department Practice," *Industrial Management* (May 1919), 55:411; Douglas, "Courses," p. 694.

27. Jacobstein, "Government Course," p. 24; Stewart, in Bureau of Labor Statistics Bulletin No. 247 (1918), pp. 72–73; Boyd Fisher to Walter V. Bingham, February 12, 1919, Bingham Papers, Box 2.

Because the Ordnance Department assigned female employment managers to installations employing large numbers of women, the course organizers had to grapple with the question of whether women should be allowed to take the training course. A compromise was reached whereby women were assigned to a training course in a special technical facility in Cleveland. In addition, the YWCA in New York and Philadelphia established classes to train women as employment managers. These were taught by Dr. Susan M. Kingsbury and Professor Anne Bezanson of the Wharton School. Boyd Fisher, in BLS Bulletin No. 247 (1918), pp. 71–72; Gilson, *What's Past*, pp. 167–168; Douglas, "Plant Administration," p. 549.

28. Kennedy, "Horse Sense," p. 68; FBVE, *Third Annual Report* (1919), pp. 28–29, 78–81.

29. Wells, in IRAA *Proceedings* (1920), pt. 2. pp. 358–361; Fisher, "Horse Sense," p. 324; FBVE, *Report* p. 81.

30. Robert W. Bruere, "Can We Eliminate Labor Unrest?" *The Annals* (January 1919), 81:97; NACS Ninth Annual Proceedings (1921), pp. 597–598; Allen Sinsheimer, "Keeping Workers Contented," *The Automobile* (March 15, 1917), 36:574; Sumner H. Slichter, *The Turnover of Factory Labor* (New York, 1921), pp. 415–416; R. C. Clothier, "The Function of the Employment Department," BLS Bulletin No. 196 (1916), pp. 7–14; Philip J. Reilly, "The Work of the Employment Department of the Dennison Manufacturing Company," *The Annals* (May 1916), vol. 65; Clothier, "The Employment Work of the Curtis Publishing Company," *ibid.*, pp. 95–110; Kelly and Allen, *Shipbuilding*, pp. 240–241; "Developing the Industrial Relations Staff," in IRAA *Proceedings* (1920), pt. 2, pp. 345–357; "Activities of the Personnel Department," NACS *Bulletin* (June 1920), 7:250–252; Ordway Tead and Henry Metcalf, *Personnel Administration* (New York, 1920), pp. 23–39.

31. K. Huey, "Problems Arising and Methods Used in Interviewing and Selecting Employees," *The Annals* (May 1916), vol. 65; Harry D. Kitson, "Employment Managers as Vocational Counselors," *Industrial Management* (March 1921), 61:211; Slichter, *Turnover*, pp. 231–245; Charles P. Avery, "The Value of the Application Form," *The Annals* (May 1916), 65:219–222; Kelly, *Hiring*, pp. 57–100; "Picking the Best Man for the Job," in The Library of Factory Management, *Labor* (Chicago, 1915), 4:32–40; H. L. Gardner, "The Employment Department: Its Function and Scope," BLS Bulletin No. 202 (1916). On the Army's testing programs, see Loren Baritz, *The Servants of Power* (Middletown, Conn., 1960); U.S. War Department, *The Personnel System of the U.S. Army* and *History of the Personnel System of the U.S. Army* (Washington, D.C., 1920); *Psychological Bulletin of the American Psychological Association* (February 1918), vol. 16; NACS *Eighth Annual Proceedings* (1920), pp. 342–366; and Daniel Kevles, "Testing the Army's Intelligence: Psychologists and the Military in World War I," *Journal of American History* (December 1968), 65:565–581.

32. NACT *Ninth Annual Proceedings* (1921), pp. 620–623; NAEM *Proceedings* (1919), p. 35; Slichter, *Turnover*, pp. 327–328; "Starting Men Right," in *Labor*, pp. 41–47; "Introducing the New Worker," in IRAA *Proceedings* (1920) pt. 2, pp. 383–396: Walter D. Scott and Robert C. Clothier, *Personnel Management* (Chicago, 1923), pp. 346–357; H. N. Clarke, "Breaking in the New Worker," *Industrial Management* (June 1919), vol. 58; Charles L. Pearson, "Introducing the New Employee," *The Annals* (May 1916), 65:229–231.

33. IRAA *Proceedings* (1920), pt. 2, p. 244; "Records that Gage Work and Worth," in *Labor*, 48–62; Arthur Williams, "The Instruction of New Employees in Methods of Service," *The Annals* (May 1916), 65:236–237; Arthur H. Young, "Harmonizing the Man and His Job," *Iron Trade Review* (February 5, 1917), 60:427; C. J. Shower, "Pontiac Centralizes Its Employment of Labor," *Automotive Industries* (July 11, 1918), 39:53.

34. Douglas, "Plant Administration," p. 551; "A Survey of Personnel Activities of Member Companies," NACS *Bulletin* (August 1920), 7:346–348; Leslie H. Allen, "The Workman's Home: Its Influence Upon Production in the Factory and

Labor Turnover," ASME *Transactions* (1918), 40:217; NACT, *Ninth Annual Proceedings* (1921), pp. 621–622.

35. J. D. Hackett, "Job Analysis as Aid to Production," *Iron Trade Review* (September 9, 1920), 67:722–724; Philip J. Reilly, "Job Analysis," in BLS Bulletin No. 202 (1916), p. 27; B. Gabine, "The Value and Application of Job Analysis," *Industrial Management* (February 1921), 61:107; P. J. Nilsen, "Job Analysis," in BLS Bulletin No. 247 (1918), p. 133.

Personnel managers were concerned that the vocational purposes for which they used job analysis might be confused with the time study methods of scientific management, which also were called job analysis. The IRAA's Committee on the Description of Occupations issued a report in 1920 which noted that personnel managers did not use job analysis "as it pertains to the machine . . . we in this Association are primarily interested in this thing as it reacts upon the worker." Similarly, the Committee on Job Analysis of the NACS said that personnel managers used job analysis "primarily for the purpose of associating the man more closely with the job. In the other case [scientific management] the job analysis is made principally from the managerial viewpoint." Thus, we see here an attempt to establish professional boundaries and an effort to distance personnel management from the purportedly inhuman methods of industrial engineering. NACS, *Eighth Annual Proceedings* (1920), pp. 167–168; IRAA *Proceedings* (1920), pt. 2, pp. 201–207.

36. *Personnel,* publication of the Committee on the Classification of Personnel for the Army (CCPA), September 11, 1918, and October 2, 1918, in Bingham Papers, Box 2; CCPA, "The Right Man in the Right Place in the Army," pamphlet, 1918, Bingham Papers, Box 2; *Trade Specifications of the U.S. Army,* War Document No. 774 (Washington, D.C., 1919).

The government used job analyses for training purposes by breaking down skilled jobs into what were called "practical instructional units," which an unskilled worker could quickly learn. Kelly and Allen, *Shipbuilding,* pp. 248–253; Charles R. Mann, "Principles Underlying Effective Training of Employees," *Corporation Training* (March 1922), 9:3–6; U.S. Training and Dilution Service, "Training Employees for Better Production," Bulletin No. 4. (1918); Roy W. Kelly, *Training Industrial Workers* (New York, 1920); C. U. Carpenter, "How We Trained 5,000 Women," *Industrial Management* (May 1918), 55:353–357.

37. Hugh L. Clary, "The Zoning of Jobs," *Industrial Management* (May 1921), 61:324–326; Herbert Feis, "The Requirements of a Policy of Wage Settlement," *The Annals* (March 1922), 100:61.

To rationalize government recruiting and to facilitate transactions between the U.S. Employment Service and employers, the Bureau of Labor Statistics launched a project in 1918 to develop standardized occupational nomenclature. Private organizations continued the project after the war. "Description of Occupations by the Bureau of Labor Statistics," *Monthly Labor Review* (February 1919), 8:441–443; John J. Swan, "Memorandum on Notes on Phases of Personnel Work of Interest Historically," December 14, 1918, Bingham Papers, Box 1; "Report of the Joint Committee on Management Terminology," January 11, 1921, Bingham Papers, Box 2; Noble, *America by Design,* p. 231.

38. Whiting Williams, quoted in "Unskilled Laborer Not Different from Well-to-Do," Harvard College *Crimson,* December 17, 1920; Gilson, *What's Past,* p. 75; Frank J. Becvar, "A Method of Grading and Valuing Operations," *The Annals* (March 1922), 100:15–18.

39. IRAA *Proceedings* (1920), pt. 2, pp. 210–211; Merrill D. Lott, "Sperry Gyroscope Company," *American Management Review* (October 1923), 12:8–9; Ordway Tead, "Tendencies Toward the Incentive Method of Wage Payment," *Industrial Management* (October 1923), 66:196–198; Merrill D. Lott, *Wage Scales and Job Evaluation* (New York, 1926).

The job evaluation plan instituted at International Harvester between 1919 and 1923 was the only major evaluation conducted prior to the 1930s. Occupational titles at the company's 23 plants were standardized. Jobs were divided into 18 groups according to a point system of relative valuation. Minimum and maximum rates were set for each group, and piece rates were made commensurate with these rate ranges. Finally, less emphasis was given to time study. *Industrial Relations* (also known as *Bloomfield's Labor Digest*) (October 21, 1922), 12:1290; Arthur H. Young, "Some Experiments in Rate Setting," speech delivered at the annual meeting of the Associated Industries of Massachusetts, Boston, October 17, 1922, in Young Papers, Speeches, vol. 1, Item 13.

40. The strike was closely followed in *Iron Age* (September 5, 1918), 102:570; (July 11, 1918), 102:93; (July 18, 1918), 102:147. Also see Bing, *Wartime Strikes,* pp. 75–78.

41. *Iron Age* (August 8, 1919), 102:332–333; (August 29, 1918), 102:535; (September 5, 1918), 102:726; (September 26, 1918), 102:755. Also see Stanley Shapiro, "The Great War and Reform: Liberals and Labor, 1917–1919," *Labor History* (Summer 1971), 12:335; and Bing, *Wartime Strikes,* pp. 200–202.

42. "Railroad Wages and Working Rules," NICB Research Rpt. No. 46 (1922); *Iron Age* (August 18, 1918), 102:320; Richard H. Rice, "Discussion of Employee Representation Plans," NACT *Bulletin* (August 1921), 8:346–363; W. D. Stearns, "Standardization of Occupations and Rates of Pay," BLS Bulletin No. 247 (1918), pp. 36–42; Stearns, "Standardized Occupations and Rates," *Industrial Management* (May 1918), 55:407–410; "Job Specification—Job Analysis," IRAA *Proceedings* (1920), pt. 2, pp. 210–211; "Grading of General Electric Employees," *Iron Age* (November 1, 1923), vol. 123.

43. S. D. Spero, *Government as Employer* (Brooklyn, N.Y., 1949), pp. 181–188; Leonard D. White, "Public Administration," in Report of the President's Committee on Social Trends, *Recent Social Trends* (New York, 1933), p. 1413; Herman Feldman, "Personnel Program for the Federal Civil Service," House doc. 733, 71st Cong., 1st Sess. (1931), vol. 14; "History of the Civil Service Merit Systems of the U.S. and Selected Foreign Countries," House Committee on Post Office and Civil Service, Subcommittee on Manpower and Civil Service, 94th Cong., 2d Sess. (1976), p. 186.

The committee's report led to the creation of the Personnel Classification Board in 1923, which was heavily involved in efforts to standardize occupational terminology, not only in government, but throughout private industry. For a very different interpretation of these events (which argues that classification was part of a "movement to standardize human beings") see Noble, *America by Design*, pp. 231–235.

44. J. B. Densmore, "Labor Turnover Meeting of the New York Section," *ASME Journal* (September 1918), 40:768; Clayton, "Destructive Recruiting," p. 59; Bing, *Wartime Strikes*, pp. 18, 23–40, 91–94, 195–203, 313; *Iron Age* (June 27, 1918), 101:1671; (July 25, 1918), 102:246; Kelly and Allen, *Shipbuilding*, p. 231.

45. Douglas and Wolfe, "Shipbuilding Labor," pp. 363–366; Harleigh Hartmann, "Should the State Interfere in the Determination of Wage Rates?" NICB Special Rpt. No. 12 (1920), pp. v, 118–125; "Job Classification on the Railroads," *Industrial Relations* (June 4, 1921), 7:697.

Some radical historians portray these techniques as an extension of employer control: Richard Edwards considers a classification system an instance of "bureaucratic control in operation"; Katherine Stone criticizes the job classification and evaluation plan adopted by the steelworkers in the 1940s for accepting and legitimating artificial distinctions between essentially similar jobs. Yet in 1919, the reformers (some of them radicals) associated with the BIR's steel industry study argued that it was "an indication of the backwardness of the steel industry that no exact classification of jobs has generally been worked out in it." They said that this encouraged an undesirable competition for jobs. Richard Edwards, *Contested Terrain* (New York, 1979), pp. 132–139; K. Stone, "The Origins of Job Structures in the Steel Industry," in R. Edwards, M. Reich, and D. M. Gordon, *Labor Market Segmentation* (Lexington, Mass., 1975), pp. 65–68; Commission of Inquiry, Interchurch World Movement, *Report on the Steel Strike of 1919* (New York, 1920), p. 271.

46. Slichter, *Turnover*, pp. 189, 356; Meyer Bloomfield, *Labor and Compensation* (New York, 1918), pp. 308–309; Boyd Fisher, "How to Reduce Labor Turnover," *The Annals* (May 1917), 71:27; Franklyn Meine, "Promotions of Factory Employees," in Daniel Bloomfield, ed., *Problems in Personnel Management* (New York, 1923), pp. 280–281.

47. Phillip J. Reilly, "Planning Promotion for Employees and the Effect in Reducing Labor Turnover," *The Annals* (May 1917), 71:136–139; Slichter, *Turnover*, p. 435.

48. "Survey Methods of Promotion," *Industrial Relations* (April 2, 1921), 7:619–624; "Promotion," *ibid.*, (December 1, 1923), 17:1761.

49. "Hiring, Discharge and Transfer: A Symposium," *Industrial Management* (August 1919), 58:242; NACT, *Ninth Annual Proceedings* (1921), p. 629; "Transfer and Promotion of Employees," *Iron Age* (June 5, 1919), 103:1519.

50. NACT, "Methods of Transfer and Promotion in Business Organizations," Confidential Rpt. No. 6 (October 1920), pp. 5–18; Paul F. Gemmill, "Methods of Promoting Industrial Employees," *Industrial Management* (April 1924), 67:238; Slichter, *Turnover*, pp. 363–368; "Periodic Rating," IRAA *Proceedings* (1920), pt. 2, pp. 313–327.

51. B. S. Beach, "Filling Vacancies from Within the Ranks," *Industrial Management* (February 1924), 67:90; *Industrial Relations* (May 26, 1923), 15:1544.

52. Gemmill, "Methods," p. 241; Grieves, in NAEM *Proceedings* (1919), p.

62; Robert S. Lynd and Helen M. Lynd, *Middletown: A Study in Contemporary American Culture* (New York, 1929), p. 66; NACT, "Methods of Transfer," pp. 3–4.

53. Slichter, "Industrial Morale," p. 178; Kelly, *Hiring*, p. 32; Charles E. Fouhy, "Relations Between the Employment Manager and the Foreman," *Industrial Management* (October 1919), 58:336; Gemmill, "Methods," pp. 240, 243, 246.

54. "Labor is Speeding Up," *Iron Age* (February 20, 1919), 103:505; John S. Keir, "The Reduction of Absences and Lateness in Industry," *The Annals* (May 1917), 71:150–155; Douglas, "Absenteeism," p. 596.

55. "The Problem of Lateness and Absenteeism: Review of Methods Used in Various Firms," *Industrial Relations* (January 5, 1921), 5:527–529; John Fitch, "Making the Job Worthwhile," *The Survey* (April 27, 1918), 40:89; *Industrial Relations* (March 23, 1923), 14:1448; Sinsheimer, "Keeping Contented," p. 574; "Studebaker Has Four Main Plans for Benefit of Workers," *Personnel* (March 1920), 2:5; "Reward for Service," *Personnel* (January 1920), 2:7.

56. Slichter, *Turnover*, p. 329; Slichter, "Management of Labor," pp. 822–823; American Management Association, "Discipline and Its Maintenance," *Management and Administration* (August 1923), vol. 6; Edward D. Jones, "Employment Management," in Bloomfield, *Selected Articles*, pp. 120–121.

57. "Driver Must Go," NACS *Bulletin* (April 1920), 7:179–182; Kelly, *Hiring*, pp. 138–141.

Sometimes, new disciplinary systems were introduced as part of the grievance procedure in an employee representation plan, and a few progressive companies like Dennison Manufacturing and Packard Motor instituted arbitration boards to adjudicate disputed dismissals. At Filene's department store, the board was elected by the employees. Eggert, *Steelmasters*, p. 115; Joseph H. Willits, "The Arbitration Plan of William Filene's Sons Company," *The Annals* (January 1917), 69:205–207; Albert B. Wolfe, "Works Committees," Industrial Relations Division, Emergency Fleet Corporation, U.S. Shipping Board (Washington, D.C., 1919); William Leavitt Stoddard, *The Shop Committee* (New York, 1919), pp. 85–86; W. Jett Lauck, *Political and Industrial Democracy, 1776–1926* (New York, 1926), pp. 151–240.

58. Earl Dean Howard, "Experience of Hart, Schaffner, and Marx with Collective Bargaining," *The Annals* (January 1917), 69:203; Bing, *Wartime Strikes*, pp. 167–168; Leonhard F. Fuld, "Employment Managers and Bolshevism," *Industrial Management* (July 1919), 58:74.

59. Tead and Metcalf, *Personnel*, pp. 245–248; "Standard Oil's New Labor Democracy," NACS *Bulletin* (June 1918), 5:207–209; Meyer Bloomfield, "What Is an Employment Manager?" *Industrial Management* (March 1917), 52:880; Reilly, "Dennison," pp. 91–93; Slichter, *Turnover*, pp. 228–242, 375–378.

60. Merlin M. Taylor, "We Can't Get Men to Stay," *Factory* (February 1918), vol. 20; "Hiring, Discharge," 20:259; Charles M. Horton, "Under New Management—Judging Men," *Industrial Management* (March 1918), 55:226; Edwin S. Blodgett, "I Quit—I No Like Job," *Factory* (March 1921), 21:473–474; Fitch, "Making the Job," pp. 87–89. Note the similarity here between the personnel

manager and the neutral labor arbitrator, a parallel that is explored in Sanford M. Jacoby, "Progressive Discipline in American Industry," in David Lipsky, ed., *Advances in Labor and Industrial Relations* (Greenwich, Conn., 1985). Indeed, employers sometimes complained that arbitrators, like personnel managers, "are uplifters. They always sympathize with the men." Julius Cohen, "The Revised Protocol in the Dress and Waist Industry," *The Annals* (January 1917), 69:191.

61. Kelly, *Hiring*, p. 35; Meyer Bloomfield, "Employment Management Department," *Industrial Management* (January 1917), 52:557.

62. "Hiring, Discharge," p. 242; William F. Johnson, "Getting the Foreman's Cooperation," *Industrial Management* (September 1918), 56:143; "Employment Office Methods" and "Relations of Employment Office and Foremen," in IRAA *Proceedings* (1920), pt. 2, pp. 261, 559–564.

63. Slichter, "Management of Labor," p. 833; Interchurch, *Steel Strike*, pp. 137, 210–211; "Report of the Committee on Labor Turnover," in NACT, *Ninth Annual Proceedings* (1921), p. 653.

64. Dudley R. Kennedy, "The Foreman of the Present and the Future," in IRAA *Proceedings* (1920), pt. 2, pp. 76–77.

65. "What's on the Foreman's Mind," *Industrial Relations* (December 11, 1920), 5:484; NACS, *Seventh Annual Proceedings* (1919), p. 394; "Employment Office Methods," p. 262; Daniel Nelson, "'A Newly Appreciated Art': The Development of Personnel Work at Leeds & Northrup," *Business History Review* (Winter 1970), 44:526–530.

66. NAEM *Proceedings* (1919), p. 31; "Relations of Employment Office," pp. 559–562; NACT, *Ninth Annual Proceedings* (1921), pp. 621–622.

67. "First Conference a Big Success," *Personnel* (November 1919), 1:1; Meyer Bloomfield, "Employment Management," *Industrial Management* (June 1917), 53:439; Roy W. Kelly, "Employment Management and Industrial Training," FBVE Bulletin No. 48 (1920), p. 91; *NAEM Proceedings* (1919), pp. 29–30; A. C. Horrocks, "The Foreman of the Present and the Future," IRAA *Proceedings* (1920), pt. 1, pp. 72–75; "Driver Must Go," pp. 179–182; D. R. Kennedy, "Training the Foreman of Industry," *Industrial Management* (January 1920), 59:68.

68. "Improving Foremanship; Trade Extension Courses for Foremen," FBVE Bulletin No. 61 (1921), pp. 9–10; FBVE, *Fourth Annual Report* (Washington, D.C., 1921), pp. 38–40; Charles W. Clark, "The Foreman and His Development," *Industrial Management* (August 1920), 60:106; Myron Barnett, "Foreman Training Courses," Report D, Bureau of Personnel Research, Carnegie Institute of Technology, Pittsburgh, 1921.

69. Joseph Willits, "War's Challenge to Employment Managers," *The Annals* (January 1919), 81:48.

6. A Different Decade: Moderation in the 1920s.

1. Stanley Lebergott, *Manpower in Economic Growth: The American Record Since 1800* (New York, 1964), pp. 512, 524.

2. See sources listed in table 6.1.

3. Irving Bernstein, *The Lean Years* (Boston, 1960), p. 67; Lebergott, *Manpower*, p. 514; National Industrial Conference Board (NICB), *Wages in the United States, 1914–1929* (New York, 1931), p. 19.

4. R. A. Gordon, *Business Fluctuations*, 2d ed. (New York, 1961), Ch. 14.

5. George Soule, *Prosperity Decade: From War to Depression, 1917–1929* (New York, 1947), p. 215; Harry Jerome, *Mechanization in Industry* (New York, 1934), pp. 45, 217–227.

6. Isador Lubin, *The Absorption of the Unemployed by American Industry* (Washington, D.C., 1929), pp. 15–18.

7. David Weintraub, "Unemployment and Increasing Productivity," in *Technological Trends and National Policy*, Report of the Subcommittee on Technology to the National Resources Committee (Washington, D.C., 1937), pp. 80–85; Sumner H. Slichter, "Technological Unemployment: Lines of Action, Adaption, and Control," *American Economic Review* (March 1932), 22:41–54.

8. Lebergott, *Manpower*, p. 510; William J. Cunningham, *The Present Railroad Crisis* (Philadelphia, 1931), p. 31; David S. Landes, *The Unbound Prometheus: Technological Change and Industrial Development in Western Europe from 1750 to the Present* (Cambridge, Mass., 1972), pp. 359–485; Ralph C. Epstein, *Industrial Profits in the United States* (New York, 1934), pp. 75–78, 122–123.

9. "Symposium on Immigration," *American Industries* (February 1923), 23:7; *Industrial Relations: Bloomfield's Labor Digest* (February 10, 1923), 14:1407, 1424. Also see Glenn A. Bowers, "Labor in Manufacturing Industries," *Manufacturing Industries* (February 1929), 17:129.

10. "Editorial," *Iron Age* (September 10, 1925), 115:699; Don D. Lescohier, "Working Conditions," in John R. Commons et al., *History of Labor in the United States, 1896–1932* (New York, 1935), 3:34.

11. T. J. Woofter, Jr., "The Status of Racial and Ethnic Groups," in *Recent Social Trends in the United States*, Report of the President's Committee on Social Trends (New York, 1933), pp. 556, 567, 574–576; Paul S. Taylor, "Employment of Mexicans in the Chicago and Calumet Region," *Journal of the American Statistical Association* (June 1930), 25:205; Paul S. Taylor, *Mexican Labor in the U.S.: Chicago and Calumet Region* (Berkeley, Calif., 1932), pp. 36–38.

12. Hope T. Eldridge and Dorothy S. Thomas, *Population Redistribution and Economic Growth in the U.S., 1870–1950* (Philadelphia, 1959), 3:251, A1–11; Sterling D. Spero and Abram L. Harris, *The Black Worker: The Negro and the Labor Movement* (New York, 1931), pp. 152–157.

13. W. A. Berridge, "Labor Turnover in American Factories," *Monthly Labor Review* (July 1929), 29:64–65; Berridge, "Labor Turnover," *Monthly Labor Review* (February 1930), 30:124–126.

14. The only national labor turnover series for the 1920s is based on data from a group of firms that subscribed to Metropolitan Life Insurance Company's industrial insurance policies. These tended to be large firms with low turnover rates. The series uses unweighted median rates that do not control for firm size, which biases the rates downward. This makes it impossible to compare data from the 1920s to the periods that preceded and followed it, because published data

from those periods are weighted mean rates. Hence the relative magnitude of the drop in rates during the 1920s cannot be gauged, although a drop no doubt occurred. The data are unrepresentative in another sense: They are based on firms that more than doubled their employment between 1920 and 1929, a time when the rest of the manufacturing sector did not grow at all. We do not know what happened to quit rates in the rest of the sector but it seems reasonable to infer that they also declined. For a complete discussion of these issues, see W. S. Woytinsky, *Three Aspects of Labor Dynamics* (Washington, D.C., 1942), pp. 18–20; Sanford Jacoby, "Industrial Labor Mobility in Historical Perspective," *Industrial Relations* (Spring 1983), 22:261–282.

15. Sumner H. Slichter, "The Current Labor Policies of American Industries," *Quarterly Journal of Economics* (May 1929), 43:429. Note that when labor market conditions permitted it—as during 1923—turnover shot up to pre-1921 levels.

16. Jacoby, "Industrial Labor Mobility," p. 274.

17. Woytinsky, *Three Aspects,* pp. 4, 19; Robert and Helen Lynd, *Middletown: A Study in Contemporary American Culture* (New York, 1929), pp. 66–68. Note that the new immigration laws were also responsible for a drop in mobility because the relatively mobile group of recent immigrants now comprised a smaller proportion of the labor force than before. See Jacoby, "Industrial Labor Mobility," pp. 274–275.

18. J. David Houser, *What the Employer Thinks: Executives' Attitudes Toward Employees* (Cambridge, Mass., 1927), pp. 50, 82. Also see Royal Parkinson, "Picturing the Quality of the Force Concisely for Executives," *Personnel* (November 1927), 4:39–42.

19. Leo Wolman, *Ebb and Flow in Trade Unionism* (New York, 1936), pp. 172–193.

20. U.S. Bureau of Labor Statistics, *Handbook of Labor Statistics,* Bulletin No. 1865 (Washington, D.C., 1975), pp. 390–391.

21. Sanford Jacoby, "Union-Management Cooperation in the United States: Lessons from the 1920s," *Industrial and Labor Relations Review* (October 1983), vol. 37; James Morris, *Conflict Within the AFL* (Ithaca, N.Y., 1958).

22. Wolman, *Ebb and Flow,* pp. 16–17, 35–37; Edwin Witte, *Historical Survey of Labor Arbitration* (Philadelphia, 1954).

23. Slichter, "Current Labor Policies," p. 396.

24. Gordon, *Business Fluctuations,* p. 251: Allen M. Wakstein, "The Origins of the Open-Shop Movement, 1919–1920," *Journal of American History* (December 1964), 51:460–475; Savel Zimand, *The Open Shop Drive: Who Is Behind It and Where Is It Going?* (New York, 1921).

25. Dudley R. Kennedy, "The Future of Industrial Research," *Industrial Mangement* (March 1920), 59:228; Sumner H. Slichter, "Industrial Morale," *Quarterly Journal of Economics* (November 1920), reprinted in *Potentials of the American Economy: Selected Essays of Sumner H. Slichter* (Cambridge, Mass., 1961), p. 169. The Red Scare even defamed the most liberal wing of the personnel management movement. The New York Legislative Investigation of Radicals (the Lusk Committee) denounced the Bureau of Industrial Research in 1920 for

containing "men who belong to the ranks of the Near–Bolshevik Intellegentsia." The bureau, which came under attack for its report on the 1919 steel strike, included on its staff such stalwarts of personnel management as Robert Bruere, Henry C. Metcalf, and Ordway Tead. See Robert K. Murray, *Red Scare: A Study in National Hysteria, 1919–1920* (Minneapolis, 1955), p. 174; Marshall Olds, *Analysis of the Interchurch World Movement Report on the Steel Strike* (New York, 1923), pp. 396, 417–431.

26. Wells quoted in Industrial Relations Association of America (IRAA), *Proceedings* (1920), pt. 1, p. 81; Casler quoted in National Association for Corporation Training, (NACT), *Bulletin* (October 1921), 8:437.

27. Edward S. Cowdrick, "What Are We Going to Do with the Boss?" *Industrial Management* (August 1920), 60:195.

28. Rodney Morrison, Jr., "Employment Office Methods," *Industrial Management* (June 1919), 57:500; J. R. Naylor, "Relation of the Foreman to the Employment Department," National Association of Corporation Schools (NACS), *Bulletin* (February 1920), 7:89–93; NACS, *Eighth Annual Proceedings* (1920), pp. 97–101.

29. Douglas, *Real Wages*, p. 445; Soule, *Prosperity Decade*, ch. 5. Note that although money wage rates fell sharply between 1920 and 1923 (along with a sharp drop in employment and hours), real wages hardly changed, due to the steady decline in consumer and wholesale prices. Clarence D. Long, "The Illusion of Money Wage Rigidity," *Review of Economics and Statistics* (May 1960), 42:150–151.

30. H. Feldman, *The Regularization of Employment* (New York, 1925), pp. 255–257; J. D. Hackett, "Layoff Compensation," *Industrial Management* (July 1920), 60:67; Leah H. Feder, *Unemployment Relief During Periods of Depression* (New York, 1936), p. 313; "Unemployment Survey, 1920–1921," *American Labor Legislation Review* (Sept. 1921), 11:210–213; Arthur H. Young, "Hours of Work," unpublished paper given to the YMCA Group, Elizabeth, N.J., March 1933, Young Papers, California Institute of Technology, vol. 3, item 51; J. E. Walters, "What's New In Personnel Work," *Personnel* (August 1932), 9:20–31. In 1919, only 4 percent of the relatively progressive firms belonging to the NACS paid layoff compensation (severance pay) to their employees, and this usually did not go to hourly workers. "Should a Dismissal Wage Be Paid?" *NACS Bulletin* (October 1919), 6:452; Edward A. Ross, "A Legal Dismissal Wage," *American Economic Review* (March 1919), suppl., 9:136.

31. Paul H. Douglas, "Personnel Problems and the Business Cycle," *Administration* (July 1922), 4:18–23; "Labor Efficiency Is Increasing," *Iron Trade Review* (July 2, 1920) 66:321; "The Efficiency of Labor Is Again Approaching Normal," *NACS Bulletin* (June 1920) 7:245–249; "Labor Returning to Prewar Efficiency," *NACT Bulletin* (October 1920), 7:459–460.

32. Douglas, "Personnel Problems," pp. 23–25; Berridge, "Labor Turnover in Factories," pp. 64–65; BLS, *Handbook*, p. 390; Wolman, *Ebb and Flow*, pp. 172–193.

33. William L. Chenery, "Personnel Relations Tested," *The Survey* (May 21, 1921), pp. 236–237.

34. "Testing Out Industrial Relations," *Personnel* (March 1921), 3:4; NACT, *Ninth Annual Proceedings* (1921), pp. 595–596.

35. W. J. Donald, "The Newer Conception of Personnel Functions," *Factory and Industrial Management* (March 1928), 75:514–515; H. H. Rice quoted in "Executive Opinions of Industrial Relations," *Personnel* (May 1921), 3:3.

36. Robert F. Lovett, "Tendencies in Personnel Practice," Bureau of Personnel Research, Carnegie Institute of Technology, *Service Bulletin* (February 1923), 5:11–12.

37. Robert Ozanne, *A Century of Labor—Management Relations at Mc-Cormick and International Harvester* (Madison, Wis., 1967), p. 175; Louise C. Odencrantz, "Personnel Work in America," *Personnel Administration* (August 1922), 9:11.

38. Ordway Tead, "The Field of Personnel Administration," *Bulletin of the Taylor Society* (December 1923), 8:240; Charles Piez, "Trends in Management: What Is the Business Outlook Today?" *Factory* (January 1, 1921), 26:32.

39. "Looking Forward," *Personnel* (January 1921), 3:6; "Holding Our Own," *Personnel* (April 1921), 3:4; Chenery, "Personnel Tested," p. 237; William H. Lange, "The AMA And Its Predecessors," American Management Association Special Paper No. 17 (New York, 1928), p. 28.

40. "Discuss Business and Unemployment," *Boston Globe,* September 28, 1921; Mary B. Gilson, *What's Past Is Prologue* (New York, 1940), p. 121.

41. "The Importance of the Labor Problem Has Not Diminished," *Automotive Industries* (January 6, 1921), 44:30; Henry S. Dennison, in *Administration* (January 1921), 1:121; Chenery, "Personnel Tested," p. 237.

42. Clarence J. Hicks, *My Life in Industrial Relations* (New York, 1941), p. 137; U.S. Congress, Senate Committee on Education and Labor, *Hearings Before a Subcommittee on Violations of Free Speech and Rights of Labor,* Supplementary Exhibits, Part 45, January 16, 1939, 76th Cong., 1st Sess., 16781, 16785, 16831.

43. Rockefeller quoted in Bernstein, *Lean Years,* p. 170.

44. "Report of the Special Conference Committee," July 15, 1920, Industrial Service Department Committee Minutes Box, YMCA Historical Library, New York.

45. Hicks, *My Life,* pp. 64–79.

46. "SCC Report," 1920; U.S. Cong., *Violations of Free Speech,* 16798, 16825, 16849–16850.

47. "Report of the Special Conference Committee, Supplement," March 1921, YMCA Historical Library; "SCC Reports," 1920; Clarence J. Hicks, "Comments," in *Human Relations in Industry,* Summary of the Eleventh Silver Bay Industrial Conference of the YMCA, New York, 1928, p. 89.

48. See the annual summaries of the Silver Bay Industrial Conferences of the YMCA, 1918–1930. At several of the conferences, Elton Mayo presented his new theory of human relations, which linked worker "pessimism" to class consciousness and radicalism.

49. "Larkin Elected I.R.A.A. President," *Personnel* (August 1920), 2:1; "Vice-Presidents," *Personnel* (October 1920), 2:1; "Industrial Conditions Cause Postponement," *Personnel* (March 1921), 3:1.

50. *Personnel Administration* (May 1922), 9:3; "Personnel Association Activities," *Industrial Management* (February 1923), 65:83; Lange, "AMA and Predecessors," pp. 19–22, 30–35; "National Personnel Association Formed by Merger, *Industrial Relations: Bloomfield's Labor Digest* (July 22, 1922), 11:1190; *Corporation Training* (January–February 1922), 9:30.

51. Boyd Fisher to Morris L. Cooke, April 11, 1922, in Cooke Papers, Roosevelt Presidential Library, Hyde Park, New York, Fisher file, Box 8. After leaving the Federal Board for Vocational Education, Fisher was a partner in Cooke's Philadelphia consulting firm, and then he was a personnel director, first at the Aluminum Castings Company of Detroit and later at Lockwood, Greene of Boston. Mary B. Gilson recalled that Fisher was "courageous to the point of sacrificing a highly remunerative job for the sake of his principles." Gilson, *What's Past,* p. 124.

52. Morris L. Cooke to Boyd Fisher, April 21, 1922, in Cooke Papers, Fisher file, Box 8. At the height of the open-shop drive in 1921, Cooke contacted other Taylor Society members for assistance in organizing an Institute of Labor and Science, to be made up of fifty prominent scientists, managers, and labor leaders. Cooke hoped that the institute would counteract the open-shop movement's propaganda and influence industrial developments, although nothing ever came of the idea. Morris L. Cooke to George L. Bell, January 21, 1921, Cooke Papers, Box 2.

53. The Personnel Research Federation was among the most liberal organizations in the professional management movement. As a result, the PRF never received much corporate support except from Industrial Relations Counselors and a handful of companies interested in applying psychological techniques to personnel management, such as AT&T, Kodak, and Western Electric. In 1928 it had only 8 corporate members. The PRF's *Journal of Personnel Research* was an academic review of research in industrial psychology, notable for including Matthew Woll on its editorial board. During the 1920s the PRF had close ties to the Taylor Society and, reflecting its vocationalist origins, to the National Vocational Guidance Association. See Personnel Research Federation, *Service Bulletin,* various issues, particularly June 1927, March 1931, and November 1931, in Bingham Papers, Box 9; and Leonard Ferguson, "Industrial Psychology and Labor," in B. Von Haller Gilmer, *Walter Van Dyke Bingham Memorial Program* (Pittsburgh, 1962).

54. "The Personnel Content of Management," *American Management Review* (April 1923), 12:3–6.

55. *Ibid.,* pp. 5–6; "The American Management Association—A Non-Engineering Society," *Management Engineering* (April 1923), 4:273.

56. U.S. Cong., *Violations of Free Speech,* 16781–16782; Sam A. Lewisohn, "Management's Part in Personnel Administration," *Personnel Administration* (August 1922), 9:3–4; E. S. Cowdrick, "The Expanding Field of Industrial Relations," *American Management Review* (December 1924), 12:3–5; Glenn A. Bowers, "Is There a 'One Best Method' in Industrial Relations?" *American Management Review* (June 1924), 13:7; W. J. Donald, "America," in *Proceedings of the 1925 International Welfare (Personnel) Congress* (Flushing, Netherlands,

1925), pp. 94–96; Arthur H. Young, "Ideals of Good Industrial Relations," address delivered at Hartford Rubber Works Company, May 20, 1926, in Young Papers, Speeches, vol. 1; L. A. Sylvester, "The Foreman as Manager," AMA Production Executives Series No. 38 (1926). In 1929, W. J. Donald of the AMA said, "We well remember the period in the personnel movement when the personnel job was supposed to be a job for the personnel man alone. We wanted entirely to relieve the line executive of the personnel function. In the last few years . . . that trend has been distinctly reversed. We are now viewing the personnel job as every executive's [i.e. foreman's] job." Donald, "Executive Training Programs," AMA General Management Series No. 107 (1929).

57. Employers also disliked the name "industrial relations department" because it evoked the liberal model: "It perhaps suggests too strongly the idea of bringing harmony out of discord . . . through the magic device of a management-controlled mediator of difficulties." National Industrial Conference Board, *Industrial Relations: Administration of Policies and Programs* (New York, 1931), pp. 42, 58.

58. Gilson, *What's Past*, p. 101.

59. Morris L. Cooke to E. O. Griffenhagen, December 22, 1926, Cooke Papers, File 38, Box 61; Cooke to Henry P. Kendall, January 2, 1929, Cooke Papers, Box 11; J. S. Keir to Henry S. Dennison, July 18, 1927, Dennison Papers, Baker Library, Harvard University, Carton 2; Morris L. Cooke to Dennison, May 24, 1927, Dennison Papers, Carton 2; Cooke to Harlow S. Person, June 18, 1926, Cooke Papers, File 138, Box 61.

60. Henry S. Dennison, "Management," in Report of the Committee on Recent Economic Changes of the President's Conference on Unemployment, *Recent Economic Changes in the United States* (New York, 1929), 2:520; Harold Porter, "Technique of Holding Council or Committee Meetings," *Personnel* (February 1928), 4:140–141; Russell L. Keppel, "Development of Foremen," AMA Production Executives' Series No. 44 (1926); Frank Cushman, "The Foreman's Place in a Training Program," AMA Production Executives' Series No. 35 (1926); E. S. Cowdrick, *Manpower in Industry* (New York, 1924), chs. 19 and 20.

61. YMCA, "Report of a Conference on Foremanship," Greenville, Penn., 1923.

62. Harold Bergen and G. Bergen, "Executive Training Programs," AMA General Management Series No. 107 (1929); R. G. Adair, "Foreman Training That Works," *Factory and Industrial Management* (June 1930), 79:1391–1397; NICB, *Industrial Relations*, p. 45; C. E. Stevens, "Foremen's Meetings on Efficiency of Operation," AMA Production Executives' Series No. 46 (1926).

As during the First World War, the Federal Board for Vocational Education subsidized foreman's training programs, especially on the railroads and in the public utilities industry. See FBVE, "Progress in Foreman Training," *Bulletin* No. 127 (Washington, D.C., 1928).

63. "Making Foremanship Effective," in YMCA, *Summary of the Industrial Conference on Human Relations and Betterment in Industry*, Silver Bay, 1924, pp. 48, 70; George F. Barbour, "The Story of Labor-Saving Machinery," pamphlet in YMCA course on "Foremanship" (c. 1922), Industrial Service Department

Committee Minutes Box, YMCA Historical Library; "Training for Leadership," *Railway Mechanical Engineer* (June 1926) 100:330–339.

64. "Putting Ideas to Work," *Factory and Industrial Management* (March 1929), 77:479–480; L. J. Parrish, "The Foremen's Club: Does It Solve the Welfare Problem?" *Factory* (April 1926), 36:648; Thomas B. Fordham, "The Growth of the Foremen's Club Movement," *Industrial Management* (June 1926), 71:339–341: W. W. Mussman, "Foremen's Clubs," *Management Record* (November 1946), 6:375; "Making Foremen's Clubs More Effective," *Railway Mechanical Engineer* (March 1926), 100:139–140; Albert Sobey, "Community Foremen's Clubs," AMA Production Executives' Series No. 45 (1926); material in Foreman's Clubs 1923–1929 Box, YMCA Historical Library.

65. NICB, *Collective Bargaining Through Employee Representation* (New York, 1933), p. 16; U.S. Bureau of Labor Statistics, "Characteristics of Company Unions, 1935," *Bulletin* No. 634 (Washington, D.C., 1937) p. 27.

66. U.S. Cong., *Violations of Free Speech,* 16495. Some personnel departments were not at all involved in the administration of the company union. See Paul F. Gemmill, *Present-Day Labor Relations* (New York, 1929), p. 55; and F. M. Dee, Jr., "Various Types of Representation Plans Designed to Fit Local Conditions," in AMA Production Executives' Series No. 49 (1926), p. 8.

67. Ozanne, *Century of Labor Relations,* ch. 7; Harold H. Swift and W. D. Richardson, "What Managerial Problems Should be Discussed in Joint Representation Meetings?" AMA Production Executives' Series No. 49 (1926), pp. 38–40; Stuart Brandes, *American Welfare Capitalism, 1880–1940* (Chicago, 1976), pp. 133–134; Rinaldo Lukens, "Employee Representation in a Single Unit Organization with Less Than 1,000 Employees," *Personnel* (February 1929), 4:114–118; Bernstein, *Lean Years,* pp. 170–173; NICB, *Experience with Works Councils in the U.S.,* Research Report. No. 50 (New York, 1922), pp. 79–110.

68. Daniel Nelson, "The Company Union Movement, 1900–1937: A Reexamination," *Business History Review* (Autumn 1982), 56:335–357; Ben M. Selekman, *Sharing Management with the Workers: A Study of the Partnership Plan of the Dutchess Bleachery* (New York, 1924); Selekman and Mary Van Kleeck, *Employee's Representation in Coal Mines* (New York, 1924); NICB, *Experience with Works Councils,* pp. 53–62, 111–121.

69. H. A. Tiedemann, "Should Employee Representation Be Applied to Scattered Groups of Wage Earners?" *Personnel* (February 1928), 4:93–98; W. F. Doherty, "Employee Representation in a Small Plant," *ibid.,* pp. 103–107; Porter, "Holding Council Meetings," pp. 140–146; Julian Aresty and Gordon S. Miller, "The Technique of Arousing and Maintaining the Interest of Foremen and Workers in Plans of Employee Representation," *Personnel* (February 1930), 6:115–132; Carroll French, *The Shop Committee in the United States* (Baltimore, 1923), pp. 61–62; NICB, *Experience with Works Councils,* pp. 55–62, 111–125.

70. Houser, *What the Employer Thinks,* p. 74. Note that some companies treated their foreman training programs as a substitute for, rather than a complement to, an active personnel management program. Arthur H. Young reported that a number of executives thought, "We don't need an employment manager, don't need a safety inspector, don't need this or that, because our foremen are all fed up on that, and it is a part of the curriculum of our shop. We take care of it."

Young is quoted in *Evaluating Personnel Work in Industry*, AMA Swampscott Conference (New York, 1924), p. 12.

71. "AMA—A Nonengineering Society," p. 274.

72. Sumner H. Slichter, "The Worker in Modern Economic Society," *Journal of Political Economy* (February 1926), 34:122; William M. Leiserson, "Contributions of Personnel Management to Improved Labor Relations," *1928 Wertheim Lectures on Industrial Relations* (Cambridge, Mass., 1929), pp. 145–147.

One may get some sense of the growth and decline of interest in, and awareness of, personnel management from the following figures on the number of articles on the subject per 1,000 American magazine and journal articles during the indicated periods:

1905–09	1910–14	1915–18	1919–21	1922–24	1925–28	1929–30
.00	.00	.14	2.05	.81	.91	.70

Hornell Hart, "Changing Social Attitudes and Interests," in *Recent Social Trends*, p. 433.

73. Houser, *What The Employer Thinks*, p. 116; Leo Wolman and Gustave Peck, "Labor in the Social Structure," in *Recent Social Trends*, p. 839; Roger E. Keeran, "Communist Influence in the Automobile Industry, 1920–1933," *Labor History* (Spring 1979), 20:216; Samuel Levin, "The Ford Unemployment Policy," *American Labor Legislation Review* (June 1932), 22:103.

74. Houser, *What the Employer Thinks*, pp. 50, 82.

75. David Brody, *Steelworkers in America: The Nonunion Era* (New York, 1969).

76. Allen M. Wakstein, "The National Association of Manufacturers and Labor Relations in the 1920s," *Labor History* (Spring 1969), 10:163–176.

77. Adelaide Clara Dick, "Personnel Work in the San Francisco Bay Region," (M.A. thesis, University of California, Berkeley, 1927), pp. 3, 6, 20, 47.

78. C. Canby Balderston, *Executive Guidance of Industrial Relations* (Philadelphia, 1935), pp. 4, 224–240; Ralph C. Epstein, *Industrial Profits in the U.S.* (New York, 1934), pp. 76–78, 92.

79. Simon Kuznets, *Seasonal Variations in Industry and Trade* (New York, 1933).

80. Balderston, *Executive Guidance*, pp. 224–240; H. Feldman, "The Outstanding Features of Dennison Management," *Industrial Management* (August, September, and October, 1922), vol. 64; Kim McQuaid, "Industry and the Co-Operative Commonwealth: Willliam P. Hapgood and the Columbia Conserve Company," *Labor History* (Fall 1976), 17:510–529.

81. NICB, *Industrial Relations*, p. 61.

82. "The U.S. Steel Corporation: Part III," *Fortune* (May 1936), 13:141; Ronald Schatz, "American Electrical Workers: Work, Struggles, Aspirations, 1930–1950," (Ph.D. dissertation, University of Pittsburgh, 1977), pp. 65–69.

83. Roy W. Kelly, *Hiring the Worker* (Boston, 1918), p. 32; NICB, *Industrial Relations Programs in Small Plants* (New York, 1929), p. 20. Note that the figures on dismissals may be misleading because at some firms the personnel department was involved only if a salaried employee was being fired.

84. Brody, *Steelworkers*, p. 267; NICB, *Small Plants*, p. 20; Paul F. Gemmill,

"Methods of Promoting Industrial Employees," *Industrial Management,* (April 1924), 67:238, 240–241; Spero and Harris, *The Black Worker,* p. 155.

85. Minutes of the International Harvester Works Managers' Meeting, November 16, 1923, courtesy of Professor Robert Ozanne; NICB, *Systems of Wage Payment* (New York, 1930), p. 7; Merrill Lott, *Wage Scales and Job Evaluation* (New York, 1926), pp. 16–17; Leon F. Alford, "Ten Years' Progress in Management, 1923–1932," typescript, 1932, in John M. Carmody Papers, Box 43, Franklin D. Roosevelt Presidential Library, Hyde Park, New York; Paul F. Gemmill, "A Survey of Wage Systems," *Industrial Management* (October 1922), 64:207–208; M. J. Jucius, "The Use of Wage Incentives," *Journal of Business* (January 1932), 5:6; Florence A. Thorne to Morris L. Cooke, April 24, 1928, Cooke Papers, Box 66. Note, however, that incentive pay rates were set by industrial engineers rather than by foremen.

86. Morris L. Cooke to Florence A. Thorne, May 16, 1928, Cooke Papers, Box 66.

87. Charles W. Lytle, *Job Evaluation Methods* (New York, 1946), pp. 110, 135; Berstein, *Lean Years,* p. 67; Lescohier, "Working Conditions," p. 85; Robert Ozanne, "A Century of Occupational Differentials in Manufacturing," *Review of Economics and Statistics* (August 1962), 44:292–299.

88. NICB, *Layoff and Its Prevention* (New York, 1930), pp. 38–39; "Report of the SCC, Supplement," March 1921.

89. NICB, *Layoff,* p. 56; Minutes of the International Harvester Works Managers' Meeting, July 6, 1931; Henry Bruere and Grace Pugh, *Profitable Personnel Practice,* (New York, 1929), pp. 38–40.

90. Lee Frankel and Alexander Fleisher, *The Human Factor in Industry* (New York, 1920), p. 16; Murray W. Latimer, *Industrial Pension Systems in the United States* (New York, 1932), pp. 708–710, 976–977; NICB, *Industrial Pensions in the United States* (New York, 1925), pp. 12–15, 62–65; NICB, *Experience with Mutual Benefit Associations in the United States* (New York, 1923), pp. 26–36; Charles M. Mills, *Vacations for Industrial Workers* (New York, 1927), pp. 236–275; Abraham Epstein, *Insecurity: A Challenge to America* (New York, 1933), p. 86; George Soule, "The U.S. Steel Corporation's Welfare Work," in *Public Opinion on the Steel Strike* (New York, 1921), pp. 249, 253–255.

91. Arthur H. Young, "Industrial Pensions," typescript, 1925, Item No. 19, *Speeches,* vol. 1, Young Papers.

92. NICB, *Industrial Pensions,* pp. 25–28; NICB, *Practical Experience with Profit Sharing in Industrial Establishments,* Research Report No. 19 (New York, 1920), pp. 18–19; NICB, *Small Plants,* p. 25; James R. Adams, "A Common Sense Attack on Labor Turnover," *Industrial Management* (November 1921), 62:302.

Firms could have used a less restrictive eligibility requirement than continuous service, such as aggregate service, but only a handful of companies chose to do this. An aggregate service provision would have opened the programs up to more workers while still maintaining a stability incentive. The fact that this wasn't done again suggests that the programs weren't primarily intended to reduce turnover but rather to strengthen the company's hold over those employees whose loyalty was considered essential, primarily skilled and non-manual workers.

93. Ralph Heilman, "Do You Keep Your Men Too Long?" *System* (April 1918), 33:540.

94. Wolman and Peck, "Labor Groups," p. 845; NACT *Bulletin* (August 1921), 9:415; "Benefit-Thrift-Budget," in IRAA *Proceedings* (1920), pt. 2, pp. 332–337; E. G. Wilson, "The Social Significance of the YMCA's Industrial Conference," *Service* (October 1927), vol. 3; NICB, *Industrial Relations*, p. 86; Sidney Fine, *The Automobile Under the Blue Eagle* (Ann Arbor, Mich., 1963), p. 8; L. Grace Sitzer, "Wrigley Doesn't Apologize for Welfare Work," *Factory & Industrial Management* (March 1929), 77:501–502.

The new welfare work also was commonly used to control indiscipline, absences, and lateness, all of which could affect a worker's vacation time or his continuous service record. See "Reduction of Absence and Tardiness," Memorandum prepared by the Industrial Relations Section, Princeton University (December 1927), pp. 3, 11–15; Mills, *Vacations*, pp. 236–275; NICB, *Pensions*, pp. 74–77.

95. "Report on Profit Sharing and Stock Ownership," in YMCA, *Summary of the Industrial Conference on Human Relations and Betterment in Industry* (New York, 1924), p. 21; Arthur H. Young, "The Function of Industrial Relations," paper delivered to the Third International Congress on Scientific Management, Rome, September 1927, Item No. 30, Young Papers, Speeches, vol. 2.

96. Those who have overestimated the importance of welfare work include Sumner H. Slichter, "Current Labor Policies," pp. 393–435; and David Brody, "The Rise and Decline of Welfare Capitalism," in John Braeman et al., eds., *Change and Continuity in Twentieth Century America: The 1920s* (Columbus, Ohio, 1968), pp. 147–178.

97. Relatively expensive programs such as pension plans tended to be concentrated in highly profitable industries like public utilities, chemicals, and communications. Arthur H. Young, "The Social Value of Industrial Relations Activities," address given at the Wharton School of the University of Pennsylvania, Item No. 40, Young Papers, Speeches, vol. 2; Latimer, *Industrial Pension Systems*, ch. 19.

98. Minutes of the International Harvester Works Managers' Meeting, September 12, 1932 and April 1, 1935; Epstein, *Insecurity*, p. 145; Brandes, *Welfare Capitalism*, pp. 107–108; Wolman and Peck, "Labor Groups," p. 846; Glenn A. Bowers, "Employment, Wages, and Industrial Relations," *Factory & Industrial Management* (June 1929), 77:1251.

The Conference Board acknowledged some of these problems, noting that, "The chief impediment to an increase in the number of employees who might benefit from industrial pensions is the service requirement. . . . A weighted composite of five surveys shows that only 5.3 percent of factory workers stay with one firm for more than twenty years. . . . Calculations made by actuaries for the purpose of determining costs of pension plans . . . indicate that for the typical median employee in industry—that is, a man about 36 years of age, the probability of remaining employed by the same company to the age of 65 is from 1 to 5 percent." NICB, *Support of the Aged* (New York, 1931), p. 30.

99. Epstein, *Insecurity*, pp. 149–151; Brandes, *Welfare Capitalism*, p. 109; Latimer, *Pensions*, pp. 845–847; Abraham Epstein, "Employees' Welfare: An Autopsy," *American Mercury* (March 1932), 25:335–342; "Industrial Plants

Abandoning Many Personnel Activities," *Automotive Industries* (August 4, 1928), 59:163.

100. "Standard Recommendations for the Relief and Prevention of Unemployment," *American Labor Legislation Review* (September 1921), 11:218–219; Meyer Bloomfield, "Steady Work: The First Step in Sound Industrial Relations," *American Labor Legislation Review* (March 1921), vol. 11; *Business Cycles and Unemployment,* Report and Recommendations of the President's Committee on Unemployement (New York, 1923); Robert Zieger, "Herbert Hoover, the Wage-Earner, and the 'New Economic System,'" *Business History Review* (Summer 1977), 51:161–189; *Waste in Industry,* Report of the Committee on the Elimination of Waste in Industry of the Federated American Engineering Societies (New York, 1921); Harlow S. Person, "Scientific Management and the Reduction of Unemployment," *Bulletin of the Taylor Society* (January 1921), vol. 6; Henry S. Dennison, "Regularization of Industry Against Unemployment," *The Annals* (March 1922), 100:102–105.

101. S. A. Lewisohn, E. G. Draper, J. R. Commons, and D. D. Lescohier, *Can Business Prevent Unemployment?* (New York, 1925); Ernest G. Draper, "Unemployment," *New York Times,* September 11, 1921; Draper, "It Can't Be Done in Our Business," *American Management Review* (September 1924), 12:3–4; "Planning and Maintaining a Regular Flow of Work and Employment," AMA Production Executives Series No. 37 (1926).

102. H. Feldman, *The Regularization of Employment* (New York, 1925), chs. 10, 11, and 16; Paul H. Douglas and Aaron Director, *The Problem of Unemployment* (New York, 1931), chs. 7 and 16; Roger W. Babson, *Actions and Reactions* (New York, 1935); "Babson's Statistical Institute," misc. material, Box 3, Bingham Papers; Dennison, "Management," pp. 504, 505–507; Malcolm C. Rorty, "The Statistical Control of Business Activities," *Harvard Business Review* (1923), 1:144–166.

103. Douglas and Director, *Problem of Unemployment,* pp. 113–117.

104. Bill Haley, "A Guarantee for Continued Employment," *Personnel Administration,* (February 1923), 11:7; Herbert Feis, *Labor Relations: A Study Made in the Procter and Gamble Company* (New York, 1928), p. 36 and ch. 10; Bryce M. Stewart et al., *Unemployment Benefits in the U.S.* (New York, 1930), p. 463; "Unemployment Agreement Made With Workers," *Personnel* (February 1921), 3:3.

105. Fred W. Climer, "Cutting Labor Cost in Seasonal Business," *Manufacturing Industries* (May 1927), 13:361; John R. Commons et al., *Industrial Government* (New York, 1921), p. 272.

106. Grace Pugh and Henry Bruere, *Profitable Personnel Practice* (New York, 1929), p. 117; *Guaranteed Wages,* Report to the President by the Advisory Board of the Office of War Mobilization and Reconversion (Washington, D.C., 1947), appendix C, p. 292; Bureau of Labor Statistics, "Unemployment Benefit Plans in the United States and Unemployment Insurance in Foreign Countries," *Bulletin* No. 544 (1931); Paul H. Douglas, "Labor Turnover," in *Encyclopedia of the Social Sciences* (Chicago, 1932), pp. 712–713.

107. Peter Temin, *Did Monetary Forces Cause the Great Depression?* (New

York, 1976), p. 6; Leverett S. Lyon, *Hand-to-Mouth Buying* (Washington, D.C., 1929); Kuznets, *Seasonal Variations*, p. 313.

108. Paul Baran and Paul Sweezy, *Monopoly Capital* (London, 1970), p. 232; Hugh G. Adam, *An Australian Looks at America*, in Bernstein, *Lean Years*, p. 60.

109. Levin, "Ford Unemployment," p. 103; Clayton W. Fountain, *Union Guy*, quoted in Fine, *Blue Eagle*, p. 15; John G. Kruchko, *The Birth of a UAW Local: The History of UAW Local 674, Norwood, Ohio, 1933 to 1940* (Ithaca, N.Y., 1972), pp. 5–6.

110. Fountain in Fine, *Blue Eagle*, p. 15.

111. Slichter, "Worker in Modern Society," pp. 115–116.

112. Epstein, *Insecurity*, pp. 347–348; Lescohier, "Working Conditions," pp. 259–262; Daniel Nelson, *Unemployment Insurance: The American Experience, 1915–1935* (Madison, Wisc., 1969), ch. 3; H. P. Dutton, "Unemployment Insurance: A Six-Year Test," *Factory & Industrial Management* (April 1929), 77:734–735; Kuznets, *Seasonal Variations*, p. 414.

7. The Response to Depression

1. Bill Severn, *Frances Perkins: A Member of the Cabinet* (New York, 1976), pp. 91–93; Irving Bernstein, *The Lean Years* (Boston, 1960), pp. 256–257; Mary Van Kleeck, "Employment or Unemployment?—That is the Question," *American Labor Legislation Review* (December 1930), 20:378–380.

2. Ewan Clague and Webster Powell, *Ten Thousand Out of Work* (Philadelphia, 1933), pp. 108–115; Bernstein, *Lean Years*, pp. 288–289, 292–301.

3. "Less Unemployment Through Stabilization of Operations," Report to Honorable Franklin D. Roosevelt by the Governor's Commission on Unemployment Problems for the State of New York (New York, 1931), pp. 3–5; Meredith B. Givens, "Unemployment," *Bulletin of the Taylor Society* (October 1930), 15:247–249; George Martin, *Madam Secretary: Frances Perkins* (Boston, 1976), pp. 215–216.

4. "Less Unemployment," pp. 7–14, 20–22.

5. "Last evening at a meeting of the Consumer's League, I had opportunity for a brief word with Frances Perkins. She tells me that the importance of stabilizing employment has suddenly become the fashion, at least with New York manufacturers. She has had in the last few days no less than 70 letters from employers who give her the impression that they are thinking of nothing else at this moment. Certainly the subject is in the air . . ." Mary Van Kleeck to Morris L. Cooke, April 8, 1930, Box 72, Cooke Papers.

6. Walker, "Third Unemployment Survey," pp. 394–397; Mabel Walker, "The Urge to Organize," *American Labor Legislation Review* (June 1931), 21:228–230; Morris E. Leeds and J. F. Springer, "Can Employment be Stabilized?" *Mill & Factory* (March 1931), 8:27–28; "Industrial Stabilization," *Factory and Industrial Management* (January 1931), 81:35–37: Ray M. Hudson, "What New England Is Doing to Stabilize Industry," *Mill & Factory* (November 1930), 9:27–28. In its Industrial Code of 1931, the Taylor Society urged industry to stabilize

employment, arguing that workers had a right to receive regular wages just like landlords receiving regular rent payments. "Industrial Employment Code," *Bulletin of the Taylor Society* (February 1931), 16:19–24; Box 69A, Cooke Papers.

7. Meredith B. Givens, "Projects and Investigations Concerned with the Investigation and Control of Unemployment," Special Research Secretary, Social Science Research Council, August 28, 1930 in Box 13, Carmody Papers; *Personnel Service Bulletin* (March 1931), 7:2–4; "Overcoming Seasonal Fluctuations," *Report of the Fourteenth Annual Silver Bay Conference on Industrial Relations,* Silver Bay, August 1931, pp. 56–57; Glenn A. Bowers, "Stabilization of Employment," *Factory and Industrial Management* (June 1931), 81:1003–1004; Edwin S. Smith, *Reducing Seasonal Employment* (New York, 1931); Swarthmore College file, Box 76, Cooke Papers.

8. "Company Plans for the Regularization of Plant Operation and Employment," Research Report, Industrial Relations Section, Princeton University (c. 1931); "Offers Unemployment Insurance to Employees," *Factory and Industrial Management* (September 1930), 80:529–530; Glenn A. Bowers, "Developments in Employment Security," *Factory and Industrial Management* (April 1931), 81:646–647.

9. Paul H. Douglas, "Can Management Prevent Unemployment?" *American Labor Legislation Review* (September 1930), 20:273–281; Ernest G. Draper, "What Employers Are Doing to Combat Unemployment," *ibid.,* pp. 282–286; "Less Unemployment," pp. 27–75; Hudson, "What New England Is Doing," p. 82.

10. Abraham Epstein, *Insecurity: A Challenge to America* (New York, 1933), pp. 247–250.

11. Sidney Fine, *The Automobile Under the Blue Eagle* (Ann Arbor, Mich., 1963), p. 351. My calculations are based on the annual range in monthly employment levels in manufacturing (the difference between the months of highest and lowest employment each year, as a percentage of the maximum level). Data is from U.S. Bureau of Labor Statistics, "Employment and Earnings Statistics for the U.S., 1909–1970," Bulletin No. 1312-7 (Washington, D.C., 1971).

12. Douglas, "Can Management Prevent Unemployment?" p. 275.

13. Glenn A. Bowers, "The Illusion of Stabilization," *Factory and Industrial Management* (October 1931), 82:497–498.

14. J. Douglas Brown, "Company Plans for Unemployment Compensation," *American Labor Legislation Review* (December 1933), 23:178; Bryce M. Stewart, *Unemployment Benefits in the United States* (New York, 1930); "Industrial Employment Code," p. 21; Ernest G. Draper, "Why Unemployment Reserve Funds?" *American Labor Legislation Review* (March 1931), 21:25–27.

15. Daniel Nelson, *Unemployment Insurance: The American Experience* (Madison, 1969), pp. 50–63; Marion B. Folsom, "The Rochester Unemployment Benefit Plan," *Report of the Fourteenth Annual Silver Bay Conference,* August 1931, pp. 19–27; "Meager List of Companies that Have Adopted Unemployment Insurance," *American Labor Legislation Review* (September 1931), 21:325; note 8, above.

16. Meredith B. Givens, "Industrial Instability and Unemployment Insurance,"

Personnel Journal (May 1936), 15:8–9; Brown, "Company Plans," pp. 176–177; Epstein, *Insecurity*, p. 153; Ronald Schatz, "American Electrical Workers: Work, Struggles, Aspirations, 1930–1950" (Ph.D. dissertation, University of Pittsburgh, 1977), pp. 81–82.

17. Brown, "Company Plans," p. 180.

18. National Industrial Conference Board, "Dismissal Compensation," Studies in Personnel Policy No. 1 (New York, 1937), pp. 5–11; "Less Unemployment," pp. 122–124; E. S. Cowdrick, "Dulling the Axe of Dismissal," *Nations' Business* (October 1930), pp. 47–49; "Hiring and Separation Methods in American Factories," *Monthly Labor Review* (November 1932), 35:1014.

19. J. M. Larkin, "The Practical Application of Employment Stabilization," *Personnel* (February 1933), 9:92; J. M. Larkin, "How Bethlehem Steel Has Effected Employment Stabilization," *Iron Age* (December 22, 1932), 130:955; Fine, *Automobile Under Blue Eagle*, p. 63; "Dismissal Wage," *Iron Age* (August 20, 1931), 128:517.

20. "Third Personnel Conference of The Goodyear Tire and Rubber Company, 1935," in U.S. Congress, Senate Committee on Education and Labor, Hearings Before a Subcommittee on Violations of Free Speech and Rights of Labor (Hereafter, *La Follette Hearings*), Supplementary Exhibits, Part 45, January 16, 1939, 76th Cong. 1st Sess., 16662–16663.

21. Al S. Ray (Personnel Director, Chicago, Rock Island and Pacific Railway) to Morris L. Cooke, February 12, 1931, Box 69A, Cooke Papers.

22. J. Douglas Brown, "Spreading Work—Emergency Measure or Fixed Policy?" *Factory and Industrial Management* (September 1931), 82:340; Bernstein, *Lean Years*, p. 306; U.S. Bureau of Labor Statistics, "Handbook of Labor Statistics," Bulletin No. 1865 (Washington, D.C., 1975), p. 176; "Spread Employment by Cutting Hours of Regular Force," *Iron Age* (November 19, 1931), vol. 128; Larkin, "How Bethlehem Steel . . . ," p. 954.

23. National Industrial Conference Board, *Effect of the Depression on Industrial Relations Programs* (New York, 1934), p. 4; Matthew S. Sloan, "The Share-the-Work Movement," *Industrial Relations* (December 31, 1932), 13:653–655; "Unemployment Relief," *Monthly Labor Review* (May 1932), 34:1046–1047.

24. Bernstein, *Lean Years*, pp. 477–478. Despite union opposition, cutting hours as a method of reducing payroll costs favored employees, while cutting wages favored employers. With hours cut, at least the employee worked less for a given level of earnings.

25. Epstein, *Insecurity*, p. 256.

26. Walter C. Teagle, "Work-Sharing Will Do the Job," *Mill & Factory* (December 1932), 11:19–21; Francis A. Westbrook, "The New Hampshire Plan," *Industrial Relations* (November and December, 1932), 11 & 12:580–582; "Annual Report of the Special Conference Committee, 1932," in *La Follette Hearings*, 16821–16822; Harold M. Davis, "Job Security Through Job Sharing," *Factory and Industrial Management* (September 1932), 83:363–364.

27. By the early 1930s, the Special Conference Committee included American Telephone and Telegraph, Bethlehem Steel, Du Pont, General Electric, General

Motors, Goodyear, International Harvester, Irving Bank, Jersey Standard, U.S. Steel, U.S. Rubber, and Westinghouse. E. S. Cowdrick, secretary of the SCC, was on the coordinating committee of the national work-sharing committee; Teagle of Jersey Standard was an SCC member.

28. Minutes of International Harvester Works' Managers Meeting, April 27, 1931, courtesy of Professor Robert Ozanne.

29. Larkin, "How Bethlehem Steel . . . ," p. 955.

30. See, for example, L. C. Walker, "The Share-the-Work Movement," *The Annals* (January 1933), 165:13–19.

31. "Thirty-Hour Bill Meets with Strong Protest," *Iron Age* (April 13, 1933), 131:595–597; Bernstein, *Lean Years,* p. 483; T. H. Gerken, "Thirty-Hour Week Would Not Work in Steel Industry," *Iron Age* (April 20, 1933), 131:613–614; Robert F. Himmelberg, *The Origins of the National Recovery Administration* (New York, 1976), pp. 175–195.

32. Glenn A. Bowers, "Unemployment: From Talk to Action," *Factory and Industrial Management* (December 1930), 80:1198; J. E. Walters, "What's New in Industrial Relations?" *Industrial Relations* (July 1932), 3:318–320; Annual Report of the Special Conference Committee, 1932," in *La Follette Hearings,* 16821; Larkin, "Practical Application . . . ," pp. 88–90.

33. NICB, *Effect of the Depression,* p. 4.

34. "Legislative Notes," *American Labor Legislation Review* (June 1931), 21:167; Samuel M. Levin, "The Ford Unemployment Policy," *American Labor Legislation Review* (June 1932), 22:103.

35. J. E. Walters, "What's New in Personnel Work—1931 and 1932," *Personnel* (August 1932), 9:29; Whiting Williams, "What's on the Worker's Mind," *Industrial Relations* (January 1932), 3:2; Edward S. Cowdrick, "Personnel Practices in 1930," American Management Association, Personnel Series No. 11 (1931).

36. For example, "Westinghouse Employee Relations," *Industrial Relations* (January 1932), 3:20–24.

37. Bernstein, *Lean Years,* p. 78; Walker, "Third Unemployment Survey," pp. 384–385; "Say Wages Will Not Come Down," *Iron Age* (August 7, 1930), 126:397; J. R. Davis, *The New Economics and the Old Economists* (Ames, Iowa, 1971).

Note, however, that the effort to hold the line on wage rates while simultaneously cutting hours may not have been entirely irrational. First, noncompetitive industries had suffered from the price deflation touched off during the 1920–1922 depression and were determined to prevent its reoccurence. In a noncompetitive environment, a reduction in hours is interpreted as a less aggressive move than a wage rate cut, and thus helps to shore up prices better than a wage cut. Second, reductions in hours and the like tended to receive less publicity than general wage cuts. To the extent that business wanted to appear patriotic, it could do so by holding wage rates steady while quietly paring labor costs in other ways.

38. U.S. Bureau of Labor Statistics, *Trend of Employment,* 1929–1931; Everett D. Hawkins and Jay Blum, "Statistical Review of 1932," *Industrial Relations* (December 31, 1932), 3:677–695; Bernstein, *Lean Years,* pp. 259–260.

39. Walker, "Third Unemployment Survey," p. 385.

40. *Ibid.*, p. 386; Bernstein, *Lean Years*, p. 261; Joseph A. Shister, "A Note on Cyclical Wage Rigidity," *American Economic Review* (March 1944), 34:111–116.

41. Hawkins and Blum, "Statistical Review," p. 617; "Building Wage Rates Must Come Down," *Industrial Relations* (January 1932), 3:59–61; "Note," *American Labor Legislation Review* (September 1931), 21:362; Bernstein, *Lean Years*, p. 259.

42. Minutes of International Harvester Works' Managers Meeting, March 30, 1931; Robert Ozanne, *A Century of Labor-Management Relations at McCormick and International Harvester* (Madison, Wis., 1967), p. 159.

43. Average size of establishment giving wage decrease obtained by forming ratio of average number of employees receiving decrease to average number of establishments giving decrease, with data from BLS, *Trend of Employment*, various issues, 1929–1933.

44. Levin, "Ford Unemployment Policy," pp. 104–105; Bernstein, *Lean Years*, pp. 313–314.

45. "Third Personnel Conference of Goodyear, 1935," *La Follette Hearings*, 16699, 16770; Fine, *Automobile Under the Blue Eagle*, pp. 123–124; Levin, "Ford Unemployment Policy," p. 106.

46. John Griffin, *Strikes: A Study in Quantitative Economics* (New York, 1939), pp. 37–44; Leo Wolman, *Ebb and Flow in Trade Unionism* (New York, 1936), p. 178.

47. Louis Adamic, "The Collapse of Organized Labor," *Harper's Monthly* (1932), quoted in Irving Bernstein, *The New Deal Collective Bargaining Policy* (Berkeley, Calif., 1950), p. 1.

48. National Industrial Conference Board (NICB), *What Employers Are Doing for Employees* (New York, 1936), p. 59.

49. "The U.S. Steel Corporation: Part III," *Fortune* (May 1936), p. 141.

50. Schatz, "Electrical Workers," pp. 134–136; "Hiring and Separation Methods in American Factories," *Monthly Labor Review* (November 1932), 35:1013; Larkin, "Practical Application . . . ," p. 92.

51. Levin, "Ford Unemployment Policy," p. 107.

52. John R. Richards, "Interviewing Industrial Employees," *Personnel Journal* (December 1930), 9:283.

53. Fine, *Automobile Under the Blue Eagle*, p. 21; "Inside Facts on General Motors Strike," *Personnel Journal* (March 1937), 15:327.

54. Charles Henderson, "Some Experiences in Managing During the Past Decade," *Bulletin of the Taylor Society* (February 1931), 16:38–40; B. C. Seiple, "Tragedy of the Aging Worker," *American Labor Legislation Review* (September 1920), 20:306–307; Lillian M. Gilbreth, "Hiring and Firing: Shall the Calendar Measure Length of Service?" *Factory and Industrial Management* (February 1930), 79:310–311; Fine, *Automobile Under the Blue Eagle*, p. 364; Frances Perkins, *People at Work* (New York, 1934), p. 162; Arthur H. Young, "Industrial Pensions," unpublished paper, January 19, 1931, Young Papers, California Institute of Technology Library; "Annual Report of the Special Conference Committee, 1933," in *La Follette Hearings*, 16830; note 18, above.

55. "Industrial Employment Code," p. 23; Walker, "Third Unemployment Survey," p. 381.

56. Thomas W. Rogers, "The Older Worker in Industry," *Industrial Relations* (July 1932), 3:352–357; Sanford M. Jacoby, "Industrial Labor Mobility in Historical Perspective," *Industrial Relations* (Spring 1983), 22:274, 277.

57. C. Canby Balderston, "Recent Trends in Personnel Management," *The Management Review* (September 1933), 22:261.

58. Epstein, *Insecurity*, p. 147; "Annual Report of the SCC, 1932," *La Follette Hearings*, 16823; Murray W. Latimer, *Industrial Pension Systems in the United States* (New York, 1932), pp. 845–847; 976–977.

59. Thomas N. Carver, *The Present Economic Revolution in the United States* (Boston, 1925); "Repurchasing Employment Stock," *Industrial Relations* (March 1932), 3:145; Eleanor Davis, "Employee Stock Ownership and the Depression," Industrial Relations Section, Princeton University (1933), pp. 18–24; Epstein, *Insecurity*, p. 86.

60. NICB, "Profit-Sharing and Other Supplementary Compensation Plans Covering Wage Earners," Studies in Personnel Policy No. 2 (1937).

61. U.S. Bureau of Labor Statistics, "Characteristics of Company Unions, 1935," Bulletin No. 634 (Wasington, D.C., 1937), p. 27.

62. "Third Personnel Conference of Goodyear, 1935," *La Follette Hearings*, 16665–16666.

63. Minutes of International Harvester Works' Managers Meetings, June 22, 1931, and April 20, 1932.

64. Balderston, "Recent Trends," p. 261; A. W. Rahn, "Does Personnel Work Need a Defense?" *Industrial Relations* (September 1932), 3:423–427. Eleven percent of surveyed companies discontinued their relief work as the depression wore on. NICB, *Effect of the Depression*, p. 4.

65. NICB, *What Employers Are Doing*, p. 23; NICB, *Effect of the Depression*, p. 12.

66. Merchants' Association of New York, "Effect of the Depression on Industrial Relations Activities," *Industrial Relations* (September 1932), 3:428–430. Also see Walters, "What's New in Personnel Work," p. 29; "Annual Report of the SCC, 1932," *La Follette Hearings*, 16825.

67. L. A. Appley, "What's New in Training Technique?" in AMA Personnel Series No. 24 (1936), p. 22.

68. Lincoln Filene, quoted in Helen Baker, "The Determination and Administration of Industrial Relations Policies," Industrial Relations Section, Princeton University, Research Report No. 55 (Princeton, N.J., 1939), p. 9.

69. William S. Leiserson, "Personnel Problems Raised by the Current Crisis," *The Management Review* (April 1933), 22:114.

70. See table 6.6. For a slightly different assessment of the importance of welfare capitalism's decline during the depression, see David Brody, "The Rise and Decline of Welfare Capitalism," in John Braeman et al., eds., *Change and Continuity in Twentieth Century America: The 1920s* (Columbus, Ohio, 1968), pp. 147–178.

71. For a similar analysis, see Richard C. Wilcock, "Industrial Management's

Policies Toward Unionism," in Milton Derber and Edwin Young, *Labor and the New Deal* (Madison, Wis., 1961), p. 286.

72. W. S. Woytinsky, *Three Aspects of Labor Dynamics* (New York, 1942).

73. Leverett S. Lyon et al., *The National Recovery Administration* (Washington, D.C., 1935); Leon C. Marshall, *Hours and Wages Provisions in NRA Codes* (Washington, D.C., 1935); Office of the National Recovery Administration, Division of Review, "The Content of NIRA Administrative Legislation: Labor Provisions in the Codes," Work Materials No. 35, Part B (Washington, D.C., 1936).

74. Lewis L. Lorwin and Arthur Wubnig, *Labor Relations Boards* (Washington, D.C., 1935), pp. 16–49.

75. Harry A. Millis and Royal E. Montgomery, *Organized Labor* (New York, 1945), pp. 193–198.

76. *Ibid.,* pp. 198–199.

77. Lorwin and Wubnig, *Labor Relations Boards,* pp. 102–117, 220–222.

78. Ordway Tead and Henry C. Metcalf, *Labor Relations and the Recovery Act* (New York, 1933), p. 184. A 1934 survey of industrial executives found them judging collective bargaining and the NIRA's labor codes to be problems of roughly equal magnitude. NICB, *Effect of the Depression,* pp. 15–16.

79. Chapin Hoskins, "The Labor Background of Business Administration," *Personnel* (August 1934), 11:4. Also see Glenn Gardiner, "Significant Changes in Employer-Employee Relations" *Personnel* (November 1934), 11:50–51.

80. "Annual Report of the Special Conference Committee, 1933," in *La Follette Hearings,* 16831; "Annual Report of the Special Conference Committee, 1934," *ibid.,* 16836.

81. E. S. Cowdrick, "Collective Bargaining in 1934," *Personnel Journal* (February 1935), 13:255. With respect to Labor Board policies, Cowdrick noted that "the amount of time and energy spent upon these policies by officials of all grades—if such an amount were obtainable—would be perfectly unbelievable to anyone not acquainted with the internal processes of industry."

82. "Coming: A Boom in Personnel Management," *Forbes* (November 15, 1933), 32:13, 33.

83. Cited in Irving Bernstein, *Turbulent Years* (Boston, 1969), p. 804, no. 2.

84. Industrial Relations Counselors, Confidential Memorandum, No. 2 (1934).

85. H. L. McCarthy, quoted in C. E. French, "The Effect of the Wagner Act on Industrial Relations," *Law and Contemporary Problems* (Spring 1938), 5:305.

86. "Industrial Espionage," U.S. Congress, Senate Committee on Education and Labor, Report No. 46, Part 3, 75th Congress, 2d. Session, 1938.

87. U.S. Bureau of Labor Statistics, "Company Unions," p. 28; Millis and Montgomery, *Organized Labor,* pp. 835, 841.

88. "Company Unions," pp. 48, 54; Fine, *Automobile Under Blue Eagle,* p. 155; Robert R. R. Brooks, *As Steel Goes . . . Unionism in a Basic Industry* (New Haven, 1940), p. 79.

89. "Company Unions," p. 74; NICB, *Industrial Relations Programs in Small Plants* (New York, 1929), p. 20; NICB, *Effect of the Depression,* pp. 8, 12.

90. The study found that of the firms whose company unions were judged to be ineffectual, two-thirds lacked personnel departments. "Company Unions," pp. 164–165.

91. "Company Unions," p. 165.

92. "Minutes of Special Conference Commitee Meeting, June 29, 1933, and October 6, 1933," *La Follette Hearings,* 16946, 16951; "Employee Representation in Chrysler Plants," *Factory Management and Maintenance* (November 1933), 91:453–455.

93. Industrial Relations Counselors, Confidential Memorandum No. 1 (July 10, 1934); "Collective Bargaining," American Management Association Personnel Series No. 19 (1935); Hoskins, "Labor Background," p. 13.

94. T. H. A. Tiedemann, "Employee Representation and the N.I.R.A.," *Personnel* (November 1933), 10:38.

95. "Annual Report of the SCC, 1933," *La Follette Hearings,* 16827–16828.

96. "Minutes of the Special Conference Committee Meeting, December 14, 1933," *La Follette Hearings,* 16953; "Company Unions," p. 68. The Bureau of Labor Statistics found these provisions among 40 percent of the company unions it studied.

97. "Company Unions," p. 72; "Goodyear Personnel Conference, 1935," *La Follette Hearings,* 16667, 16756; "Annual Report of the SCC, 1935," *ibid.,* 16839.

98. "Company Unions," pp. 159, 163; F. W. Pierce, "Basic Principles of Wage and Salary Administration," *Personnel* (May 1935), 11:111–113; "Goodyear Personnel Conference 1935," *La Follette Hearings,* 16658, 16665–16666.

99. Millis and Montgomery, *Organized Labor,* p. 847.

100. National Industrial Conference Board, *Industrial Relations Programs in Small Plants* (New York, 1929), p. 20; NICB, *What Employers Are Doing,* p. 15; J. W. Reinhardt, "The Foreman's Club Comes Back," *Personnel* (May 1937), 13:156–157; "Regular Foremen's Meetings?" *Maintenance Engineering* (September 1932), 90:364; Gardiner, "Some Personnel Aspects of Production," pp. 30–33.

101. Industrial Relations Counselors, Confidential Memorandum No. 2 (1934); "Third Personnel Conference of Goodyear," *La Follette Hearings,* 16731; "Annual Report of the SCC, 1933," *ibid.,* 16832; Burnham Finney, "Today's Foremen Are Bigger Men," *Iron Age* (December 6, 1934), 134:24–26.

102. "Human Relations Win," *Factory Management and Maintenance* (October 1934), 92:536; "Films Teach Foremen Tact," *Factory Management and Maintenance* (October 1940), 98:62–63.

103. H. P. Larrabee, "These Foremen Speak Freely," *Factory Management and Maintenance* (January 1938), 96:81–82.

104. Note the parallel here to the FBVE's activities after World War I. See Charles Prosser and Thomas H. Quigley, *Vocational Education in a Democracy* (Chicago, 1949), ch. 17.

105. R. C. Oberdahn, "Organizing for Supervisory and Executive Training," AMA Personnel Series No. 47 (1941), pp. 15–19; "Foreman Training," *Factory Management and Maintenance* (March 1935), 93:S1–S16; Karen L. Jorgenson-

Esmaili, "Schooling and the Early Human Relations Movement: With Special Reference to the Foreman's Conference, 1919–1939," (Ph.D. dissertation, University of California, Berkeley, 1979), pp. 222–236.

106. Reinhardt, "Foreman's Club," pp. 152–154; Robert D. Leiter, *The Foreman in Industrial Relations* (New York, 1948), pp. 82–83; assorted material in "Foreman's Clubs" box and "Industrial Department Committee Minutes" box, YMCA Historical Library, New York.

107. International Harvester Works' Managers Meeting Minutes, December 3, 1933. Also see Gardiner, "Significant Changes," p. 51; Hartley W. Barclay, "The Forgotten Man," *Mill & Factory* (September 1934), 15:25.

108. Reinhardt, "Foreman's Club," p. 156; IRC Confidential Memorandum No. 2 (1934).

109. Guy Wadsworth, Jr., "Cross-Currents in Industrial Relations," *Personnel* (May 1940), 16:174–182.

110. Cowdrick, "Bargaining in 1934," p. 255.

111. See comment by William S. Knudsen of General Motors in Finney, "Today's Foremen," p. 26.

112. Note 100, above; Baker, "Determination and Administration of Industrial Relations," pp. 44–45; U.S. Bureau of the Census, *Historical Statistics of the United States, Colonial Times to 1970* (Washington, D.C., 1976), pp. 139–145.

113. Cowdrick, "Bargaining in 1934," p. 255.

114. Harold B. Bergen, "Improvement of Employer-Employee Relations," *Management Record* (June 1940), 2:67.

115. Lorwin and Wubnig, *Labor Relations Boards*, pp. 167–174.

116. *Ibid., pp.* 170, 317.

117. "Minutes of Personnel Conference, 1936, Goodyear Tire and Rubber," *La Follette Hearings*, 16753–16754; Russell L. Greenman, *The Worker, the Foreman and the Wagner Act* (New York, 1939).

118. Minutes of International Harvester Works' Managers Meetings, August 27, 1934.

119. *La Follette Hearings*, Part 6, 2513.

120. *La Follette Hearings*, 16750, 17035–17037.

121. NICB, *What Employers Are Doing*, p. 26.

122. H. B. Bergen, "Personnel Policies in the Light of the New Deal," *Personnel* (August 1934), 11:21–22; C. H. Murray, "Wage and Salary Administration in the American Rolling Mill Company," *Personnel* (November 1934), 11:37–46; NICB, "Job Evaluation," Studies in Personnel Policy No. 25 (1940), pp. 10ff; Samuel L. H. Burk, "A Case History in Salary and Wage Administration," *Personnel* (February 1939), 15:93–129.

123. Bergen, "Personnel Policies," p. 24; *La Follette Hearings*, 16659–16660.

124. Fine, *Automobile Under Blue Eagle*, p. 364.

125. *Ibid.*, pp. 250–257; Lorwin and Wubnig, *Labor Relations Boards*, pp. 353–364.

126. Elmo Roper, "What American Labor Wants," *The American Mercury* (February 1944), p. 181; NICB, "Factors Affecting Employee Morale," Studies in Personnel Policy No. 85 (1947); NICB, "Dismissal Compensation," Studies in

Personnel Policy No. 50 (1943), p. 3; Sumner H. Slichter, *Union Policies and Industrial Management* (Washington, D.C., 1941), pp. 132–134.

127. Paul A. Raushenbush, "Wisconsin's Unemployment Compensation Act," *American Labor Legislation Review* (March 1932), 22:11–18; Harold H. Groves and Elizabeth Brandeis, "Economic Bases of the Wisconsin Reserves Act," *American Economic Review* (March 1934), 24:38–52; Office of War Mobilization and Reconversion, *Guaranteed Wages,* Report to the President by the Advisory Board (Washington, D.C., 1947), p. 292.

128. Office of the NRA, "Labor Provisions in the Codes," p. 20; Fine, *Automobile Under Blue Eagle,* pp. 120–122.

129. *Ibid.,* pp. 351–368; Herman Feldman, *Stabilizing Jobs and Wages* (New York, 1940), pp.83–86.

130. Lorwin and Wubnig, *Labor Relations Boards,* pp. 170–173, 317, 365; Sanford Jacoby, "Progressive Discipline in American Industry: Origins, Development and Consequences," in David Lipsky ed., *Advances in Industrial and Labor Relations* (Greenwich, Conn., 1985).

131. NICB, *What Employers Are Doing,* p. 59; table 7.2, above.

132. Bergen, "Personnel Policies," pp. 19–20; H. B. Bergen, "Developing Promotional Opportunities," *Personnel* (February 1939), 15:208–212; Helen Baker, "Company Plans for Employee Promotions," Industrial Relations Section, Princeton University, Report No. 58 (1939).

133. P. W. Schubert, "If Fixed Salaries Were Not Fixed," *Mill & Factory* (July 1934), 15:34; L. A. Appley, "What's New in Training Technique?" AMA Personnel Series No. 24 (1936), p. 22. Also see Paul Mooney, "How Should Facts Regarding Personnel Policies Be Presented to Executives to Aid in Reaching Decisions?" *Personnel* (August 1935), 12:141–143.

134. Harry A. Millis and Emily Clark Brown, *From the Wagner Act to Taft-Hartley: A Study of National Labor Policy and Labor Relations* (Chicago, 1950), pp. 67–70; Richard Polenberg, "The Decline of the New Deal, 1937–1940" in John Braeman, Robert Bremner and David Brody, eds., *The New Deal* (Columbus, Ohio, 1975), pp. 246–266.

135. Wadsworth, "Cross Currents," p. 177. Also see William P. Clarke, "Making the Collective Agreement Work," in *Addresses on Industrial Relations: 1939,* University of Michigan Bureau of Industrial Relations Bulletin No. 9 (Ann Arbor, 1939), pp. 53–60; Robert N. McMurry, "The Supervisor's Function in Labor Relations," *Factory Management and Maintenance* (July 1941), 99:84.

136. T. G. Spates, "An Analysis of Industrial Relations Trends," AMA Personnel Series No. 25 (1937), p. 24. Also see A. B. Gates, "Looking Forward in Industrial Relations," *Personnel* (August 1935), 12:150–153; Ordway Tead, "New Duties in Personnel Work," *Personnel Journal* (June 1937), 16:36–45.

8. Another Great Transformation, 1936–1945

1. U.S. Bureau of Labor Statistics, "Handbook of Labor Statistics," Bulletin No. 1865 (Washington, D.C., 1975), pp. 105, 389; Lloyd Ulman, "The Development of Trades and Labor Unions" in Seymour Harris, ed., *American Economic History* (New York, 1961), pp. 404–406.

2. Minutes of International Harvesters Works' Managers Meeting, June 3 and June 24, 1935, courtesy of Prof. Robert Ozanne; *La Follette Hearings*, 16809–16812, 17022–17024 (see note 20, ch. 7 above).

3. Thomas G. Spates, "Industrial Relations Trends," American Management Association Personnel Series No. 25 (1937), p. 24.

4. *La Follette Hearings*, 17035–17037.

5. "Note," *Personnel* (February 1937), 13:73. Also see Helen Baker, "The Development and Administration of Industrial Relations Policies," Industrial Relations Section, Princeton University, Report No. 55 (1939), pp. 15–17.

6. C. E. French, "The Effect of the Wagner Act on Industrial Relations," *Law and Contemporary Problems* (Spring 1938), 5:300; "Industry and Its Employees," *Factory Management and Maintenance* (January 1937), 95:45–46; Homer D. Sayre, "Successful Employer-Employee Relations," *NAM Labor Relations Bulletin*, No. 13 (May 18, 1936).

7. For example, see George S. Gibb, *The Saco-Lowell Shops* (Cambridge, Mass., 1950), pp. 345, 805.

8. Clinton S. Golden and Harold Ruttenberg, *The Dynamics of Industrial Democracy* (New York, 1942), p. 120.

9. Sumner, Slichter, *Union Policies and Industrial Management* (Washington, D.C., 1941), pp. 105–107. It also is possible that the overwhelming concern with job security stemmed from a desire to protect new forms of communal stability from the disruption caused by unemployment. The decline in job and geographic mobility during the 1920s had created newly stable working class communities centered around the workplace. Sanford Jacoby, "Industrial Labor Mobility in Historical Perspective," *Industrial Relations* (Spring 1983), 22:261–282.

10. Frederick Harbison, "Seniority in Mass Production Industries," *Journal of Political Economy* (December 1940), 48:851–864; Harbison, "Seniority Policies and Procedures as Developed Through Collective Bargaining," Industrial Relations Section, Princeton University, Report No. 63 (1941).

11. Ronald Schatz, "American Electrical Workers: Work, Struggles, Aspirations, 1930–1950" (Ph.D. dissertation, University of Pittsburgh, 1977), pp. 122–123. Also see Frederic Meyers, "The Analytic Meaning of Seniority," Proceedings of the Eighteenth Annual Meeting, Industrial Relations Research Association (1966), pp. 1–9.

12. Frederick H. Harbison, "The Seniority Principle in Union-Management Relations," Industrial Relations Section, Princeton University, Report No. 57, (1939), p. 11.

13. A. C. Sprague, "Seniority Program at the B. F. Goodrich Company," *Personnel* (May 1938), 14:158–167; T. O. Armstrong, "Seniority Record Boards," *Personnel* (January 1942), 18:239–242.

14. Charles A. Myers, "Personnel Problems of the Postwar Transition Period," Prepared for Committee for Economic Development, New York, 1944; NICB, "Company Policies on Military Service and War Jobs," Studies in Personnel Policy (SPP) No. 52 (1943); NICB, "Seniority and Reemployment of Veterans," SPP No. 65 (1944); Ruth M. Milkman, "The Reproduction of Job Segregation by Sex: A Study of the Changing Sexual Division of Labor in the Auto and Electrical

Manufacturing Industries in the 1940s" (Ph.D. dissertation, University of California, Berkeley, 1981), pp. 241–250.

15. NICB, "Seniority Systems in Nonunionized Companies," SPP No. 110 (1950), p. 13. Also see, "Operation Dixie," *Modern Industry* (August 15, 1946), 12:51. This describes how southern firms prepared for postwar union organizing drives. "Seniority," it reported, "is getting recognition before becoming a union demand."

16. H. Ellsworth Steele, W. Myles, and S. McIntyre, "Personnel Practices in the South," *Industrial and Labor Relations Review* (January 1956), 9:250.

17. *Ibid.*, 250.

18. NICB, "Curtailment, Layoff Policy and Seniority," SPP No. 5 (1938), p. 8; NICB, "Seniority Systems," p. 11.

19. Industrial Relations Counselors, *Memorandum to Clients,* No. 35 (February 10, 1938).

20. Slichter, *Union Policies,* pp. 106–107; William H. McPherson, *Labor Relations in the Automobile Industry* (Washington, D.C., 1940), pp. 131–132; Donald Anthony, "Rubber Products," in Harry A. Millis, ed., *How Collective Bargaining Works* (New York, 1945), p. 659.

21. W. Rupert MacLaurin, "Workers' Attitudes on Work Sharing and Lay-Off Policies in a Manufacturing Firm," *Monthly Labor Review* (January 1939), 48:52.

22. Frederick H. Harbison, "Steel," and Anthony, "Rubber Products," in Millis, *How Collective Bargaining Works,* pp. 554, 659; Schatz, "American Electrical Workers," pp. 141–144; McPherson, *Labor Relations in the Auto Industry,* p. 132.

23. "Employment Stabilization," Bureau of National Affairs, Personnel Policies Forum Survey No. 24 (April 1954), pp. 11–13; Office of War Mobilization and Reconversion and Office of Temporary Controls, *Guaranteed Wages:* Report to the President by the Advisory Board (Washington, D.C., 1947), pp. 27–34, Slichter, *Union Policies,* p. 154. Some have argued that imperfect experience rating under unemployment insurance provides another incentive for employers to choose layoffs. See James Medoff, "Layoffs and Alternatives Under Trade Unions in U.S. Manufacturing," *American Economic Review* (June 1979), 69:380–395.

24. Daniel J. B. Mitchell, *Unions, Wages and Inflation* (Washington, D.C., 1980), p. 95.

25. Philip Selznick and Howard Vollmer, "Rule of Law in Industry: Seniority Rights," *Industrial Relations* (May 1962), 1:102–103.

26. Schatz, "American Electrical Workers," pp. 150–151; Harbison, "Seniority Policies and Procedures," p. 53.

27. Sidney Fine, *The Automobile Under the Blue Eagle* (Ann Arbor, Mich., 1963), p. 362; McPherson, *Labor Relations in the Auto Industry,* pp. 103–108; Slichter, *Union Policies,* p. 128; Robert R. R. Brooks, *As Steel Goes . . . Unionism in a Basic Industry* (New Haven, 1940), pp. 213, 231; Sanford M. Jacoby, "Union-Management Cooperation in the United States During the Second World War," in M. Dubovsky, ed., *Technological Change and Worker Movements in the Modern World* (Beverly Hills, Calif., 1985).

28. *Guaranteed Wages,* p. 297; "Can Industry Guarantee an Annual Wage?" *Factory Management and Maintenance* (July 1945), 103:82–87; NICB, "Annual Wage and Employment Guarantee Plans," SPP No. 76 (1945), p. 9.

29. *Guaranteed Wages,* pp. 293–297.

30. McPherson, *Labor Relations in the Auto Industry,* pp. 107–109; L. K. Urquhart, "Employee Security," *Factory Management and Maintenance* (February 1937), 95:S357–S368; "And Now—Secured Incomes," *Factory Management and Maintenance* (December 1938), 96:33, 104–105; "Notes on Personnel Administration," *Management Record* (January 1940), 2:9.

31. NICB, "Assuring Employment or Income to Wage Earners: A Case Study," SPP No. 7 (1938); NICB, "Reducing Fluctuations in Employment," SPP No. 27 (1940), pp. 5–12; Herman Feldman, *Stabilizing Jobs and Wages* (New York, 1940); C. S. Craigmile, "Factors Upon Which Employment and Income May Be Stabilized," *Better Industrial Relations Through Better Understanding,* Summary Report of the Silver Bay Industrial Conference, New York, August 1939, pp. 22–27; Marion B. Folsom, "Stabilization of Employment and Income," *Management Record* (February 1939), 1:17–24; "Industry to Get Report on Job Regularization," *Factory Management and Maintenance* (March 1940), 98:102–104.

32. Charles A. Myers, "Employment Stabilization and the Wisconsin Act," *American Economic Review* (December 1939), 29:708–723; Industrial Relations Counselors, *Memorandum to Clients,* No. 51 (March 29, 1940); Emerson P. Schmidt, "Employment Stabilization and Experience Rating," *Personnel* (May 1940), 16:163–174. The federal experience rating provisions were part of Title II of the 1935 Social Security Act.

33. See note 11, chap. 7; NICB, "Dismissal Compensation," SPP No. 50 (1943), pp. 7–8; American Management Association, "Annual Wages and Employment Stabilization Techniques," Research Report No. 8 (1945), pp. 18–19.

34. NICB, "Selecting, Training and Upgrading," SPP No. 37 (1941), p. 8.

35. Clinton S. Golden, "Making the Collective Agreement Work," in *Addresses on Industrial Relations: 1939,* University of Michigan, Bureau of Industrial Relations, Bulletin No. 9 (Ann Arbor, 1939), pp. 71–72; Helen Baker, "The Industrial Relations Executive and Collective Bargaining," *Society for the Advancement of Management Journal* (July 1939), 4:105–107; Golden and Ruttenberg, *Industrial Democracy,* pp. 139–143.

36. *LaFollette Hearings,* 17035–17037; T. O. Armstrong, "New Methods in Promotion and Hiring," *Personnel Journal* (January 1936), 14:280; G. I. MacLaren, "Promotion from the Ranks," *Personnel* (May 1937), 13:157; Helen Baker, "Company Plans for Employee Promotions," Industrial Relations Section, Princeton University, Report No. 58 (1939), pp. 38–48; Harold B. Bergen, "Developing Promotional Opportunities," *Personnel* (February 1939), 15:208–212; Whiting Williams, "Management's Industrial Relations Problems," American Management Association Personnel Series (PS) No. 22 (1936), pp. 20–22.

37. Baker, "Plans for Promotions," p. 8. Also see Baker, "Development of Industrial Relations," pp. 40–41.

38. French, "Effect of the Wagner Act," p. 301. Also see C. G. Eubank, "Standard Instructions," *Personnel* (August 1937), 14:10–14.

39. Baker, "Development of Industrial Relations," pp. 21–26; John E. Christ,

"Employee Handbook Answers All Questions," *Factory Management and Maintenance* (November 1941), 99:66–67, 166–168.

40. NICB, "Written Statements of Personnel Policy," SPP No. 79 (1947), pp. 4–5; H. F. Lange, "Getting Company Policies Across to Employees," in *Addresses on Industrial Relations: 1939*, pp. 13–24; NICB, "Employee's Handbooks," SPP No. 45 (1942); C. R. Dooley, "Application of Industrial Relations Policies," in *Addresses on Industrial Relations: 1940*, University of Michigan, Bureau of Industrial Relations, Bulletin No. 10 (Ann Arbor, 1940), pp. 23–26; Harold B. Bergen, "Basic Factors in Present-Day Industrial Relations," *Personnel* (November 1937), 14:47–48; P. D. Fairbanks, "Development and Use of Employee Manuals," in *More Production Through Sound Industrial Relations*, Proceedings of the 25th Silver Bay Industrial Conference, July 1942, pp. 113–117.

41. Brooks, *As Steel Goes*, p. 211.

42. Golden and Ruttenberg, *Industrial Democracy*, p. 170.

43. Bergen, "Basic Factors," pp. 50–52; A. F. Kindall, "Job Description and Rating," and Edward N. Hay, "Job Evaluation by the Point Method," *Personnel* (February 1938), 14:122–132; L. J. King, "Job Evaluation," *Society for Advancement of Management Journal* (May 1938), 2:93–98.

44. AMA, "Compensation Problems and Training Technique Today," PS No. 24 (1936), pp. 4–10; A. L. Kress, "How to Rate Jobs and Men," *Factory Management and Maintenance* (October 1939), 97:60–70; J. E. Walters, "Rating the Job and the Man," *Factory Management and Maintenance* (June 1937), 95:S393–S404; Material on Industrial Relations Counselors in Case 4, Louis E. Kirstein Papers, Baker Library, Harvard University, Graduate School of Business Administration.

45. Helen Baker and John M. True, "The Operation of Job Evaluation Plans," Industrial Relations Section, Princeton University, Report No. 74 (1947), p. 13. Also see A. L. Kress, "Putting Job Rating to Work," in AMA PS No. 49 (1941), pp. 4, 27; Charles W. Lytle, "Job Evaluation—A Phase of Job Control," *Personnel* (May 1940), 16:192–197.

46. W. S. Woytinsky, *Labor and Management Look at Collective Bargaining* (New York, 1949), pp. 146–147.

47. Jack Stieber, "Union Viewpoints on Job Evaluation," in University of Minnesota Industrial Relations Center, *Job Evaluation Practices* (Minneapolis, 1950); Sar Levitan, "Union Attitudes Towards Job Evaluation," *Industrial and Labor Relations Review* (January 1951), 4:268–274.

48. M. E. Nichols, "Rating Employees," *Addresses on Industrial Relations: 1939*, pp. 109–122; Milton Olander, "Merit Ratings in Industry," *NAM Labor Relations Bulletin* (September 1939), 30:4–8; Kress, "How to Rate," pp. 65–70.

49. Loren Baritz, *The Servants of Power* (Middletown, Conn., 1960), p. 161; R. S. Livingstone, "Policies for Promotion, Transfer, Demotion and Discharge," in *For National Unity: Better Industrial Relations*, Proceedings of the 24th Silver Bay Industrial Conference, July 1941, pp. 82–89.

50. NICB, Plans for Rating Employees," SPP No. 8 (1938); NICB, "Employee Rating," SPP No. 39 (1942); Industrial Relations Committee, American Iron and Steel Institute, "Merit-Rating of Employees," *Personnel* (August 1938), 15:6–17.

51. Randolph S. Driver, "A Case History in Merit Rating," *Personnel* (May

1940), 16:137–162; Samuel D. Marble, "A Performance Basis for Employee Evaluation," *Personnel* (January 1942), 18:217–226.

52. Asa S. Knowles, "Merit Rating and Labor Management," *Personnel* (August 1940), 17:29–41.

53. Arthur W. Kornhauser, "The Technique of Measuring Employee Attitudes," *Personnel* (May 1933), 9:99–107; R. S. Uhrbrock, "Attitudes of 4430 Employees," *Journal of Social Psychology* (1934), 5:365–377; Harold B. Bergen, "Finding Out What Employees Are Thinking," *Management Record* (April 1939), 1:53–58; Richard Hull, "Measuring Employee Attitudes," *Management Record* (November 1939), 1:165–172; "Asked Employees How They Felt," *Factory Management and Maintenance* (November 1937) 95:63; David G. Moore, "How Do Our Employees Feel About Us?" *Personnel Conference Record,* Sears, Roebuck Company, Chicago, November 1946; James C. Worthy, "Discovering and Evaluating Employee Attitudes," address before the American Management Association, October 3, 1947, unpublished.

54. Kornhauser, "Measuring Employee Attitudes," p. 100.

55. "Annual Report of the Special Conference Committee, 1936," *La Follette Hearings,* 16850; Minutes of Special Conference Committee Meeting, May 21, 1935, *La Follette Hearings,* 16907; John W. O'Leary, "Industry Has a Public Relations Job to Do," *Factory Management and Maintenance* (March 1936), 94:96–98; NICB, "Personnel Activities in American Business," SPP No. 20 (1940), p. 12.

56. *Ibid.,* pp. 19–29; NICB, *What Employers Are Doing For Employees* (New York, 1936), p. 26; Robert Ozanne, *A Century of Labor-Management Relations at McCormick and International Harvester* (Madison, Wis., 1967), pp. 94–95.

57. Material on Industrial Relations Counselors, Case 4, Kirstein Papers; NICB, "Trends in Company Vacation Policy," SPP No. 21 (1940), and "Developments in Company Vacation Plans," SPP No. 13 (1939); F. W. Pierce, "Basic Principles of Wage and Salary Administration," *Personnel* (May 1935), 11:113.

58. NICB, "Company Pension Plans and the Social Security Act," SPP No. 16 (1939), p. 26; AMA, "Economic Security: Pensions and Health Insurance," Personnel Series No. 20 (1935), pp. 18–19; Industrial Relations Counselors, "Memorandum to Clients," No. 38 (September 15, 1938), p. 2.

59. Thomas G. Spates, "An Objective Scrutiny of Personnel Administration," AMA Personnel Series No. 75 (1944), p. 5; Arthur H. Young, "Employee Relations—Asset or Liability?" address to the 48th Anniversary Convention of the California Bankers' Association, Young Papers, California Institute of Technology, Speeches, vol. 4, no. 68; Lawrence Appley, "Industrial Relations in Wartime," in *More Production Through Sound Industrial Relations,* Proceedings of the 25th Anniversary Silver Bay Industrial Conference, July 1942, p. 8.

60. Charles S. Slocombe, "Meet C.I.O. on Its Own Ground," *Personnel Journal* (May 1937), 16:2.

61. Thomas G. Spates, "Spark Plugs of Democracy," *Personnel* (January 1942), 18:187–194; C. L. Huston, "Design for the Future of Industrial Relations," *Personnel* (July 1943), 10:24–32; Neil W. Chamberlain, *The Union Challenge to Management Control* (New York, 1948), pp. 77–81.

62. Wade E. Shurtleff, "Top Management and Personnel Administration," AMA

Personnel Series No. 144 (1952), p. 5. Also see Frederick H. Harbison and John R. Coleman, *Goals and Strategy in Collective Bargaining* (New York, 1951), p. 45.

63. NICB, "Organization of Personnel Administration," SPP No. 73 (1946); J. Walter Dietz, "New Trends in Personnel Policies," *Personnel* (February 1940), 16:99.

64. Thomas G. Spates, "Industrial Relations Trends," AMA Personnel Series No. 25 (1937), p. 16.

65. "The Annual Report of the American Management Association: Activities and Finances," AMA General Management Series No. 133 (1937), p. 6.

66. Hicks helped to set up the Industrial Relations Section at Princeton in the 1920s. By 1940, there were industrial relations centers at Cal Tech, MIT, Queens (Canada), and Stanford. Clarence J. Hicks, *My Life in Industrial Relations* (New York, 1941); Case 4, Kirstein Papers; "Enlarging Influence of Special Conference Committee Activities, May 1936," *La Follette Hearings*, 16871.

67. For an excellent analysis of management's legislative efforts to change the Wagner Act, see Howell J. Harris, *The Right to Manage: Industrial Relations Policies of American Business in the 1940s* (Madison, Wis., 1982).

68. Harold F. North, "The Personnel Man's Functional Relationships," AMA Personnel Series No. 45 (1940), pp. 17–18; Charles A. Drake, "What Is Wrong with Personnel Management?" *Personnel* (November 1941), 18:121–128; Charles A. Drake, "Developing Professional Standards for Personnel Executives," *Personnel* (March 1943), 19:646–655.

69. NICB, "Principles and Application of Job Evaluation," SPP No. 62 (1944), p. 7.

70. Harold B. Bergen, "The Handling of Grievance as a Present Day Employment Relations Problem," *NAM Labor Relations Bulletin* (June 25, 1938), 28:7–9. Also see William V. Owen, "Decentralize Personnel Work," *Personnel Journal* (June 1940), 19:65–68; Joseph E. Moody, "Handling Grievances," in *For National Unity: Better Industrial Relations*, Proceedings of the Silver Bay Industrial Conference, 24th Year, July 1941, pp. 63–65; Baker, "Industrial Relations Policies," p. 55.

71. Arthur H. Young, "Industrial Relations and the Foreman," speech given at California Institute of Technology, May 2, 1942, Young Papers, Speeches, vol. 4, no. 70; AMA, "Compensation Problems and Training Technique Today," Personnel Series No. 24 (1936), pp. 4–6; Albert L. Kress, "Changing Functions of the Foreman," in *Better Industrial Relations for Victory*, Proceedings of the 26th Silver Bay Industrial Conference, July 1943, pp. 120–125.

72. Lawrence A. Appley, "The Foreman's Place in an Employee Educational Program," AMA PS No. 33 (1938), pp. 27–28.

73. Frank Rising, "Union for Foremen," *Personnel* (February 1940), 16:94–95; "The Foreman Looks to Management," *Management Record* (May 1939), 1:69–74.

74. Norman G. Shidle and Leslie Peat, "Industry's Forgotten Man," *Forbes* (May 15, 1940); Don D. Lescohier, "The Foreman and the Union," *Personnel* (August 1938), 15:18–25. Note that a postwar survey found that 34 percent of foremen felt that union stewards undermined their authority; 13 percent felt this

way about the personnel department. "Here's Your Modern Foreman," *Modern Industry* (July 1947), 14:60.

75. Ira B. Cross, Jr., "When Foremen Joined the CIO," *Personnel Journal* (February 1940), 18:277.

76. Sumner H. Slichter et al., "Report and Findings of a Panel of the NWLB in Certain Disputes Involving Supervisors," *War Labor Reports* (1945), 26;645–753; Rising, "Union for Foremen," pp. 94–96; NICB, "Foreman Compensation," SPP No. 30 (1941).

77. Slichter et al., "Report and Findings," pp. 655–656; AMA, "The Unionization of Foremen," Research Report No. 6 (1945), pp. 11–26; Robert D. Leiter, *The Foreman in Industrial Relations* (New York, 1948), pp. 85–95.

78. North, "Functional Relationships," pp. 20–21; C. S. Coler, "Employee Training Programs," in *Addresses on Industrial Relations: 1940*, pp. 88–89; Lescohier, "Foreman and the Union," pp. 20–24; T. J. Connor, "Conferences Make the Supervisor," *Factory Management and Maintenance* (May 1940), 98:69–72; H. L. Humke, "Types of Foreman Training," *Advanced Management* (September 1937), 2:144–148.

79. H. W. Anderson, "Should Foremen Be Unionized?" AMA Personnel Series No. 90 (1945), p. 18; J. W. Reinhardt, "The Foreman's Club Comes Back," *Personnel* (May 1937), 13:156; W. W. Mussman, "Foremen's Clubs," *Management Record* (November 1946), 8:375; Industrial Department Committee Minutes box, YMCA Historical Library; Thomas B. Fordham, "The Growth of the Foremen's Club Movement," *Industrial Management* (June 1926), 71:339–341; Charles Copeland Smith, *The Foreman's Place in Management* (New York, 1946), pp. 63–74.

80. Leiter, *The Foreman*, pp. 82–83; NICB, "Foreman's Compensation," p. 4; Coler, "Employee Training," pp. 88–89.

81. E. J. Benge, "Industrial Relations for Small Plants," *Factory Management and Maintenance* (May 1940), 98:62, 152–162; P. M. Jones, "Personnel Policies and Practices Survey," *Personnel Journal* (October 1941), 20:122–128; Baker, "Industrial Relations Policies," pp. 27–30.

82. "Some Notes on Employment Records," *NAM Labor Relations Bulletin*, No. 23 (July 23, 1937), p. 29; Thomas R. Jones, "Why Employment Relations?" *NAM Labor Relations Bulletin*, No. 36 (March 1941), pp. 5–10; William Girdner, "Procedure on Discharges," *Personnel* (February 1938), 14:118–121.

83. NICB, "Selected Interpretations of the Fair Labor Standards Act," Management Research Memorandum No. 8 (1942); Russell L. Greenman, "Adapting Personnel Programs to Current Labor Legislation," *Personnel* (February 1939), 15:138–144.

84. "Personnel Managers Beware," *Personnel Journal* (February 1944), 22:274–280; "How Much 'Personnel' in Your Plant?" *Modern Industry* (February 15, 1946), 11:35–39; AMA, "How to Establish and Maintain a Personnel Department," Research Report No. 4 (1944), pp. 3, 11. As the postwar data in the following table indicate, size was highly correlated with the existence of a personnel specialization within the firm; unionism also was important, although not as much as size:

Proportion of Firms With Personnel Specialization

SMALL (under 250)		LARGE (over 250)	
Nonunion	Union	Nonunion	Union
38%	51%	86%	92%

From Steel, Myles, and McIntyre, "Personnel Practices," p. 247; and H. E. Steele and H. Fisher, Jr., "A Study of the Effects of Unionism in Southern Plants," *Monthly Labor Review* (March 1964), 87:267.

85. NICB, "Organization of Personnel Administration," SPP No. 73 (1945), p. 85; Dale Yoder, *Personnel Management and Industrial Relations,* 3d ed. (New York, 1948), p. viii; R. A. Sutermeister, "Have Plenty Personnel People," *Personnel Journal* (June 1943), 22:62–67. As union-management relations became more routinized during and after the war, there developed specialized labor relations sections within the personnel department. Very rarely was the labor relations function housed in a separate department of equal status. These sections handled collective bargaining and contract administration. NICB, "Company Organization Charts," SPP No. 64 (1944); "Organization of Personnel Administration," pp. 8–60; "Are You Pessimistic About Postwar Labor?" *Modern Industry* (March 15, 1944), 7:64–77.

86. Joel Seidman, *American Labor from Defense to Reconversion* (Chicago, 1953); Nelson Lichtenstein, *Labor's War at Home: The CIO in World War II* (Cambridge, England, 1982); U. S. Department of Labor, *Termination Report of the National War Labor Board* (Washington, D.C., 1948), 1:63–70, 80–100. The new CIO unions were aided by the NWLB's orders to insert union security clauses in their contracts. Fifty-eight percent of the NWLB cases in which union security was an issue involved CIO unions. Sanford Jacoby and Daniel J. B. Mitchell, "Development of Contractual Features of the Union-Management Relationship," *Labor Law Journal* (August 1982), 33:515.

87. *NWLB Termination Report,* p. 65; C. L. Shartle, "New Selection Methods for Defense Jobs," AMA Personnel Series No. 50 (1941), p. 40; Roy M. Dorcus and Robert D. Loken, "Survey of Personnel Workers," *Personnel Journal* (January 1943), 21:251–254.

88. The "net effect" of labor shortages, said an AMA report, "has been to discourage submissiveness on the part of labor." AMA, "Constructive Discipline in Industry," Research Report No. 3 (1943), p. 6. Also see W. I. Newman, "Breaking the AWOL Habit," *Factory Management and Maintenance* (October 1942), 100:110–111; *Investigation of the National Defense Program,* Hearings Before a Special Committee Investigating the National Defense Program, Part 17, U.S. Senate, 78th Cong., 1st Sess. (Washington, D.C., 1943), 6986–6987, 7007, 7017–7018, 7029; King MacRury, "Measuring Absenteeism," *Management Record* (January 1943), 5:106–107.

89. NICB, "Personnel Activities in American Business (Revised)," SPP No. 86 (1947), p. 32; NICB, Personnel Forms and Records," SPP No. 87 (1947); "Use the Right Selection and Testing Methods," *Factory Management and Maintenance* (August 1943), 101:96–105.

90. ´ The Employment Ceiling Headache and What to Do About It," *Industrial Relations* (July 1944), 2:4–5, 32–33; Paul A. C. Koistinen, "Mobilizing the World War II Economy: Labor and the Industrial-Military Alliance," *Pacific Historical Review* (November 1973), 42:443–478; "Industrial Manpower Controls," AMA Personnel Series No. 60 (1942), pp. 3–32.

91. NICB, "Employment Procedures and Personnel Records," SPP No. 38 (1941), p. 3; J. P. Woodard, "Select the Right Workers," *Factory Management and Maintenance* (August 1945), 103:84–91.

92. NICB, "Time Schedules in Job Training," SPP No. 55 (1943); "Operating Under Manpower Controls," AMA Personnel Series No. 64 (1943), pp. 3–42; Shartle, "Selection Methods," pp. 30–31; "Manning Tables," *Factory Management and Maintenance* (November 1942), 100:74–82; "Set Up a Manpower Control Program," *Factory Management and Maintenance* (August 1944), 104:81–88. These tables also were used to justify draft deferments for workers considered essential by an employer.

93. *Manpower Problems in Detroit*, Hearings Before a Special Committee Investigating the National Defense Program, Part 28, U.S. Senate, 79th Cong., 1st Sess. (Washington, D.C., 1945), 13539, 13799–13801; Bartley Whiteside, "Methods of Training Workers Quickly," *For National Unity*, Proceedings of 24th Silver Bay Conference (1941), pp. 68–72; Office of Production Management, Labor Division, "Expediting Production Through Training," Bulletin No. 2A (1941); War Manpower Commission, Bureau of Training, *The Training Within Industry Report, 1941–1945* (Washington, D.C., 1945), pp. 128, 223–235.

94. Dooley in Office of Production Management, Labor Division, "Upgrading Within Industry," Bulletin 2 (1940), p. 2. See also H. C. O'Sullivan, "Upgrading— For Effective Utilization of Manpower," *Factory Management and Maintenance* (February 1944), 102:113–116; NICB, "Selecting, Training, and Upgrading," SPP No. 37 (1941).

95. Carrol R. Daugherty and Milton Derber, "Wage Stabilization," in Colston Warne, ed., *Yearbook of American Labor: War Labor Policies* (New York, 1945), p. 170; Garret L. Bergen, "War's Lessons in Personnel Administration," AMA Personnel Series No. 94 (1945), pp. 39–41; NICB, "Time Schedules," pp. 3–5; *NWLB Termination Report*, pp. 275–277.

96. Dooley in "Upgrading," p. 2. Also see Slichter, *Union Policies and Industrial Management*, pp. 160–162.

97. "Why War Workers Strike," *Modern Industry* (March 15, 1945), 10:47.

98. Edward N. Hay, "Union-Management Cooperation in Job Evaluation," *Management Record* (June 1945), 7:151–155; Lee Hill and Charles R. Hook, Jr., *Management at the Bargaining Table* (New York, 1945), p. 59; Richard Lester, "Company Wage Policies," Industrial Relations Section, Princeton University, Research Report No. 77 (1948), pp. 21–22.

99. NICB, "Principles and Application of Job Evaluation," SPP No. 62 (1944), pp. 3–4; Helen Baker and John True, "The Operation of Job Evaluation Plans," Industrial Relations Section. Princeton University, Research Report No. 74 (1947), p. 19; *NWLB Termination Report*, pp. 240–243; Daugherty and Derber, "Stabilization," pp. 168–169.

100. Richard Feise, "Aircraft—A Mass Production Industry," in Warne, ed., *Yearbook*, pp. 262–266; Arthur P. Allen and Betty V. H. Schneider, *Industrial Relations in the California Aircraft Industry*, West Coast Collective Bargaining Series, Institute of Industrial Relations, University of California, Berkeley (1956), pp. 21–23.

101. *NWLB Termination Report*, pp. 252–258; Robert Tilove, "The Wage Rationalization Program in U.S. Steel," *Monthly Labor Review* (June 1947), 64:967–982; R. Conrad Cooper, "The U.S. Steel Wage Classification Program," AMA Personnel Series No. 114 (1947), pp. 3–15; Jack Stieber, *The Steel Industry Wage Structure* (Cambridge, Mass., 1959), pp. 4–11.

102. Lester, "Wage Policies," pp. 16, 38–41.

103. "Trends in Employee Health and Pension Plans," AMA Personnel Series No. 118, (1948); Bergen, "War Lessons," pp. 37–39. That the growth of fringe benefits cannot entirely be attributed to the NWLB may be seen from the rapid postwar and post-NWLB increase in the number of workers covered by some type of negotiated health and welfare plan: it more than doubled between the end of the war and early 1947. Jacoby and Mitchell, "Contractual Features," p. 516.

104. Chamberlain, *Union Challenge*, p. 79; Harry A. Millis and Emily C. Brown, *From the Wagner Act to Taft-Hartley* (Chicago, 1950), pp. 564–568.

105. Ernest Dale, "The Guaranteed Annual Wage," *Personnel* (November 1944), 21:146–151; "What the Factory Worker Really Thinks," *Factory Management and Maintenance* (October 1944), 102:91.

106. In true diplomatic fashion, the NWLB recommended that the President conduct a national study of the issue. In 1945 Roosevelt appointed a study board that issued its final report in 1947. *Guaranteed Wages*, pp. 186–187.

107. Reuther quoted in Jack Chernick and George Hellickson, *Guaranteed Annual Wages* (Minneapolis, 1945), p. 58; Solomon Barkin, "The Challenge of Annual Wages," *Personnel Journal* (April 1946), 25:374. Also see A. D. H. Kaplan, *The Guarantee of Annual Wages* (Washington, D.C., 1947), pp. 13–48; Joseph L. Snider, "The Annual Wage Concept and Management Planning," AMA Personnel Series No. 105 (1946), pp. 13–22; "CIO Goals," *Modern Industry* (June 15, 1946), 12:133–134.

108. "Guaranteed Employment and Wages," in U.S. Bureau of Labor Statistics Bulletin No. 1091, *Labor-Management Contract Provisions, 1950–1951* (1952), p. 32; Lee H. Hill, "Management's Objectives," *Industrial Relations*, (April 1945), 2:36; "Industry Climbs on Annual Wage Wagon," *Modern Industry*, 12 (October 15, 1946), 12:29; Murray W. Latimer, "Management Weighs the Annual Wages," AMA General Management Series No. 135 (1945), pp. 10–23; NICB, "Annual Wage and Employment Guarantee Plans," SPP No. 76 (1946).

109. NICB, "Written Statements," pp. 21–34; Matthew Radom, "Maintaining Regularized Employment," AMA Personnel Series No. 105 (1946), pp. 3–11. Calculations of the annual percentage change in peak-to-trough monthly employment levels for the U.S. manufacturing sector show the following trend: 1919–1940 = 11.48; 1941–1946 = 14.98; 1947–1970 = 6.0. See note 11, ch. 7, above.

110. *NWLB Termination Report*, p. 113.

111. "Comments on Management Problems," *Management Record* (June and November 1942), 4:175, 360; James M. Talbot, "How Can Discipline Be Maintained Under Today's Labor Conditions?" *For National Unity*, Proceedings of the 24th Silver Bay Conference (1941), pp. 96–99; Jacoby and Mitchell, "Contractual Features," p. 515.

112. W. J. Graham, "Arbitration of Labor Disputes," *Personnel* (February 1941), 17:177–184; Edwin Witte, *Historical Survey of Labor Arbitration* (Philadelphia, 1954); Sanford Jacoby, "Progressive Discipline in American Industry," UCLA Institute of Industrial Relations, Working Paper No. 60 (1983).

113. Chamberlain, *Union Challenge*, p. 292.

114. AMA, "Constructive Discipline," p. 15. See also L. H. Hill, "Company Organization of Manpower," AMA Personnel Series No. 63 (1943), p. 7.

115. "The Development of Foremen in Management," AMA Research Report No. 7 (1945), pp. 4–15; "Final Authority to Discharge," *Management Record* (March 1944), 5:63; *Manpower Problems in Detroit*, 13128; Lichtenstein, *War at Home*, p. 117.

116. Chamberlain, *Union Challenge*, pp. 79, 270–276; NICB, "Foreman Training in the Anthracite Industry," SPP No. 66 (1944); Loren Baritz, *The Servants of Power* (Middletown, Conn., 1960), pp. 183–185; Robert A. Sutermeister, "Training Foremen in Human Relations," *Personnel* (July 1943), 20:6–14.

117. Robert C. Reed, "How to Develop Labor Policies, Make Them Work, and Assure That They Are Carried Out," *More Production Through Sound Industrial Relations*, 25th Annual Silver Bay Industrial Conference (1942), pp. 105–106.

118. *Training Within Industry*, pp. 204–222, 128; War Manpower Commission, Bureau of Training, TWI Service, "The Development of TWI: Program Development Institute" (December 15, 1944), and "The TWI Program: Management and Skilled Supervision" (June 1944); Walter Dietz, "Training New Supervisors in the Skill of Leadership," *Personnel* (January 1943), 19:604–608.

119. Twenty-two percent of nonunion hourly workers in 1954 had access to a grievance procedure, although only one-third of these terminated in arbitration. Orme Phelps, *Discipline and Discharge in the Unionized Firm* (Berkeley, Calif., 1959), p. 6.

120. Moody, "Handling Grievances," pp. 63–65; Stephen Habbe, "How Not to Have Grievances," *Management Record* (June 1949), 11:247–249; Raymond S. Livingstone, "Labor Relations in a Non-Unionized Company," AMA Personnel Series No. 99 (1946), pp. 10–11; "Stopping Grievances Before They Grow," *Modern Industry* (February 15, 1947), 13:49–64; "Billy Rose of Labor Relations," *Modern Industry* (December 1947), 14:67–71. Grievance systems usually were found in companies that had personnel departments. In the nonunion sector, a company with a personnel department was two times more likely to have a grievance procedure than a company without a department; personnel departments provided the independence necessary to ensure the procedure's integrity. Steele, Myles, and McIntyre, "Personnel Practices," p. 250.

121. Bergen, "War's Lessons," pp. 27–29; E. H. Adriance, "Decentralizing

the Staff Personnel Function," *Personnel* (September 1947), 24:116–122; "How Much 'Personnel'?" pp. 35–39.

122. Industrial Relations Counselors, "Foremen's Unions," *Advanced Management* (July–September 1944), 9:110–117; Hill, "Organization of Manpower," p. 7; Edward Salner, "Are Foremen Overtrained?" *Personnel* (March 1944), 20:295–299.

123. Guy B. Arthur, Jr., "The Status of the Foreman in Management," AMA Personnel Series No. 73. (1943), pp. 3–5; B. V. Moore, J. E. Kennedy, and G. F. Castore, "The Status of Foremen in Industry," *Personnel* (January 1947), 23:250–255; Slichter et al., "Report and Findings," pp. 688, 696, 704, 712–715, 740–746.

124. *Ibid.*, pp. 679–680, 684–686, 691–695, 710–714, 718, 724; "The Facts About Foremen," *Factory Management and Maintenance* (September 1944), 102:82–92; Walter M. Mirisch, "Temporary Organizational Advancements in Industry," *Personnel* (November 1944), 21:152–155.

125. Slichter et al., "Report and Findings," pp. 656–663; Charles P. Larrowe, "A Meteor on the Industrial Relations Horizon: The Foreman's Association of America," *Labor History* (Fall 1961), 2:259–287; Edwin H. Cassels, "Foreman Unionism—Its Legal Status," AMA Personnel Series No. 96 (1945), pp. 3–12; C. G. McQuaid, "Detroit Foremen Fight for Recognition," *Industrial Relations* (June 1944), 2:6–7, 33–35; Robert H. Keys, "Should Foremen Bargain Collectively With Management?" *Modern Industry* (August 15, 1943), 6:121–126.

126. For a discussion of management's legislative and lobbying efforts to quash foremen's unions, an effort that resulted in section 14(a) of the Taft-Hartley Act, see Harris, *The Right to Manage*, ch. 4.

127. AMA, "Development of Foremen," pp. 56–67; D. W. Weed, "Status and Compensation of Supervisors," in *More Production Through Sound Industrial Relations*, Proceedings of the 25th Anniversary Silver Bay Industrial Conference, July 1942, pp. 132–136; Glenn Gardiner, "The Foreman's Management Job," in *For Maximum Production, Better Industrial Relations*, Proceedings of the 28th Silver Bay Industrial Conference, July 1946, pp. 38–45; Grosvernor S. McKee, "Handling Foremen's Grievances," in *ibid.*, 99–107.

128. Smith, *The Foreman's Place*, pp. 63–75; "Foremen Are Definitely Part of Management," *Supervision* (June 1944), 6:6; W. W. Mussmann, "Foreman's Clubs," *Management Record* (November 1946), 8:375. The YMCA also changed the name of its national organization from the National Council of Foremen's Clubs to the National Council of Industrial Management Clubs.

129. Bergen, "War's Lessons," pp. 27–29, 44; John Pfiffner, "The Relation of the Foreman to Staff Departments," *Personnel* (July 1945), 22:59–61; "Tying Supervision Into Management," *Modern Industry* (October 15, 1946), 12:38; Guy B. Arthur, Jr., "A Scrutiny of Personnel Practice," AMA Personnel Series No. 111 (1947), pp. 6–15; "How Much 'Personnel'?" pp. 35–39; Paul Pigors, "The Challenge for Personnel Administration," *Personnel* (March 1947), 23:294–301.

130. Industrial Relations, Counselors, "Foremen's Unions," p. 116; "Here's Your Modern Foreman," *Modern Industry* (July 1947), 14:54–64; Adriance and

Beck, "Decentralizing," pp. 116–122; AMA, "Development of Foremen," pp. 15–30.

131. Glenn Gardiner, "The Operating Executive and the Personnel Department," AMA Personnel Series No. 121 (1948), p. 6; Harris, *Right to Manage*, p. 83.

132. Chamberlain, *Union Challenge*, p. 77; *Manpower Problems in Detroit*, 13174–13175; Frederick H. Harbison and Robert Dubin, *Patterns of Union-Management Relations* (Chicago, 1947), pp. 45–51.

133. J. Stevens Stock and Harriet Lubin, "Indices of Personnel Management," *Personnel* (July 1946), 23:6–16; Guy B. Arthur, Jr., "The Status of Personnel Administration in Management," AMA Personnel Series No. 102 (1946), pp. 32–35; L. E. Schmidt, "Methods of Evaluating a Personnel Program," AMA Personnel Series No. 111 (1947), pp. 24–30; "How Much 'Personnel'?" pp. 35–36.

134. "Should Industrial Relations Men Be Given Professional Status?" *Industrial Relations* (December 1946), 4:27–28; Charles A. Drake, "Developing Professional Standards for Personnel Executives," *Personnel* (March 1943) 19:646–655; "The Profession of Personnel Administration," *Personnel Journal* (January, 1946), 24:265–269; Dale Yoder, "Professional Associations in Manpower Management," *Personnel Journal* (June 1948), 27:43–46.

135. Thomas H. Patten, *The Foreman: Forgotten Man of Management* (New York, 1969); Donald E. Wray, "Marginal Men of Industry: The Foremen," *American Journal of Sociology* (January 1949), 54:298–301.

Conclusions

1. Sumner H. Slichter, *The Challenge of Industrial Relations* (Ithaca, N.Y., 1947), p. 35; Slichter, "Are We Becoming a 'Laboristic' State?" *New York Times Magazine*, May 16, 1948, reprinted in John T. Dunlop, ed., *Potentials of the American Economy: Selected Essays of Sumner H. Slichter* (Cambridge, Mass., 1961), p. 255.

2. Clark Kerr, "The Balkanization of Labor Markets," in E. Wight Bakke et al., *Labor Mobility and Economic Opportunity* (Cambridge, Mass., 1954), p. 96.

3. Arthur M. Ross, "Do We Have a New Industrial Feudalism?" *American Economic Review* (December 1958), 48:903–920.

4. U.S. Bureau of Labor Statistics, *Handbook of Labor Statistics—1975 Reference Edition* (Washington, D.C., 1975), p. 130; Stephan Thernstrom, *The Other Bostonians: Poverty and Progress in the American Metropolis, 1880–1970* (Cambridge, Mass., 1973), pp. 228–232.

5. Joseph Shister, "Labor Mobility: Some Institutional Aspects," *Proceedings of the Third Annual Meeting of the Industrial Relations Research Association* (1950), pp. 42–59; James Medoff, "Layoffs and Alternatives Under Trade Unionism in U.S. Manufacturing," *American Economic Review* (June 1979), 69:380–395.

6. On immigration and emigration levels, see U.S. Bureau of the Census, *Historical Statistics of the United States* (Washington, D.C., 1960), pp. 56, 64.

Note that there was an increase in the average age of the manufacturing labor force between 1940 and 1960; this was both an effect and cause of the decline in job mobility. John Pencavel, *An Analysis of the Quit Rate in American Manufacturing Industry* (Princeton, N.J., 1970).

7. Peter Doeringer and Michael Piore, *Internal Labor Markets and Manpower Analysis* (Lexington, Mass., 1971); Oliver E. Williamson, *Markets and Hierarchies: Analysis and Antitrust Implications* (New York, 1975), ch. 4; Arthur M. Okun, *Prices and Quantities: A Macroeconomic Analysis* (Washington, D.C., 1981), pp. 26–133.

Another problem with theories based on turnover is their implication that internal labor markets arose because of some historic shift in turnover cost patterns. However, I have found no evidence that such a shift occurred. If anything, there is reason to believe that job skills became less, rather than more, idiosyncratic over time, as discussed in chapter 4. These problems reflect the ahistorical character of turnover-based and other implicit contract theories of the labor market. The theories offer timeless and universal explanations for phenomena that are relatively recent (quasi-permanent employment relationships) and, to some extent, uniquely American (sticky nominal wages). Hence, as noted in my introduction, the theories are simply rationalizations of postwar American practices.

8. Robert M. Solow, "On Theories of Unemployment," *American Economic Review* (March 1980), 83:3. Also see George A. Akerlof, "A Theory of Social Custom, of Which Unemployment May Be One Consequence," *Quarterly Journal of Economics* (June 1980), 94:749–775.

9. Clark Kerr, "What Became of the Independent Spirit?" *Fortune* (July 1953), 48:110; Harry Braverman, *Labor and Monopoly Capital: The Degradation of Work in the Twentieth Century* (New York, 1974).

10. Jürgen Kocka, *White-Collar Workers in America, 1880–1940* (Beverly Hills, Calif., 1982), pp. 96–97, 269–270. As the Lynds discovered when they visited Middletown in 1924, one result of the white-collar employee's job security was steady employment: Only 2 percent of Middletown's white-collar men were jobless during 1924, whereas during the year 43 percent of its working-class men experienced at least one spell of unemployment lasting more than a month. Robert S. and Helen M. Lynd, *Middletown: A Study in Contemporary American Culture* (New York, 1929), pp. 33–56.

11. A Massachusetts court noted in 1908 that the word "salary" was "more frequently applied to annual employment than to any other, and its use may impart a factor of permanency." *Maynard v. Royal Worcester Corset Co.*, 200 Mass. 1. (1908). Also see J. William Schultze, *Office Administration* (New York, 1919), p. 213.

12. William H. Whyte. *The Organization Man* (New York, 1956), p. 129; National Industrial Conference Board, "Personnel Practices in Factory and Office: Manufacturing," SPP No. 194 (1965), passim.

13. Reinhard Bendix, *Work and Authority in Industry* (New York, 1956), pp. 294–297.

14. Frank B. Miller and Mary Ann Coghill, "Sex and the Personnel Manager," *Industrial and Labor Relations Reveiw* (October 1964), 18:32–44.

15. For an insightful discussion of management's efforts on behalf of the Taft-Hartley Act, see Howell John Harris, *The Right to Manage: Industrial Relations Policies of American Business in the 1940s* (Madison, Wis., 1982).

16. As this is meant to imply, the differences between the AFL and the CIO were not as great as commonly is supposed. The new industrial unions relied on a job control system that first had been devised on an interfirm basis by nineteenth-century craft unions (the "guild" system), and which was later redefined on an intrafirm basis by the AFL's printing, railroad, mining, and apparel unions (the "manorial" system). In the workplace, unlike the political arena, very few of the CIO's demands were entirely new.

Index